WHY WE CAN'T AFFORD THE RICH

WHY WE CAN'T AFFORD THE RICH

Andrew Sayer

First published in Great Britain in 2016 by

Policy Press
University of Bristol
1-9 Old Park Hill
Clifton
Bristol BS2 8BB
UK
Tel +44 (0)117 954 5940
e-mail pp-info@bristol.ac.uk
www.policypress.co.uk

North American office:
Policy Press
c/o The University of Chicago Press
1427 East 60th Street
Chicago, IL 60637, USA
t: +1 773 702 7700
f: +1 773 702 9756
e:sales@press.uchicago.edu
www.press.uchicago.edu

British Library Cataloguing in Publication Data
A catalogue record for this book is available from the British Library

Library of Congress Cataloging-in-Publication Data
A catalog record for this book has been requested

ISBN 978-1-4473-2086-9 paperback

Cover design by www.thecoverfactory.co.uk
Front cover image: www.istock.com
Printed and bound in Great Britain by TJ International,
Padstow
Policy Press uses environmentally responsible print partners

Contents

List of figures

Acknowledgements

Many thanks to:

- all the investigative journalists, academics, bloggers, activists and campaigners who have exposed the processes that support the rule of the rich and the denial of climate change;
- the Economic and Social Research Council for a Fellowship in 2004–05 which allowed me to get started on moral economy, as did a sabbatical from Lancaster University;
- Colin Gordon, Emmanuel Saez, Mike Norton, John Hills and Tom Palley for permission to use their data or graphs; to New Society Publishers for Figure 5.1, the Resolution Foundation for Figure 12.2, and the Global Commons Institute for Figure 21.1.
- Bob Jessop for regularly alerting me to sources of data and alternative news and, with the usual disclaimers, for comments on much of the text – for which thanks also to Dean Curran, Norman Fairclough, Dimitri Mader, Kevin McSherry, David Tyfield, Dick Walker and John Urry;
- Danny Dorling and an anonymous reviewer for invaluable suggestions;
- John Allen, John Baker, Gideon Calder, Aditya Chakrabortty, John Christensen, Mick Dunford, Michael Edwards, Norman and Isabela Fairclough, Tony Fielding, Neil Foxlee, Russell Keat, Kathleen Lynch, Kevin Morgan, Betsy Olson, John O'Neill, Diane Perrons, Kate Pickett, Karen Rowlingson, Balihar Sanghera, Clive Spash, Richard Wilkinson, Ruth Wodak and the Language, Ideology and Politics group at Lancaster, Linda Woodhead, Erik Olin Wright and many others for discussions, advice, data and encouragement;
- all those other friends who kept asking 'when is it coming out?' while, in the nicest possible way, distracting me from finishing it: Ann McChesney, Pat Batteson, Dinah Brown, Eric and Cecilia Clark, Isabela Fairclough, Steve and Anne Fleetwood, Anne-Marie Fortier, Bridget Graham and Tom Fairclough, Costis Hadjimichalis and Dina Vaiou, Frank Hansen and Helle Fischer, Iain Hunter and Sue Halsam, Ruth Joyce, Richard Light,

Grazyna Monvid, Celia Roberts, Georg Schönfeld, Judy Sebba and Brian Parkinson, Eeva Sointu, Sue Taylor, Liz Thomas, Jill Yeung and Karin Zotzmann;

- my other colleagues at Lancaster for friendly collegiality, and Karen Gammon, Jules Knight, Kate Mitchell, Cathlin Prill and Rachel Verrall for good-humoured and excellent administrative support in the department, despite understaffing;
- Alison Shaw, Laura Vickers and the Policy Press team for encouragement, advice and support;
- my daughter Lizzie, especially, as always.

I will be giving all royalties from this book to a selection of charities and organisations pursuing equality and economic justice.

Foreword

Andrew Sayer has written a very good book which does much more than its title suggests. As well as explaining why we can't afford the rich, it also explains why we go on doing so. The ideology that the rich shower on us is meant to justify their privilege, but it turns the truth completely inside out. When inequality reaches the insane levels it has done, the rich depend on hoodwinking us all into thinking that they are the source of jobs, prosperity and everything we value. But, to paraphrase George Monbiot, once we stop believing this, either governments have to tackle inequality or revolutions arise. So Sayer's piece-by-piece unpicking of the economic justifications of the rich is an important political act.

Although this book has a light touch that masks the impressive scholarship which has gone into it, and is free of jargon and sometimes funny, to say it is a 'good read' would belie its seriousness of purpose. Above all, Sayer is concerned to help our societies surmount what he rightly calls a 'diabolical double crisis' – at once economic and environmental. But too often reading books or articles on the threats the world faces becomes little more than a form of consumerism. We read them to feel well informed – hopefully better informed than others. And it is easy to feel that the more threatening the problem under discussion, the more exhilarating it is as the plot of a 'whodunnit'. Being well informed adds to our cultural capital and gives us more to say, but let us make sure this book also makes us part of the solution.

On the interface between the environment and inequality, Sayer quotes Pacala, saying that 7 per cent of the world's population is responsible for 50 per cent of all greenhouse gas emissions. But even if we in the rich world give up flying, do without a car and eat little or no meat, we would probably reduce our total (direct and indirect) carbon emissions by no more than a third – only a modest contribution to the 80 or 90 per cent we need to achieve.

Fortunately, well-being and high carbon emissions are not inseparable. Countries achieve high levels of happiness and life expectancy at a fraction of the carbon emissions per head of population produced by many of the richest countries, including

Britain and the USA. The truth is that the rich developed societies are very inefficient producers of well-being – particularly those with bigger income differences between rich and poor. According to WHO figures, over 20 per cent of the populations of the more unequal rich countries are likely to suffer forms of mental illness – such as depression, anxiety disorders, drug or alcohol addiction – each year. Rates may be three times as high as in the most equal countries. At the same time, measures of the strength of community life and whether people feel they can trust others also show that more equal societies do very much better. As discussed in *The Spirit Level* (Penguin, 2010), tackling inequality is an important step towards achieving sustainability and high levels of well-being.

As the populations of the developed world have gained unprecedented standards of comfort and material prosperity, further increases in those standards make less and less difference to well-being. But what *has* become critical to well-being is the social environment and the quality of social relations. There is abundant research showing that social life and relationships are essential to both health and happiness. However, very large material inequalities mean that status becomes more important and social life is increasingly impoverished by status competition and status insecurities. Social anxieties and our worries about how we are seen and judged are exacerbated. The result is that people start to feel that social life is more of an ordeal than a pleasure and gradually withdraw from social life – as the data show.

But by intensifying status insecurities, inequality also drives consumerism, which is the biggest obstacle to sustainability. Any idea that we should consume less will be opposed as if it were an assault on our social standing and quality of life. But by reducing inequality, we not only reduce the importance of social status but, at the same time, we also improve social relations and the real quality of life. Reducing inequality is the first step towards combining sustainability with higher levels of well-being.

The main reason why inequality has increased over the last generation in so many countries is that the incomes of those already rich have increased so much faster than everyone else's. The super-rich now see themselves as superior beings who are doing us a kindness by living amongst us. As Sayer so clearly shows, if we are to reduce inequality and stop the zombie-like extraction of more and more fossil fuel, we have to bring the economic and political dominance of the rich to a close.

Richard Wilkinson
Emeritus Professor of Social Epidemiology,
University of Nottingham

ONE

Introduction

> There's class warfare, all right, but it's my class, the rich class, that's making war, and we're winning. (Warren Buffett, estimated 'worth' $44 billion, Chairman and CEO of Berkshire Hathaway, quoted in the *New York Times*, 26 November 2006)[1]

We are seeing an extraordinary phenomenon: for years the rich have been pulling away from the rest, with the top 1% taking an increasing share of national wealth, while those on low to middling incomes have got progressively less. And the rich continue to get richer, even in the worst crisis for 80 years – they can still laugh all the way to their banks and tax havens as the little people bail out banks that have failed. Meanwhile a new kind of bank is multiplying – providing food for those who can no longer make ends meet. Austerity policies fall most heavily on those at the bottom while the top 10%, and particularly the top 1%, are protected. Generally, the less you had to do with the crisis, the bigger the sacrifices – relative to your income – you have had to make. Youth unemployment has soared – in Spain and Greece to over 50%; this is an outrageous waste of young lives, and in many countries it's become clear that young people are unlikely to experience the prosperity their parents enjoyed. How ridiculous that the answer to our economic problems is seen as wasting more of our most important asset – people. Meanwhile a political class increasingly dominated by the rich continues to support their interests and diverts the public's attention by stigmatising and punishing those on welfare benefits and low incomes, cheered on by media overwhelmingly controlled by the super-rich.

But, while the divide between the rich and the rest has certainly grown, how can it be claimed that we can't afford the rich? Here's a short answer.

Their wealth is mostly dependent ultimately on the production of goods and services by others and siphoned off through dividends, capital gains, interest and rent, and much of it is hidden in tax havens. They are able to control much of economic life and the media and dominate politics, so their special interests and view of the world come to restrict what democracies can do. Their consumption is excessive and wasteful and diverts resources away from the more needy and deserving. Their carbon footprints are grotesquely inflated and many have an interest in continued fossil fuel production, threatening the planet.

Of course, this brief summary leaves out many qualifications, not to mention the actual argument and evidence. Some readers may agree straightaway, some may have a few objections, but others may respond with incredulity, perhaps outrage, for to claim that we can't afford the rich is to imply that they are a *cost* to the rest of us, a burden. Aren't the rich wealth creators, job creators, entrepreneurs, investors – indeed, just the kind of people we need? Don't entrepreneurs like Bill Gates deserve their wealth for having introduced products that benefit millions? Aren't the rich entitled to spend what they have earned how they like? What right has anyone to say their consumption is excessive? Couldn't the rich cut their carbon footprints by switching to low-carbon consumption? Wouldn't the world miss their philanthropy and the 'trickle-down effects' of their spending? In fact, isn't this book just an example of 'the politics of envy' – directed at those whom former UK Prime Minister Tony Blair used to call 'the successful'? Shouldn't we thank, rather than begrudge, these 'high net worth individuals'?

It's the objections regarding the alleged role of the rich in wealth extraction, as opposed to wealth creation, that present the biggest challenge and occupy the bulk of this book, though I'll attempt to answer other objections too. In the process it will become clear that this is not about the politics of envy – a cheap slur used by those who want to duck the arguments and evidence – but *the politics of injustice*. I don't envy the rich, in fact I regard such envy as thoroughly misguided. But I resent the unjust system by which the rich are allowed to extract wealth that others produce and to dominate society for their own interests. What's more, this is not only unjust but profoundly dysfunctional and inefficient, and it creates inhumane, rat-race societies.

The time is ripe for examining where the wealth of the rich comes from. The Occupy movement has very successfully highlighted the growing split between the top 1% and the 99%, and the dominance of politics by the 1%. The rich have made a remarkable comeback since the 1970s – the end of the post-war boom – rapidly increasing their share of national income in a large number of countries, Britain included. As Figure 1.1 shows, we are now getting back to early 20th-century levels of inequality between the rich and the rest. Having cornered 'only' 5.9–9% of total income before tax in the UK in the early 1950s through to 1978 – 'The Golden Age of Capitalism' – the top 1% of 'earners' now hoover up 13%.

Figure 1.1: Top income shares in the UK, 1913–2011

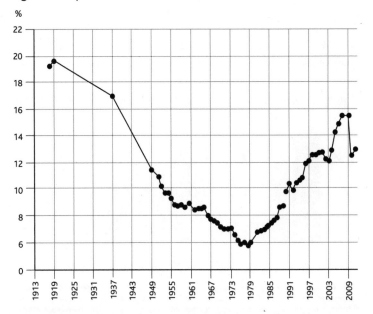

Source: Alvaredo, F., Anthony B. Atkinson, A.B., Piketty, T. and Saez, E., The world top incomes database, http://topincomes.g-mond.parisschoolofeconomics.eu/

U-shaped curves like that of Figure 1.1 are most striking in the US, the UK, Canada, Ireland and Australia. Sweden and Norway have shallower U-shaped curves. Italy, Spain, New Zealand and Argentina have also seen a return of the rich, albeit with more fluctuations. China, of course, has seen a dramatic rise in top incomes in recent years. The return of the rich is much more limited in France, Denmark and Japan, which have more L-shaped curves. In Germany, the share of national income taken by the 1% has stayed fairly flat but at a relatively high level since the war. In the Netherlands and Switzerland the income shares of the top 1% have fallen since the post-war boom.[2]

Figures 1.2 and 1.3 provide another way of showing what's happened where the rich have come back, this time in the world's leading capitalist economy, the US. The five bars on the left split the population into equal numbers of people, so the bar on the left is the poorest fifth (or 0–20th percentiles), the next bar the next poorest fifth and so on. In both figures the five bars on the right show the divisions within the richest 5% or twentieth of the population.

First (Figure 1.2), the situation during the early post-war period. This was a time when the majority of the population shared in the post-war boom, with low-income households doing slightly better than others and the top 5% growing at slower rates, albeit from

Figure 1.2: Change in average household real income in the US, 1947–79

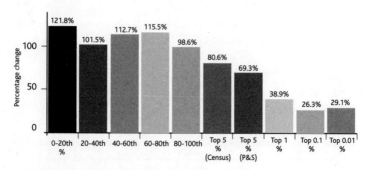

Source: Data from Census Bureau and Economic Policy Institute compiled by Colin Gordon. Incomes include transfers. Average top incomes (market income only) from Piketty and Saez, *World top incomes database*. Top 5% figures shown from both sources, http://www.epi.org/blog/growing-growing/

Figure 1.3: Change in average household real income in the US, 1979–2012

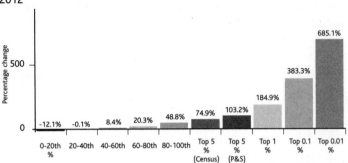

Source: Data from Census Bureau and Economic Policy Institute compiled by Colin Gordon. Incomes include transfers. Average top incomes (market income only) from Piketty and Saez, *World top incomes database*. Top 5% figures shown from both sources, http://www.epi.org/blog/growing-growing/

a higher base. But from 1979, things turned around completely (Figure 1.3). It couldn't be clearer. From 1979, the majority of incomes stagnated or grew only slowly, while the poorest fifth suffered a substantial loss and the rich roared ahead, swallowing up most of the spoils of economic growth, with the top 0.01% enjoying a 685% rise in real income![3] This divergence has continued since the crash; indeed the gulf is widening as a result of austerity policies, which disproportionately hit those on low to middle incomes, contrary to the rhetoric of 'We're all in it together'.

In fact, the inequalities *within* the top 1% are much greater than between them and the 99%. Those in the top 1% in the UK have incomes ranging from just under £100,000 to billions.[4] What's more, the richer they are, the faster their income has grown: the top 0.5% have increased their share faster than the rest of the 1%, but not as fast as the top 0.1%, while the top 0.01% (ten-thousandth) have enriched themselves even faster.[5]

Inequalities in *wealth* – the monetary value of individuals' accumulated assets minus their liabilities (debts) – are even wider than income inequalities, and increasing. In the US, the top 1% own 35% of the nation's wealth and the bottom 40% a mere 0.2%! In the UK in 2008–10, the members of the top 1% each had £2.8 million or more (14% of the nation's wealth), though, given the opportunities for the rich to hide their wealth, this is almost certainly an underestimate (Figure 1.4). Twenty-eight per cent of wealth in the UK is inherited, not earned.[6] Half of the population had wealth of less than £232,400, and the poorest 10% had less than £12,600:

Figure 1.4: Distribution of total wealth between households, 2008–10, Great Britain

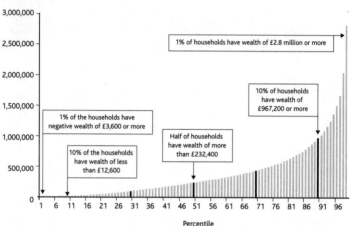

Source: Hills, J., Bastagli, F., Cowell, F., Glennerster, H., Karagiannaki, E, and McKnight, A. (2013) 'Wealth distribution, accumulation, and policy', Centre for the Analysis of Social Exclusion, CASEbrief 33. Derived from ONS analysis of July 2008 to June 2010 wave of Wealth and Assets Survey. Total wealth includes private pension rights as well as personal possessions, net financial assets, and housing (net of mortgages). Each column represents the wealth of one per cent of households.

Changes in the 1%'s share of wealth over the last 100 years again form a U-shaped curve. What is also clear is that, over the last 40 years, *within* the 1% that growth in wealth has been concentrated at the top: in the US, the top 0.01% have gone from having less than 3% of national wealth in the mid-1970s to over 11% in 2013 (Figure 1.5). Those making up the rest of the top 0.1% have seen their share go up from less than 6% to almost 11% in the same period, while the rest of the top 1%'s wealth share has remained fairly level. So the richest one-thousandth – currently those with more than $20 million – own over a fifth of the country's wealth.

Figure 1.5: Wealth at the top in the US: changes in shares of US national wealth within the 1%

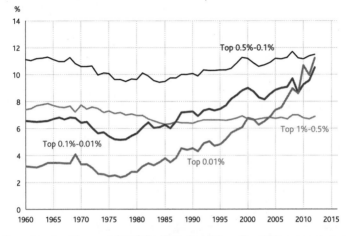

Source: Saez, E. and Zacman, G. (2014) 'The distribution of US wealth, capital income and returns since 1913', http://gabriel-zucman.eu/files/SaezZucman2014Slides.pdf

The global picture is far more extreme, indeed astonishing.

Owning the world: figures from Oxfam

- The richest 80 people in the world own as much as the poorest half of the world's population, all 3.5 billion of them!
- 48% of the world's wealth is now owned by just 1% of the population.[7]
- The wealth of the richest 1% in the world amounts to $110 trillion. That's 65 times the total wealth of the bottom half of the world's population.
- Seven out of ten people live in countries where economic inequality has increased in the last 30 years.[8]

Have the rich got richer because those at the top have become more enterprising, dynamic wealth creators? Are today's capitalists – or entrepreneurs, as they like to call themselves – so much better at leading economic development than their more moderately paid predecessors of the post-war boom? The economic data suggests the opposite. Growth rates have been slower than in the post-war boom.

The rich are clearly not taking the same share of faster growth, but an increasing share of slower growth. So how have they done it?

The rich are not only getting a bigger proportion of nations' gross incomes, but keeping more of it, thanks to massive drops in top rates of taxation (Figure 1.6).[9] From the 1930s onwards, tax rates on the rich soared, topping 90% in the UK, the US, France and, briefly, Germany. It's hard to believe this now when they have fallen to less than 50%, with many governments repeatedly trying to drive them down still lower. The sky did not fall down when top rates of tax were high, indeed the economies of these countries boomed, yet we are now told in severe tones that taxing the rich merely restrains growth.

Figure 1.6: Top individual marginal income tax rates, 1900–2011

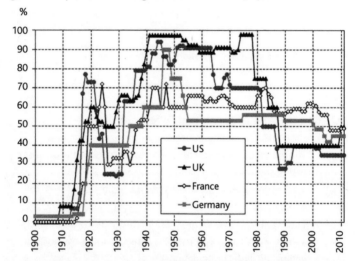

Source: Piketty, T., Saez, E. and Stantcheva, S. (2011) 'Optimal taxation of top labor incomes: a tale of three elasticities', Working Paper 17616, National Bureau of Economic Research, MA

We are now experiencing the deepest recession since the Great Depression of the 1920s and 1930s, but whereas then the reaction under the US New Deal was to impose high taxes on the rich and tightly regulate finance, this time round neither of these things is happening on either side of the Atlantic. The rich have got away with it and the financial sector is free to do more damage again.

My title is intended to provoke a critical examination of the rich, but the argument is directed not at particular individuals but at the *sources* of their wealth and power and the ways in which these are justified. It's always tempting to seek particular individuals who, we suppose, embody all the worst features of the situation – those who have been richly rewarded for failure, for irresponsible handling of risk, for limitless greed, for destabilising banks or threatening people's pensions and homes, for example. Many books on the financial crisis have told the stories of the rise of financial giants – 'Masters of the Universe' as they liked to call themselves – and their subsequent falls; or, more often, their ability to shift the consequences of their failure onto others and stay on top. But focusing just on individuals actually lets the causes off the hook – the rules, institutions and situations that they're allowed to take advantage of. It's also tempting to dwell on greed, but while there is plenty of evidence of it, mere expressions of disapproval have little effect; they fail to deal with the circumstances that encourage it. As long as these remain, then there will be some who can exploit them to the detriment of the many: if it's not the present incumbents, it will be new ones. To be sure, they, like the rest of us, have some responsibility for their actions, but we need to look beyond this to the circumstances that allow them to get rich at the expense of others. So this is not a book of tirades against rich or super-rich individuals: where I do mention particular people it's only to make more general points.

To show why we can't afford the rich we need to do more than find out just how rich they are and describe how they got their money and spend it. We need to do something that most books on the rich and the financial crisis fail to do – question the *legitimacy* of their wealth. But it *is* important to realise just how rich the rich are. I don't want to put readers off with an indigestible mass of figures, but some are needed, especially as few people realise how unequal our society is and just how wealthy the rich are.

First, whom do I mean by 'the rich'? How rich is rich? Is it an absolute number? £100,000+ per year, £1 million+ per year? Or a percentage: the top 1% or 0.1%?

Both absolute terms, like 'millionaire', and relative ones, like the 1%, are useful. And we should distinguish income (a flow over a period of time) from wealth (as the market value of someone's total accumulated assets, minus any debts). The distribution of wealth is far more unequal than the distribution of income.

So where do I draw the line between the rich and the rest? For much of this book I'll be talking mainly about the top 1% in terms of share of national income and fractions within that. Particularly for the UK, it turns out that in counterposing the 1% to the 99%, the Occupy protestors hit upon a crucial divide, even if they didn't realise it. Danny Dorling, the radical statistician and social geographer, shows that, over a century (1910–2009) in the UK, the shares of total income of those within the different fractions of the top 1% changed together, and rose and fell in the *opposite* direction to the shares of the bottom 99%: when the 1% got more, the 99% got less. And that's not just because the income shares of these two groups have to sum to 100%. It could have been the top 20% gaining as the bottom 80% lost, or the top 35% relative to the bottom 65%, or a more complex picture. But it wasn't: the main dividing line was between the 1% and the 99%. While it's been mostly the bottom 90% who have lost relative to the 1%, even the shares of national income received by the 9% above them but below the top 1% have fallen slightly over the last 20 years as the share of the rich has gone up. In other words, in the UK, even the best-off of the 99% now have more in common with the rest of the population than with the top 1% as regards how their share of national income has evolved.[10] In the US the boundary isn't quite so sharp, with the 4% below the top 1% getting a slight increase in share of national income since the post-war boom, though nothing like as big an increase as those above them, but it's at the top of the 1% where the big gains have been made.

But the problem of the rich isn't just a matter of quantity of income or wealth, but one of where the money they get comes from. I'll be arguing that the richer people are, the higher the proportion of their income is likely to be unearned, through being based on power rather than some kind of contribution. So there's a qualitative difference too.

This becomes important when we think not about how rich is rich, but how much is too much. At what level does income and wealth become excessive or unjustifiable?[11] Is it:

- more than the equivalent of what they have contributed (so that they are being subsidised by others, and without good reason)?
- more than others can afford to pay them?
- more than they need or is necessary for their well-being?
- more than their share of the planet's resources?

The answer is that it depends on what particular problems we're talking about. If it's carbon footprints and climate change, then it includes many of us in the rich countries, though people in some countries (the US, Australia) have much greater CO_2 emissions than others, like France and Sweden. If the whole world emitted as much CO_2 as the US, we'd need five planets to absorb the carbon emissions. Though the US's population is only 5% of the world's, it accounts for a quarter of the world's CO_2 emissions.[12] Generally, the higher your income, the bigger your carbon footprint is likely to be. Otherwise, for most of the issues dealt with in this book, those who arguably have too much are much smaller in number even within the rich countries of the world. Nevertheless, as we'll see, climate change is the biggest threat of all.

Unimaginable wealth

References to millions, billions and trillions have become familiar since the 2007 financial crisis and, as many have said, it's hard to appreciate just how big such numbers are. We know £1 billion (£1,000 million) is a huge sum, but cannot imagine it. Here's one way. Imagine you were given £1 every second until you had £1 billion. You might think you would soon reach that figure – after all, after just one hour you'd already have £3,600. But you'd actually have to wait over 31 years and 8 months. So billionaires are astonishingly wealthy. As for trillions (1,000 billion), the unit now often used for estimating the sums needed for bailing out the financial crisis, the time you would need to accumulate £1 trillion is nearly 32,000 years.

In 2011, the wealth of US households with more than $1 million, according to Deloitte auditors, amounted to $38.6 trillion, with an estimated $6.3 trillion hidden in offshore accounts. Deloitte forecast that the wealth of the world's dollar millionaire equivalents will reach $202 trillion, or roughly four times current global Gross Domestic Product, by 2020.[13]

How people underestimate inequality

Lots of studies of people's views of inequality show that they drastically underestimate just how unequal their societies are.[14] Figure 1.7 is from one such study, by Michael Norton and Dan Ariely in the US. At the top it shows the actual distribution of wealth in the United States – with the top 20% owning about 84% of total wealth in the country. The next 20% have about 11%, and so on. The bottom 20% and the next-to-bottom 20% don't even show up because their share of total wealth was too tiny to represent on the graph! The middle bar summarises what a sample of 5,000 Americans thought was the actual distribution. As is clear, they mistakenly imagined that the top 20% own less than 60%. But even though they radically underestimate how unequal their society is, they *still* think it's much too unequal. The bottom bar presents what they think would be a fair distribution![15]

Figure 1.7: Wealth distribution in the US: actual, estimated and ideal

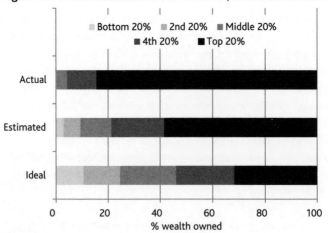

Source: Based on data from Norton, M.I. and Ariely, D. (2011) 'Building a better America – wealth quintile at a time'. *Perspectives on Psychological Science*. 6(1), pp 9–12.

Similarly in the UK: an ICM poll of 2,034 people found that they thought that *ideally* the top fifth should get 25% of the wealth and the bottom fifth 15% of the wealth. They *guessed* that in practice the top fifth got 40% of the wealth and the bottom 20%. But *actually*, the top fifth of households get 60% of the wealth (including pensions) and the bottom fifth less than 1%![16]

In the UK, to get into the top 1% of individuals in terms of net income after deducting tax and national insurance, you need to clear at least around £80,000 per year.[17] But the average gross income of the top 1% is £250,000, with some, of course, getting far more than that. In the US in 2012, to get into the top 1% you needed an income before tax of at least $393,941, but the average for the 1% is $1.26 million.[18] The distribution of income *within* the top 1% is itself highly unequal: to get into the top 0.1% (the top thousandth of the population) required an income of at least $1.55 million, and to get into the top 0.01% at least $7.2 million. And the higher up they are, the faster their share of national income has grown over the last 40 years.

The richer people are, the more of their wealth tends to be in financial form – shares, bonds and other financial investments. Financial wealth formed 13% of the total wealth of the top 10% wealthiest, most of it concentrated in the top 1%, but less than 4% for the bottom 50% of the distribution.

The richest 1,000 people have become vastly more wealthy over the last 15 years and, after a brief post-crisis dip, have bounced back to become even richer. In 2014 Britain had 104 billionaires, compared with just 53 in 2010. In the US, Emmanuel Saez found that in the 2009–11 'recovery' the 1% actually gained at the expense of the 99%. So it certainly wasn't a recovery for the vast majority. Just in 2009–10, the top 0.01% (ten thousandth) captured 37% of this additional income, gaining an average of $4.2 million per household.[19] The wealth of the top 400 US households equals that of the bottom 50% of the population. The box shows how the situation has developed in the UK.

Collective wealth of the UK's 1,000 richest people

1997 = £98 billion
2008 = £413 billion
2010 = £336 billion
2012 = £414 billion
2013 = £450 billion
2014 = £519 billion
2015 = £547 billion
Source: Sunday Times Rich List

That £547 billion would fund the UK state pension bill for 3.7 years, or the public health system for 4.7 years. It's also 9.8 times the size of the country's annual welfare bill.[20] It's worth pausing to let these figures sink in; the UK has 63.9 million people and yet many of their most important needs could be met several times over just by the collective wealth of the richest 1,000. (Could there be a solution here?) When people worry about the effect of an ageing population on the pension bill and the NHS bill, we need to remember that just the annual growth of the wealth of the super-rich could easily pay for it. This is a ridiculous and obscene misallocation of resources. And why should we celebrate the growth of the financial sector, but see the growth of the health sector as a problem?

Globally, according to the Bloomberg Billionaires website,[21] the top 100 billionaires controlled $1.9 trillion in 2012, adding $240 billion that year. Oxfam calculates that just over a quarter of this – $66 billion – would have been enough to have raised everyone in the world over the $1.25 per day poverty line.[22]

Who are the rich?

Predictably, the richer they are, the more likely they are to be men – 84% of the top 1.0–0.1% in the UK, and over 90% of the richest 0.1% taxpayers (about 47,000 adults) are male. The UK's top 1% live mainly in London and the South-East of England, where the summits of most organisational hierarchies are located. The bottom half of the top 1% includes small business owners, top managers and top health professionals, but the higher up you go within the top 1% the more likely are individuals to be involved in the financial and property sectors, and the greater their reliance on income from capital gains, dividends, stocks and shares and other financial assets.

With a 'net worth' of $76 billion, Bill Gates of Microsoft is the richest person in the world, according to the 2013 Forbes list of billionaires. Second, with $72 billion, and for many years the first, is Carlos Slim Helu, a Mexican who took over his country's telecommunications industry when it was privatised – a nice example of the consequences of privatising state monopolies. Warren Buffett, whose candid statement about class war heads up this introduction, is fourth. The richest woman, at ninth, with $52.5 billion, is Christy Walton, who inherited part of the Walmart fortune. Three other members of the Walton family are in the top 20. Rupert Murdoch, the media mogul, with $13.5 billion, comes in at 78th.[23]

Very few of the rich and super-rich are celebrities. The wealthiest, Steven Spielberg, with $3 billion, is 337th on the Forbes list. Next is Oprah Winfrey, at 442nd with $2.7 billion. In the UK, the *Sunday Times* often uses a montage of photos of celebrities to publicise its Rich List, but as in the US, few of them reach the upper levels. The highest (2012), Paul McCartney, with £665 million, owes his high position partly to marrying Nancy Shevell, an American heiress. Author J.K. Rowling, came in at 148th, the Beckhams at 395th. Most of the super-rich above them are unknown to the vast majority of British people.

The top six in the UK are all foreign nationals resident in the UK, attracted by special tax deals open to them: Alisher Usmanov (first, with £13.3 billion) owns Russia's biggest iron ore producer; second is another Russian, Leonard Blavatnik, who's involved in a range of industries including music, aluminium, oil and chemicals; in third place, the Hinduja brothers inherited their father's conglomerate, with interests in power, automotive and defence industries in India and overseas; Lakshmi Mittal, in fourth place, is an Indian-born steel magnate who owes much of his wealth to buying up former Soviet state enterprises when they were privatised; Roman Abramovich (fifth), from Russia, best known in the UK for his ownership of Chelsea football club, owns an investment company with interests in a wide range of sectors, particularly oil; Norwegian-born Cypriot citizen John Frederiksen (shipping and oil) is sixth. 'Non domiciles', like these individuals, take advantage of a rule unique to the UK and Ireland that allows those who can claim to be linked to some other domicile to escape UK tax on their income and capital gains in all of the rest of the world, providing they do not bring the money into the country.[24] At eighth, the richest British-born person on the list is the Duke of Westminster, with £7.8 billion, who inherited property in Lancashire, Cheshire, Scotland and Canada and prime sites in London.[25] Although only a minority of the super-rich around the world list their speciality as finance, most of those in non-finance business are nevertheless also heavily involved in finance, in playing the markets and making deals[26] and, of course, steel, power or telecommunications companies and the like are chosen for financial gain.

Why have the rich got a bigger share?

The return of the rich over the last four decades has been closely associated with developments in capitalism. Most important has been the rise of a new political economic orthodoxy, called *neoliberalism*.[27] Initiated aggressively by Margaret Thatcher and Ronald Reagan in the 1980s, it was consolidated with more stealth by their successors, New Labour as well as Conservative, Democrat as well as Republican. Now, after the crash of 2007–08 and in the ensuing recession – exactly when it has most clearly failed – it is being imposed with renewed vigour. It has three key features.

1. *Markets are assumed to be the optimal or default form of economic organisation*, and to work best with the minimum of regulation. Competitive markets supposedly reward efficiency and penalise inefficiency and thereby 'incentivise' us to improve. Governments and the public sector, by comparison, are claimed to be inferior at organising things – monopolistic and prone to complacency, inefficiency and cronyism. Governments should therefore privatise as much as possible. Financial markets should be deregulated and there should be 'flexible labour markets' –

political code language for jobs in which pay can fall as well as rise and in which there is little security. Where parts of the public sector can't be privatised, league tables should be established and individuals, schools, universities, hospitals, museums, and so on should be made to compete for funds and be rewarded or penalised according to their placing. Democracy needs to be reined in because the ballot box can't match markets in governing complex economies; people can express themselves better through what they buy and sell. Unsurprisingly, neoliberals keep their anti-democracy agenda under wraps.

2. The rise of neoliberalism also involves a *political and cultural shift* compatible with its market fundamentalism. Through a host of small changes in everyday life, we are increasingly nudged towards thinking and acting in ways that fit with a market rationality. More and more, the media address us as self-seeking consumers, savvy investors, ever pursuing new ways of supplementing our incomes through 'smart investments'. Risk and responsibility are transferred to the individual. Job shortages are no longer acknowledged, let alone seen as a responsibility of the state: there are just inadequate individuals unable to find work: 'skivers', 'losers'. No injustice, just bad choices and hapless individuals. The word 'loser' now evokes contempt, not compassion. Those unable to find jobs that pay enough to allow them to cope and who still need the welfare state are marginalised, disciplined and stigmatised as actual or potential cheats. State health services and pensions are run down and replaced by private health insurance and private pensions. You're on your own, free to choose, free to lose, depending on how you navigate through the world of opportunities and dangers. Instead of seeing ourselves as members of a common society, contributing what we can, sharing in its growth, pooling risks and providing mutual support, we are supposed to see ourselves as competing individuals with no responsibility for anyone else. Want to jump the queue for medical services? Click here. Want to give your child an advantage? Pay for private tuition. We should compete for everything and imagine that what is actually only possible

for the better off is possible for everyone; everyone can win simultaneously if they try.

We are expected to see ourselves as commodities for sale on the labour market, but also as 'entrepreneurs of the self'. Hence the rise of the cult of the curriculum vitae (résumé) and self-promotional culture. Education is increasingly debased by efforts to turn it into a means for making young people in this mould. Some people – probably many readers of this book – may want to resist these tendencies, but in a neoliberal society it is impossible to avoid them totally, not least because in so much of life using markets (disguised as 'choice') and competing in league tables have become the only choices we can make.

3. Neoliberalism has ushered in a *shift in the economic class structure* of the countries it has most affected. It involves not only a shift of power and wealth towards the rich, marked most clearly by the weakening of organised labour in industrialised economies and the enrichment of the 1%, but a shift of power *within* the rich: from those whose money comes primarily from control of the production of goods and services, to those who get most of their income from control of existing assets that yield rent, interest or capital gains, including gains from speculation on financial products. The traditional term for members of this latter group is 'rentier'. Many of the changes noted in 1 and 2 above benefit them. Neoliberalism as a political system supports rentier interests, particularly by making the 99% indebted to the 1%. More on this in Part One.

Many have tracked and attacked the first two elements; not enough have paid attention to the third.

A different approach: 'moral economy'

The deregulation and spectacular growth of finance are central to neoliberalism and the rise of the rich – and to the biggest economic crisis since the Great Crash of 1929. There has been a small avalanche of books on the financial crisis of 2007, some of them illuminating, many merely providing superficial narratives of successive financial disasters and the key players in them, served up with journalistic brio. Some critiques have targeted the hubris of the financial sector, identifying mismanagement, poor judgement and questionable legality. But some have seen the credit crunch and recession as evidence of something more basic – capitalism's crisis-prone nature.

Why We Can't Afford the Rich isn't just about the financial crisis, dire though it is. It's about what underpins and generates such crises – the very architecture of our economy. It treats the economy not merely as a machine that sometimes breaks down, but as *a complex set of relationships between people*, increasingly stretched around the world, in which they act as producers of goods and services, investors, recipients of various kinds of income and as taxpayers and consumers. The problems it identifies are as old as capitalism, though they have become much more serious with the rise of finance over the last 40 years. It goes beyond a focus on irrationality and systemic breakdown, to injustice and the moral justifications of taken-for-granted rights and practices. It's not only about how much people in different positions in the economy should get paid for what they do, but about whether those positions are legitimate in the first place. Is it right that they're allowed to do what they're doing?

There is of course a long history of critiques of capitalism aimed at different targets: alienation, insecurity and poverty; the treadmill of working and consuming; economic contradictions and irrationalities; and environmental destruction. There are useful things to learn from all of these critiques, but at the current time, when the rich have increased their power so much, and inequalities have widened, I believe we need a new line of attack, one that focuses on the institutions and practices that allow this to happen. Too many books on economic justice, and especially on the economic crisis, take as given the very institutions and practices that need questioning. This book is about the injustices of some long-standing economic relations that have come to a head in the crisis.

It could be described as an example of 'moral economy'.[28] By this I mean not moralising about greed but assessing the moral justifications of basic features of economic organisation. It's about the huge differences between what some are able to get and what they do, need and deserve. What people should get is a difficult issue, particularly where it's a matter of what we think people deserve or merit, but in the case of the rich, it can be shown that what they actually get has more to do with power. I shall argue that basically, the rich get most of their income by using control of assets like land and money to siphon off wealth that others produce. Much of their income is *unearned*. What's more, over the last 35 years, particularly with the increasing dominance of the economy by finance – 'financialisation', as it's sometimes called – the rich have become far richer than before by expanding these sources of unearned income.

This book is not only about money and goods, but about the very language of economic life, for the history of our modern economy is partly one of struggles over how to describe or categorise economic practices, as this affects what we see as acceptable or unacceptable: words like 'investment', 'speculation' or 'gambling' invite different evaluations. Who wouldn't prefer to be called an 'investor' rather than a speculator or gambler? But what do such terms mean and what practices fit them? When a top banker is described as having 'earned' £x million, we might question what 'earned' means in such a context: is it just what they've managed to extract from the economy? This struggle over words has been largely won by the rich and powerful, so how we speak about economic life systematically conceals their activities. Mainstream economics has proved to be a helpful if largely unwitting accomplice to this process, fearful of anything that might be construed as critical of capitalism.

To show why we can't afford the rich we need to go into some basic economic matters, but in a different and yet simpler way than usual. Most basically, we need to remember something that has been forgotten in modern mainstream economics: economics is about *provisioning*. As anthropologists and feminist economists have reminded us, it's about how societies provide themselves with the wherewithal to live.[29] Provisioning requires *work* – producing goods, from food and shelter through to clothes and newspapers, and services, such as teaching, providing advice and information, and care work. Almost all provisioning involves social relations between people, as producers, consumers, owners, lenders, borrowers and so on. It's through these relations that provisioning is organised. Some kinds of provisioning take place through markets; some do not. The market/

non-market boundary does not define the edge of the economy: unpaid work in preparing a meal for someone is as much an economic act as preparing pizzas for sale – or selling computers or insurance.

Most economists and political theorists think of economic actors only as independent, able-bodied adults, forgetting that they all started off as helpless babies, unable to provide for themselves and dependent on others, and who sooner or later reach a stage where, whether for reasons of illness, disability or age, they become unable to contribute to provisioning themselves and others. There is nothing exceptional about these conditions. We all go through them: they are universals. We can never pay back our parents for all the work they did for us, just as future generations will never be able to pay their parents back. *Dependence on others, particularly across generations, is part of being human*; it derives from the fact that we are social animals, 'dependent rational animals', as the philosopher Alasdair MacIntyre put it; we cannot survive on our own.[30] Robinson Crusoe depended on having been brought up in society; the newborn Crusoe wouldn't have lasted more than a few hours on his own. And like Crusoe we depend on the resources of the earth to survive; we cannot flourish if we damage the planet.

No one would deny the right of children to be fed ('subsidised') by their parents when they are too young to contribute anything in return. But would it be OK for me to buy up the company that currently provides your water and slap an extra 10% on your bills so that in effect you subsidise me, enriching me greatly? Would that be a defensible form of dependence? Or if I seized a park or beach that you had visited regularly all your life and charged you for access, would that be all right?

Dependence can be defensible or indefensible; it depends. Because we are so dependent on each other, there are always likely to be questions of fairness and justice where economic activities are concerned. Are you being paid fairly? Is it right that some get so much/little, and pay so much/little tax? Should students pay for their university courses? Should you get interest on your savings? Should there be more/less/no child benefit? More money for carers, or none? Who should pick up the bill when a company goes bankrupt, and who should pay for clearing up a derelict site left by deindustrialisation? Who should pay for pollution? These and other such questions are about *moral economy*. I believe we need to think much more about them – about whether our familiar economic arrangements are fair and justifiable, instead of taking them simply as immutable facts of life – or equally bad, as matters of mere subjective 'preferences', or 'values', beyond the scope of reason.[31]

Individuals may sometimes give more than they get, or get more than they give, for justifiable reasons, as in the case of parent–child relations, but sometimes they do so for no good reason other than power. Sexist men free-ride on the domestic labour of women for no good reason. This free-riding is particularly likely where people or organisations are very unequal in power. Minority control of key assets that others need is a crucial source of power and inequalities.

Because they can

Important though it is to think about moral economy, it's different from *explaining* economic arrangements. Few of our ways of doing things in economic matters are arrived at through democratic decision or careful deliberation on what is good and fair. Most are products of power. Usually, the best explanation of what people do and what they get in economic matters is *because they can*. Why do chief executive officers (CEOs) of big companies pay themselves such vast amounts? Because they can. They may offer justifications, but these are not only invariably feeble but redundant. They can get their pay rises even if the majority of people think they're unjustifiable. And usually the fuss over their pay hikes dies down in a week or two anyway. Equally, when we ask why care workers get so little for doing work that clearly benefits people, the answer is because that's all they *can* get, given their limited power. What we think people *should* justifiably get or contribute is one thing, and what they can actually get is another. Justifications and explanations are usually different. Many of the defences of existing economic institutions are surprisingly weak, but particularly if people start treating those arrangements as natural – as 'just how things are' – they can persist on the basis of power.

The landowner and the stranger

Here's an example of a taken-for-granted economic institution – private ownership of land by a minority. You may know the story of the stranger who trespassed on a landowner's land and was told to 'get off my land', whereupon the stranger asked the owner how he got this land. 'From my father', was the answer. 'And where did *he* get it from then?' 'From his father' . . . , who got it from his father, and so on. 'So how did one of your ancestors get this land in the first place?' asked the stranger. 'By fighting someone for it', said the landlord. 'Right', said the stranger, 'I'll fight you for it. If it was all right for your ancestor to seize the land in the first place, it must be all right to seize it back now. And if it *wasn't* all right for them to seize it, it *should* be seized back now!'

The story is striking but it's not clear what a better alternative might be. Would private ownership of land be OK if it was divided up equally so everyone had some? Or should land be publicly owned with individuals renting plots from the state, with the use of the rent revenue to be decided democratically? What the story does, at least, is jolt us out of our uncritical acceptance of the institution of minority land ownership. At this time of crisis we need much more jolting.

Mainstream economics takes the particular features of capitalism – a very recent form of economic organisation in human history – as if they were universal, timeless and rational. It treats market exchange as if it's the essential feature of economic behaviour[32] and relegates production or work – a necessity of all provisioning – to an afterthought. It also focuses primarily on the relationship between people and goods (what determines how many oranges we buy?) and pays little attention to the relationships between people that this presupposes.

It values mathematical models based on if-pigs-could-fly assumptions more than it values empirical research; so it pays little attention to real economies, having little to say about money and debt, for example! Predictably, the dismal science failed to predict the crisis. When the UK's Queen Elizabeth asked why no one saw the crisis coming, the economists' embarrassment was palpable.

I'll be drawing on the work of thinkers who had a more critical view, including, in chronological order, Aristotle, Adam Smith, Karl Marx, John Maynard Keynes, the Christian socialist R.H. Tawney and many recent so-called 'heterodox economists' and political commentators. Significantly, many of the latter *did* predict the current crisis.

Capitalism: a mixed bag

While this is as much a critique of capitalism as a critique of the rich, capitalism is both good and bad in a host of ways. There is no doubt, in particular, that it has produced unprecedented growth in technology and science and led to the integration of formerly largely separate parts of the world, as eulogised by Marx and Engels in *The Communist Manifesto*. Marx and Engels were less prescient as regards the improvement in living standards for many workers, who turned out to be better off being exploited than not being exploited, though that does not mean there were no losers or that there cannot be better alternatives to capitalism.

The media have a depressing tendency to favour simple stories of good versus bad over ones that portray the world as a complex mix of good and bad. This book should not be seen as ignoring the benefits capitalism has brought; nor, in criticising it, to be legitimising the state socialism of the former Soviet Bloc. 'Neither Washington nor Moscow (former or contemporary!)' would be my slogan. A recent Russian saying goes: 'Marx was completely wrong about communism, but damn, it turns out he was right about capitalism!' I don't think he was entirely right about capitalism by any means, though his thinking on its dynamics and on its generation of inequalities was more illuminating than most. But I'll draw on plenty of other thinkers too, many of them in varying degrees critical of Marx. If you're wondering whether I'm a Smithian, Marxist or Keynesian or whatever, my answer in each case is yes and no: yes where I think they're right, no where I think they're wrong.

The belief in a just world

For New Labour and Conservatives it's become an article of faith to deny that the rich are rich because others are poor. To get ahead, any career politician has to parrot this claim; it helps to keep corporate funders of their political parties happy, as well as media owned by the super-rich. No evidence or argument is needed, apparently; they just have to profess the belief, as if swearing on the Bible. This book shows that whatever they might want to believe, the rich are indeed rich largely at the expense of the rest.

How tempting it is for not only the rich but also the merely comfortably-off to imagine that, through their own efforts and special qualities, they deserve what they have, disregarding the fact that by the accident of birth they were born into an already rich country and in many cases an already well-off family within it that gives them significant advantages. How easy to overlook that they rely on getting cheap products made and grown by people from poor countries, who are no less hard-working or deserving but can be paid much less because they have little alternative.

But it's not only the rich who believe that they deserve their wealth. Many in the rest of the population think so too: 'they've earned it so they're entitled to it' is a common sentiment, even among those on low incomes. This is an example of what US psychologist Melvin Lerner called 'the belief in a just world'.[33] In economic matters, it's the idea that, roughly speaking, we get paid what we deserve and deserve what we get paid. Believing the rich deserve their wealth may seem a pleasingly generous sentiment, though assuming the poor also deserve their lot does not. It produces an unwarranted deference to the rich. As Lerner noted, the belief in a just world is a delusion, a kind of wishful thinking. Who wouldn't want to live in a just world, where need was recognised and effort and merit rewarded, while their opposites were not? But it doesn't follow that we do.

Understandably, since the 2007 crash, people have become more critical of the rich, especially those identified as bankers. Yet, according to recent surveys of public attitudes, they are even more critical of those at the bottom, scorned as 'welfare mothers', 'chavs', 'trailer trash', 'scroungers' and so on. What's more, it seems that as societies become more unequal, their members become less critical of inequality![34]

The rule of the rich

Economic power is also political power. The very control of assets like land and money is a political issue. Those who control what used to be called 'the commanding heights of the economy' – and increasingly that means the financial sector – can pressure governments, including democratically elected ones, to do their bidding. They can threaten to take their money elsewhere, refuse to lend to governments except at crippling rates of interest, demand minimalist financial regulation, hide their money in tax havens and demand tax breaks in return for political funding. Investigative journalists have revealed the circulation of individuals between political posts and positions in key financial institutions, and the role of powerful lobby groups in maintaining the dominance of unregulated finance, even after the crash. Prominent financial institutions have been involved in illegal money laundering, insider dealing and manipulation of interest rates, yet in the UK no one has been prosecuted and, where banks have been fined, the fines have not been imposed but arrived at by negotiation, as 'settlements'! They have infamously pocketed gains while the losses they have incurred have been dumped on the public, who have suffered substantial drops in income and services as a result. Of course, many politicians are already from an upper-class background in which supporting the rich is as natural as breathing, but even if they are not, 'our representatives' have become increasingly unrepresentative of the majority of the population at large. Even if they want to resist, they face an environment dominated by financial interests.

Spending it

The problem of the rich goes beyond issues of how they get their money, to how they spend it. Their massive spending on luxuries distorts economies, diverting producers from providing goods and services for the more needy. It's a waste of labour and scarce resources. In some cases, it makes things worse for those on low incomes, for example, by driving up house prices beyond their reach. The super-rich have so much that there is no way they can spend all of it on things they can use, so they recycle the rest into further rounds of speculation, buying up property, companies and financial assets that generate little or no productive investment, and merely siphon off more wealth that others have produced.

No one treads more heavily on the earth than the rich. Private jets and multiple mansions mean massive carbon footprints. Yet the inconvenient fact is of course that even though most of us have smaller footprints, in the rich countries they are still seriously in excess of what the planet can absorb. Even if we could afford them in money terms, we cannot afford high-carbon, high-consumption life-styles if we are to stop runaway global warming.

We are in deep trouble, not just because of the economic crisis, but because it's overshadowed by a bigger and more threatening crisis – climate change. The solution to the economic crisis is widely thought to be growth. But that will only accelerate global warming. The rich countries need to switch to steady-state or 'degrowth' economies to save the planet, but capitalism needs growth to survive; it's in its DNA. Soviet state socialism proved no better environmentally. We need a different model.

If that seems a gloomy conclusion, there is a very important and positive counter message: that beyond a certain level, attained already by most people in rich countries, well-being is not improved much by further increases in wealth, and well-being tends to be higher in more equal countries. Above this threshold, well-being *is* improved by greater equality, reductions in stress, exercise, being with others, both caring for and being cared for, developing interests and skills and projects and experiencing the world at large beyond the confines of narrowly defined jobs. Ending the rat race will do us, and the planet, a lot of good.

Outline of the book

The basic argument – expressed in my opening short answer – is simple. In the longer answer that follows there are of course some complexities, but I'll try to restrict these to the ones that make the most difference in practice. At many points, you may think of objections. While I'll try to answer some of these as I go along, in some cases I'll save them up until I've finished making points that are strongly interlinked. So I ask readers to be patient: the answer to your objection may lie a few pages on. I deal with some minor objections and qualification in the notes at the back of the book, and it's there you'll find the sources and references I draw upon. While it's probably best to read the chapters in sequence, the text is broken up by boxes with examples and asides that can be read in any order.

Part One, A Guide to Wealth Extraction, begins by showing how three familiar words – 'earnings', 'investment' and 'wealth' – can lead us astray in thinking about economic matters, effectively concealing a great deal about how our economy works. It then presents a crucial key to understanding the sources of the wealth of the rich: the distinction between earned and unearned income. The chapters that follow explain the different forms that unearned income takes in the contemporary economy. It ends with some common objections that people tend to make in defence of the incomes of the rich, such as their alleged powers of job creation, entrepreneurship and, more technically, promoting efficiency in the coordination of the economy.

Part Two, Putting the Rich in Context, deals first with how far our wealth depends on the labours of previous generations. Second, it examines the determinants of earned income, highlighting the much-overlooked implications of the division of labour between high-quality and low-quality jobs, and the inequalities these generate. Third, it exposes the myth of the level playing field or meritocracy, in which our position in society reflects our effort and abilities. In so doing, it sets the rich in a wider context of the reproduction of economic inequality.

Part Three, How the Rich Got Richer, deals with the build-up to the crisis over the last 40 years and the role of the rise of the rich in this, showing how the massive expansion of the financial sector has enabled a tiny minority to get rich by taking advantage of the opportunities it affords for wealth extraction on an unprecedented scale. It goes on to explain the origins of the wealth of some of the key beneficiaries of the financial boom – financial intermediaries, CEOs and big property owners.

Part Four, Rule by the Rich, for the Rich, shows how a finance-dominated elite subordinated democracy, ensuring that governments supported the interests of the rich, including their use of tax havens to hide their wealth. It explains the remarkable success of the rich in making others pay for the crisis, while diverting attention from what they have done and continue to do.

Part Five, Ill-gotten and Ill-spent, takes a critical look at how the rich spend their money, how it distorts the economy, wasting resources and labour and encouraging those below them to emulate their wasteful consumption. Worse, the rich threaten the planet. It also shows that well-being in the rich countries is not enhanced by ever greater consumption of material goods.

The conclusion highlights the diabolical double crisis in which we live – on the one hand, a deep financial crisis, on the other hand, the threat of runaway global warming. Business as usual is not an option. We need radical change – including rethinking what economic activity is for, and what kind of lives we want to lead – so we have to go back to basics. Though I can't provide a manifesto, I'll try to signpost *some* of the new ways of doing things that are needed.

Plenty of people are angry about the current crisis and the way they are being made to pay for it even though it was not of their making. In the old industrialised countries many will face years of unemployment, more debts than previous generations did, difficulty in paying for housing, lack of state support, bigger bills for basic utilities and a shrunken and underfunded public sector. Those who, through the lottery of birth in a highly unequal society, find themselves growing up poor are being blamed and despised for the lack of opportunities open to them. But we need to recognise the major part in all this played by the rise of the rich. As Tawney, a much under-rated radical thinker from the early 20th century, said: 'what thoughtful rich people call the problem of poverty, thoughtful poor people call with equal justice a problem of riches'.[35]

PART ONE

A guide to wealth extraction

Any economy depends on people contributing to provisioning as well as consuming what has been provided. Not everyone is able to contribute but everyone needs to consume to live. Those who can contribute – whether farming, producing machines or software, delivering products, teaching, training, caring and so on - usually don't mind supporting at least some others who are unable to work, certainly if they are their loved ones or part of their community, and sometimes beyond too. But some people can get an income by extracting wealth from the economy simply through their control of key resources that others need but lack, and by charging them for their use.

As we'll see, this is the key to the exceptional wealth of the rich. Access to mechanisms of wealth extraction, rather than wealth creation, is what marks them out. To understand why we can't afford the rich, we need to look into how this is done. Part One examines the main methods of wealth extraction.

But it so happens that the very vocabulary we use to describe and understand economic practices in our economy is systematically misleading. Even simple words like 'earnings' and 'investment' are dangerously ambiguous and conceal a great deal. We need to open up how these simple terms are used, so as to guard against mystification. And we also need to revive a distinction that used to be part of our economic vocabularies: between earned and unearned income. Chapters Two and Three explain these matters. Only when we've done this can we understand wealth extraction in all its guises.

The classic big three mechanisms of wealth extraction are rent, interest and profit from ownership of enterprises, but there are other, less obvious ones. The remaining chapters in Part One deal with these in turn, except for the last chapter, Chapter Eight, which answers some of the most common objections in defence of the rich, such as the claim that they create jobs and are special, entrepreneurial, innovative and hence deserving people, and that their wealth benefits others by 'trickling down'. It also answers the most likely objections to come from mainstream economists.

TWO

Three dangerous words: 'earnings', 'investment' and 'wealth'

In economic language, as in any language, a single word can mean quite different things. Words like 'earnings', 'investment' and 'wealth' may seem humdrum and innocuous, but they mask important economic, moral and political differences in contemporary life. They prompt ideas and assumptions about economic practices that guide what people do, but they do so in a way that conceals a great deal. For example, it's easy to suppose that because the rich are 'investors' they have 'earned' their wealth, so everything's perfectly right and proper. If we are to understand the problem posed by the excessive concentration of wealth, we need to crack open these words to reveal the crucial differences they hide, because they affect how we evaluate what we and others do, including the rich. Let me illustrate:

'Earnings'

When someone says 'I've earned £x this year', they could just mean that they have been paid £x. But, especially if they say it with emphasis – 'I've *earned* that £x' – they're likely to be implying that they have *deserved* what they have been paid; they may feel they've put in a lot of effort and done a good job. Some languages have separate words for these things, but English and many others do not. Slippage between the two meanings is very useful in leading people to assume that people get paid what they deserve. So it's not unusual for those on quite low incomes to say of the rich: 'Oh well, they've earned it so they're entitled to it'. It allows the rich to imagine that they are both deserving and special, and that those on low incomes are inferior.[1] It also allows 'earners' of all kinds to imagine that taxation takes away what they deserve.

There are many reasons why income and wealth have little to do with merit and effort. To understand them we need to look not only at where income and wealth come from, but also at what enables and encourages merit and effort in the first place. Much of this book is concerned with these matters.

'Investment'

Investment is surely a good thing: the word has a halo. We need to invest for the future, training people, building better infrastructure and communications networks, improving technology and so on. In these cases, investment involves the provision of resources that enable the production of goods and services or the development of skills that wouldn't otherwise exist. But this honorific term is arguably the most dangerously ambiguous word in our economic vocabulary, at least in camouflaging the sources of wealth. It's often used for quite different practices from the above, such as lending money to others at interest (who may just spend it on consumer goods instead of investing it), or buying existing assets like property, gold, works of art or shares in the hope that their price will rise.

Two quite different concepts of investment are involved here.

1. *Object-focused definitions.* These focus on what people or organisations invest *in* (e.g. infrastructure, equipment, people) and its usefulness and benefit in the future. A school or a wind farm or a railway or a training programme can provide long-term benefits by increasing our capacities. They enable the production of new goods, services and skills – things with useful qualities, or *use-values* in the language of political economy: a better teaching environment, a cleaner source of energy, a better means of travel, a more skilled workforce and so on. Or it might involve repairing or replacing worn-out equipment. These are examples of what we might call real or objective investment.
2. *'Investor'-focused definitions.* These focus on the financial gains to the 'investor' from any kind of spending, lending, saving,

purchase of financial assets or speculation – regardless of whether they contribute to any objective investment, or provide anything socially useful. In other words, instead of focusing on the benefits of the investment in terms of use-values, the focus is on how much money it yields to the investor. The financial sector uses the term 'investment' mainly in this sense, because it is largely indifferent to where its money comes from: £1 million derived from an objective investment is no different from £1 million obtained as interest on a loan, or through stock market speculation; money is money and masks all such crucial distinctions. As long as there's a good chance of it bringing a financial return, then gambling, including gambling with other people's money, gets called 'investment'. A tollbooth set up on a bridge for extracting money out of the bridge's users, could, in contemporary economic parlance, be called an 'investment' for the owners, even though the bridge already existed and no maintenance or improvements were made by the tollbooth owners.

Why does this matter? Because using the same word for different things allows people to mistake wealth extraction for wealth creation. The first meaning of investment refers to attempts to create wealth, the second to attempts to extract it. This indifference as to whether individuals or institutions are funding genuine investment or merely vehicles for providing money for the 'investor' is a major irrationality of capitalism, and the way we use the word 'investment' helps to conceal it.

There is no necessary link between the practices identified by these two usages of the term. While you might get a return on a genuine investment, you might not; even if it yields you nothing personally, it may still have produced material benefits somewhere – perhaps a hospital at the other end of the country that you'll never need. You might even lose money on it, but it could still be an investment in the first sense if it brings benefits to someone. Parents may feel the effort they put into bringing up their children is like this. From the point of view of the second definition, such cases would be seen as *bad* investments.

Equally, those usages that focus merely on financial gains can refer to actions that produce no objective investment in anything whatsoever; indeed they may, like asset stripping, have negative effects by sacrificing long-term objective investment for short-term gains made from closing down production and selling stuff off. Speculators almost always call themselves 'investors'.

Even the feelings associated with these two uses of the word are likely to be different: in the first case we might experience the satisfaction of having done something productive, whether for ourselves or others; in the second case there might be a more self-regarding feeling of having been prudent or clever, and an enjoyment of the money – we are 'smart investors'. Yet investors in this second sense often haven't a clue if any productive investment results from their savings or dealings on financial markets. As long as they get a reasonable return, then why should they care? But of course, it matters for the development of the economy. Banks invite us to think of our assets and savings as our 'investments', and offer to help us make them 'work harder' for us. This is especially ironic where things that we used to regard purely in terms of their use – our house as our home, for example – are treated as things we should regard as an 'investment', for the money they can bring in.

The rise of the second usage relative to the first reflects the emergence of 'financialised' capitalism, which prioritises making money out of money, instead of the tricky business of organising people to produce goods and services. It's truly extraordinary that we treat these different things as one and the same without even noticing. Even radical commentators often slide between the two meanings. For those who depend on investment in this second, investor-oriented sense, the slippage is a useful source of mystification, including self-mystification. It conceals not only a difference in functions, in how things work, but a moral difference – between contributing to the creation of something useful and just getting a return, no matter what.

In the absence of a different word, from now on I will put investment in the second sense in scare quotes or call it 'financial investment'. Such 'investment' is not necessarily derived from investment in the productive sense; it may be, but it may just be a means of siphoning off money from elsewhere in the economy.

'Wealth'

To uncover what this word conceals we need first to clarify something about money. Money has many functions and effects but the most important for the argument here is that it ultimately functions *as a claim on the labour and products and services of others*. It's a claim that they don't have to accept, but if they need money to live, and are willing to sell us something we want at a price we can accept, then our claim will be successful. This means that money only has value if others have things they want to sell us in return for it. And people from whom we buy things are likely to accept our money only if they're confident that, when they in turn want to buy something, the money will be accepted. So money is only trivially a thing – coins or notes. Much more importantly, it's a social phenomenon – an IOU, a symbol of a social relation between people, involving confidence and trust.

It's also a form of power: the rich have vastly more claims on the labour of ordinary people than vice versa. Although market evangelists like to compare markets to a kind of democracy, because everyone can use their money to 'vote' for what they want, it's a ridiculous comparison, as the voters have hugely unequal numbers of votes to cast, so that the rich minority can outvote the rest. And as we'll see, while most people have to produce goods and services to get money, the rich can also get money without producing, by getting it from those who do produce. But even though money is a form of power over others it is nevertheless ultimately dependent on goods and services being produced for sale. Contrary to the way some talk about economies simply as systems in which people buy and sell stuff from and to each other, we need to remember that the stuff needs to be produced first. If not, then pretty soon there will be nothing to buy or sell.

So what about wealth? In accountancy terms, our wealth is the market value of all our assets or possessions minus all the amounts ('liabilities') we owe to others. Unlike income, which is a flow of money in a given time period, wealth is usually defined as the market value of a stock or accumulation of things that have monetary value at a point in time. But again, there's a different sense of wealth that is not to do with money but with the usefulness and the import of things for us. We may treasure certain things because of what they do for us or mean to us, regardless of whether they'd fetch a price if we were to try to sell them. This is wealth in the use-value sense of goods and services, infrastructure and accumulated knowledge and information that enable us to do things and live well. Again, without goods and services, mostly the product of human labour, money would be worthless.

In a way, our current economic crisis is one in which this basic truth has been forgotten and people have imagined that money can be made just from money. If we remember only the financial sense of the word 'wealth', we will be like those people who, Oscar Wilde said, 'know the price of everything and the value of nothing'.[2]

Wisdom on wealth

For Aristotle, true wealth consists in things and practices that are useful in themselves, not the accumulation of property or money.[3] Money is just a means to an end, and to imagine it's an end in itself is a form of madness. For John Ruskin, 'A thing is worth what it can do for you, not what you choose to pay for it.' We sometimes include other things: some say 'your health is your wealth', and sometimes we stretch the word to cover everything that enriches our lives – friendship and love, nature, art, literature, science, music, dance, sport and so on. Ruskin also memorably said: 'There is no wealth but life. Life, including all its powers of love, of joy, and of admiration.'[4] At the end of this book, I'll argue that, rather than consider such comments as poetic indulgences, we should keep them in mind when trying to devise a better way of organising our economy and society – indeed, it's unrealistic to imagine that we can save the planet and improve the lives of the worst-off unless we do so.

You may have noticed a parallel between these three terms and their different uses. Just as we use the word investment both to refer to a process with useful results in terms of what people can do and as something that merely gives a provider of money a financial return, so wealth itself can be thought of in two parallel ways – as useful, beneficial things and relationships, or as whatever our possessions would fetch on the market. Similarly, earning can imply doing something that justifies a reward, or just a payment. In each case there's one meaning that has to do with useful activity (use-value) and another meaning that has to do with what people can get in money terms ('exchange-value'). In each case there may be occasions when the two aspects go together and perhaps have some interdependence, and other occasions where they need not. If we want to understand anything about the problem of the rich, and indeed the sorry state of the world, we need to avoid confusing these different meanings.

THREE

Income: earned or unearned?

To uncover the most important reason why we can't afford the rich, we need to rediscover the distinction between *earned* and *unearned* income. This distinction has been fundamental to the history of political economy, socialist thought and taxation. Indeed, it's still implicit in the categories used in our tax returns. It sounds prosaic, but it's hugely important. Politically, it's dynamite, for it implies that the income of the wealthiest people is largely undeserved. Interestingly, while the distinction has a long history, it has fallen out of use over the last 40 years – just the period when the unearned income of the rich has ballooned.

Let's take earned income first. Roughly speaking, this is what waged and salaried employees and self-employed people get for producing goods and services. I don't mean to suggest that the size of their pay exactly reflects what they deserve, but that their pay is at least conditional on contributing to the provision of goods and services that others can use. The relation between what we might think people deserve for their work – however we might want to measure that – and the amount of pay they actually get is pretty loose, as we'll see later. Nevertheless, their income is earned in the sense that it's *work-based*, and the goods or services they help to produce and deliver have *use-value*, such as the nutritious and tasty quality of a meal, or the educational benefits of a maths lesson, or the warmth provided by a heating system. So there are *two* criteria here: earned income is dependent not just on working, but on work that contributes directly or indirectly to producing use-values.[5] This is important because, as we'll see shortly, it's possible to work without producing any useful goods or services, and indeed in a way that merely extracts money from others without creating anything in return.

Some earned income is deferred. National insurance contributions paid by employees out of their earnings provide for a state pension in retirement and certain other benefits. So just because someone is receiving benefits without currently working it doesn't mean that their income is necessarily unearned; they may just be getting back what they had earned but not used earlier.

Many products and services are sold in exchange for money in markets, and so have not only use-value but *exchange-value*; they can be exchanged for other things for sale, by using money. But many are not produced for sale but funded by taxes, providing income for state sector workers, such as police officers, public librarians and school teachers. Public sector workers, no less than private sector workers, can produce wealth – useful goods and services. These goods and services have costs of production – the labour, the materials and energy they use, the training they require. Unpaid labour can produce vital goods and services too, like family meals, childcare and eldercare, though there are arguments for paying carers via the state. No society can exist without care work, but nobody ever got rich by doing it.

So we can reject the old prejudice that unless work produces a material object – something you can drop on your foot – it's unproductive. What could be more productive and socially useful than teaching a child to read, for example? (People who parrot the glib saying 'Those who can, do; those who can't, teach' need to do some thinking for a change.) Non-material services – whether they provide advice and information, healing, training, education or entertainment – can be hugely beneficial. And if we expect to have specialists in these things, as well as in material production, then giving them an income both rewards and compensates them for their work and enables them to do it. We can also ditch the prejudices that unless work generates money it's of no value, and that only the private sector produces wealth. As we've just seen, money and financial wealth have value only if there are goods and services for sale, but goods and services that are made available for free, like school lessons, can also be produced.

Some work has a more indirect relation to the production and distribution of goods and services, but is nevertheless necessary for efficient provisioning. Accounting is needed to monitor and manage the use of money in organisations; a police force is needed to protect people and property; and organisations that sell things need some workers simply to log the transfer of the title of ownership of the goods from the organisation to the buyer and to take money in return (this is primarily what check-out workers do in supermarkets).[6]

While earned income depends on providing goods or services, unearned income does not. It takes two very different forms.

1. *Donated or warranted unearned income – or simply 'transfers'*. Some forms of unearned income are freely given to their recipients, usually on the grounds that they cannot be expected to work to earn it. Children, the elderly and sick and those unable to do paid work may get this kind of unearned income, whether provided by families or by the state. In these cases the unearned income is generally deemed to be warranted on the basis of *need*, though of course love usually comes into it within families. In fact, we don't even think of it as unearned because it's so clearly warranted. Producers are unlikely to object to having to produce a bit more than they themselves consume in order to support them. There might be some individuals who resent supporting anyone but themselves, but of course if we all thought this it would be the end of society. We all depend on the care and support of others for important parts of our lives.

   And of course, while we might be public spirited enough to support something that we might not ever use, because it's good for others and part of what a civilised society should have, there will usually and quite reasonably be an element of self-interest in it too: who knows what mishaps and illnesses may befall us in future? Self-interest and what is in the general interest are not always opposed, indeed sometimes they're complementary.[7] It's not selfish of me to try to keep healthy, but it's in my self-interest, and in so doing I'm avoiding burdening others unnecessarily. But sometimes we can't avoid problems. Vulnerability is part of the human condition. So it makes sense to pool those risks and share in the construction of a safety net. If we share in supporting such a system, it can be a source of rights, not just gifts. Rights are obligatory, but gifts are discretionary and tend to position the recipient as deficient. As Ken Loach's film *The Spirit of '45* so powerfully reminds us, before the British welfare state was undermined and stigmatised by neoliberals, it was something to be proud of and part of – as workers, users and contributors through our taxes. Private insurance, by contrast, is provided on the basis not of need, but of ability to pay. In the US, in the absence of an adequate state health system, 48.6 million people couldn't afford health insurance in 2012.[8] (46.8 million Americans were living below the official poverty line at the time.) Many more had insurance that covered only less serious conditions. In such a situation, accidents and illness can have a devastating impact on people's lives: loss of jobs and homes, failure of small businesses and rapid descent into poverty. When British people get an email or letter from a private health company inviting them to bypass a National Health Service struggling to survive chronic underfunding, the implication is 'pay us – and tough on those who can't afford it – so we can feed a hefty proportion of the money through to our shareholders'.

In practice, just who is deemed to be entitled to transfers varies between societies, but it's generally based on a mixture of moral commitment, sense of duty and fairness, recognition of similar self-interests, cultural norms and political decisions regarding what the government needs to provide in benefits in order to get elected. It's a common source of argument in democratic politics. The prime justification is usually that the recipients are needy and cannot reasonably be expected to work for an income, or that there are insufficient jobs for them. But it's also a matter of collective and individual prudence. Transfers are *needs based*.

2. *Extracted unearned income.* This is very different. Unearned income can also be *extracted* by those who control an already existing asset, such as land or a building or equipment, that others lack but need or want, and who can therefore be charged for its use. The recipients of this unearned income can get it regardless of whether they are capable of working and hence of *earning* an income, and regardless of whether those who have to pay consider it fair. If the asset, say a house, already exists, then there are no costs of production apart from maintenance costs. Those who

receive unearned income from existing assets do so not because they are in any sense 'deserving' – they have not contributed anything that did not previously exist – or because they are judged by others as needy and unable to provide for themselves – but *because they can*. It's power based on unequal ownership and control of key assets. This is what J.A. Hobson, writing in the 1930s, called 'impropery'.[9] In most cases they have this power of control by virtue of property rights that legally entitle them to control an existing asset and dispose of it as they wish. This kind of unearned income is *asset based*. *It's central to the argument of this book.*

So, whereas earned income is work based and depends on producing use-values, transfers (or donated unearned income) are warranted on the grounds of needs, while unearned income based on control of assets has no warrant other than power.

Scroungers? Skivers?

Neoliberal politicians and the tabloid press regularly attack those on welfare benefits as 'scroungers' – or 'skivers' in the latest version from the UK Coalition government. In so doing they are echoing a distinction that goes back centuries – the distinction between the deserving and the undeserving poor. As historian John Welshman has shown, over the last 120 years social scientists have repeatedly been commissioned to find evidence for it, have done their researches and come back empty handed.[10] Terms like scrounger and skiver applied to those on benefits are a disgraceful slander against fellow citizens. Here are five reasons why.

- Many people who currently get state benefits *have* made contributions of work in the past or may do in the future, including paying National Insurance, and all of them will have paid tax in some form – even if they haven't paid income tax, they will have paid VAT on much of what they buy. One way or another, all but the very youngest members of society are taxpayers. So they are contributing as well as receiving; indeed, many are just getting deferred earned income. Maybe we should call it an entitlement rather than a 'benefit', which suggests an act of charity.

- Typically, the unemployed are in and out of work as short-term jobs become available, rather than unemployed permanently. And thanks to declining real wages since 2008, the numbers of 'the working poor' have risen, substantially exceeding the out-of-work poor.[11]
- Many are unable to work because of debilitating illnesses or serious impairments. In the UK the current ConDem coalition has waged a shocking campaign against the sick and disabled, attempting to force people who are in no condition to work to find work or face benefit cuts.
- Many do important *unpaid* work caring for others. There's more to work than employment, and more to wealth than money. Care work is vital for well-being. It needs to be supported.
- Many are unemployed because there are not enough jobs to go round. This is the glaring fact that neoliberals and a largely uncritical media always resolutely avoid. In the last three years, estimates of the ratio of jobseekers to vacancies in the UK ranged between 5:1[12] and 8:1. In some localities, for every vacancy there are 20 people looking for a job. No matter how hard they work on upgrading their skills, the ratio is unlikely to change. Revealingly, unemployment is concentrated in localities with a history of major job losses and disinvestment. The unemployment rate doesn't vary across the country because people in one part of the country are feckless 'skivers', while elsewhere they are industrious – or 'strivers' as the UK Chancellor of Exchequer, George Osborne, called them. Eight – or five – into one doesn't go, George.

Any reasonable and civilised society would feel obliged to support such people. We should turn our attention to the undeserving at the other end of the income scale.

There's a further question to be asked about unearned income that unfortunately is all too often overlooked: How can it be possible for someone to live without producing anything? If they're consuming goods and services – in the case of the rich, in vast quantities – but not contributing to their production, then who is producing them? The answer can only be this: *for it to be possible for some to consume without producing, others who are producing goods and services must be producing more than they themselves consume. In other words, others must be producing a surplus.* Even though they may be getting a wage or salary, *part of their labour must be unpaid.* As the Christian socialist R.H. Tawney put it in 1929 (hence the gendered language): 'The man who lives by owning without working is necessarily supported by the industry of someone else, and is, therefore, too expensive a luxury to be encouraged.'[13]

Some people may get a mixture of unearned and earned income. Some workers, for example, may own a second property that they let out for rent and that provides them with some unearned income on top of their earned income. Some may manage to make money on their houses, when prices rise, and some may get income from shares on top of their incomes from work, though in both cases it's mostly the better-off who get these opportunities. As we'll see, there are other ways in which people may get a mixture of both sources of income. We shouldn't expect to be able to classify everyone unambiguously as getting their income from one just source or the other; the distinction between the sources of income remains clear even if some individuals have more than one. Our tax returns require us to distinguish them.

Unearned income derived merely from ownership of assets is problematic, *whoever* benefits from it, because it relies on power rather than contribution or need. In the case of the very rich, as we shall see, it is power rather than contribution that accounts for most of their income. The fact that many ordinary people benefit from small amounts of asset-based unearned income shouldn't allow us to miss the elephant in the room: the rich get so much more of this undeserved income than others. In the US, political economist Michael Hudson writes:

> The richest 1 per cent of the population receive 57.5 per cent of all the income generated by wealth – that is, payment for privilege, most of it inherited. These returns

– interest, rent and capital gains – are not primarily a
return for enterprise. They are pure inertia, weighing
down markets. They do not 'free' markets, except by
providing a free lunch to the wealthiest families. The
richest 20 per cent of the population receives some 86
per cent of all this income . . .[14]

We can now look at the major kinds of unearned income that political
economists have identified, starting with the least contentious one
– rent – and going on to interest and the more contentious case
of profit, and then on to others such as shareholding and 'value-
skimming'. This will take a while because some of them, particularly
interest on loans, have far-reaching implications; but, especially in
these times of crisis, property bubbles and unpayable debts, we need
to understand them if we are not to be victims of them. These are
all forms of wealth extraction, and they all primarily benefit the rich.

FOUR

For rent ... for what?

As soon as the land of any country has all become private property, the landlords, like all other men, love to reap where they have not sowed, and demand a rent even for its natural produce. The wood of the forest, the grass of the field, and all the natural fruits of the earth, which, when land is held in common, cost the labourer only the trouble of gathering them, come, even to him, to have an additional price fixed upon them. He must then pay for the licence to gather them; and must give up to the landlord a portion of what his labour either collects or produces. This portion, or, what comes to the same thing, the price of this portion, constitutes the rent of land. (Adam Smith)[15]

Men did not make the earth.... It is the value of the improvement only, and not the earth itself, that is individual property. (Tom Paine)[16]

Roads are made, streets are made, railway services are improved, electric light turns night into day, electric trams glide swiftly to and fro, water is brought from reservoirs a hundred miles off in the mountains – and all the while the landlord sits still. Every one of those improvements is effected by the labour and at the cost of other people. Many of the most important are effected at the cost of the municipality and of the ratepayers. To not one of those improvements does the land monopolist as a land monopolist contribute, and yet by every one of them the value of his land is sensibly enhanced. He renders no service to the community, he contributes nothing to the general welfare; he contributes nothing even to the process from which his own enrichment is derived. ... the unearned increment in land is reaped by the land monopolist in exact proportion, not to the service but to the disservice done. (Winston Churchill)[17]

If land is owned by a minority, then because everybody needs land to live on, and new land can't easily be produced, the landowners can charge others rent for the right to use 'their' land. As the land and any minerals or other useful properties that it has already exist, the rent is not a payment for the creation of something useful; there are no costs of production to pay for. Nor does ownership in itself make land more productive. Only if the landlord improves the land or builds something on it is any of their income earned, and then only to the extent that users are paying for the work of improvement – the costs of production – rather than anything more. Any more is what the American reformer Henry George – and later, Winston Churchill – called 'the unearned increment'. But even where landlords buy land in order to put up buildings to let out, the tenants are usually not just contributing to the cost of producing the building but paying pure economic rent on top of that. Michael Hudson, estimates that 33–35% of US national income goes on rent. Although income from rent is often called 'earnings', it is not. As Tawney observed, rent is like a private tax on the industry of others.[18]

A person who derives unearned income from ownership of existing assets or resources is known in political economy as a *rentier*. The Duke of Westminster, Britain's eighth-richest person and a major landowner,[19] is a prime example.

This familiar system of private landownership and private rentiers can be inverted. If the land is owned by the state, it can be rented out to individuals and organisations, and the unearned income in this case goes to the state, whether central or local, where it can, in principle, be used for democratically controlled purposes; so, as John Stuart Mill put it, 'it can become a rent-charge in favour of the public'. Earlier Tom Paine wrote, 'Every proprietor owes to the community a *ground rent* for the land which he holds.'[20] Alternatively, under the private system, the rent could be taxed. In the infancy of modern taxation, it seemed obvious that the first thing that should be taxed was unearned income from rent. How strange – and interesting – that modern governments would rather tax earned income than unearned income!

As Adam Smith correctly recognised, the unearned income of the rentier depends on producers producing a surplus over and above what they consume themselves. *Rentiers free-ride on others' work*. If someone gets £1 million from rent, that money can only have any value if there are goods and services for sale that they can buy with it. Therefore surplus goods and services have to be produced by others somewhere. The unearned income of adult, able-bodied rentiers is unwarranted and undeserved. We should challenge it.

Land values, and with them rents, tend to rise over time, especially as cities develop and infrastructure is improved, so the unearned increment rises. This is 'development gain', and it's unearned – a windfall. Lots of people are small-time rentiers without realising it, and benefit from development gain. If you buy a house for £150,000 and do no more than maintain it in its existing condition, and later sell it for £200,000, then the profit (after deducting inflation) is unearned income – a windfall gain. But it's the rich who benefit most.

'Billionaires' Alley' – or Benefits Street for the super-rich

On The Bishops Avenue in London, Britain's second-richest street, a third of the mansions are standing empty. They are owned mostly by extremely wealthy foreign nationals and registered in tax havens. Most of them are occupied for only a minority of the year, partly for tax avoidance reasons, and some have been empty and left to decay for years. Despite the deterioration, their market value has soared by millions – not thanks to anything their owners have done to the property – but merely as a side-effect of the wider development of London. Their owners bought them as 'investments' – a way of free-riding on wealth produced by others in the form of 'development gain'.[21]

Rather than impose a 'mansion tax' on such owners, the government has instead chosen to impose a punitive 'bedroom tax' on low-income people in state housing who have a spare bedroom, pricing some of them out of their houses, and despite the lack of smaller properties for them to go to. To them that have shall more be given, and from them that have not, shall be taken even that which they have.

From land to patents, Wi-Fi, stars and celebrities: economic rent

We're used to thinking of rent as something we pay for using land or property, but economists have extended the use of the term to cover other things that provide a means of extracting unearned income by controlling an existing scarce asset.

Because the supply of land is almost entirely fixed, demand for it usually exceeds supply, allowing owners to extract a rent from non-owners. But the supply of some other goods can also be restricted by power, with or without legal enforcement. Any business that has a monopoly of a product or technology or has a captive market can push up its prices beyond what it would obtain in a competitive situation, so that part of its income is rent. In the case of major infrastructure like railways or information technology networks, where there are benefits from having a common set of technical standards for all users so that they can interact, the provider of the common technology can use this 'natural monopoly' to extract rent from users. When businesses lobby (and bribe!) governments to approve technical product standards and regulations that favour their own company by giving them a monopoly, they are seeking economic rent. The need for compatibility in information technology has enabled Microsoft to extract vast rents from sales of its Windows operating system; the prices far exceed the costs of producing the software. Owners of patents on particular technologies can extract rent by charging others for its use. On a smaller scale, hotels and other businesses that sell Wi-Fi access – which, once installed, has minimal costs – are extracting rent from users.

There are intermediate cases too of 'soft power' where goods are provided, but as a means of getting rent: social networking sites provide users with ways of keeping in contact with people but their income is mainly economic rent from letting out advertising space.

Businesses can compete not only by providing better products more cheaply but by 'rent-seeking', that is, seeking control of assets and resources that can be used to extract rent from users. Joseph Stiglitz, former Chief Economist at the World Bank, claims that the return of the rich is largely the result of a massive growth in rent-seeking, particularly in the financial sector. He argues that this not only transfers income from one group to another, but has a negative effect on the economy because it diverts resources from productive uses that create wealth, to mere wealth extraction.[22] Instead of being reinvested in production, the money is merely siphoned off to the unproductive rentier.

Carlos Slim Helu, for many years the richest man in the world, owns 90% of the telephone landlines in Mexico, and 80% of the mobile phone networks, an extraordinary politically mediated windfall of economic rent.[23] Chrystia Freeland reports that Slim's income is equivalent to the average annual salary of 400,000 Mexicans.[24] The Russian and Indian oligarchs who figure prominently among the super-rich owe much of their wealth to buying up existing businesses, often at knock-down prices, particularly through the privatisation of former state-owned enterprises. Privatisation of public utilities, like water and railways, a hallmark policy of neoliberalism, decisively favours rentier income.

How to extract rent from ordinary people via water, electricity, railways, roads and hospitals

In the UK, all these things used to be wholly controlled by the state via nationalised industries. They were state owned and were often monopolies, charged with supplying infrastructure and services, and paid for by ordinary people either directly or via taxes. They did this with varying quality; sometimes producer interests outweighed consumer interests, but they weren't burdened with having to make continual short-run profits for shareholders (on which see below) and the government was accountable for their performance. When they were privatised, they became private monopolies for substantial periods, providing companies with a guaranteed source of income. True, they had to compete for those contracts, but once they had got them, they could enjoy the opportunity to soak the public. Contrary to the hype, they don't need to be 'enterprising'. Water bills have nearly doubled since privatisation,[25] but this is no longer the government's problem. As James Meek points out, at least when they were nationalised, the rich could be charged more than the rest in taxes to fund them, and so helped to redistribute to low-income households. But once they were privatised – and this first happened during a period in which top rates of tax fell to 40% in the UK – the rich could pay what to them were trifling sums for their services, while the rest had to pay dearly.[26] Politicians may wring their hands when privatised suppliers push their prices up far above inflation, but it's also out of their hands.

But there's another new area in which rent-seeking is advancing. 'Intellectual property' may sound dull, but it's opened up huge new possibilities for companies to extract rent from others, with major consequences. Intellectual property is the ownership of ideas and the representation of those ideas, covering trademarks, patents (allowing ownership of inventions – tangible or virtual – for specific periods of time) or copyright, protecting authorship of books, music, art, images and films, again for specific periods of time. For a period they have a monopoly over selling the idea or product themselves, or can license it out to others at a fee.

It may be costly for an individual or company to come up with an invention; knowing that they can recover those costs helps motivate them to innovate. And they would rightly feel aggrieved if others could immediately copy and sell their invention and free-ride on it. If inventors can get a patent, then they have ownership of their invention, and can charge others for borrowing it. This provides a compromise between allowing them to recoup their costs and getting the benefits of allowing others to use and develop the innovation further. But while it's one thing to allow inventors to recoup their costs, it's quite another to use patents or copyright to charge others far over and above this. This not only impedes the spread of innovations and their benefits but allows the patent owner to charge others what are effectively rents, so they become a form of wealth extraction.

NewYork filmmaker Kirby Ferguson observes that while we happily borrow, copy and benefit from the ideas of those who have gone before us, without a thought, many of us are reluctant to let others use 'our' ideas unless they pay us for doing so. When Walt Disney produced films like *Snow White*, *Pinocchio* and *Alice in Wonderland*, he borrowed the stories freely from the public domain, but when the copyright on his films ran out, he lobbied to have it extended. And as the late Steve Jobs said, 'We [Apple] have always been shameless about stealing great ideas.' Yet Apple is famously quick to litigate against any companies who borrow or appear to borrow Apple's ideas. As Ferguson puts it, 'Most of us have no problem with copying (as long as we're the ones doing it).'[27]

In recent decades, the scope of 'intellectual property' claims has expanded these sources of rent extraction, most notably in seeds,[28] software and business methods and in so-called 'financial innovations' such as new types of derivatives. Whereas patent law protected specific inventions, software claims can be much looser and broader in their coverage as designers have sought to expand the range of their claims. Sixty-two per cent of all patent disputes are now over software. As intellectual property rights have grown, litigation has itself become big business, not only extracting huge rents but stifling the emulation and adaptation of ideas that are so important for the growth of knowledge and culture.[29] You can come up with an idea and sue someone for reproducing it, even if you had no intention of using it yourself. Not surprisingly, intellectual property is the subject of feverish activity and struggle.

Sports, TV and film stars and musicians often come to mind when people think about the rich – the likes of Tiger Woods, Lionel Messi, Paul McCartney, Angelina Jolie and Oprah Winfrey – even though they make up a tiny proportion of the rich, and hardly any of the super-rich. They are clearly examples of people who do things that many people value as special, that enhance the lives of their followers. Surely their income, though enormous, is earned? If no one wanted to follow them, they wouldn't be rich.

In many cases, although they have to work extremely hard at their skills, they owe at least part of their advantage to genetics, whether it be the exceptional height of basketball players, the capacity of endurance athletes for benefitting from fitness training, or the cheekbones, eyes and long legs of a model. Like land or the natural fertility of the soil, these aspects of their success are not the product of work and training, but are inherited assets.

Take the example of football stars: in the UK Premiership, footballers' annual pay averages £1.16 million. Although they clearly have thousands of followers, one British survey of attitudes to economic inequality found that footballers were at the bottom of the public's 'deservingness list', even below city bankers.[30] But first we should remember that there aren't many of them – fewer than 500, representing only 0.00076% of the UK population, and far fewer than the more anonymous (and wealthier) rich of the corporate sector. They can charge much more to perform than what it cost them to develop and use their skills, significant though those costs might have been. If thousands, perhaps millions, of people are willing to pay to watch them, then while the charge to each might not be large, the sum of these payments will be. Not surprisingly, players' wages take up the majority of the vast revenues of leading football clubs (70% of the UK Premiership clubs' revenue[31]). Small differences in ability may make huge financial differences, determining whether clubs can enter elite competitions and win trophies and lucrative advertising and sponsorship deals.

Some fans may feel the players deserve their pay, but even if there are others who think they should be more modestly paid, they may still be willing to pay the £20 or £40 per game or whatever it costs to see them. Either way, the players get these wages because they can, even if some fans think they shouldn't. If all elite players' pay across the main leagues were reduced by 50%, there's no reason why they couldn't play as well. Standards of skill and fitness have surely improved over the years, but if players' incomes now are 20 times what they were, say, 40 years ago, it doesn't mean that their skills and efforts have increased by the same amount. The main change has been in the size of the audience or markets, and this is largely a result of developments in information and communications technology, especially in TV money, and in sponsorship by advertisers and sales of kit.[32] Their growth has far outstripped the supply of stars: in fact, by definition, stars are small in number, and in some cases they have unique qualities.

The same goes for today's top music and film stars. Their income doesn't reflect simply what they contribute, but economic rent; in effect, the expansion of the customer base by global media has increased the amount of economic rent they can collect. But stars differ from other recipients of economic rent in one important respect: unlike someone needing a place to live, those who pay to hear their music or watch them act or play do so freely rather than under duress. Whereas the landlord offers a disservice, they offer a service, though it's more expensive than it needs to be.

There are also particular 'stars' in some lines of business – often designers and technologists – who have the edge in skills and know-how, or at least reputation over others – and can therefore push up their salary to include what is effectively economic rent. The more universities are rewarded financially and in league tables for employing star academics, the more those individuals can demand in pay. It's often called pay for performance, but again, these employees' performance is largely unaffected by pay: it's just a matter of status bargaining, of charging as much as they can.

FIVE

Interest ... for what? *or* We need to talk about usury

Interest today rewards no genuine sacrifice, any more
than does the rent of land. (J.M. Keynes, 1936)[33]

Especially if you're young, you're probably worried about debts –
credit cards, student loans, car loans; and if you want to buy a house
– which for most people means taking on even bigger debts – how
will you ever be able to afford it? For many the debt crisis isn't just
something out there they've read about. Politicians may have spun
the idea of 'a nation of owners', but 'a nation of borrowers' would
be more apt.

Debt, and more specifically interest on loans, needs closer
examination. It's the second major form of unearned income. It's a
more complex case than rent, but it has much in common with it too.
Where rent derives from controlling assets such as land and property,
for interest, the relevant asset here is money that can be lent out to
others. In fact, political economist Ann Pettifor calls interest 'money's
rent'.[34] It assumes a huge importance in neoliberalism. Particularly
in the middle of a debt crisis of unprecedented proportions that
threatens economies and ordinary people's lives, we need to be clear
about the nature of interest. It's common to think that charging
interest on loans is only fair, and also a good way of encouraging
people to lend. But in many ways it's economically dysfunctional,
and arguably socially unjust: indeed, the two problems are linked.

What's more, it's widely assumed that when we borrow from
banks or use our credit cards, we're borrowing existing money that
others have deposited there. Actually, as we'll see, this is far from

the truth, for the money the banks lend is *created* by them, out of nothing – yet of course they still charge us interest on it. The media and most conventional economists are quick to criticise when a state-controlled central bank 'prints more money', and to raise the alarm about stoking inflation, but they either don't know or don't want to admit that most new money is routinely created by private banks, with little regulation and public accountability. But more of that later. First, we need to deal with interest itself, assuming for now that the money being lent already exists.

Even after the debt crisis of 2007, interest charges have an easy ride in popular thinking today. The lender, it would seem, is doing the debtor a favour, for which she should be grateful. The lender may after all be a saver, someone who prudently 'invests' in a savings account and who imagines (mostly wrongly, as we'll see) that their savings will be lent on to businesses for productive investment, so that their actions support the economy too, in a happy conjunction of self-interest and public benefit, with interest as the reward. The debtor, however, is more clearly in a position of inferiority, deficiency, *owing*; the very word 'debt' signals this. Debtors who fall behind with their repayments – be they ordinary individuals or governments – should surely pay up, shouldn't they? A promise is a promise. If the debts were to be cancelled – or 'forgiven', as they used to say, as if being in debt were a sin – those prudent lenders, those financial benefactors, would lose out; worse, the debtors would not learn their lesson, and they would soon come to expect to be subsidised by others! This is how many people think about debt. In the words of Nicholas Mirzoeff, a New York University professor active in the Occupy Wall Street movement,

> Debt has become the means of subjecting everyone – from sovereign nations to homeowners and victims of payday loan sharks – to a mixture of ersatz morality and threats. Pay your debts or else you're a bad person or bad country, and so bad things will happen to you.[35]

By such means, creditors maintain ideological as well as economic dominance.

On the other hand, precisely because 'debt' has a negative tone, we may prefer to think of its positive flip-side, 'credit'. The consumer finance industry has played this option brilliantly. In a remarkable social transformation, where once debt was seen as a burden and source of shame, now, under the more appealing label of 'credit', it has come to be seen as an entitlement and an index of social inclusion. (In some situations businesses will only accept credit cards in payment, so without one you are excluded.) Where once ordinary people could obtain loans only by enduring a testing session with their local bank manager, financial institutions now bombard us with offers of 'easy credit'. Credit cardholders can easily forget the difference between paying for something with their own money and borrowing to pay for it. The 'credit-worthy' can buy a house, a car and other products now, rather than at some point in the future when they have enough money. Having a mortgage admits us to the ranks of respectable property owners. With a 125% mortgage you could not only buy a house but furnish it too, all on credit. How generous! The offer of credit seems like a vote of confidence in our prudence and ability to earn money in the future. Yet, as Maurizio Lazzarato says, 'The credit card is the simplest way to transform its owner into a permanent debtor.'[36] And debts discipline people to work to repay their debts, providing their creditors with unearned income on a long-term basis.

There is also *hidden interest*. Businesses regularly borrow money at interest and pass on the cost to consumers. Those credit cardholders who pay off their debts every month and imagine that they're not paying interest are wrong: the retailers selling us stuff on our credit cards have to pay interest anyway and they pass it on to us in the price of the goods. The German economist Helmut Creutz calculated that in his country, 38% of the price of drinking-water is hidden interest, as is 77% of the rent on government-subsidised housing and 40% of the cost of a typical bundle of goods bought by a German household.[37]

But there's a different and much older way of talking about interest on debt: as *usury*. As David Graeber shows in his remarkable book, *Debt: The First 5000 Years*, usury has been understood and resented for millennia, and is still condemned by some religions, for example Islam.[38] The objections are not directed at lending and borrowing as such, but at lending at interest. This pre-modern term may sound anachronistic and negative, with its associations of exploitation and grinding oppression. Its condemnation by stern religious voices, often dismissed as 'fundamentalist', may not be appealing either, and we may be tempted to dismiss it as dogma backed by arbitrary, supposedly divine, authority. Talk of 'interest' may sound more modern, rational and non-judgemental, though we do still use 'usurious' to describe excessive rates of interest.[39] Yet the critique of usury has much to tell us today, as we are learning – the hard way. Precisely because paying interest on loans and getting it on savings are thoroughly normalised in modern life, we can easily fail to note the peculiarity of the practice. We need to step back to get a better view, and the critique of usury can help.

The first thing to note is something that the concept of usury puts centre stage – that debt is a social relation between lender and borrower, not merely a sum of money. Put like that, it may seem too obvious to mention, but we easily forget it in a world where debt is an 'asset' that can be bought and sold and can become an object of financial speculation, and where we read of debts as pure quantities – often of astronomical size – with little or no indication of who owes what to whom. Historically, the most important form that this social relation takes is between those who have spare cash and those who lack cash. In such cases, the economic inequality between the relatively rich and the relatively poor is a precondition of the debt relation being set up in the first place. If the real interest rate – interest after adjusting for inflation – is zero, then the transaction is at least equal, even if the context that prompted it is not. But if the real rate of interest is positive, the inequality increases because repayments exceed the amount borrowed, and in effect the lender can take advantage of the relative weakness of the debtor. Unless the debtor defaults, when the loan is paid off the net flow of money is from the poor to the rich. Interest payments thus allow the better-off to 'hoover up'[40] money from those with low incomes. On a global scale, loans – usually called 'aid' – to Third World countries *produce a net flow from poor countries to rich*: in 2005 an estimated $40.4 billion of aid to the very poorest countries yielded $43.2 billion in debt service.[41]

Like rent, interest is asset-based unearned income that accrues without any effort. There may be some administration costs in providing a loan, but these tend to be low and can be charged to the borrower. Like rent, interest presupposes that those who produce goods and services for their income produce a surplus that the lenders can buy with their unearned income. Like rent, therefore, interest is parasitic on producers. As Michael Hudson puts it, it is a 'deadweight cost' on the economy.[42] It is not merely a transfer, a zero-sum game (where gains equal losses), but a negative-sum game – that is, one that, other things being equal, leaves the economy worse off.

Blocking a possible misuse of the argument

In societies in which National Socialism or fascism took hold, the argument that asset-based unearned income was parasitic was hijacked and used explicitly or implicitly in a specifically anti-Semitic way, to attack Jewish people involved in finance. Neo-Nazi and other anti-Semitic groups elsewhere have also used it. I have found in giving talks on this book, specifically in Germany and Austria, that a common response has been that words like 'parasitic' provoke disturbing reminders of that tendency, and that it is risky to reintroduce them. I have not had the same response from UK or Scandinavian audiences – presumably because of their different histories or ignorance of the history of anti-Semitism. Many centuries before fascism, the association between finance and Jews arose because, while Christianity prohibited usury, though not *borrowing* money at interest, Jewish beliefs restricted it to lending at interest to *non*-Jewish borrowers. (Christianity also at times used an insider–outsider split for restricting usury.) Further, money lending was one of the few occupations that Jews living in Christian and some Muslim societies were *allowed* to have. (In Austria, for example, they were not allowed to own land, or be farmers or manufacturers until emancipation in the early 19th century.) By such means usury was both tolerated and forbidden, while anti-Semitism created a scapegoat and a target of resentment.

So let me both acknowledge that hypocritical history and the despicable, appalling, anti-Semitic consequences that followed, and dissociate myself completely from it and the related rhetoric: my argument has absolutely nothing to do with religion or ethnicity, or other groups constructed via generalised stereotypes. It is about the problem of getting unearned income purely on the basis of control of existing assets that others need; it can be done by anyone, and is done today by people of many different religions and none, sometimes unwittingly, as in getting windfalls from house price inflation. This is something we all need to think about if we want a fairer society, while robustly condemning any who try to hijack and pervert the argument for anti-Semitic purposes. A bad use of an argument should not drive out a good one.[43]

In the case of compound interest, as charged on credit card bills, unpaid interest is added to the principal and subsequent interest is calculated on the basis of this enlarged sum, so that debts can increase exponentially – a fact of enormous significance. *At 5% compound interest, the principal doubles every 14 years.*

Compound interest means that, *unlike* rents, which are generally fixed for certain periods, and unlike profit from production, interest payments can provide the lender with continual *increases* in their unearned income. This is unsustainable. Unless the rate of interest is below the rate of growth of the economy, debts will pile up to the point where they become unpayable. Exponential growth of anything eventually leads to crises. In nature, processes may grow exponentially for a while but then growth typically slows down and flattens out. The exceptions include the growth of cancers.

Compound interest – 'the worst thing in the world'?

'All that we had borrowed up to 1985 was around $5 billion, and we have paid about $16 billion; yet we are still being told that we owe about $28 billion. That $28 billion came about because of the injustice in the foreign creditors' interest rates. If you ask me, what is the worst thing in the world? I will say it is compound interest.' (Former Nigerian President Olusegun Obasanjo speaking after the G8 Summit in Okinawa, Japan in 2000)[44]

Albert Einstein called it 'the most powerful force in the universe', and US magnates J.P. Morgan and John D. Rockefeller 'the 8th wonder of the world'. Napoleon apparently wondered how the human race had not been devoured by compound interest.[45]

The problem here is not credit but interest, and worst of all, compound interest. Credit is a useful way in which money – claims on others' labour – can be provided for those who can put it to use. Capitalism has always required credit as part of its normal workings – at the least to cover temporary gaps between outgoings and revenues. Without it firms would be continually held up by having to wait for payments to come in before they could pay for a new round of production. Credit oils the wheels of production and commerce by tiding businesses over at such times and enabling them to reap the huge economies of routine, continuous activity, instead of being held back by wasteful disruptions. Large-scale, long-term investments in which returns lag behind outlays by many years may also require credit. Such 'productive' loans, as Adam Smith called them, in contrast to 'consumptive' loans, are paid off through the gains they bring in output. They encourage higher output, efficiency and growth than would be the case if businesses had to wait until they had enough cash before undertaking investment. But the higher the rate of interest, the more these gains are siphoned off by lenders, reducing the benefits to the economy.[46]

'Consumptive loans', including mortgages and credit cards, allow consumers to bring forward purchases, and so may boost growth for a while, though in the long run their consumption is reduced by the burden of paying off the interest. Whatever the benefits of credit, interest charges add deadweight costs, diminishing those benefits. This depression of consumption and investment by the payment of interest is sometimes called 'debt deflation'.

Lenders generally demand higher rates of interest from those who are more at risk of defaulting. In the US, the poor pay 50–60% more in interest on auto loans than the better-off. From the point of view of the lender, this may be rationalised as a form of insurance against risk, but it has the ironic effect of making those in a weaker position for getting credit even more likely to default. This is a prime contradiction of usury. High rates of compound interest are a recipe for the impoverishment of debtors. Further, the lender usually demands some form of collateral from the debtor, so that in the event of default, the debtor has to give up some of their assets to the lender. According to The Money Charity, in 2014 in the UK, a home was repossessed every 20 minutes.[47] So, having taken advantage of the inequality, the creditor is then allowed to *dispossess* the debtor. In recent decades, at the international level, a common means of dispossession has been demands by the International Monetary Fund and World Bank that debtor countries sell off their public utilities to private businesses as a condition of getting better credit terms.

In the case of 'debt bondage', the lender effectively enslaves the debtor, who has to work for the lender in order to pay off their debt – which of course, they may never be able to do; that's the intention. Though banned in international law in 1956, it continues in various forms in some countries.[48] It may have ceased in most of the world, but when debtors plead inability to pay, the creditors can still call the tune, dictating to the debtor. As the critics of usury argued long ago, it allows the rich to take advantage of the borrowers' poverty and make them their servants.

We see something close to this in Europe today, with holders of government bonds (that is, lenders to governments) – mostly large private banks and 'investment' funds – demanding that debtor countries such as Greece, Ireland and Spain – or, more accurately, ordinary people in such countries – tighten their belts, and their governments sell off public assets in return for concessions. The Greek state has been selling off land and property to outsiders in order to pay back its debts, providing them with profit through dispossession. More on this in Part Three.

For the rich, lending money, even at modest rates of interest, can provide a good income. With a real interest rate (that is, net of inflation) of just 3% per year, someone with a spare £1 million can, without working, secure an income from lending it of £30,000 after one year. This is well above the median household income of £23,208 in 2011–12, which is likely to be mostly *earned*, from working 1,700 hours or so. After 10 years' compound interest at 3%, the lender's initial 'investment' will have grown to £1,343,916. In practice, the rich can get higher rates of return than this. And of course, ultimately, the millionaire rentier's interest must be paid for by those who actually produce goods and services.

> ## Modern usury
>
> In early 2014 the average UK household debt, including mortgages, was £54,472 – or £6,018 excluding mortgages. Daily interest payments on personal debt are £162 million.[49] To their cost, many people do not realise how high rates of interest can be: high or 'usurious' rates of interest have become common for consumer credit, with some store cards charging rates of interest well above 20% per year. In Britain the annual percentage rate of interest on Homebase and Dorothy Perkins cards in 2014 was 29.9%.[50] £1.5 billion of transactions are made with plastic cards every day. So-called payday loans – small loans for short periods of time – are in a league of their own, incurring enormous rates of interest – Ferratum charges a typical Annual Percentage Rate of interest of 2,591%, while Wonga, the highest-profile payday lender in the UK, charges 5,853%.[51] That might sound downright nasty, but Wonga advertises its loans through television commercials featuring puppets of loveable, funny old people – Betty, Earl and Joyce – making small talk. This is how contemporary usury is deodorised. 'Easy credit' is the most expensive. No wonder its founders, Errol Damelin and Jonty Hurwitz, had made £50 million between them.[52]

Despite the remarkable normalisation of debt, there are still situations where we would regard charging interest on loans as unethical, indeed outrageous. Imagine you're currently having a hard time paying your bills, so you ask a comfortably-off friend to lend you some money. They answer, 'Yes, but only if you pay me interest at x%' – perhaps compound interest. Such a response would threaten the relationship, for your so-called friend would clearly be taking advantage of you. It would turn what would otherwise be seen as a generous act into something mean spirited and exploitative. And of course it would seem even more outrageous if they demanded that you should hand over your assets if it turned out you couldn't repay. So, while we might accept interest as a fact of life in impersonal economic dealings, in our personal lives we generally do not, indeed we find it *objectionable.*[53] And we refuse it for reasons similar to those given in traditional critiques of usury, be they religious or secular: it allows the rich to take advantage of the weakness of the poor.[54]

Yet there are some strange contradictions in everyday thinking about usury. While the interest the so-called friend wanted to charge would be regarded as unreasonable, indeed outrageous, the interest that institutional lenders like banks charge is just seen as a necessary cost. And of course, we may still expect interest on our savings, though we don't notice that this means that someone, somewhere, will have to pay us that unearned income.[55] One person's interest is always another's debt.

Notwithstanding this contradiction, the example of the friend demanding interest makes clear that interest changes a situation in which the lender's temporary sacrifice is matched by the borrower's eventual repayment into one where the lender gains at the expense of the borrower, for the value of the repayments exceeds the loans (unless inflation wipes out the lender's gains). *As creditors are normally better off than debtors, interest serves to widen inequalities.* Helmut Creutz estimated that in Germany, the bottom 80% of people in the income distribution pay out far more interest on loans and hidden in the prices of goods than they get back on savings – not surprisingly, for few of them can afford to save much. Those in the next 10% get roughly as much interest as they pay out, while those in the top 10% get more than they pay out, and within that group the richest of course enjoy the biggest surplus (Figure 5.1). In Britain, the Positive Money researchers estimate that only the top 10% get more in interest than they pay out, and of course it's the 1% who get the most.[56] This redistribution through interest on debt is a major cause of inequality.

Interest payments made by people on their mortgages, credit cards, car loans, payday loans and so on provide banks and other financial institutions with a major source of unearned income to 'invest' in a host of ways, often by re-lending it to others to extract still more. Similarly:

> Government debt . . . can be thought of as a means
> for upward redistribution of income, from ordinary
> taxpayers to rich bondholders. Instead of taxing rich

people, governments borrow from them, and pay them interest for the privilege. Consumer credit also enriches the rich: people suffering stagnant wages who use the VISA card to make ends meet only fatten the wallets of their creditors with each monthly payment.[57]

Figure 5.1: Comparison of household interest payments and interest returns in Germany, 2000

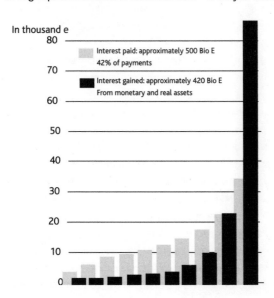

Comparison of interest paid and gained
In 10 groups of households of 3.8 million each – in the year 2000

Source: Kennedy, M. (2012) *Occupy money*, New Society Publishers

Another day older, and deeper in debt: neoliberalism and the middle class in the US

Harvard Law Professor Elizabeth Warren has tracked what has happened to the middle class in the US since the 1970s. Throughout this period, men's wages flat-lined. At the same time many women entered the labour force and contributed to family incomes.

She looked at how much families getting the median annual income saved and how big their 'revolving debts' were (mainly credit card debts, which can be carried forward continually). In 1972, households getting the median annual income saved 11% of their income, and their revolving debts were only 1.4% of their income. By 2005 such households had negative savings of 1.4% and debt amounted to 15.6% of their income.

By 2005 such families were spending everything that the women's pay added to family income, plus everything they used to save, and yet still went into credit card debt to the tune of 15% of their incomes. Why? Warren shows that it wasn't a result of over-spending on everyday goods: spending on things like clothing, food, appliances actually *fell*, though all the real costs of these items had *fallen*, not risen, too. But over the same period mortgage costs for a three-bedroom and one-bathroom house went up by 76%; even though interest rates fell, house price inflation went through the roof. Meanwhile health insurance went up by 74% and taxes by 25%. Of course, payments for housing, health insurance and taxes can hardly be postponed, unlike renewing a car or buying new clothes. At the same time, the health services to which health insurance gave access contracted and pushed up the risk of illness or injury threatening family income. Families with children have become much more subject to bankruptcy, mostly because of loss of job, medical problems and/ or family breakdown. Indeed Warren found that more children lived in families that had gone bankrupt than that had split up.

This is exactly what you'd expect of neoliberalism: an increasing proportion of ordinary people's income has gone on paying for property – effectively rent – and on interest on debt, and hence into the hands of rentiers, while formerly partly socialised costs funded by progressive taxation are privatised and borne by a more restricted group of taxpayers.[58]

Those who lend at interest certainly don't want borrowers to default on repayments, but if borrowers clear their debts and fail to borrow anew, that's bad news for lenders, as it stops their unearned income; if borrowers can be kept in a state of indebtedness, needy yet just solvent, able to pay off compound interest, then that's ideal for lenders. And of course, with compound interest, when the borrower gets into difficulties, short of defaulting altogether, *the lender benefits even more*. In the sober language of political economy, it is an extremely 'regressive' form of redistribution of income. This means there's a strong whiff of hypocrisy and deceit about the portrayal of debtors as morally deficient – whether it's indebted individuals, companies or whole nations – for the creditors' continued unearned income depends on these debts being renewed! That's why some creditors charge penalties to those who pay off their debts early.

The rich would rather lend to the rest at interest and enlarge their unearned income than have to pay taxes to support them. Neoliberal governments obligingly cut the taxes of the rich, sell off public assets to them and replace government spending on education with loans to students that will yield interest. Governments then have to borrow more from the private sector to fund the public sector, thereby increasing the power of the rich and their ability to dictate policy. As Maurizio Lazzarato puts it, 'repaying is a duty, lending is an option'.[59]

But there are some situations in which the rich themselves are borrowers, so it's a different kind of social relation of debt. It costs them less to do so than it costs the rest of us because they are the most 'credit-worthy' and have the most assets to use as collateral. Not only do they get charged lower interest than the poor, because they are seen as a lower risk, but any given interest rate is less onerous for a rich borrower than for a poor borrower for the simple reason that a pound is worth much more to a poor person than to a rich person. Wealthy individuals and corporations, including financial institutions, borrow from other wealthy sources in order to finance takeovers of companies and speculative ventures, in the expectation of getting more money than they have to pay back in interest.

Economists often encourage us to think of economies as masses of exchanges. I give you this money in exchange for that thing you want to sell. Once we have made the exchange, our obligations to each other are at end. But debt relations are not like this, for they last until they're paid off. This leads us to a further argument against usury: *interest charges make a claim on the future.* Because lending at interest must ultimately be backed by increased output of goods and services, it requires continual growth, though at present the amount of debt far exceeds what economic growth can pay off. As Philip Coggan comments: 'In the last forty years, the world has been more successful at creating claims on wealth than it has at creating wealth itself.'[60] At a micro-scale, individual borrowers may be able to pay off interest by cutting their current spending – accepting austerity, we might say. But at the scale of a whole economy, things work differently: if many cut their consumption, this means that firms' sales go down, causing them to lay off workers; and those who lose income find it still harder to pay off debts. So government-imposed austerity only makes things worse, stifling the growth that is needed to pay off the debt. Unless debts are cancelled (the creditors 'take a haircut', as they say in financialese), economic growth is needed to enable debtors to pay off interest. Debt with interest places demands on economies that may be simply unachievable, and are likely to be environmentally unsustainable. And insofar as they control the future, debts project the lenders' dominance into the future.

As long as growth continues and debts are not too large, usury may be tolerated, but if we enter a period of zero growth, whether by choice or necessity, then it becomes intolerable. It's extraordinary that compound interest is allowed. While rates of interest that merely compensate for inflation are reasonable, so that the value of the money that's repaid to the lender is the same as that of the loan in the first place, the more rates of interest exceed the rate of inflation, the more unacceptable they are.

So goes our modern, secular critique of usury. It appeals not to divine or other arbitrary authority but to criteria of fairness and human well-being. Of course, there are defences of interest on credit, but before we consider them, there's a common misunderstanding of bank lending and where credit comes from that we need to rectify.

It's a misunderstanding that has long allowed the financial sector to escape serious scrutiny, and there's a risk the delusion may persist.

How banks create money for nothing and charge us interest for it

> The essence of the contemporary monetary system is creation of money, out of nothing, by private banks' often foolish lending. (Martin Wolf)[61]

> I believe it is absolutely fundamental to understand that banks do not intermediate already existing money. They create money and credit *ex nihilo, de novo*. (Adair Turner, former Chair of the UK Financial Services Authority)[62]

> Capitalism is issuing money to itself and claiming it as profit. (Mary Mellor)[63]

For most people, it's natural to think of interest in terms of their own savings and debts, and to assume that loans are always loans of someone else's savings. Banks, it's imagined, lend out our savings to others and make money on the difference between the interest they pay on deposits and the interest they charge on loans. In this view, banks are 'intermediaries', linking hard-working, prudent savers to investors in the economy's future.

This picture is seriously misleading. It is not just that banks lend out much more than they borrow from us, on the assumption that we and other savers will not draw out our savings all at once. This is the widely taught story of 'fractional reserve banking'. The important point is that they have the power to *create* electronic money in the form of interest-bearing credit (or debt, from the point of view of the borrower) simply by typing the figures into the borrower's account. They *create* such deposits rather than wait for them to come in.[64] When we borrow from a bank, or from a credit card company, we are *not* drawing upon existing money that they already have. In fact 'lending' money is hardly the right word, inasmuch as that implies that they've already got the thing they're lending![65] Conventional economic theory may claim that investment (lending) is determined by saving, but that is nonsense; it is mostly dependent on the creation of credit money.[66] The prime consideration in assessing whether to make a loan is the risk of default and whether the borrower has sufficient collateral.[67] The costs of production of this 'credit money' are negligible, and so, *in this case it is clear that the principal as well as the interest are unearned.* Rather than the bank doing the borrower a favour by lending other people's savings to the borrower, the borrower is doing the bank a favour by allowing it to create money – and a source of unearned income in the form of interest. As Ann Pettifor puts it, banks 'extract money from the productive sector in a manner that can fairly be described as parasitic'.[68] Their interest charges are a private tax on borrowers.

When the television news reports increases in the money supply they love to show film of banknotes being printed, but most money in modern economies is electronic money, created as credit by banks, merely entries in digital accounts, almost costless to 'produce'. They have a licence not only to create money but to extract interest in the process. To be sure, the central bank has a monopoly on producing coins and notes, but cash has declined dramatically relative to digital money; in the UK, it forms less than 5% of all money.[69] As we borrow from one bank, get paid from our employer's account with another bank and pay bills by direct debit to other bank accounts, no coins or notes need be exchanged. In so far as banks still need money in the form of cash, they can borrow this from the central bank without limit, passing on the cost of the interest charges to their own customers.[70]

In effect, banks can *create* 'fictitious capital'. Here, the unearned income in the form of interest is dependent not on the existing surplus of goods and services but on future surpluses. Ultimately, even though the money isn't usually lent for productive investment, it's necessary that *somehow* future production will grow to provide the goods and services for sale on which the interest yielded is a claim.[71] That depends on the whole economy – which of course particular lenders of fictitious capital don't control.[72] It's a gamble. Although creation of fictitious capital can facilitate growth, it is all too easy for it to be created at a rate far exceeding the growth of production, and indeed this has happened with a vengeance over the last 30 years, resulting in the current crisis.

Given the economic importance of credit creation and the power it gives to banks, one might think that it would be tightly monitored, but in the UK it is not:

> There is no monitoring of whether newly created credit is used for transactions that contribute directly to GDP or not. Credit financing trading in existing assets, real or financial, does not contribute to GDP, but instead contributes to unsustainable asset inflation. Nowhere is there oversight of whether credit contributing to GDP is used for productive or consumption transactions (the latter creating more direct inflationary pressure).[73]

As we shall see, in practice credit money goes primarily to trading in existing assets.

Yet the creation of credit money can be a good thing. In its absence borrowers are dependent on those who have savings or reserves that they can lend out. Credit creation undermines the monopoly of lenders of existing money and promises lower interest rates, allowing economies to escape from dependence on them. This is not the way things have turned out, however, for private banks have used it for their own gain. In so far as the creation of credit money is useful, we have to assess whether private banks – governed by a tiny, self-interested elite – or some other kind of organisation should perform it, and how whoever does it should be regulated. Should the economic development of societies be constrained by the need to provide private banks – which have their own interests and shareholders – with unearned income? Or should credit creation be undertaken by democratically accountable public banks, to support real investment at minimal rates of interest? This is something neoliberals strenuously resist; they value their little-known private source of unearned income.

The dominance of private credit money implies that we should change the way we think about debt. Those who don't know about it are inclined to think of interest as a reward to someone for lending out their hard-earned pay to others. Lenders, it seems, are thrifty and prudent, borrowers less so, perhaps, and interest payments reward the former for their virtues. Though this homely moral tale might seem appealing, strictly speaking, any interest that exceeded the administrative costs of lending out the money would still be unearned income. But much credit has no such 'honourable' origins. So we should stop thinking as if it did.

But what about the case *for* interest? As we'll see, the standard arguments don't acknowledge the existence of credit money created by private banks, but there are other problems with them too. Let's look at the usual defences.

The consenting adults/entitlement defence

In this view, as adults we have every right to contract freely with others who want to borrow or lend and who are willing to pay or accept interest. It is up to us what we do with our property and who we contract with and, beyond providing a few safeguards against fraud and coercion, the state has no business in the matter. This is a classic, liberal economic argument. In some of the more right-wing versions it loads all the responsibility for avoiding deceit onto the borrower. Those low-income, sub-prime borrowers who defaulted and lost their homes should have had more financial savvy, and the lenders should feel no guilt about having taken advantage of the asymmetry of information and knowledge. It's a hard competitive game. 'Your mortgage is not my problem', as the Tea Party slogan goes. In the softer versions, interest is fine, provided there's no deceit or duress.

But what is duress where debt is concerned? Take parents on low incomes who find they can't afford to buy Christmas presents for their children, and so borrow, probably at very high rates of interest, to do so. Right-wingers might say that the freely taken, uncoerced decisions of free individuals present no problem. But consider the shame involved for the parents and the sense of lack of worth of the children if they had not done this. The situation is actually a form of duress. Or consider student loans.[74] In the absence of grants, few students can afford to fund their time at university without going into debt. They may feel that the risks of not having a degree are such that debts, including interest charges, are a cost they just have to pay. Although there's no coercion, the fact that it's harder for young people to get a job, let alone a good one, without a degree, means that this too is effectively another form of duress. This is not to say that all borrowing is like this: some credit cardholders overreach themselves quite unnecessarily, for example.

But anyway, we should be wary of sliding from the classic liberal idea that people *ought* to be able to contract with one another to lend and borrow, as if they were equals, to the assumption that in practice such relationships *are* ones of equality. Yes, we all have the right to borrow and lend, and are formally equal in that respect. But in practice much debt depends on economic inequality – on some having more power than others, either through having spare money to lend or, as in the case of the main source of money – banks – having the right to create credit money. Usury exploits that inequality.

The abstinence defence

Another line of defence of interest argues that it's compensation for the deferred use of the money. Assuming that the creditor prefers having a given sum – say £1,000 – now to having it in, say, five years' time, then, if they are to lend it to others, they deserve compensation for that deferral, so that they will be willing to go without it. According to the abstinence defence, in classic Protestant fashion, interest is a reward for not spending![75]

That people do necessarily value future wealth less than present wealth is questionable, actually: people who are worried about their pensions may not, for example. From the point of view of the environment, valuing the future less than the present is asking for trouble, and penalises future generations who will have to bear the costs. In many cases, rich creditors have no intention of spending their spare cash but see it precisely as a means by which they can get unearned income by lending it out. And, as we've seen, banks profit from creating new credit money, not by deferring the use of existing money. They don't have a rival activity that they need to be encouraged to abstain from. They hardly need compensating for what they would rather do anyway – and do at little real cost to themselves!

That would be like compensating a glutton for eating. In any case, in practice, interest is determined not by appeal to arguments about what people deserve but by the relative power of the would-be lenders and borrowers.

The risk defence

If we lend some of our money to someone, especially a stranger, we are taking a risk, and arguably deserve compensation for doing so, in the form of interest. And the more risky the loan, the higher the interest rate should be. Interest rates also regulate flows of credit: high rates encourage creditors to lend, and deter borrowers from taking excessive risks. (Although, again, if you're desperate, you may have to.) Differences in interest rates are useful to financial 'investors' in assessing risk. It's true, of course, that borrowers can default, and not all loans are secured by collateral – such as the mortgagee's house – so the lender may sometimes lose; but while the risk argument is stronger than the previous two defences of interest, it avoids some important facts.

First, as we saw, charging higher interest rates to borrowers regarded as risky increases the risk that the borrowers will get into trouble! This is obvious both for low-income people in debt and for public debt, as we see in Europe now, particularly in the Greek case. In demanding higher rates of interest on loans to countries that are deemed to have weak economies, bondholders – mostly private banks – make them still weaker and less able to repay.

Second, the risks are not usually shared equally between lender and borrower. This is hardly surprising, for credit presupposes a power imbalance evident in the very fact that the borrower has to turn to the lender for assistance. If the borrower gets into difficulties, perhaps through events beyond their control, the lender expects the interest, regardless, and compound interest allows them to benefit still more from the borrower's difficulties. As Pettifor comments: 'Unlike wages and profits, the gains from usury are fixed regardless of whether value has been added or losses made.'[76] Where the loan is funding a risky real investment that turns out to be successful, it seems reasonable for lenders to share in the gains with the borrower, for they have helped to enable the investment. But if that's so, then it is also reasonable for them to share in any losses, for the lender has made a bad investment by supporting a venture that failed. This is consistent with the idea of markets rewarding and penalising people according to the relation between demand and supply. Some forms of credit are regulated to ensure that gains and losses are shared in this way – for example in Islamic banking, at least in principle[77] – but in modern liberal economies the lender gains in either case. And in the event of bankruptcy, lenders usually have a claim to the firm's assets.

The risks are also unequally shared because, through tax breaks and bankruptcy laws, states give more protection to creditors than to enterprises involved in producing useful goods and services. At a global level, governments of the most powerful countries, the World Bank and the International Monetary Fund can impose punitive policies on debtor countries. Like the heavies sent round to collect people's debts, they are the global creditors' enforcers.

Third, the more the risks fall on the borrower, the less need the lender has to worry about whether to make the loan. If, on the other hand, the risks are shared, so that the lender bears some of the risk if the borrower gets into difficulties, then they are likely to be more cautious about making the loan, and more likely to assess the investment closely and offer advice to reduce the risk. In other words, an asymmetry between lender and borrower encourages reckless lending and unwise investment. Instead of 'we're in this together, so let's both make sure it works', the logic becomes 'it's your problem, I want my interest, whatever'. Instead of sharing in a real investment, the lender can treat the arrangement as merely a financial 'investment'. And the lender can always take out insurance on the loan and pass the costs on to the borrower.

Fourth, as a matter of fact, *contrary to their image as institutions that lend for risky investments in new production, banks do very little of this.* Rather than lend against means of repayment that are not yet in existence, most of their loans are for buying existing property – 70% in the US and the UK[78] – and in so far as they lend to firms, it's mostly for buying back their own shares (on which more later) and for amassing funds to take over other firms – a mere change of ownership rather than real investment. In today's world, businesses of any size finance most of their real investment internally, from retained earnings, not loans. According to Hudson, US banks lend mostly for the acquisition of property for rent.[79] In such cases, the loan helps to enable another source of unearned income, as takings in rent are used to pay off the loan. Further, much of the vast expansion of debt in recent years has been in consumer credit, such as for buying cars, rather than for investment purposes. You may think the money you have deposited in your bank is being used to support economic development, but in practice very little of it is. Banks have failed in their most basic function.

Fifth, on top of the inequality of the economic context in which debt is likely to be taken on, there is also typically an asymmetry of information that favours the lender and pushes risk onto the borrower. In the US, as Joseph Stiglitz writes, powerful, voracious banks are engaged in 'predatory lending' in the sub-prime housing market to 'the least educated and financially unsophisticated in our society by selling them costly mortgages and hiding details of the fees in fine print incomprehensible to most people'.[80] Again, this is not to say that borrowers never have any responsibility for their debt. Predatory lending and irresponsible borrowing feed off each other, though it still provides the lender with unearned income.

Sixth, there's a more technical point that's become important in financialised economies: if the lender can sell on the debt as a security – a financial asset that promises to yield the buyer a flow of unearned income – to some other organisation, then the asymmetry in the distribution of risk is all the greater. Offloading the risk allows the lender to issue more credit and escape capital controls on the ratio of loans to cash reserves. Apologists call this managing or distributing risk, but all too often it has just encouraged more risky lending. More on this when we come to the financial crisis. Worst of all, when banks are deemed 'too big to fail', they have less reason to manage risk prudently, for they know that if they get into trouble they will be bailed out by taxpayers. The very fact that one group of people's debts can be treated by another group as assets – as a reliable source of income – should give us pause.

Finally, the risk defence tries to treat charging interest at rates related to risk purely as a matter of prudence. In its populist forms, the risk taker is a daring character – made of stronger stuff than ordinary mortals – but also smarter, someone who can spot opportunities that others miss, and yet prudent too – as the term 'risk manager' implies. The more prosaic truth is that they mostly lend against existing assets, are concerned only with their own returns, not with the consequences for the wider economy, and are generally taking advantage of the relative weakness of borrowers.

The pragmatic defence: interest is the only way

Credit is critical in capitalism. Imagine that there was a high rate of saving, but savers simply hoarded spare cash, stashing it under their mattresses for a rainy day; this would stall the economy because, unless there is enough money circulating, producers will not be able to sell their goods. And credit would be beneficial in any non-capitalist economy too. The pragmatic defence is simply that the only way you're going to get credit is by offering interest to the lender, even though, as a deadweight cost, interest reduces the benefits of credit. Interest encourages the recycling of spare cash and allows it to be put to effective work. It's a necessary evil. This clearly doesn't apply to credit money created by banks, though it would seem valid otherwise. Credit oils the wheels of commerce – and while interest encourages lubrication, it also throws in some grit as well.

In principle, if not always in practice, usury is forbidden in Islamic banking and those with savings are encouraged to bank them without expecting interest, in order to benefit the public good, and credit is channelled into real investment and for helping the less fortunate.[81] But in much of the world, apart from lending to friends and relatives, moral incentives to lend without interest don't work. In the absence of strong support for such moral economic principles, the most realistic option is to regulate interest, and to create publicly accountable banks that can issue credit money at low or zero interest for purposes that benefit the economy as a whole, instead of extracting the maximum unearned income out of whomever they deem credit-worthy.

The pragmatic defence of interest might apply to lending out and borrowing existing money, but, given that most of us borrow from banks that create credit money out of nothing, it has limited relevance.

Whatever we think about the 'justifications', they are beside the point when it comes to *explaining* what happens here: *lenders charge interest because they can, not because they can show that they deserve it or because it's good for the economy as a whole.* And of course the lenders usually charge as much as the market will bear. Whatever the 'justifications', it fits our definition of unearned income.

So, let's sum up.

Interest payments have been the big growth sector in unearned income in recent decades and are central to our current economic crisis. Though it's common to imagine that it's 'only fair' that people – or countries – should pay their debts, what's fair about interest, especially compound, when it involves the needy subsidising the rich? We need to talk about modern forms of usury. Whereas most of the defences of interest are from the standpoint of the lender, talking about usury draws attention to the social relation between lender and borrower in context – usually an unequal one – and considers both parties.

Credit is useful, indeed essential for an efficient modern economy, but interest is unearned income and a deadweight cost on economies; it redistributes wealth upwards and it places huge burdens on future generations. It's therefore ethically questionable and dysfunctional, so rates of interest are best minimised. Other ways of allocating credit are needed.

Whoever controls the allocation of credit, whether through using savings deposits or by creating credit money, has considerable power, for they control 'the commanding heights of the economy' and can shape its development. But where private banks are allowed to do this, the only responsibility that goes with this power is to their depositors (creditors) and shareholders. As far as they are concerned it doesn't matter what the loans are for and what their wider economic impact might be, so long as they stay in profit and keep share values rising. This ensures that financial 'investment' has little relation to real investment. Today's financial elite has come to imagine – extraordinarily – that extracting interest payments from people, businesses and governments is a form of wealth creation. For them, money is money, so who cares where it comes from?

SIX

Profit from production; *or* Capitalists and rentiers: what's the difference?

This brings us to the last of the big three forms of wealth extraction, and the one most associated with critiques of capitalism: profit from production, whether taken by private owners or by shareholders.

In everyday talk we tend to use the word 'profit' loosely to refer to any surplus of revenue over costs, regardless of the circumstances in which it arises. If you buy some goods for £10 and manage to sell them to someone else for £15, you might say you've made a profit of £5. But for your £5 to have any value, there must be some other goods or services on sale somewhere that you can buy with it, and of course they have to be produced. If producers produce only enough to cover their costs, then there can be no profit. Only if they produce and sell more than this can there be any profit. So, while profits can appear in such exchange of goods for money, the origin of profit in a whole economy can't be in exchange: it must be in production. For it to be possible for some to make profits systematically by buying cheap and selling dear, somewhere in the economy a surplus of goods must be being produced.

Imagine an economy of small, worker-owned cooperatives producing goods and services for sale in markets. Each cooperative has to decide how much of the revenue it gets from those sales to take as their pay, and how much to invest or save. Whether they call the difference profit or something else, it's clear that it's the difference between the value of what they produce and all the costs – wages, buildings, materials, equipment, energy and so on – that go into producing it. If they don't produce and sell goods or services with

83

a value that is greater than these costs they won't make any surplus or profit.

But cooperatives account for only a small proportion of businesses today. In a capitalist society, most businesses are privately owned by capitalists – or shareholders, though we'll come to them later. In this case the workers, as employees, do not own the business, nor its equipment, buildings, materials – nor, amazingly, do they have any ownership rights to the things they produce through their own work! Thanks to the strange property laws that have come to be taken for granted in capitalism, no part of the fruits of their labour is theirs to sell.[82] If it were, they could decide on what proportion of the revenue that the business brought in they could take as pay, be they managers or ordinary workers, and what should be done with the remaining surplus. But, as they own neither the so-called 'means of production' nor the output, they have little power and are dependent on those who do own them – the capitalists. (I'll explain why I don't use the more flattering term 'entrepreneur' in Chapter Eight.)

We've seen that landlords and money lenders, as rentiers, get their money from controlling existing assets. Capitalists own already existing means of production, so are they any different from rentiers? The answer is yes and no.

Almost everything we need has to be produced, and this almost always requires means of production. But apart from things like cooking equipment, most of us lack the means of production to produce the things that we need and hence are dependent on those who do own or control those means of production. So, most people, whether they consider themselves working class or middle class, are dependent on others – those who own means of production and who are willing to employ them – for making a living. In a capitalist society, most means of production are privately owned by a minority. In the classic sense,[83] a capitalist is someone who owns means of production and uses it to employ others to produce goods and services at a profit. (In public corporations the ownership is shared by shareholders, but what matters here is not whether ownership is vested in a single person or in a company on behalf of shareholders, but the origin of profit.) Capitalists can take advantage of this dependence and employ people to work with their means of production to produce goods and services for sale. But from the point of view of capitalists, there's no point in doing this unless they can make a profit, and this depends on the workers producing goods and services that are worth more than what the capitalist spent on hiring them and paying for materials, equipment, energy and so on. Otherwise their profits would be zero. So workers' wages are such that they are unable to buy back the equivalent of what they have produced. Their pay reflects not what they contribute, but what is needed to get them to do their jobs. More on what determines pay later.

Some may be tempted to object here that competition between capitalists encourages innovation and unprecedented economic development, from which workers have surely benefitted. The first point is certainly true, the second often true. But neither point contradicts what I have just argued!

At the same time, without a workforce, the owners can do nothing with their means of production. So there is an interdependency between workers and capitalist employers; they both need each other. But it is employees who are in the weaker position. In effect, they have to convince capitalist employers that they will be profitable to employ.[84] Some employers now even ask job applicants outright: 'What are you going to do to make me a profit?' It may be brazen, but from their point of view it's absolutely the relevant question. With the rise of neoliberalism over the last 30 years, this dependence has been culturally reinforced as young people have been encouraged to see themselves as marketable, and to work on their CVs so as to persuade employers to take them on, while educational institutions have been pressured into making it their priority to prepare students for the labour market.

Means of production are certainly important, indeed vital, for they boost the productivity of each worker, enabling them to produce far more than would otherwise be the case. One could easily think that since the machinery and computers make a difference here, the owner or 'provider' of such equipment should get the benefits. Mainstream economics, as ever the sycophant of the powerful, sometimes justifies capitalists' profit as a return for their contribution of capital, meaning means of production. But merely *owning* means of production does not make it productive; to make it productive you have to *use* it, operate it, and the pure capitalist leaves this to employee workers and managers. Owning a fast-food chain and its equipment and living off the profit that its workers produce is not like grilling burgers all day. Owning a chain of residential care homes for the elderly and living off the profit is not like doing the labour of washing, dressing, feeding and caring for the residents. Nor is it like doing the managerial work of organising the home. *Ownership itself produces nothing.*[85] If the means of production were owned by the workers in a cooperative, then the difference between their pay and other costs and the revenue their products brought in would accrue to them rather than to a capitalist, though of course that revenue would come from putting the productive equipment to work, not from mere ownership. In a cooperative, the benefits of using means of production are shared by those who use them to produce, instead of being pocketed by those who just own but who do no work.

Pure capitalists – that is, ones who merely own their firms and delegate management to others – are not contributing to wealth creation, but just using their power relative to that of employees to appropriate the difference between costs and the value of what the workers (and managers) produce.[86] *Their income is unearned.* Like rent, it is dependent on the private control of an existing asset, not productive contribution.

But not all capitalists play such a passive role; some get involved in managing their businesses. In such cases they can be called *working capitalists*; their profit is *partly earned* (in so far as they help to organise and plan the work) and *partly unearned* (in so far as their ownership of scarce assets allows them to take advantage of the dependence of workers and extract profit). One cheer for the working capitalist, we might say.

All organisations need managers: as Marx commented, a single violinist does not need a conductor, but an orchestra does.[87] Yet managers, however necessary they are, do not have to be owners. The conductor does not need to own the instruments and have sole control over the revenue that the orchestra earns. She could be an employee, or co-owner appointed by fellow workers.

Popular models of capitalists – such as the 'dragons' on the UK television programme *Dragons' Den*, in which would-be capitalists try to get the dragons' backing for new business ventures – tend to be of working capitalists rather than pure capitalists. As such they appear more legitimate. The dragons may offer business advice to the novice, but it's significant that what they're interested in is a share of the ownership of the new businesses so that they can cream off profit, not merely payment for advice. And of course, the workers employed in the businesses are rarely (never?) mentioned on the programme.

In these respects, pure capitalists profiting merely from owning businesses producing goods and services look very much like rentiers. But there's also a difference. Even though their income is unearned, it has a 'saving grace': it is at least dependent on supporting productive activity. A landlord who gets her income solely from rent is indirectly benefiting from the surplus that those who produce goods and services make, but she has no constructive role in wealth generation in the first place. While pure capitalists also depend on this surplus for their profit, they are also instrumental in making the generation of that surplus possible, and can make a profit only as long as this is the case. For Marx, whereas the capitalists funded production, those who merely made money out of money by lending or speculation belonged to 'the class of parasites'.[88] Further, as the political economist David Ricardo and, later, Marx, Henry George and many subsequent commentators have argued, capitalists and landlords and other rentiers have opposed interests, for rent puts up living costs for workers, creating upward pressure on wages, and it creates overheads for capitalists who rent land from the landlords. In both cases, it squeezes profits from industry. Interest on loans also cuts into capitalists' profits; not surprisingly, where firms can finance their investment internally from their own profits, interest free, they tend to do so.

Once again, income sources and individuals don't have to correspond one to one. Capitalists involved in productive capitalist businesses increasingly wear several hats by getting not only profit on the goods and services produced, but also interest payments on credit issued to customers or 'investments' on the stock market.

The saving-grace factor is strengthened by the fact that individual capitalist enterprises are in competition with others, and any that make below-average profits are liable to lose out to those that make higher profits. This obliges individual capitalist firms to make economies or to innovate if they are to stay in business. There are many ways of doing this. Some, such as simply cutting costs, like pay and pensions, or making workers work harder, have their limits (workers won't work for nothing,[89] and they can't work at just any speed). But the most radical and repeatable way of being competitive is to introduce more advanced and efficient means of production, or new, more attractive products that displace earlier ones. It is this pressure of competition and its effects on production that makes capitalism both dynamic and revolutionary, as Marx and Engels so eloquently acknowledged in *The Communist Manifesto*. So, on the one hand, the profit of the capitalist involved in production is parasitic, like that of the rentier, but on the other hand, it also depends on keeping the host organisms alive and supporting their growth. However, as we shall see in Part Three, under neoliberalism, the pressure to produce short-term profits and the increased mobility of capital have meant that capitalists have become less interested in long-term productive investment and more interested in plundering companies for profits, continually moving on to new ones to repeat the exercise.

While we are lauding some aspects of capitalism we might note another paradox. Although workers have to produce goods and services whose value exceeds the costs of production, including wages, they may be better off being exploited in this way than being unemployed or working in the informal sector, and hence not being exploited at all by capital. But then, if they owned the firms they worked for and didn't have to provide others with unearned income, they could be better off still.

But, you may say, isn't this model of individual capitalists owning companies rather dated? Aren't most big companies owned by shareholders and run by employee managers? Let's turn to them.

Shares and dividends: a bizarre institution

'Our first duty is to our shareholders.' In the 'shareholder spring' of 2012, shareholders were praised for trying to assert their rights over greedy CEOs. Almost always, shareholding is given an easy ride as a legitimate practice that needs defending from any rival source of power. It seems so much part of the furniture of economic life that it is only when we try to justify it that we notice what a strange phenomenon it is. Having been a marginal phenomenon in the post-war boom, in recent decades the power of shareholders has increased enormously with the growth of the so-called shareholder movement, playing a major role in causing the crisis.

Stocks and shares provide an important source of unearned income, though many people assume that they are rewards for investment. They give the owner dividends – an entitlement to a share of the profits of the company for which they are issued – though the amount depends on how much profit the company makes, if any, the type of share and the strategy of the company. They also give voting rights at company meetings, though it's major institutional shareholders such as pension funds and insurance companies that tend to dominate on such occasions. Most importantly, the existence of a market in shares means that as a company's share price rises or falls as its profits and expectations of profit change, they can be bought and sold in order to make gains. On the face of it, the dividends look like a reward for investing in the company and for taking a risk: there may be no dividends if the company is doing badly,[90] and if the company goes bankrupt the shareowners will lose their outlay, though no more than this: hence the term 'limited liability'.

But appearances are deceptive, for over 97% of share deals are second hand – bought and sold on the secondary market. So if, like most 'investors', I buy existing shares, the money I pay goes to the previous owner, *not* to the company itself; in other words, I have bought an entitlement (and one that could last indefinitely) to a probable stream of future income from a company, without making any real investment in it.[91] As Tawney put it, shares 'yield an income irrespective of any personal service rendered by their owners'.[92] Even if I buy the shares first hand, direct from the company when it makes an 'initial public offering' as it's called, so that the money can be used by it for real investment (though it could use it for other purposes, including buying up existing assets), it's not clear why I should be entitled to an indefinite reward rather than a time-limited one or one that's capped at some level. At least when one buys bonds issued by a company (that is, lends it money, rather than buying shares), the interest payments on the bond are limited, though they are still unearned income. On the other hand, the bondholder has in general to be repaid, regardless of the fortunes of the company, and so she carries little risk, unlike the shareholder.

But most buyers of shares are hoping to make money not so much from dividends but from buying and selling shares at the right time as their prices go up and down so that they make a profit. Nearly two-thirds of share income comes from price increases, less than one third from dividends.[93] A firm that is making above-average profits is likely not only to pay high dividends but find its share value rising, benefitting shareholders. It may also be able to use its shares as collateral for short-term borrowing. Where, as happened from the 1980s, more and more people and institutions enter the market for shares, such that demand exceeds supply, share prices overall will go up, allowing an inflation of share values – which many mistake for evidence of economic growth, and of prudence and enterprise on the part of the 'investor'. If demand rises for ordinary products like computers or cars, we expect the supply to increase. If the price of such products rises, we expect fewer people to buy them; but more to buy them if the price falls. But the stock market doesn't work like this. The supply of new shares is limited because companies are wary of triggering a fall in share prices. And 'investors' want to buy shares that are expected to rise in price, so the stock market is radically different from ordinary product markets.

An early lesson: the Matthew principle

When I was a boy I saved up most of my pocket money in the hope of being able to afford to buy a car when I got to 17. (Growing up in the 1950s and having parents from Yorkshire, thrift and deferred gratification were instilled into me.) By the time I reached my early teens, which was also the time when I learnt how to calculate interest in mathematics at school, I came to realise that I had no chance of achieving my goal. My Post Office savings account would never grow fast enough at the low rates of interest it offered, or even if I got more money by delivering newspapers before school. I started to wonder how some people became rich and how their wealth could exceed even what high salaries could provide on their own. Then I discovered that you can get a higher return on shares and through speculation, though they were riskier than my boring Post Office account; but then you had to buy shares in amounts that were far beyond what I could expect to afford in the foreseeable future. It seemed you had to be rich to get rich. I also discovered that rich people tend to have rich parents and to inherit money. I hadn't heard about 'unearned income' then, but I did think it was unfair. It was becoming clear that wealth didn't have much to do with merit and effort, though I wanted to believe that it did. I hadn't thought much about need as a criterion of distribution at the time, though the welfare state, particularly the NHS, state housing and public education, was based on it. But neither need nor merit were relevant here; rather, 'to them that have, shall more be given' was the rule.

Referring to shareholders, John Maynard Keynes called for the 'euthanasia of the rentier, of the functionless investor'.[94] Commentating more broadly on the joint stock enterprises, that is, companies owned by shareholders, he wrote:

> The divorce between ownership and the real responsibility of management is serious within a country, when, as a result of joint stock enterprise, ownership is broken up among innumerable individuals who buy their interest to-day and sell it to-morrow and lack altogether both knowledge and responsibility towards what they momentarily own. But when the same principle is applied internationally, it is, in times of stress, intolerable – I am irresponsible towards what I own and those who operate what I own are irresponsible towards me. There may be some financial calculation which shows it to be advantageous that my savings should be invested in whatever quarter of the habitable globe shows the greatest marginal efficiency of capital or the highest rate of interest. But experience is accumulating that remoteness between ownership and operation is an evil in the relations among men, likely or certain in the long

run to set up strains and enmities which will bring to nought the financial calculation.[95]

Or, as Doug Henwood puts it, 'They're walking arguments for worker ownership.'[96]

In effect, this implies a widening gulf between financial 'investment' and real investment, between the pursuit of financial gain from whatever sources are available and the necessary business of creating new infrastructure, technology and training, and between those who gain from productive activities without contributing to them and those who contribute to them and usually gain less from them. Before Keynes railed against the functionless investor, Tawney wrote:

> It [the share] is a title to property stripped of almost all the encumbrances by which property used often to be accompanied. It yields an income and can be disposed of at will. It makes its owner the heir to the wealth of countries he has never travelled to and a partner in enterprises of which he barely knows the name.[97]

Shareholders are usually absentee owners. By diversifying their holdings, they are able to capture unearned income from a range of sources, rather than being bound to a single, specific property as the single private owner is. And their ownership can be as fickle as they wish. The fetish of liquidity – being able to sell everything quickly – reinforces the abandonment of all responsibility and commitment: shares are bought and sold purely for personal advantage, regardless of the interests of those, particularly employees, who have a long-term interest in and commitment to their work but who enjoy no claims on the profits it generates. Yet outsiders who buy shares in the company, usually second hand, have rights to part of that revenue in the form of 'distributed profits'. Worse, the greater the power of shareholders, the more likely workers are to lose their jobs as management seeks to cut costs and pay more to shareholders.

The controversy over share ownership has a long history. Its legitimacy was widely contested for nearly two centuries,[98] though it was the limited liability that caused most concern – the fact that, unlike full private owners, shareowners could at most lose their outlay, and would not be liable for any debts incurred by the firm. But even though the dust has long since settled on that struggle, the legitimacy of this strange economic institution is just as dubious. What is bizarre about it is not so much the limited liability but the fact that it can be an asset providing unearned income without time limit; while the downside risks are limited, the upside gains are not.[99]

The stock market is both a market in which these claims to unearned income are bought and sold, and a market for the control of companies. The prices at which shares exchange are a reflection of the valuations and expectations of shareholders with regard to dividends and future price changes. When the price of shares slumps, and millions of pounds are 'wiped off' the stock exchange, this doesn't mean that the real economy has been affected by companies disinvesting from producing goods and services. The reduced share prices may merely mean that the company has less collateral for raising loans – but then large companies generally finance real investment by ploughing back their profits, not by borrowing.

The idea that shareholders are enabling productive investment, and in so doing have some claim to a share of the returns, is now largely myth. It applied in the 19th century, when middle-class shareholders helped to fund the construction of railways in the UK, but shareholding is now largely decoupled from real investment and amounts to a game in which shareholders compete for gains without having contributed to real investment. Instead of taking the legitimacy of absentee shareholding for granted, we should recognise it for what it is: a means by which uncommitted owners can benefit from the contributions of committed, dependent employees.

Yet aren't we all complicit in this? Aren't many people's pensions 'invested' in shares? And hasn't shareholding become more common amongst ordinary people? Don't many people put some of their savings into managed investment funds, via Individual Savings Accounts (ISAs) and the like, where they benefit indirectly from rising share prices and get tax privileges in the process? Indeed, doesn't it allow ordinary people to share in the wealth of the country?

Given that many people's pensions depend on the generation of unearned income from shareholding and speculation, and given that many have derived unearned income from house-price inflation, a larger number are at least small-time rentiers as well as being employees. Although they are only bit-players in the rentier game, their largely passive involvement is ideologically significant in that it habituates 'ordinary' people to rent-seeking as a source of income, and they may imagine the rich rentiers are working for them. The money pages of newspapers encourage them to think of this as merely being prudent and smart, as if these qualities alone legitimised their unearned income.[100] More importantly, such investment locks the fortunes of many ordinary people into the strategies of voracious financial institutions. Thus, in the recent crisis many have deplored the irresponsibility of financial capital in its use of ordinary people's savings, creaming off commission and fees and failing to safeguard their pensions.

But we're not all rentiers now.

Firstly, personal share ownership in the UK has actually *fallen* proportionately in the last 50 years, from 54% of shares on the London Stock Exchange in 1963 to 10% in 2010, and the amount owned is usually small. The richest 1% of the population own more than the rest put together.[101] The idea of a 'popular capitalism', touted at the time of Margaret Thatcher's wave of privatisations in the 1980s, in which everyone would own shares, predictably did not materialise. Most of the shares from the privatisation of nationalised industries that the public were allowed to buy were quickly sold on to large institutional 'investors' in order to make quick gains. So the privatisations of the 1980s did not produce popular capitalism, though it has to be said that this one-off source of unearned income was popular at the time.

Secondly, only about half (51%) of the adult population and 40% of households in Britain have their own pensions, with their pension contributions 'invested' on their behalf by institutional investors, leaving over half the population inadequately covered for their old age.[102] Occupational pensions and personal pension plans, on average, invest over two-thirds of their capital on the stock market.[103] To the extent that individual pension holders become 'investors' they do so mostly by having a high- and secure-enough earned income to be able to save and 'invest'; they are only part-time rentiers at most.

'The fortunate 40%' – as the Manchester University Centre for Research on Socio-Cultural Change (CRESC) team call them – hold 80% of all UK savings, an increasing share of which has gone into pensions and life assurance. The increased supply of these savings has fuelled a major inflation of share values, from which the 40% have benefitted.[104] In the 1990s the flow of these funds onto the stock market equalled that of productive investment by all industrial and commercial companies in the UK.[105]

Thirdly, unearned or rentier income in the form of dividends and profits from share dealing does not become any less problematic just because the recipients include not only the rich but some of the comfortably off. There is absolutely nothing democratic about it. Once again, 'to them that have, shall more be given' (along with tax concessions) sums it up. It is not earned income but asset-based unearned income, a function of power.

The fortunate 40% may be small-time rentiers via their pensions and capital gains, but most of their income is earned income from their jobs, and many of them will pay out more in interest on loans and rent to major rentiers than they get back in their indirect 'investment' in shares through their pensions. We should remember too that, while rentiers ultimately need workers to produce the goods and services on which their unearned income is a claim, workers and the rest of us do not need them; pensions can be more rationally and justly funded via the state, according to democratically agreed taxation.

Owners or shareholders versus employees: who are the stakeholders?

We need to keep asking why owners, especially shareholders, only interested in what their shares will bring, have near-exclusive influence over companies, while employees have none. We take this blatantly unjust arrangement for granted, as if it were 'just the way things are', rather than the product of historical struggles in which power rather than reasoned argument has won out. Capitalists own the output and revenue that their workers produce not because they have done something to deserve ownership of it but because they can.

The problem here is not simple private property: owning a house does not make you a capitalist, because you don't use it to employ people to produce goods and services in order to make a profit. You may make a profit – capital gains – when you sell your house, but that's not from employing people and taking some of the value of what they produce. The problem is the lack of restriction on the concentration of ownership of means of production into the hands of a minority, and the lack of rights to ownership of both means of production and output for employees.

In the pre-history of capitalism in Britain, merchants used to buy materials like yarn and 'put it out' to cottagers scattered across nearby rural areas to work up into cloth, pay them a sum of money for this and then sell the output on at a profit. But they found that the cottagers developed a habit of selling some of the output themselves so that they got the profit instead. This was used by some merchants as an argument for bringing workers together under one roof where they could be supervised directly and prevented from 'embezzling' what they were making. Capitalist property rights provide legal backing for this strategy.

SEVEN

Other ways to skin a cat

Rent, interest and profit are the classic trio of sources of wealth extraction, but there are some important other ways to do it too.

Capital gains, asset inflation and bubbles

Rentiers can benefit not only from rent or interest but from 'capital gains' – increases in the market price of their assets. Though they may need to sell them in order to realise the gains, even if they hang on to them the paper gains improve their accounts, and increase the value of their collateral, should they wish to borrow.

Asset inflation is a key feature of neoliberalism. When there's an increase in demand for cars or cakes, there might be an initial rise in price, but more cars or cakes will be produced in response, so the price is likely to be driven down again. But where assets like shares or houses are concerned, increases in demand can be fuelled by increased availability of bank credit, and this tends to produce little response in terms of supply, so the price climbs. An increase in the price of assets may make the owners better off on paper in terms of financial wealth – potential claims on goods and services for sale – but it does not reflect any additional wealth creation, so ultimately the increase must come at the expense of others, including those unable to afford to buy such assets.

As we saw, over the last 30 years share prices have risen, not because of economic growth but simply because demand for shares grew steadily with the rise of big institutional 'investors', driven by increasing numbers of people taking out private pensions and financial 'investments', while the supply of shares was fairly static. Rising share prices in turn drew in more buyers wishing to enjoy these gains, which only pushed the prices higher. This positive feedback generated asset inflation – an effortless increase in unearned wealth. As William Tabb puts it, 'The buying and selling of claims to wealth can . . . become a self-levitation process in which, as prices of paper claims rise, the assets can be used as collateral to borrow still more and buy more assets, driving prices higher in a seemingly endless loop.'[106]

As long as this process continues, the rentier's free ride gets bigger. Eventually, when people are no longer willing or able to pay the higher prices, the bubble bursts. Those who 'get out the room before the door closes' – that is, sell up before prices plummet – stand to make capital gains, while those who don't stand to make big losses, especially if they've borrowed to buy the assets. Some 'investors' may know very well that a bubble is building up, and know that others know it too, but that is not likely to deter them from trying to profit from it. After all, if they don't, others will.

When asset bubbles burst, the losses in value may be measured in billions, or even trillions. But these are paper values; it doesn't mean billions are lost in the production of goods and services. This is small comfort for those who borrowed large sums against the inflated paper values of houses or other assets they were buying and who find that they still have to repay those sums when values collapse. The irrationality of bubbles is cranked up where financial institutions enter the loop by increasing lending for buying the assets, causing credit-driven asset inflation.

Housing bubbles are the most familiar case. In Britain, homeowners were tempted to take out outsize mortgages (absurdly, often over 100% of the current market value of the property) or remortgage their houses, in the belief that house prices would rise and would thus cover the cost. Because credit was easy to get, buyers could pay more for housing, and so house prices *did* rise – encouraging still more lending, on the grounds that the collateral was an appreciating asset. As long as house prices rose faster than the rate of interest, buyers were winning. Rising prices produce little response from house-builders in terms of increasing the supply of housing because they want to avoid risking a fall in prices and rents. They accumulate 'land banks', but they only build on these when the prospective profits are highest, thereby creating artificial scarcity.[107] They can make more money from building and selling a few houses while prices rise than from building many and risking a lower price. Planning restrictions on new developments can also help to maintain this scarcity. And you can't build houses in a region where it's cheap to do so, and ship them to where the prices are highest.

The streams of interest payments that banks get from borrowers, and the possibility of selling them on to other financial institutions and lending afresh to a new set of customers, tempt banks to offer credit to more marginal – that is, low-income – borrowers, enticing them with 'teaser rates' of interest to start with, quickly followed by high rates and debt charges. This, of course, is the fateful story of sub-prime mortgages.

When existing house owners hear of local house prices rising, they may be tempted to seize the moment and sell. But if too many others do this in the hope of realising their capital gains, it may swamp the market and send prices plummeting. The bubble can survive only as long as the number of houses actually up for sale remains smaller than the number of house hunters. But demand-side changes could burst the bubble too: it takes only a small disturbance, such as some house buyers losing their jobs, for the rising market to collapse. Some lose their homes, others end up finding themselves in 'negative equity' – with a house worth less than their debts but still having to repay them. Markets for assets, especially where credit plays a major role, are inherently unstable and prone to boom and bust cycles.[108]

How neoliberalism uses housing to support rentier interests

Since neoliberalism took hold in Britain in the 1980s, governments have acted in ways that have produced massive house-price inflation and increases in unearned income for rentiers. It's probably not intentional: it's doubtful if they even know what 'rentier' means. Author James Meek has brilliantly tracked the history.[109] First Margaret Thatcher's government allowed local authority tenants to buy their houses at massively discounted prices, but prevented the local authorities from using the money to build more houses for rent to replace them. This was the largest privatisation in Britain, worth £40 billion. Naturally, this was a popular policy with those who bought their houses, but it diverted money paid as rent to mortgage lenders. The councils lacked sufficient money to improve their existing properties for rent, which of course led to their deterioration and helped the growth of a new stigma attached to council housing and its tenants. New Labour did not reverse this policy.

As private sector rents went up, the flow of state money into housing benefit payments for those on low incomes also rose (much more than would have been needed for such tenants in local authority housing), but most of this went straight to the landlords. Since the 1980s housing supply has failed disastrously to keep up with the increase in demand that has resulted from a combination of population increase and reduction in the number of persons per household. Annual new house building has fallen from 400,000 units in 1970 to 120,000 in 2010. So it's no surprise that from 1997 up to the crash in 2008, house prices trebled. It has allowed those who buy to let to claim £13 billion of tax relief on the interest they pay on their mortgages and on what they claim to pay on maintenance[110] – a direct subsidy to rentiers. Most recently, through its 'Help to Buy' scheme, the Coalition government has assisted house buying by those who are already well off (the scheme supports purchases of up to £600,000 at a time when the average house price is £247,000 and the 5% deposit required is beyond the reach of most low-income buyers). Bereft of ideas for reviving productive investment, the government has resorted to starting a new house-price bubble to produce the impression of recovery in time for the next general election. Who said neoliberal governments were anti-inflation?

Using a house as a cash machine has become a cliché. As house prices rose, and hence their collateral increased, house owners were encouraged to remortgage so that they could 'unlock the value' of their house and get cash up front for whatever purpose they liked – buying a new car, paying for a holiday, a wedding or children's education costs. The 'value unlocked' is unearned income from asset inflation. It does not depend on producing goods and services; in fact, it diverts resources from productive activity. True, some homeowners may improve their houses, building extensions, improving insulation or whatever, and may rightly feel that they deserve a higher price as a result. But that wouldn't be an example of house-price inflation, because the use-value of the house would have been enhanced; any buyer would be getting more. Rising house prices are meat-and-veg to newspapers, which typically treat them as a right of the prudent middle classes, while occasionally remembering to bemoan the downside for first-time buyers who face rising prices. Absurdly, even though they're a consequence of insufficient new housing and excessive credit, they are widely treated as evidence of economic health, and politicians know that they help to win elections.

A common subject of political cartoons and comedy sketches in the 1980s was dinner parties at which the middle classes boasted about how much their house prices had risen. Their smug self-congratulation might occasionally be tinged with embarrassment, in faint recognition that this was a matter of luck, but then, as successful people, they felt they deserved it anyway. An inflated sense of entitlement is a common vice of the better-off.

Increasingly, homeowners are encouraged to see their houses not merely as homes but as 'investments', indeed they may even think of their mortgage debt as an investment! Some may see it as a step towards becoming rentiers in their own right. But why should anyone expect the price of a house to rise even when nothing has been done to it? When you buy a second-hand car or bike you expect to pay less than the original price. Why doesn't the same apply to housing? Some tried to justify it, saying it allowed ordinary home-owners to share in the economic growth of the country. Sometimes it did, yet this was not a sharing of the surplus based on democratic decision, as in the case of needs-based transfers, but a privatisation by just part of the population of wealth produced by others.

House price inflation and New Labour

From the website of Shelter, the UK charity for the homeless:

If food prices had risen at the same rate as house prices over the last 40 years, a chicken would cost £51.18.

Four pints of milk would be £10.45, and a loaf of bread would set you back £4.36. We wouldn't accept this with food. So why accept it with housing?

Unless something changes, a generation will struggle to afford a home of their own.[111]

Showing its neoliberal credentials, in 2005 New Labour encouraged 'more people to share in increasing asset wealth: homes are not just places to live. They are also assets ... Support for home ownership will enable more people on lower incomes to benefit from any further increases in the value of housing assets.'[112]

This is the classic neoliberal error of confusing asset inflation with wealth creation, expanding rentier gains in the process, mainly benefitting the better off, while putting homeownership further out of reach for those on low incomes.

Much of the population of countries like the UK is caught up in this irrational process, and some actively pursue it for capital gains, though it isn't straightforward, as house sellers are usually buyers too, so any gains are likely to be lost immediately unless they downsize. Second-home owners are in a better position when they come to sell because they don't need to buy again; the use-value of the house as home is less important than its market value as a financial 'investment'. Many have gone further and got 'buy-to-let' mortgages, using the rent to pay off their debts.[113] Yes, they are taking a risk, for their 'investment' may fall in value, but their risk taking makes no contribution to the real economy whatsoever. Any gains are ultimately parasitic on others' work.

Of course, there may be extenuating circumstances; someone who has an inadequate pension may be able to use capital gains on their house to provide themselves with an income in retirement; who can blame them? And they are only small-time rentiers. But that's a private solution and leaves the underlying structural problems untouched: inadequate state pensions that can't provide people with sufficient needs-based income in retirement; inadequate wages that prevent many from saving; private landownership that allows owners to free-ride on others; and the existence of a free-for-all (which means a game biased in favour of the already well-off) in the scramble for asset-based unearned income. Yes, a pay-as-you-go state pension is effectively a transfer from young to old, but it is one that can be decided upon democratically rather than prised out of others through the control of existing assets.

These irrationalities reflect a broader one that stems from the parasitic nature of rentiership. Rentiers have a love–hate relationship with inflation; when money gets cheaper, the interest they are paid is worth less: lending a £1,000 for a year at 3% interest when inflation is 3% means that their unearned income is effectively zero. But low or near-zero real interest rates are good news for borrowers, and good for the economy because they minimise the deadweight costs. Not surprisingly, powerful rentier interests lean on governments to prioritise limiting inflation. Of course, since borrowers are also consumers, unless their incomes keep abreast of inflation, they lose out from inflation on the prices of consumer goods. The neoliberal governments of the 1980s and 1990s covertly supported rentiers by publicly supporting consumers' interests in price stability. But there's one kind of inflation that rentiers love: asset inflation; this is neoliberalism's dirty secret. It redistributes wealth from those who lack assets and have to rely on earned income to those who have them and can use them to get unearned income.

Value-skimming

Rent, interest, profit from production and capital gains from asset inflation are not the only sources of unearned income. Many have made fortunes in the financial sector by arranging major transactions such as mergers and takeovers, involving many millions of pounds, by taking a small commission. Although the percentage may be small, the sums are large. In effect, they are standing next to a big till,[114] and it is easy for them to put their hands in it without breaking any laws. It is in their interest to promote as many transactions as possible – that is, as many transfers of ownership of assets as possible – regardless of whether there is any social benefit in this; they stand to gain handsomely even though it may be just 'churning'. Lawyers too can profit from the complicated legal work accompanying many major financial transactions. According to Michael Hudson, in the

US the average duration for holding a share is 20 seconds, and the average currency investment is held for 30 seconds. No doubt some of the transactions are beneficial for the economy, enabling greater economic efficiency, but some are merely forms of indirect wealth extraction gained by helping others extract it in return for a share of the takings.

The CRESC researchers call this 'value-skimming' and show that financial intermediaries have been major but hidden beneficiaries of the growth of the financial sector. High-income but largely anonymous financial intermediaries far outnumber the much-publicised CEOs. The researchers estimate that in the City of London there are about 15,000 senior intermediaries employed at a principal or partner level in investment banking, hedge funds and other kinds of trading and private equity, as well as those providing support services in law and accounting.[115]

What about the working rich? Getting paid for wealth extraction

For some, all this talk of rentiers and wealth extraction on the basis of mere ownership and control of key assets may seem strange, given that today most of the rich get the bulk of their income in the form of salaries, and apparently only a minority from capital gains, dividends or interest payments and the like. So often a contrast is drawn between the idle-rich rentiers of the past and the 'working rich' of today. The latter phrase has become popular in recent years, and not surprisingly, because it appears to provide the rich with a self-evident justification. Since they work for their income, it can't be unearned – can it? – and they can't be rentiers. Hasn't the rentier of the past been replaced by the salaried executive of today?

'Rentier' is indeed an old term, and when it's used today, writers often like to quote John Stuart Mill's famous description from 1848: 'They grow richer, as it were in their sleep, without working, risking, or economizing. What claim have they, on the general principle of social justice, to this accession of riches?'[116] Actually, some of them would also have been active rentiers when they were awake, working to find more sources of rent, interest and capital gains.

But the question remains: how can income in the form of salary for work be 'unearned'? It can if the work involves extracting unearned income through rent-seeking, interest-charging or any of the other methods covered in this book. 'Even today's rent-seeking plutocrats work for a living – Carlos Slim or the Russian oligarchs owe their fortunes to rents they've captured themselves, not to estates conquered by distant ancestors,' writes Chrystia Freeland.[117] Remembering the definitions in Chapter Three of earned income as conditional on producing goods and services ('use-values'), and unearned income as derived from control of existing assets that others lack but need, then the salary earned – or rather received – by someone whose work consists of extracting rent or interest and getting control of new sources belongs to the second category.

If you work for a salary for a rentier organisation, like a loan or property company – and, increasingly, 'non-finance' companies have been getting involved in such activities too – then you are a *rentier-at-one remove*. Even critical commentators and researchers like Paul Krugman and Thomas Piketty miss this point and take even salaries paid to the top 0.1% at face value. In the US, those in the top 0.01% get most of their income from salaries, whereas a century ago their equivalents got most of their income from capital gains.[118] But revenue from rent, interest, profit, capital gains, speculation and other sources of unearned income can be paid out as 'salary' to executives or, indeed, to more lowly workers in rentier organisations. The recipients are indeed more likely to be top executives than simple owners. The new rentiers who have flourished under neoliberalism compete with others for the assets with the highest returns from all around the world.

Some of the rich claim to be 'self-made' rather than merely the heirs of rich parents: in the US, Forbes classified 840 of the 1,226 people in its 2012 billionaire league table as 'self-made', but that doesn't mean they have necessarily 'made' 'their' wealth through their own contributions: they may merely have extracted it themselves. Rent or debt collection needn't take the form of knocking on doors for payment; it can involve buying debt to get access to interest payments and speculating on asset inflation. Continually seeking the maximum gains by using money to get more money can be a full-time job, and the competition is tough.[119] (In their defence many of the rich may claim to work particularly long hours, but then so do many people on low and middling pay.[120] Is a top financial sector employee on £3 million a year working 150 times as hard and effectively as the employee on £20,000 a year?)

And, given the size of the winnings from occupying top positions, there is likely to be fierce competition for them. Other things being equal, these competitions are likely to be won by the most hard-working and clever (and maybe best-connected), but they are competing for access to positions that allow them to extract wealth produced by others and, indeed, require them to do so. Particularly if they work for primarily rentier organisations, this means that their pay doesn't necessarily reflect productive contribution. (As we saw, even if it isn't a rentier organisation, their position still allows them to take a bigger share than others, over and above what their contribution might warrant.) So the fact that they are smart and workaholic doesn't mean that they deserve their huge salaries.

In the UK, it's no surprise that the biggest concentration of the top 0.1%, with gross incomes of over £351,137, is in jobs where wealth-extraction opportunities are prominent – in financial intermediation (30%) and real estate, renting and other business activities (39%). Bonus payments are heavily concentrated at the top of the income distribution; the top 1% of employees get 40% of their annual pay in bonuses, while the bottom 90% get only 5% of their pay in bonuses. In the financial sector, over 25% of pay is in the form of cash bonuses, again heavily concentrated at the top, and often supplemented by bonuses in shares and options.[121] Nor is it a surprise that 34% of the top 0.1% are company directors, and 24% of those in the rest of the top 1% are too, for this is a job that allows control over the disposal of company revenues.[122] Those at the top are always likely to look after themselves before others.

Apart from top executives, some well-placed employees with scarce skills that are in demand may also be able to enter the 1%. Hospital consultants and top lawyers are in such positions, and not surprisingly employees in legal and health services figure prominently in the top 1%, albeit mostly in the lower half of it. In these cases, they almost certainly are making productive contributions too, but simply by virtue of their scarcity and the bargaining power that derives from that they are in a strong position to take a larger share than would otherwise be the case.

At the same time as we acknowledge the prominence of the salaried rich, we should not lose sight of the fact that the higher one goes up the income pyramid, the greater the proportion of income that comes from non-salary sources. In the UK the top 0.1% receive 17% of their income from 'investments', as compared to 7% for the average taxpayer, and of course in the case of the former it's 17% of a far larger income. Taking into account other sources of income such as benefits and pensions, the 1% receive a lower share of their total income from employment than does the average taxpayer. The richest 1–0.1% receive 61% of their income from employment and the richest 0.1% get 58%, as against 69% for the average taxpayer[123] (who may also be eligible for democratically approved transfers such as disability benefit). And let's remember, only the top 10% – and within that, mostly those at the top – tend to receive more interest than they pay out.

As we'll see, the rise of finance and neoliberalism has involved a major shift of power from productive capital to rentier interests.

What about speculation?

Speculation has rarely had a good press, but in the current crisis it has attracted more suspicion and contempt than usual, carrying associations with 'casino banking' and 'gambling with other people's money'. It is not just that speculators have taken outrageous risks but that their gains are seen as undeserved, particularly when set against the modest rewards that most people get for providing useful work. Is this fair? Or is speculation actually a misunderstood but socially beneficial activity?

We've already seen how terminology can mislead in economic matters. Dutch professor of politics Marieke de Goede has shown how the history of finance has seen continual struggles over the use of favourable and unfavourable terms for its practices – such as 'investment', 'speculation', 'gambling', 'fraud' and 'the work of the devil'.[124] Repeatedly, those with an interest in these activities have tried to stretch the use of favourable terms to cover more questionable practices, so speculators call themselves 'investors'. We see this now too in the talk of 'managing risk'. 'Speculation' is a slightly less odorous term than 'gambling', but little different. Yet, there are some defences of it that claim it's beneficial for economies, and not just for individual speculators.

Let's get one misconception out of the way immediately. It's tempting to say that all real investment is speculative in so far as it involves making a guess about whether a new product or practice will succeed and taking a risk. Deciding whether to invest in expanding food production might involve taking risks, and trying to predict future prices is helpful in making such a decision, but it is very different from simply betting on food or any other prices. The former is productive, the latter not, though there may be some indirect benefits, as we shall see. Attempting to treat these different things as the same is just one way of legitimising speculation.[125]

Speculation involves buying and selling in order to make a financial gain, not in order to use something. Though speculators may trade in commodities like oil or wheat that can be used, they have no personal interest in consuming them. Like gamblers betting on horses, they are not part of the business of breeding, training and racing horses, but hope to make money nevertheless. At its simplest, speculation may involve taking advantage of price differences in different places at the same time ('arbitrage'): buying products where they are plentiful and cheap and selling where they are scarce and expensive; or borrowing where interest rates are low in order to lend the money out where rates of interest are high.

With the development of electronic trading, much financial speculation has become a finely tuned and automated practice. Minute differences in prices of tradeable assets can be taken advantage of in microseconds.[126] The percentage margins may be minute and ephemeral, but where the transactions involve many millions of pounds and can be made continually, thousands of times per second, the gains are substantial.

Speculators are not necessarily a separate group of specialist actors particularly inclined to risk taking; they can be pension funds or any financial or indeed non-financial institution, or just individuals with spare cash. That the savings and pension contributions of millions of people are 'invested' speculatively in financial products is clearly of concern, not only from the point of view of the future economic security of those people, but because they form the equivalent of a human shield for the activities of those in charge of their money – the fund managers and their teams. On the upside of bubbles they may do well, though the fund managers and associates themselves make sure that they take a big cut for themselves. While they are likely to have the accumulated personal wealth to ride out the inevitable crash, the small savers whose money they use may not. So, when the dot.com bubble burst, for example, pension funds took much of the hit. Predictably, it was not the use of their money for speculating on asset bubbles that was held to be the main threat to the pensions system but the increasing longevity of pensioners and the 'generosity' of their pensions.

Speculation can also involve seeking to take advantage of price changes over time. In futures markets, the speculator contracts to buy something in future at an agreed price, such as a barrel of oil in a month's time or a foreign currency in a year's time. If it turns out, as the speculator hopes, that when the time comes the market price has risen above this, she can profit from the lower agreed price by selling on to ordinary buyers at the new market price. Alternatively, speculators can buy 'options' to buy or sell a commodity at a particular price at a certain time in the future (the expiration date). If it's an option to buy at a certain price they gain if the market price at that time is higher. If it's an option to sell, they gain if the market price at that time is lower. If things don't turn out as hoped, the speculator loses only the cost of the option, as they can opt not to exercise it. Or they can do both and bet both ways. These are relatively simple examples of 'derivatives' – financial instruments that can be created, in effect, to bet on the movement of prices of just about anything: oil, copper, shares, bonds, interest rates, currencies, royalties or non-price measures like the temperature. They can even be related to the value of other derivatives.

But before we go into speculation further, we need to consider a related practice: *hedging*. Hedging is a way of reducing the risk of losses in one activity by trying to ensure that they are offset by gains in another. For example, an airline's profits are vulnerable to fuel price rises, so it may decide to protect itself by entering into a futures or option contract to buy fuel at a given price at a future date. Or it may buy shares in oil companies in the hope of benefitting from price rises. Hedging may be socially beneficial if it reduces risks and provides economic security to businesses and employees, and thereby creates a more stable climate for long-term investment. It doesn't reduce the underlying risk – just the exposure of certain economic actors to it. The downside is that it reduces pressure to do something about the underlying risk – or worse, the sense of security that it provides may encourage more dangerous risk taking.

Hedging can take place only if would-be hedgers can find people to bet against them. If you want to be able to buy aviation fuel at a certain price next month, you've got to find someone who will agree to sell it to you at that price at that time, or as they say, someone 'to take the other side of the transaction'. If it's a futures contract, they may think that the market price will actually end up lower than the one the hedger has agreed to pay. If it's an option to buy at a certain price, they may feel it's worth betting against the hedger, and that the price of the option is itself worth having. Either party may also be able to sell the option on if they see profit in doing so. As the day nears on which the futures contract matures, holders may find that others are willing to pay a good price for it. But whatever the case, it takes two to tango.

So speculation and hedging are frequently complementary, and the boundary between them is fuzzy. While some companies may hedge against exposure to the risks peculiar to their line of business by using derivatives, traders can use the same kind of derivatives – particularly options and futures – merely to make money.[127] Instead of hedging against a possible loss, they may just decide to bet on something, regardless. In turn, speculators may try to hedge these bets. So we might say that hedging and speculation have a moebius-strip relationship, sometimes appearing as on opposite but complementary sides, sometimes on the same side (Figure 7.1). Either way, when it comes to defending these activities, 'hedging', with its connotations of prudence, sounds better than 'speculation'.

Figure 7.1: The hedging–speculation moebius strip

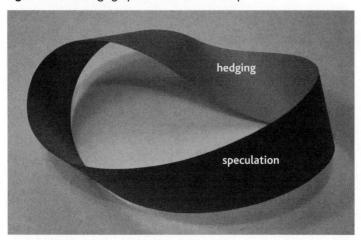

Source: http://en.wikipedia.org/wiki/Mobius_strip

There are some common defences of speculation, though, and they don't always dress it up as hedging. Here's one from a practitioner:

> 'Like hundreds of thousands of other traders, I try to predict the prices of common goods a day or two or a few months in the future. If I think the price of an item will go up, I buy today and sell later. If I think the price is going down, I'll sell at today's higher price. The miracle is that in taking care of ourselves, we speculators somehow ensure that producers all over the world will provide the right quantity and quality of goods at the proper time, without undue waste, and that this meshes with what people want and the money they have available…. when a harvest is too small to satisfy consumption at its normal rate, speculators come in, hoping to profit from the scarcity by buying. Their purchases raise the price, thereby checking consumption so that the smaller supply will last longer. Producers encouraged by the high price further lessen the shortage by growing or importing to reduce the shortage. On the other side, when the price is higher than the speculators think the facts warrant, they

sell. This reduces prices, encouraging consumption and exports and helping to reduce the surplus.'[128]

So speculators, in this view, help to make the market work, and perhaps even encourage investment to meet increased demand; they don't intend to do so, but supposedly this is an unintended consequence of their actions.

The example of speculating on a poor harvest is hardly an appealing one, precisely because food is so essential and because crops take a long time to grow and so producers usually can't increase production quickly, and there may not be surpluses elsewhere that could be imported. Food crises and disruption of trade by wars are good news for speculators. And if there are just a few speculators and they buy up most of the output in advance they may be able to hold consumers to ransom; of course it's in the interest of speculators that there are shortages and price differences that they can take advantage of. But where production and consumption can respond relatively quickly, speculation, at least in this form, may make the markets work more efficiently, better coordinating the behaviour of producers and consumers and producing benefits that go beyond the speculators' gains. The trouble is that a great deal of speculation is in asset markets, like the market for shares, which don't work like markets for products whose supply can be increased easily. Making markets that facilitate the extraction of unearned income for rentiers work 'better' is neither ethical nor rational for economies. Defenders hope that such accessible examples of speculation will allow them to get away with claiming that all or most forms of speculation are therefore OK. As George Cooper notes, it's a favourite trick of economists to use homely examples of products like bread, for which supply and demand adjust to one another in a way that tends to stabilise the market, as a basis for making universal claims about the miraculous properties of financial markets.[129]

Consider some other examples.

First, speculation in property markets. Property developers typically buy up plots close to city centres, in the hope of converting them to a new use, usually commercial and office development, that will allow higher rents to be charged than for the present uses. As we've seen, they tend to accumulate plots as 'land banks' and postpone development until prices are rising. In the meantime, the existing buildings are usually left to decline, producing the typically decaying environments of our inner cities, with all the social costs that go with them. In this case, far from the speculation causing an increase in supply, it holds it back.

Many companies, particularly from China, are buying up land in Africa in anticipation of an increased demand for food and biofuel crops and rare minerals, so as to extract rent from producers in the future. Where mainstream economics would see this as self-evidently justifiable in that it promotes 'the highest and best' – that is, most profitable – use of resources, such developments invariably have major social and environmental costs that fall on others. Local producers may lose their land and economic security as a result. As always, we have to ask 'efficient for whom?' and 'in whose interests?'. Just because the pursuit of self-interest in markets sometimes produces wider benefits, it does not follow that it always does.

Consider also the 'carry trade', a form of speculation consisting of borrowing money in countries where the rate of interest is low (such as Japan in 2007) and lending it or 'investing' it in countries where the prevailing rate is higher, pocketing the difference. In 2007, Japanese yen were among the sources of finance behind the US sub-prime lending crisis. This tends to put downward pressure on the higher interest rates and upward pressure on the lower rates. This may benefit borrowers in the former case – or stimulate predatory lending. In the countries where interest rates are low, perhaps as a matter of policy for supporting investment, the carry trade switches funds away, undermining such policies. Attempts at national self-determination of economic development are frustrated.

Speculators can make money on both sides of a bubble – not only buying in order to sell on the upside, but 'short-selling' on the downside. The latter practice works like this Imagine that prices of certain common, frequently traded shares, such as those of an oil company are expected to fall or already falling. The short-seller agrees to borrow some shares from an existing owner for a period of time, say six months, for a fee. If he (usually he) then sells them straightaway for, say, £10 each, and then later, when the price has fallen to £7, buys the same number of shares back at that price, he will then be able to return them to the original owner having made £3 per share minus the fee for borrowing them. It sounds counter-intuitive, but it works. (Clearly, the shares or whatever asset or commodity is being short-sold need to be homogenous or 'fungible' like gold or currencies or popular shares so that the seller can rely on being able to buy the same amount back.) By fuelling price falls, this supposedly makes markets work more efficiently. Yes, it does seem strange that anyone is allowed to sell something that does not belong to them! But then the financial sector often does things that aren't allowed elsewhere.

But there is a further twist that has become important in recent decades and has played a major role in the crisis. Here, speculation has taken on an increasingly turbo-charged, and more dangerous, form by using 'leverage'. This is simply the practice of placing bigger bets by using borrowed money. If buying £100,000 of futures contracts is likely to give you a gain of £100,000 (100% profit), borrowing £1 million to buy more should, other things equal, give you £1 million profit. Even though you have to pay interest on the loan, it will be dwarfed by your profit; if it's 5% interest, then that's 'only' £50,000 to pay, leaving you with £950,000 clear – much better than the paltry £100,000 you'd get if you just used your own money. The attractions may seem irresistible. The more the trade is leveraged, the bigger the gains – provided you bet right! If the bet fails, you are in deep trouble, for you have to repay £1,050,000, having just lost the principal! So leverage multiplies gains and losses, and hence risk.[130] Some banks levered their money 30 times – that is, borrowed 30 times their capital in order to make bigger 'investments' (in other words, bet with other people's money) and get more profit, which meant that if as little as a 30th of their 'investments' failed they would be in trouble. Hence, leverage has played a major role in the crisis. It is not simply 'risk management' or 'risk taking', like investing in a new technology that may possibly fail to deliver, but *risk creation*. Those whose money is being used may find that it is they and not the speculator who takes the risk and has to pick up the bill. The phenomenon of speculators keeping their gains while offloading any losses onto others has been a key feature of the crisis.

'Debt' or 'leverage'?

While the word 'debt' has a negative ring to it, the word 'leverage' is positive; indeed it is now often used as a verb, as we leverage our assets in order to reach for the stars. Forgetting that Archimedes' lever had a purchase point, the financial engineers aspire to move the world without securing the land on which they stand. (Robin Blackburn, 2008)[131]

So what's the overall verdict on these practices? Considered on its own, hedging seems prudent, but it is closely coupled with speculation, whose benefits are more ambiguous. The same goes for a host of financial instruments and practices. They have to be checked out case by case, to see if they produce any social benefit. In general, speculation is an activity that can yield unearned income on the basis of control of money as an asset, and while it sometimes produces some beneficial effects too, it can also, particularly if leveraged, create huge risks. As Nicholas Shaxson puts it: 'A little speculative trading in [financial] markets improves information and smooths prices. But when the volume of this dealing is a hundred times bigger than the underlying volume of trade, the result has proved to be a catastrophe.'[132] The enormous amount of energy that has gone into speculation is symptomatic of an economy that struggles to make profit from production and seeks to make it instead by betting on prices.

Where markets are dominated by a few key players, there is scope not just for speculation, but for *market manipulation* and *insider trading*. This is especially true of the financial sector, dominated by a handful of enormously powerful companies. Each has fingers in hundreds of pies and therefore has access to information that others do not. In particular, they often have advance knowledge of events that markets will respond to, such as takeover bids, or an increase in a company's profits, and so they can buy shares before their price is driven up, and sell them at a profit. But it's hard to detect. A report produced by the UK's Financial Services Authority with the wonderful title of 'Measuring Market Cleanliness' found a lot of muck, estimating that over 30% of transactions on the London Stock Exchange involved insider dealing.[133] In the dot.com bubble, investment banks talked up the prospects of the particular new companies in which they had stakes so as to be able to sell them at a premium. It didn't matter to them when the bubble burst in 2000 at their gullible clients' cost, because they had already realised their capital gains.

Investment banks can also play off different customers or clients against one another, and bet against them. They sold credit derivatives that they knew to be overvalued to their clients, while betting against them by buying credit default swaps that paid out when the derivatives crashed: a classic heads-we-win-tails-they-lose strategy. Like arms dealers profiting from arming both sides in a war, they can 'help' both sides in competitive struggles.

> Goldman Sachs now finds itself on so many sides of a deal simultaneously that the mind boggles. Goldman's merchant bank arm competes with clients (and counts them as customers), and its proprietary arm may trade against them. At the same time as it represents a firm, it could be shopping for its sale, attempting to buy it for itself, or competing for an acquisition on behalf of another client.[134]

And it is investment banking above all that has concentrated wealth at the top.

Hedge funds: the Wild West of financial 'investment'

Hedge fund managers are among the fattest of the fat cats, often making far more money than CEOs of major companies and banks. They've become major predators in the financial ecosystem, though like any species they are also dependent on others, in this case particularly on investment banks that provide much of the funding and intermediary services they use – indeed many banks and insurance companies have their own hedge funds.[135] In the US, their best years were 2007 and 2009, with a brief dip in between when the recession hit. The top 25 managers made an average of over a $1 billion each in 2009, with John Paulson topping the charts at $4.9 billion.[136] How do they do it?

Hedge funds are privately owned businesses that 'invest' large sums from rich 'investors', whether individuals or financial institutions like insurance companies and investment banks. Being private, they escape many of the regulations that apply to other financial institutions, which of course makes them attractive 'investment' outlets for the public companies. They may use hedging to protect themselves against losses, but they mostly use financial instruments aggressively rather than defensively, profiting from leveraged speculation on changes in the prices of assets, whether they be stocks, bonds, currencies, commodities like gold, copper or oil, or derivatives, and by buying up bankrupt and undervalued companies.

They seek to profit from both rises and falls in prices, by buying assets in the hope that they will rise in price, or short-selling where they expect prices to fall. These are not merely responses to market shifts but ways of influencing those shifts, for example by inflating bubbles: they are weapons, not tools, as Ewald Engelen and co-researchers argue.[137] On 'Black Wednesday', 16 September 1992, multi-billionaire George Soros made £1 billion by short-selling sterling – in anticipation of its being ejected from the European Exchange Rate Mechanism. In effect, he saw that the pound was overvalued, took on the Bank of England when it made frenzied efforts to defend the currency, and won.[138] When the previously much-lauded Northern Rock bank got into trouble in 2008, hedge funds short-sold its shares and then bought them up when they'd hit rock bottom.[139] When, in 2013, the UK's Royal Mail was privatised by issuing shares at far below the market price, it was an aggressive hedge fund that became the largest shareholder.

Hedge fund managers' remuneration system is distinctive: most get 2% of assets, regardless of whether they make a profit or loss, and 20% of profits. Given the amounts 'invested', this can give them extraordinary wealth. And as the profits count as 'capital gains', they are taxed at a low rate. In the US they pay just 15% on profits. No wonder so many hedge fund bosses are super-rich.

All these kinds of wealth extraction that we've looked at – rent, interest, profit, shareholding, value-skimming and speculation – primarily benefit the rich, those who can afford to use assets to extract unearned income from the 99%. It's true that many of the better-off within the 99% have pensions that depend on the generation of unearned income from shareholding and speculation, and a few may own shares too. Many have derived unearned income from house-price inflation, so a larger number of people are at least small-time rentiers as well as being employees. Although they are only bit-players in the rentier game, their largely passive involvement is ideologically significant in that it habituates 'ordinary' people to rent-seeking as a source of income, helps to legitimise what principally benefits the rich and allows people to imagine that the rich rentiers are working for them. The money pages of newspapers encourage them to think of this as merely being prudent and smart, as if these qualities alone legitimised their unearned income.[140] It also makes the fortunes of many people dependent on self-interested financial institutions, that use their savings, cream off commission and fees and fail to safeguard their pensions.

The rentiers will of course deny that their wealth comes at others' expense, preferring to see it as self-made wealth creation. They are deluded. While these ways of extracting wealth have grown massively in the last three decades and played a major role in the crisis, the basic mechanisms have long been in place. This is why this book is not just about the crisis but about the basic mechanisms of the capitalist economy that concentrate wealth in a few hands.

EIGHT

Don't the rich create jobs? And other objections

Obviously, these claims are controversial, so before proceeding with a fresh set of arguments, this is a good point to pause and address objections. There are two kinds of objection that I want to deal with here: first those voiced regularly in the media and in everyday life, and then some more technical counter-arguments from mainstream economists.

Don't the rich create jobs?

'When did you last get a job from a poor person?' So goes my favourite American Tea Party slogan. The Americans are good at slogans but the Tea Party specialises in discombobulatingly daft ones. *Of course* you won't get a job from a poor person, we wearily concede, but it doesn't follow that the rich create jobs, as if they have special powers that turn their gains into a gift of jobs to the rest of us. US billionaire Nick Hanauer is refreshingly honest about this: 'If it was true that lower taxes for the rich and more wealth for the wealthy led to job creation, today we would be drowning in jobs.'[141] So why hasn't the spectacular shift in income and financial wealth to the rich over the last four decades led to unprecedented jobs growth?

First of all, we need to ask what the rich and super-rich do with their spare money. They generally use it to try to get even more, through either real investment or financial 'investment'. In the latter case, whether by betting on market movements or buying income-yielding assets, or the many other ways unearned income can be extracted, their actions are unlikely to result in net job creation. Some 'investment' is used to buy up firms in order to sell off parts of them – to *asset-strip* them, in other words. This is likely to result in job losses, and indeed may reduce the ability of the firm to produce in the long run.[142] Many companies have boosted their profits by cutting jobs. In the US, Scott Thompson, the CEO of Yahoo!, on a salary package of $27 million per year, axed 2,000 jobs in April 2012 – about 14% of the company's workforce – following six major lay-offs in the preceding four years.[143]

But even if the rich *do* fund real investment in productive businesses – in equipment, training, new infrastructures or whatever – this may or may not result in job creation. Some businesses need to employ more people if they are to expand, but some do not: they may make more profit by reducing the number of workers they employ, whether by intensifying work for the remaining workers or automating their jobs. Either way, as Nick Hanauer makes clear, hiring more workers 'is a course of last resort for the capitalist'. Extra workers may enable more output, but if firms can find other ways of expanding output that are cheaper, they will.

So, even productive investment may be either job-increasing or job-decreasing. The last few decades have seen plenty of 'jobless growth' in advanced industrial economies. Contrast that with the post-war boom of the 1950s and 1960s, when the rich controlled a much smaller percentage of wealth than now: then growth was job-creating overall and real wages grew.

In the economy as a whole, the number of jobs depends primarily on the level of total or 'aggregate' demand. As Hanauer argues, ordinary people create jobs simply by spending their money. Job numbers are most likely to rise when people and businesses are spending more. Aggregate demand is not within the control of individual businesses: it's their environment. Businesses can't grow unless demand increases. The current crisis of capitalist economies owes much to the fact that aggregate demand in many rich countries has been stagnant for decades, and only buoyed up by massive expansion of consumer credit. It has therefore become harder to make profits out of producing goods and services. As both cause and consequence of this, there has been a major relative shift in investment, or rather 'investment', in the last 30–40 years from so-called non-financial companies (that produce goods and services) to financial companies that make money directly from money.

But you might ask why a shift in the proportion of national income going to the rich should make a difference to aggregate demand. Isn't it just a change in who has the spending power rather than a change in the total spending power? The answer is that the rich use a smaller proportion of their money for buying goods and services than do other people. Those on low incomes cannot afford to save because they need to spend all they have just to get by, and if they get an increase it's likely to be spent on basic things or paying off debts. Those in the middle may be able to save a little, and if they get more, then both their spending and saving can be increased. Hanauer puts it more simply: someone who earns a hundred or thousand times more than the average person is not likely to spend it on a hundred or thousand cars and houses. Yes, they may spend eye-wateringly large sums on themselves, but it's likely to be a considerably lower proportion of their overall income than for most people. In Keynes' terms, the rich have a lower 'marginal propensity to consume' than the rest of us. So, other things equal, redistributing income to the rich lowers aggregate demand, and redistributing downwards increases it.

This means that 'trickle-down' arguments are wrong. Yes, the rich employ a few servants and provide demand for accountants, tax advisors and luxury services, but far fewer jobs result from this than would be case if their income were redistributed back to ordinary people with a much higher propensity to consume. The best way to get money to cascade down from the rich to the rest is to tax them – or stop them extracting it in the first place! As Ann Pettifor argues, any trickle-down effect is dwarfed by the reverse 'hoovering up' effect of rent and interest in directing money to the wealthy.[144]

So, to come back to the Tea Party slogan: jobs are created by those who control the means of production and finance, subject to the constraints of demand and costs. Those with little money don't create jobs because they lack the means of production to employ anyone to work; where would they get the capital to do so? But that doesn't mean we have to depend on the rich. More modestly paid owners and managers of firms and other organisations, including co-ops, can create jobs too, where aggregate demand allows. Or the state can. If it provides services for sale, like public transport, and demand for them increases, then, unless it can find ways of increasing productivity, it is likely to have to increase employment. The state can also create jobs where the services it provides are free to the user, as in schools; it can just raise or redirect taxes to pay for more jobs in education.

But there's another twist here. For an individual capitalist, say, owning a fast-food chain, it makes sense to minimise the wage bill for any given level of output; but it's also in their interest that other organisations pay good, indeed rising, wages because that will mean bigger sales of burgers and of other goods, to the advantage of all businesses. As Marx and Keynes pointed out, this is one of capitalism's contradictions: the interests of capitalists in general are in conflict with the interests of individual capitalists. Neoliberalism ignores this problem of collective action and encourages capitalists to pursue their individual interests – to their ultimate cost. For a while there seemed to be a way round this through globalisation, by employing people where labour is cheap and selling their products where incomes are high, but the resulting 'hollowing out' of jobs, particularly in manufacturing in the rich countries, also depressed demand there.

One more twist: the rich, collectively, have another reason for restricting job creation. If employment grows too much, it is likely lead to wage inflation, as workers, now less fearful of unemployment, bid up their pay. That would squeeze profits. And wage inflation would also hit the rich as rentiers, because it would erode the value of the debts owed to them. This is why the rich pressure governments to hold down inflation, and high levels of unemployment help.

'Enterprise': aren't the rich the entrepreneurs?

Here's another case of how words can mislead. Rentiers don't call themselves rentiers, and not many capitalists call themselves capitalists, but many of each like to call themselves 'entrepreneurs'. Upbeat terms like 'entrepreneur' and 'enterprise' can be stretched to cover things that don't deserve them.

To be enterprising is to be resourceful, innovative, determined and bold, showing initiative and engaging in risky ventures that turn novel ideas into realities, with beneficial effects; these are surely good qualities. Who wouldn't like to be seen as enterprising, or better, as an entrepreneur? But what's problematic about these words is the company they often keep.

'Enterprise', as a quality or virtue, is what linguists call a non-count noun, but as a count noun – 'an enterprise', 'enterprises'[145] – it is often seen as synonymous with private business, as is the term 'entrepreneur'. This of course has the neat effect not only of associating the *virtue* of enterprise with the private sector but of setting up an implicit contrast with the public sector, which is seen as un-enterprising by comparison. No argument is needed to support this implicit claim because this use of the word seems to make it a matter of definition: private businesses are enterprises, therefore their owners are entrepreneurs – special, enterprising people – and whatever is not a private business cannot be enterprising.

But if we think about it, we can see that:

1. An entrepreneur or enterprising person does not have to be a capitalist, although already having a lot of money certainly helps to *fund* business, perhaps an enterprising one. However, significant innovation takes considerable time and resources, so particularly where businesses are under pressure to deliver shareholder value in the short term, this may *stifle* entrepreneurial behaviour. The spectacle of major firms spending more on buying back their own shares, so as to push their price up, than they spend on research and development makes a nonsense of the idea that they are enterprising in the sense of innovative and risk-taking.
2. Many communities have people who set up new things, for example, running festivals or sports events, starting a community bank or charity or setting up local 'freecycle' systems so members can give away unwanted items to others who need them. Such people are entrepreneurs – social entrepreneurs, we might say – but not capitalists. Cooperatives can be entrepreneurial too.
3. The state – *yes, the state!* – so often portrayed as rule bound and sluggish, and lacking the spur of competition, can also be entrepreneurial. Even though it usually has a monopoly in certain activities, the public sector sometimes engages in enterprising ventures, such as setting up the National Health

Service, establishing the Open University in the UK, high-speed rail services or launching space probes. As we show later, governments have repeatedly fostered fundamental research and borne the risk of ventures failing. Ability to withstand failure is essential if people are to have the freedom to think 'outside the box', for most innovations, like most new small businesses, fail. The road to success is paved with failures; if there's no room for failure, then people – whether they work for the state or private firms – become conservative and risk averse. And again, enterprise needs *patient* money, for major innovations can take over a decade to turn into successful products. Market competition may help to drive innovation, but competition for *quick* gains is more likely to be a brake, especially on major innovation. Obsession with liquidity – with being able to sell off any fixed assets like machinery, buildings or research divisions the minute they fail to yield gains – stifles innovation in production.

4. Pure (non-working) capitalists are *not* entrepreneurial – they merely own the means of production and extract profit from businesses, delegating any control and direction of activities to managers, who may or may not be enterprising.[146] Their short-term demands may inhibit enterprising behaviour.

5. Working capitalists may or may not be enterprising: while successful innovations may make firms profitable, there are other ways of making a profit, such as squeezing labour or suppliers. (It's a sad day when we treat wage cutting as 'enterprising'.)

6. As American economist William J. Baumol noted, enterprise may be used in devising new forms of rent-seeking that damage rather than benefit the economy ('unproductive entrepreneurship', as he called it).[147] Rentiers may find new ways of extracting rent or interest, but while they might like to think of themselves as enterprising in this respect, they are unproductive – worse, a drain on the productive economy. All sorts of ingenious financial instruments have been designed, often by 'quants' – first-rate mathematicians employed by financial institutions – for value-skimming and speculation. While the quality of enterprise involves being willing to take risks, a lot of risk taking is not entrepreneurial: all sheep are animals, but not all animals are sheep.

As we saw earlier, when speculators claim to be entrepreneurs because they take risks, they flatter themselves.

7. Workers may be enterprising, but their scope for realising their potential in this respect is limited by lack of money and security and restrictions on what they are allowed to do at work. Alternatively, they may fear that their bosses will take the credit (both financial and symbolic) for their enterprising activity. Those who want to develop new products and ways of doing things usually have to leave and become self-employed or set up a small business.

8. Finally, the romance of the entrepreneur is like the romance of the individual scientific genius; it is rarely simply individuals who do innovative things on their own, but more often groups or networks, and all are indebted to the accumulated knowledge and infrastructure that they inherit from their society. More on this in Part Two. Wittingly or unwittingly, celebrations of 'entrepreneurs' in the media serve to render invisible the workers on whom they depend.

So, for all these reasons, we should be sceptical about the idea that the rich are entrepreneurs and thereby deserve their wealth.

Sometimes, though, an owner of a firm – a capitalist – *is* enterprising, perhaps developing a new product from which millions of consumers benefit. Don't they deserve their wealth?

The Jobs/Dyson defence: don't truly innovative people deserve all they get?

Steve Jobs, the late CEO of Apple computers, was said to have been 'worth' $8.3 billion. If you were given a dollar every second, it would take 266 years to get that much. In the UK, James Dyson, famous for his Dyson vacuum cleaners, was estimated to be worth £2.65 billion (84 years at £1 per second), according to the 2012 Sunday Times Rich List.

People like Jobs and Dyson are exceptional. But *they are rare amongst the rich* in creating new products of value. Paul Krugman points out that 'very few of the top 1 percent, or even the top 0.01 percent, made their money that way. For the most part, we're looking at executives at firms that they didn't themselves create. They may own a lot of stock or stock options in their companies, but they received those assets as part of their pay package, not by founding the business.'[148] So Jobs, Dyson or indeed Mark Zuckerberg of Facebook are exceptional as regards their role in developing brilliant new products that have benefitted millions, but they are not representative of the super-rich, even though they are useful poster boys for them.

But we still need to ask questions: first, how much would they have got if they hadn't *owned* (much of) their firms? And second, to what extent did they depend on technologies developed by others?

Regarding the first question, although they are working, indeed entrepreneurial, capitalists, rather than pure capitalists, as (part) owners they are able to take the profit produced partly by others. Key research and development employees and managers responsible for important innovations may get higher pay than other workers, not least to stop them going to another firm, but unless they can get shares or share options they do not get the chance to even approach the kind of rewards that owners can.

Regarding the second question, it's easy to swallow the usual media tales of heroic individuals doing it all themselves, or at least starting off on their own – the maverick-kids-in-garages stories. But research on innovation reveals a different picture of the involvement of multiple individuals, groups and agencies in which people interact and build on the achievements of others. If there appear to be 'breakthroughs' they are typically the final stage in long processes of learning that involved many people. As we'll see in Part Two, so much of our wealth depends on those who have gone before us. In computing, the graphical user interface involving mouse, pointer, icons and hypertext, adopted by Apple and Microsoft, had already been invented, as Bill Gates has acknowledged. Key innovations in electronics, including the microchip and the development of the internet itself, were funded not by private money but by the US government's Department of Defense.[149] Similarly, the development of the algorithm behind Google was funded by the US National Science Foundation, and the technologies behind the iPhone – GPS and touchscreen display – were also dependent on state funding.

To be sure, Steve Jobs and others were brilliant at taking these and developing them into consumer products, but they were building on what others had done. And it's not just in electronics that the private sector depends on innovative work done within the state: 75% of radical new drugs in the US pharmaceutical sector are the product of research funded by the National Institutes of Health; similar stories are to be found in less glamorous sectors like construction.[150]

Rather than simply be dazzled by the brilliance of the products and the nice stories of the rise from obscurity to fame, we need to take a more sober look at what has enabled these employers' wealth.[151] We might agree that the likes of Jobs and Dyson deserve more than ordinary workers, though we'd probably differ on just how much more they should get. But let's not kid ourselves, these innovative capitalists do not ask their workforces or the general public: 'How much do you think I deserve for my contribution?' (Jobs would have had to go to China to consult the bulk of the manufacturing workforce, including those at one of Apple's chief suppliers, Foxconn, a company that made headlines for the high number of worker suicides, under-age labour and oppressive working conditions. Dyson would have had to go to Malaysia, as he moved his factory there from England to cut costs, especially labour costs.) Such employers get what they get because they can, and the crucial reasons for this are the availability of existing technologies and private ownership. And let's remember that it's not uncommon for employees who come up with inventions to find that they are effectively stolen from them by their employers, who then get the benefit.[152] So, at best, two cheers for innovative working capitalists.

'They'll just go to another country and take their money with them ...'

'... if we tax them too much, or otherwise restrict their power.' This point is frequently wheeled out, as if the rich were major wealth creators, possessing rare powers, and therefore people whom we must do all we can to attract.

British Conservative politician John Redwood's defence of this belief is a common one: 'The problem is the rich do not have to hang around if you seek to make them too poor. They have the best lawyers and accountants. They can go on strike when it comes to investing and developing businesses. They can go off shore.'[153] This is right on all three counts: yes, there are no restrictions on them taking 'their' wealth elsewhere; yes, they can afford the best legal and financial servants; and yes, they can hold countries to ransom by refusing to invest. But of course, *accepting* these facts as if they were immutable adds up merely to saying 'might is right'. We need to challenge their arbitrary power.

Redwood also resorts to the tired old trickle-down and job-creator claims: they employ 'small armies of professional advisers [and] set up businesses and create jobs'. We've already dealt with these well-worn myths. Their advisors will no doubt help them evade tax, in fact the likelihood is that most of their money has already gone to other countries, particularly tax havens. They could indeed disinvest from any country that didn't provide a 'competitive' (in other words low tax, low regulation) environment, escaping their duties as good citizens. Unrestricted movement of capital, and governments' support of rentier businesses, allows them to pick and choose where to go in order to avoid tax and maximise profits. But capitalism was much more successful when it had top rates of tax of 80% and over, restrictions on capital movements and the top 0.01% controlled a much smaller share of wealth than now.

And actually the threats to leave are exaggerated:

> If it were the case that higher taxes caused wealth to flee we would expect to see an exodus of the wealthier citizens of Sweden, Denmark, Norway and France – the countries with the highest tax rates. A glance at the latest Forbes billionaires list reveals that of four Norwegians on the list all live in Norway, the two Danes live in Denmark, five of the nine Swedes live in Sweden, and eight of the ten French live in France.[154]

The new small entrepreneur

In talking about this book with friends I've found that the most common objection to my argument goes like this:

> What if someone sets up a small business with savings or by borrowing money, perhaps by remortgaging their house? In so doing they're taking a major risk. They work hard. Let's say the business turns out to be successful; so they start employing people, and build up the business into a significant venture, from which they can draw a high income, and indeed become rich. Surely they've deserved their wealth, especially as they've created jobs on the way?

To answer this, we need to look at the stages in the development of this new firm.

In the first place, the founder is self-employed or co-owns it with a partner, or possibly employs one or two people, often family members. At this stage she is what political economists call a 'petty commodity producer'. If she's successful and demand for the product increases, she may then employ more workers. As she does so, she gradually shifts to becoming a *working capitalist*, that is, an owner of means of production who employs others to work for her, but who also still does some work, usually planning and management. Workers are only likely to be employed if they can not only cover their own costs and that of the materials they use, but produce enough to make a profit over and above this – *to which, thanks to capitalist property rights, they are not entitled*. For example, if each worker produces goods and services worth 20% more than they cost to employ plus other costs, under capitalist property rights, that 20% belongs to the owner, to be used as she sees fit – for her own consumption or for investment, speculation or whatever. As the firm grows and the owner relies more and more on employees to produce the output, an increasing proportion of the owner's income comes from this surplus.

Eventually, she may be able to stop working altogether and delegate management to employee managers, and become a pure, that is, non-working capitalist, and still draw profit from the business. She may then be able to take over other firms and live off their profits too, and use them to get still more unearned income from rent or interest or other capital gains.

So we might agree that the person who starts a successful business and then employs a workforce deserves credit, and indeed some extra income, but, especially in the long run, the source of their profit comes primarily from being able to take advantage of capitalist property relations that allow them sole ownership of the revenue received by the firm for the goods and services that the workers have mostly produced. Unfair outcomes can have clean origins.

Other objections and slogans

'I do not believe you can make the poor rich by making the rich poor.'[155]

Another palm-to-forehead, exasperating slogan. No one said either that the rich should be made poor – or indeed that the poor should be made rich. But, given the dependence of the rich on wealth extraction, and the low marginal propensity to consume of the rich, redistributing income from rich to poor would be a positive-sum game, expanding aggregate demand and increasing employment, which in turn would create more demand.

'I believe that the way to help the poor is not to take from the rich but to make the pie bigger through economic growth.'

The implication is that we need inequality in order to get growth. Not only does this not make any sense in terms of transfers of unearned income, investment and the marginal propensity to consume, but the empirical evidence on the relation between economic growth and inequality at national levels shows there is no such relation.[156] On the contrary, capitalism grew faster when it was more equal. But we should note also how, in today's debased political culture, saying 'I believe x' is taken to be more convincing than 'the evidence shows that x': apparently, belief trumps evidence, and those who bother to look at the evidence are accused of not knowing what they think, or being a 'flip-flop person', as John Kerry was called in the US election of 2004.

'A rising tide lifts all boats' – or yachts.

This tired old cliché has the same discombobulating effect on thinking about economic matters. The message is supposedly that everyone benefits from economic growth, the hidden premise being again that inequality is necessary for that economic growth. It's a *dis*analogy. Yes, we may rather like the attractive imagery, but people are not like boats, and the economic growth is not like a tide: it's characteristically uneven and it's not at all unusual for some groups to lose out in not just relative but absolute terms during periods of growth. That politicians and media pundits still trot out this phrase shows how a picturesque analogy can disarm critical thinking and replace it with wishful thinking. But it's doubtful that even the ruling elite believe this themselves: in a secret report for the super-rich, Citigroup, the international financial conglomerate, used the following headline: 'Rising tide lifting yachts'.[157]

An objection from mainstream economics: 'allocational efficiency'

> We should always keep in view the enormous economic benefits that flow from a healthy and innovative financial sector. The increasing depth and sophistication of financial markets promote economic growth by allocating capital where it is most productive. (Ben Bernanke, Chair, US Federal Reserve, 2007)[158]

Contemporary mainstream economists are most likely to object to my arguments so far by complaining that I am ignoring the contribution of rent, interest, speculation, private profit and so on to 'allocational efficiency'. The rich, it might be claimed, boost this through their 'investment', and their wealth is their reward for doing so. What does this mean? As we shall, see there are two versions of this concept that need to be distinguished, but which are commonly confused.

In one version it's claimed that in any economy resources need to be allocated across different activities where they're most wanted and needed and most productive. In our everyday lives, we often seek to do this at least in an approximate, 'good enough' fashion.

Even hunter-gatherers have to decide how to spend their time if they are to be able to survive and live well, though the solution may have become settled as a matter of convention.[159] Since this applies to all societies to some degree it can be said to be a 'transhistorical' concept. In modern societies, one of the things financial systems, whether privately or publicly run, are supposed to do is to move underused or idle resources, particularly savings, to where they can be used more productively. This, surely, makes luminous sense?

It does, but it is frequently used as a cover for a quite different version of allocational efficiency that is specific to capitalism, in which resources are allocated to where expected rates of financial return are highest. This is what 'investors' or lenders do, and, in the process, economic growth is allegedly maximised and, supposedly, everyone benefits: their money is working hard for them, as they say. But the highest expected rates of return could be where labour is most exploitable; or where consumer incomes are highest (the rich can outbid the poor, and the wants and needs of thee poor are massively under-represented in markets relative to those of the rich); or where prospects for extracting rent are best; or where asset inflation is highest (the latest bubble); or where taxation is lowest. It could fund logging in Sumatra, or mining in Peru, or luxury apartments in Dubai or London, or buying up land in Africa to rent out, or buying shares and bonds and other sources of unearned income, or simply moving money to a tax haven.

Further, where, as in contemporary capitalism, liquidity and short-termism are at a premium, long-term investment and people's security may be threatened by this constant shifting of funds to where rates of return are highest. This may have damaging effects on efficiency in the long run. Differences in rates of return in capitalism do not simply reflect differences in 'productiveness' or needs or priorities. Some things which are very much needed – for example, good-quality care for old people with low incomes – cannot easily be provided for profit, so this capitalist kind of allocational efficiency ignores them.

So the usual trick of mainstream economists and the business media is to pass off *capitalist* allocational efficiency as no different from the first, transhistorical kind. Only to the extent that it does assist the creation of wealth can it be said to be beneficial. Even then, we still have to decide to whom the gains should go.

Some defences of private renting use a similar kind of reasoning. It's argued that rent performs a *rationing function* by allocating land and property – to whichever user can make best use of them. Thus, in a city the most sought-after land tends to be in the centre, the most accessible part, so users who (a) most need it and (b) can most afford it will bid the most for it, and landlords will rent to them. This is supposedly rational because it results in scarce city-centre land being allocated to 'the highest and best use'. Yet these are weasel words, for again the rich can outbid the poor, regardless of the relative strength of their needs or the uses to which they can put the land. In London, the rich are pushing up prices so much that cleaners, teachers and health workers needed in the city cannot afford to live there. This is rationing land not simply according to who can make the best use of it, but according to who can afford it. If everyone had the same income, then the prices they were prepared to pay for a piece of land, or indeed for anything, would reflect the strength of their desire for it relative to others'. But where there are major income inequalities, what people are prepared to pay also reflects their differing purchasing power.[160]

But even in so far as rent *does* help to ration land and property in a rational way, this does not serve as a defence of private landownership. Public ownership of land, with the state renting to private individuals and organisations, could allow the same rationing function, while the revenue would go into the public purse instead of the pockets of private rentiers. Beware of economists and others who use the rationing functions of rent to justify private ownership of land. It's a non-sequitur.[161]

This sleight-of-hand is an instance of a more general kind of dubious argument.

Typically, their arguments about financial activities go like this. First, some beneficial effects of the practice (such as creating credit money) are noted, so as to show that it has a useful function. Next, it's claimed that everything is therefore fine and those involved should be left alone to get on with it. The first issue is about the usefulness of a given function, but the second step glosses over further vital questions:

if it is found to be socially useful, who – or which organisations – should be allowed to perform this function, how should the rewards be distributed and how much should they be taxed? The financial services sector doesn't welcome scrutiny of the first question and typically claims that only insiders have the expertise to assess it; it certainly would not welcome the other issues being raised, as they put into question its property rights.

Mainstream economists are likely also to object to our distinction between earned and unearned income, on the grounds that it involves 'making value-judgements', a phrase unthinkingly used in mainstream economics to mean 'judgements without justification'.[162] But of course we have provided justifications – to do with whether income is merely asset based and whether economic practices contribute to the production and distribution of goods and services or are merely rent-seeking. Not making such a distinction has the effect of condoning unproductive and, indeed, parasitic activities. (To condone something, one also has to make a value-judgement. The issue is not whether we can escape value-judgements, but whether the arguments supporting them stand up.) For economists, anything that sells, be it food, guns or the latest derivatives, must be meeting a need[163]: otherwise it wouldn't sell! No moral judgements are needed, according to this capitalist logic.

While we're on the subject of objections from mainstream (or 'neoclassical') economics, this is a good place to say something more about the basics of that approach, for its influence is enormous, dominating not only educational curricula but government policy thinking, especially with the rise of neoliberalism. It believes itself to be a predictive science but overwhelmingly failed to predict the crisis. It not only offers theories of economic processes but shapes their development by influencing economic practices themselves. Despite its professed belief in the value of free competition, it monopolises the production of economic knowledge in universities by excluding alternative or 'heterodox' economists (who were better at predicting the crisis) from positions of power and from publishing in the journals it controls.[164] In Britain it also controls the panels that assess university research in economics, and hence how research is rated and rewarded by government funding.

Its view of economic processes is decidedly peculiar, seeing economic life as primarily a matter of people exchanging goods, with production – which all societies need in order to survive – pushed into the background. In other words, it looks at the world through market lenses. Even though not all societies rely on markets, all societies need to produce in order to survive. Yet, from the first pages of any mainstream economics textbook, the market blinkers are firmly in place, so it will start with how what we buy is influenced by prices, and how prices are influenced by supply and demand. Both are true, but they miss what this exchange presupposes: the social organisation of people engaged in provisioning – producing and distributing goods and services in various divisions of labour. When it does address production it frequently theorises it as a matter of exchanges between individuals. In this way it immediately heads in the wrong direction.

Mainstream economics' view of efficiency is particularly one sided. In a society where markets are widespread, and each individual can exchange freely with others, then if they can agree prices it is in their interest to do so. If A has more x than she wants, but not enough y, whereas B has more y than she wants, but not enough x, it is in their interest to exchange, assuming they can agree on a price – effectively, how much of x for each unit of y. When they have exchanged in this way, both are better off, so there has been an improvement in the 'utility' that A and B derive from their property, and the allocation of resources has improved. Because resources have moved to those who value them the most – or, as they usually forget to say, *and are also able to pay for them* – one might be tempted to call this wealth creation, but this is actually only a redistribution and revaluation of existing wealth. True, wealth is not just any goods and services, but those that are deemed worth something by people who might use them, and distribution to those who want them is likely to increase their welfare. But that doesn't mean that value is merely subjective so that wealth can be wished into existence. If that were the case, wishful thinking could remove all economic problems.[165] But goods and services have to be produced before they can be sold.

In the neoclassical view of what a rational economy would be like, everything is potentially up for sale, everything would have a price, because only then can people assess whether they could gain from exchanging things. So economic efficiency is thought of primarily in terms of market exchange, and whether all resources have been moved to where they give their holders maximum utility. Any restriction on this, for example by governments fixing a minimum wage, or unions engaging in collective bargaining, therefore reduces economic efficiency thus defined. From this, economists tend further to claim that economic growth will be restricted, since growth will surely be fastest when goods are deployed where they bring most benefit (or rather, make most profit). Rates of return on different possible 'investments' are continually shifting, so markets must be as active as possible so as to allow traders to shift their 'investments' as fast as possible to what are or are expected to be the most profitable things. If too much wealth is tied up in fixed resources, rather than in liquid form as money, it can't take advantage of potential gains.

A similar argument is used to defend share dealing – it allows control of a corporation to go to those who are willing to pay the most for it, and supposedly, they will be the ones who can run it most efficiently (profitably). If companies don't do things that make the price of their shares rise, it makes it easier for others to buy them up and take them over and try to extract more profit from the business. So an active market for companies can develop, leaving them prey to takeovers.

How absurd to suppose that speculative 'investment' in financial assets (which, ultimately, are claims on the labour and products of workers) can be as economically beneficial as direct real investment in infrastructure, skills, production and distribution! But it isn't just a flimsy rationalisation of unfettered markets; it's also a useful cover for rentier interests. Never mind their wealth extraction, let's put our faith in possible increases in 'allocational efficiency' through ever more rapid responses to prices.

PART TWO

Putting the rich in context: what determines what people get?

> The entire process of bargaining, by which the apportionment of work and of its product is determined, is seen to consist in a struggle where economic strength, not justice or humanity, is the decisive factor. (J.A. Hobson, 1929)[1]

Misunderstandings of how the rich get their wealth are underpinned by wider misconceptions about the causes of economic inequalities in general – not just between the 1% and the 99%, but within the latter. Many people think the rich deserve their wealth, because they believe that right across the board people *generally* get what they deserve. Even if we take out those whose income is mainly unearned, there are still significant inequalities within the rest. Don't highly skilled people doing responsible jobs, like surgeons, get paid more than unskilled workers like cleaners because they deserve more? Doesn't this explain the inequalities between them, and show them to be fair? It actually appears to be true. But, as we'll see, this takes a lot for granted that needs to be questioned.

Surveys on attitudes to economic equality show that people are concerned not only with what people *get* in terms of income but also with what they *contribute*, in terms of work. And they expect there to be some relationship between the two.[2] I agree that we should consider contributions as well as what people get – 'distribution'; after all, the chapters so far are an attack on unwarranted free-riding on others' work by the rich. To deal with these questions we need to widen the scope of the argument to look at what produces economic inequalities within society as a whole. The answers take us deep into the basic structure of our societies.

The kind of wishful thinking involved in the belief in a just world may be partly the product of an understandable desire to avoid painful feelings of resentment at injustice and what might seem like mean-spiritedness. It's tempting to jump to the conclusion that economic inequalities are basically fair, without investigating what *does* determine people's incomes. When we do look at this in practice, we find that the issue of differences in what people seem to deserve shrinks considerably, because their jobs and income depend so much on other things; we realise that we don't live in a just world.

The justifications of pay are one thing, the determinants quite another. If we are going to get anywhere in understanding these things we need to look a much bigger picture, and ask to what we owe our wealth. What determines what we get? Part Two answers this, first in broad terms regarding differences in wealth between different societies, then in relation to the determinants of pay within any particular society. It ends by attacking the myth of 'a level playing field' that underpins ideas of meritocracy.

NINE

To what do we owe our wealth?
Our dependence on the commons

> How long can the benefits conferred by many generations of development continue to be siphoned off by elites rather than allowed to flow back to society and the people at large? (Gar Alperovitz and Lew Daly, 2008)[3]

It might seem from what I've said so far that wealth depends purely on people producing goods and services. But they don't do it on their own, from scratch, but mainly by using and building on what's already been produced, on what today's society inherits from yesterday's, and by drawing upon nature's resources. This is our common inheritance – or simply 'the commons'.

Compare today's earnings now with those of people in the 19th century; workers today are of course much better off. But this is not because they are working any harder or are more deserving than their ancestors. They are producing far more output for each hour they work – in the US, output per person per hour is estimated to have increased 15-fold since 1870[4] – but that's because they are working with better technology, in better-organised workplaces, in a society with faster communication and distribution systems. So the difference in wealth is a result of society as a whole being more productive. The accumulated intelligence, know-how and investments of successive generations are what have made us so productive now. Without them we would be desperately poor. Yet we so easily fail to notice our enormous debts to the past and imagine that our pay is simply a reflection of our personal merit and effort or contribution. Some of this inheritance may be privatised by a minority – and not the ones who created it! – with far-reaching implications for the production and distribution of wealth, but I'll come to that in a bit.

Most of what we so easily attribute to our own intelligence and efforts is the hard-won product of previous generations' thought and labour, to which any one of us can rarely add more than a little. Indeed, the more this inheritance grows, the smaller our additions in proportion to it. In their important book, *Unjust Deserts*, Gar Alperovitz and Lew Daly quote this halting challenge from the Bible:

> What do you have that you did not receive? And if you received it, why do you boast as if it were not a gift? (1 Corinthians 4:7)

It's a little bit exaggerated, for however important this inheritance, we cannot just live off the past without adding something ourselves – some work is required just to use the common inheritance. But it reminds us of our dependence on what nature and our ancestors have provided. None of us can really claim to be 'self-made'.

The commons vary geographically. If we imagine picking 10 people randomly from the world's population, the best predictor of their income or wealth would probably be their country of origin. If they're from Norway or the US they're probably richer than if they're from Nigeria or Uganda, notwithstanding the inequalities within each of those countries. Why these geographical differences?

As a youngster growing up at the time when some of the British Empire had yet to be dismantled, I remember a popular racist myth that people were poor in certain countries because they were lazy or unintelligent, while the British were enterprising and industrious, and hence richer. This of course is nonsense. If you think of virtually any occupation that is found in a wide range of countries – teacher, labourer, engineer, doctor, retailer, call centre operator – in most cases their pay is higher in rich countries than in middling or poor countries, though this has nothing to do with how hard they work or how intelligent they are. Again, rich countries have a higher level of technological development, and their workers tend to use more of this technology than do their counterparts in poorer countries, so things can be produced more easily, quickly and cheaply, even though wages and salaries are relatively high. So, at a global level, a good predictor of an individual's standard of living is the level of development of what Marx called 'the forces of production' – the knowledge, skills, resources, technology, infrastructure and equipment – available to them in their country.

Alperovitz and Daly begin their book by quoting billionaire Warren Buffett: 'society is responsible for a very significant share of what I have earned [sic]'.[5] Buffett, and also Bill Gates, head of Microsoft, acknowledge that they would not be where they are were it not for the fact that they were born into a very rich, technologically advanced society and they have been beneficiaries of a vast inheritance of knowledge, particularly science. It was no less a figure than Isaac Newton who said 'If I have seen further than others, it is by standing on the shoulders of giants'. If Buffett and Gates had been born into a society without an electricity supply, without a history of scientific development, we would not have heard of them. Of course, these facts alone do not explain why they are so much richer than other people from their own country – for that we would need to consider other factors, especially the privatisation of parts of the commons and its use as a source of unearned income; but they do underscore the importance of what we inherit for our current standard of living.

The commons go beyond the forces of production, to *institutions*, in the broad sense of tried and tested ways of doing things. It would be enormously inefficient to have to invent new ways of doing things each time we acted. Indeed, it is thanks to our ability to rely on institutions that we have time to do anything new. We are indebted to our legal and political system, for example, for enabling us to live in the way we do.

The commons also includes *cultural* goods, knowledge and wisdom. Authors, artists or composers, no less than scientists or entrepreneurs, can innovate only by using the materials, genres and ideas available to them that others have provided; innovation doesn't come out of the blue but from new combinations of what already exists. So the commons extends from the most basic to the sublime – from roads and sewage systems to the most treasured works of art and science. We tend to take them for granted, but it's worth pausing to think where we would be without them; most of our everyday activities would be simply impossible. We would be ignorant and helpless – scratching at the earth with our hands for a living.

In his book *The Country and The City*, Raymond Williams urged us to look at the rural landscape not as a 'view' but to 'think it through as labour' – to ponder the immense amount of work that had gone into making it, in clearing land, digging ditches, building villages, tending woods and so on.[6] It is sobering to look at this inheritance as a whole – urban as well as rural – in this way and realise how much we owe to those who made it.

Finally, and most fundamentally, the commons includes the *environment*: energy, minerals, rivers, oceans, soils, flora and fauna and climate, or 'the biosphere'; indeed this part of the commons is the basis for the rest of it. It is far from 'untouched': our environment has been extensively transformed by human labour over many millennia; the material products of that labour, from bread to computers, are just transformations of natural substances. The environment constrains and enables everything that we do. Two farmers may put the same effort into growing crops, but their yields and incomes may differ according to their local soils and climates, and previous work in draining or irrigating the land. Some might think their equal efforts deserve equal rewards, but what they actually get is likely to be unequal.

So it's clear that the commons – technological, institutional, cultural and environmental – are geographically uneven, comprising different cultures and language communities, of which most of us know very little outside our own. This means that to a significant extent our wealth depends on the lottery of birth. Again, what do we have that we were not given? Not much.

Inequalities between countries in the level of development of the commons, especially the forces of production, are the source of another mechanism favouring the strong over the weak: unequal exchange. When a rich country like the US trades with a poor one like Bangladesh, not just the rich, but everyone in the rich country benefits from getting cheap goods, provided by cheap labour. Most of Europe has benefitted from this unequal exchange for over two centuries, from cotton and cocoa to jeans, electronic goods and call centre services. For any given traded product, the workers in the poor country have to work much longer to be able to afford it than do their counterparts in rich countries. Even if they're working in state-of-the-art factories producing tablet computers, as some Chinese suppliers of western firms are, their pay is still low. To be sure, this has a lot to do with the huge supply of labour and limited employment rights to protect workers, but it's also because the overall level of development of productive forces in the economy as a whole is still relatively low. That those of us in rich countries can get goods so cheaply from poor countries has of course nothing to do with what anyone deserves or needs. Markets simply don't operate with regard to such considerations.

Passing it on

While the commons pre-exists each of us, it needs continual renewal if it is not to decline. Literature and science have continually to be reinterpreted, re-evaluated. And they have to be passed on. 'If you can read this, thank a teacher' was a slogan used by a teachers' union a long time ago. Everyone is indebted to their teachers, parents and all those who have made the effort to help us discover the wonders of the commons, even if we didn't always enjoy the experience. To be sure, as some of them may have reminded us occasionally, they couldn't learn it for us – we had to make an effort. In the process, we not only inherit and reproduce the commons, but may help to develop it.

Remembering the challenge from Corinthians, when someone claims that they deserve extra money or praise for their skills and expertise, we might ask to what extent they are mistaking their own contribution for that of their teachers. In so far as we owe our abilities to an organised system of education, we are indebted to that system. The reason more people are literate in Britain now than 200 years ago is not that we are cleverer or make more effort now, but because we have a public education system. This, too, is part of the commons.

So here's the second key point: what we can contribute depends not only on the state of the commons – the technological, institutional, cultural and environmental inheritance that we are born into – but on the education that helps us to get access to it. We should broaden this to include our whole upbringing, particularly early family life. We are brought up among the advantages or disadvantages of our parents, and absorb these influences, developing a feel for the game in which they live, and our aspirations and expectations tend to correspond to them. No wonder the child of affluent, cosmopolitan parents who have a second home in France is likely to do better in French at school than the child whose parents' income doesn't stretch to holidays abroad.[7]

Controlling the commons

There are other things besides geography and education that govern our access to the commons underlying our wealth: namely, *power and property rights*. To make a productive contribution of any kind we need access to the particular materials and information necessary for the specific kinds of work we are doing. So we need control over the relevant property and equipment, and in many cases ownership provides this. If anyone can help themselves to the cook's equipment, the taxi driver's car, the doctor's stethoscope or the farmer's land, the cook, the taxi driver, and so on, cannot do their work.

But this situation where workers own or at least control the means of production they use is enjoyed by only a minority today. As Marx clearly saw, it's very different from the kind of property in means of production that dominates modern capitalism. This allows a massive centralisation of the ownership and control of means of production into the hands of a minority, so that they can then extract unearned income from the majority as a condition of allowing them to benefit from the use of the technological inheritance. In Tawney's words, the result is that the means of production become not 'a means of work but an instrument of gain or the exercise of power, and . . . there is no guarantee that gain bears any relation to service, or power to responsibility'.[8] Ownership is divorced from work, and from the workers. Thus, most of the property of the rich takes the form of 'rights of various kinds, such as royalties, ground-rents, and, above all, of course, shares in industrial undertakings, which yield an income irrespective of any personal service rendered by their owners'.[9] Unearned income, in other words.

The concentration of private ownership has occurred partly through simple dispossession of small producers, usually by confiscating the land on which they depend, partly through their being outcompeted and taken over by more successful businesses, and partly as a way of controlling large-scale, complex means of production such as power stations, that can't function when split up into separate bits. Of course, there are huge efficiency benefits in the concentration of some kinds of production into a few large units and centralising their control, but there are other forms of control and ownership that can avoid enabling a minority to corner those benefits and free-ride on the labour of the majority, such as cooperatives or state ownership.[10] The need to have centralised control over large organisations does not justify capitalist ownership and control.

So, under capitalism the parts of our heritage that are most crucial for economic and political power have been turned into the private property of a minority. This privatisation of the inherited fruits of past labour – or 'dead labour', as Marx called it – is crucial for understanding inequality and the dominance of the rich. As long as other people need to draw on the commons, then anyone who has property rights over parts of it – whether land, minerals, buildings, technology, works of art, genetic material or intellectual property – has power over those who don't and can make them pay for it. Much of the commons are social in origin and therefore its benefits should be treated as social wealth, not something that Johnny-come-lately rentiers can divert into their own pockets.

An important objection from the Right

The Right often challenge any questioning of capitalist property rights by saying that to remove them would deny people the freedom to produce, or even to do what they want with their property. Since no one would be responsible for the upkeep and use of means of production it would be neglected or misused. Alternatively, if central state planners try to organise it, they will inevitably lack the detailed and often tacit knowledge that the producers have on the ground, and in trying to conduct it from above will make a mess of it, as happened in the former Soviet Bloc. As the neoliberal guru Friedrich

Hayek argued, in a society with a complex division of labour such as our own, only those actually involved in particular specialisms within that economy can know what their specific needs are – how many and what kind of widgets are needed for producing other widgets and so on. We need private property in the means of production to encourage producers to make responsible, well-informed use of property, and to allow them to buy what they need and to sell what they produce in markets. The price system will automatically organise them, rewarding those who produce what others want, and penalising those who don't.[11] So, private property in the means of production allows ownership to correspond with function, power with responsibility.

This is right in some respects – that's why it's important – but seriously wrong in others. In particular, it tries to legitimise capitalist ownership, which may involve businesses as large as BP, Toyota or Microsoft, by treating them as no different from homely examples of self-employed workers and small businesses. The word 'producers' covers both. In effect, it appeals to a pre-capitalist model of tiny family businesses that clearly needed to own their tools and control their work. This is a characteristic strategy of argument in mainstream economics, and neatly hides the inequality between employer and employee and conceals the enormous difference in power between a self-employed person and owners of large firms. In fact, this is why they like to talk about 'market society' rather than capitalism, because it hides these relationships. In taking this line of argument, Hayek ironically played into the hands of Marx and Tawney's arguments, for, although Hayek didn't realise it, his was unwittingly a defence of ownership of means of production by those who *work* it, not of capitalist ownership – which denies workers any such rights.

There are indeed important arguments against the state trying to control those kinds of economic activity that depend on local knowledge; such control not only separates power and responsibility but results in information loss by disempowering particular producers.[12] But it's not the only alternative to capitalist control: cooperatives enable decentralised ownership and control in the hands of those who do the work, aligning power more closely with responsibility and know-how. They are free from the straitjacket of a central plan telling them what to do, and free from the associated political authoritarianism of the Party, which went with state socialism. And they still face the discipline of the market, which allows consumers to decide whether they want their products, and so producer power cannot develop at the expense of consumers, and it allows the benefits of markets for coordinating local knowledge and encouraging the experimentation that Hayek highlighted and Marx failed to appreciate.

What about *private* inheritance?

You might be wondering about the legitimacy of inheritance in the more common sense of gifts and bequests in wills. It's difficult to estimate how much of personal wealth is inherited, but in the US the estimates average out at 50%. It's certainly a major source of inequalities. Since the 1980s, inheritance has made a comeback as a source of income, approaching 19th-century levels in France, while inheritance taxes have been severely cut from their high levels during the mid-20th century in France, the UK and the US.[13] People feel strongly about this; especially in unequal societies, many defend tax-free inheritance.[14]

How would you respond to these two questions?

1. If people choose to leave money to others when they die, should it be taxed, and if so, by how much?
2. Is it all right for the children of the rich – already given an arbitrary advantage through the lottery of birth in unequal societies – to get a large windfall gain and keep all of it?

Did you feel the same about them? I suggest that you might accept untaxed inheritance more easily in considering the first question, because it focuses on the rights of the giver: surely people should be allowed to do what they want with their money? They've paid taxes throughout their lives, so why shouldn't they give what's left to their chosen others when they die, if that's what they want? As Republicans and Conservatives like to put it, inheritance tax is a 'death tax', and therefore wicked.

But considering just what seems right from the point of view of the donor ignores the elephant in the room – the fact that we are born into different positions in a hugely unequal society and inevitably inherit many of our parents' advantages or disadvantages. The second question, focused on the recipient, highlights this. All the evidence on inequality and social (im)mobility shows that if you want to get on in life, the best thing to do is – like David Cameron or George W. Bush – choose your parents carefully. Large inheritances just reinforce these arbitrary inequalities. Six of the ten richest people in the US inherited fortunes. Those inequalities have nothing to do with differences in merit.

The geek and the heiress

As Thomas Piketty explains, the richest person in France, Liliane Bettencourt, heiress to the L'Oreal cosmetics empire, 'who never worked a day in her life', saw her wealth increase from $2 billion to $25 billion between 1990 and 2010. Bill Gates, who clearly does work, saw his wealth increase from $4 billion to $50 billion in the same period.

Both saw an annual real return on their wealth of 10–11%. Such people can live in incredible luxury on a minute percentage of their wealth and 'invest' the rest.[15] Bettencourt is simply a rentier, Gates a combination of working capitalist, albeit one who has profited from a near-monopoly in operating systems, and rentier.

Some might object that though the recipients may not *deserve* an inheritance, they are *entitled* to receive it, as it was given freely to them. This is actually a common view in popular thought, not just among the rich. As you can imagine, philosophers have had a field-day with that distinction.[16] But then, if we want to make entitlement a key criterion, is it not bizarre that we think it's OK to tax the income of those who work to provide goods and services for others, so they share in the burdens of supporting society, but think it's wrong to tax those who just get a windfall without doing anything?

But, from what I've said earlier, you may be thinking: aren't bequests in wills exactly an example of a free transfer – the legitimate form of unearned income where people give to those they love or to whom they think needs it? Who wouldn't want to be able to do this? Being able to give people things is not only necessary, in so far as we all need care, but a much under-valued source of well-being for the donor as well as the recipient. (Not being able to afford to give is one of the deprivations of poverty.) But major windfalls for the recipient – usually already well off – are another matter, and they're not needs based, unlike the support that people with disabilities receive, or public education, funded by the taxes we pay. And asking whether people should be able to leave large sums of money to others without being taxed not only ducks the issue of inequalities but leaves aside the question of whether the donor's money was earned or unearned, or indeed whether it in turn was inherited. Work alone is unlikely to make you rich; you need to get unearned income for that.

So I recommend that inheritances should be quite heavily taxed – at least as heavily as income. If you want equality of opportunity, you have to have rough equality of the circumstances in which people grow up and live.

Whereas inherited income used to be thought of as undeserved and hence appropriate for taxation, in Britain the rich have campaigned successfully to cut such taxes, using the usual trick of scaring the middle classes that inheritance tax will seriously impact on them. Actually, it's only on the estates of couples who leave property worth more than £650,000 that inheritance tax is payable – amounting to a mere 3% of the population. As Polly Toynbee comments:

> Why do they call the top 3% 'middle class'? That's the trick Conservatives play, deliberately conflating the interests of the very few with the interests of the genuine 'middle'. What is 'middle'? A mere 13% earn enough to reach the 40% tax band starting at £35,000, let alone pay any inheritance tax. Yet every average home-owner (price £250,000) is falsely stirred up to fear inheritance tax so that they will support the rich in their never-ending fight to avoid it. This paltry tax only brings in £3.1bn a year.[17]

Forty-two per cent of inherited wealth goes to just the richest 5%. Only 13% of the population inherit more than £2,000![18] And actually, the seriously rich tend to avoid inheritance tax by hiding their wealth in 'trusts' anyway.

Rather than congratulate ourselves on our wealth, or on being 'self-made' men and women, we should open our eyes to our vast debts to our common inheritance from nature and the labours and achievements of previous generations, and to our parents and teachers. But though we all need this inheritance, some are in a position to privatise and control others' access to parts of it, and thereby use it to extract rent and profit out of them. It's key to wealth extraction. And the rich can pass on their wealth to their children as windfalls, through their wills.

TEN

So what determines pay?

We may be able to add only a bit to what those before us have provided, but it is a vital bit, and of course work takes up much of our lives. Not surprisingly, we want to feel that we and others are fairly rewarded for it. We don't want others free-riding on our efforts if they have no good reason for doing so.

In a capitalist economy, what people get is largely a function of power, not of moral or democratic judgement. However strongly we may feel about what would be fair and just, we have to remember that our incomes aren't determined by people sitting around and deciding what we need or deserve. When an organisation decides it needs to create a new job, the person who draws up the job spec might possibly think about what someone doing it might deserve, but the finance department is likely to make sure they don't set the pay higher than is necessary to get an employee of the required standard.

Do individuals' incomes reflect the value of what they contribute?

We have already dealt with one major reason why workers in general *don't* get paid the equivalent of what they have created: as long as there are rentiers and capitalists, workers have to produce enough not only to cover their own pay, but also to provide those owners with unearned income. They also provide transfers or warranted unearned income for those too young, old, sick or disabled to work. *So the existence of unearned income of either kind means that, in general, those who produce goods and services will get paid less than the value of what they produce.* (And remember, these workers could be anywhere; in a global economy they don't have to be in the same country as those who get the surplus.)

It's still possible for at least some productive workers to get paid more than they have contributed, perhaps by taking advantage of a particular source of power, such as having control over a key bit of technology on which their firm depends, or having specialist skills and knowledge, or a management role; in such cases they would be partly subsidised by their fellow, less powerful employees.[19] Differences in what employees get paid depend heavily on how much power they have in terms of skill, know-how and authority. Authority comes not merely from a particular kind of personality: it depends on occupying a recognised role. Your boss can thank that role for his or her authority over you. So, while skills and authority enable people to make contributions that others can't, they also give them power relative to others, which is likely to be reflected in pay.

Is everyone pulling their weight?

As the surveys of public opinion on economic inequality show,[20] this question concerns many people greatly: everyone, they feel, should contribute what they can, at least while they are young and fit enough to do so, and income should, where possible, be earned by doing something useful. It seems that what people contribute to the economy varies enormously: don't some work, while others are unemployed? Don't some do simple, unskilled work that anyone can do, while others do complex, demanding, responsible work? Surely some are not pulling their weight? In fact, aren't they scrounging – free-riding on others' labour? Yet, as we shall see, these unequal contributions have little to do with motivation and effort, or even intelligence and merit.

All our own work?

It's often hard to assess what is 'all our own work'. The economy does not consist of self-sufficient Robinson Crusoes, but of people whose work is interdependent through divisions of labour, whether within households, places of employment or between different locations. In fact, such is the interdependence among the many tasks performed by workers within an organisation that it is often hard to say exactly what each contributes. If we feel under-appreciated at work, we might be tempted to take some time off so that others notice the difference – but then again, they might not! Probably, though, they would feel the extra burden of having to cover for us. Work is a lot more social than we generally realise, though that doesn't mean that the contributions of each are equal: some get more help than they give. Workers often complain that their managers take credit for what they have done (while blaming workers for management's mistakes).[21] Owners can take not only the recognition but the financial rewards too.

Take the idea that people should contribute what they can. In a team, if someone who's perfectly capable of contributing takes it easy and free-rides on the efforts of the others, the rest of the team are likely to feel a sense of injustice and to complain. Or consider a traditional household where women do the bulk of housework and men free-ride on it. This is a common source of domestic arguments that are based on a similar sense of injustice regarding individuals' contributions. Such feelings are about what philosopher Paul Gomberg calls 'contributive injustice'.[22] When discussing economic inequality, most philosophers talk about 'distributive justice' – what people *get* in terms of resources and rewards; but in these cases it's also what people contribute, particularly in terms of work, that matters.

In such situations, we might say there's a contributive injustice as regards the *quantity* of work that people contribute. But it's not that everyone is expected to contribute exactly the *same* quantity: if it's manual work we do not expect an elderly person to contribute as much as a young, fit person. We might also want to make allowances for other responsibilities that people have – for example, expecting a smaller contribution from a single parent with young children than from someone with no care responsibilities.

Those who have jobs often resent the long-term unemployed and other benefit claimants, because this looks like another example of contributive injustice. (Actually, most of those on benefits have usually previously contributed by paying taxes and National Insurance contributions.) Neoliberal governments regularly smear the unemployed for being allegedly workshy and irresponsible, or for having sunk into 'welfare dependency', and this helps to distract public attention from the rich and their wealth extraction and tax avoidance. But whereas the free-riding team member can easily start pulling their weight and the sexist husband can start doing more housework, unemployed people in areas where there are not enough jobs to go round can't find non-existent jobs. Surveys of public opinion show that the majority judge those below them much more harshly than those above them,[23] and although in recent years rich bankers in particular have come in for more criticism, hostility towards them is still less than towards those at the bottom. Neoliberal governments and media work hard to keep it that way, so resentment is directed downwards.

Here the problem is not merely individual but structural – a consequence of job shortages. These are normal in capitalism – more in recessions than in booms, and more in areas of deindustrialisation, like Liverpool or Detroit. To the extent that such areas have any jobs at all, they tend to be low paid and unskilled. Right-wing politicians love to point to individuals from disadvantaged backgrounds who, through heroic struggle, find a job and then get ahead, and they castigate others for not doing the same. But where there are not enough jobs to go round, it's a zero-sum game: if one person gets a job, it means that another does not. The same applies even if the jobseekers upgrade their skills. Yet, with boring predictability, the neoliberal media turn stories of lack of jobs into tales of lack of skills, or 'welfare dependency'.

This fallacy of imagining that what is possible for one must therefore be possible for all – a fallacy of composition, as logicians call it – is a staple of neoliberal politics and evangelists of meritocracy; it's central to the so-called 'American Dream'. The unemployed cannot will jobs into existence. As we saw earlier, the number of jobs depends primarily on aggregate demand – spending by consumers, firms and the state.

But there is another kind of contributive injustice in modern economies, and again, it concerns a familiar situation.

Hogging the nice work and offloading the bad

Highly paid workers such as doctors and lawyers may feel that they deserve their pay because they are doing work that is highly skilled and demanding, and that it's only fair that those doing unskilled work like cleaning or labouring should be paid less. On the face of it, this might seem reasonable, at least if there is free competition for the different jobs, for then the best-qualified should get the best jobs.

Just a job, or meaningful work?

Are jobs a burden, just something people have to do in order to get money, something for which they need 'compensation'? Or are they a benefit, a source of interest and fulfilment? It depends, of course, on the quality of the work. It's great to feel you are doing something worthwhile and getting recognition for it – as well as decent pay. Many have more negative or mixed feelings about their work, but these are likely to relate to how tedious, interesting, stressful, varied, challenging, responsible or sociable it is. Work can be far more than a means to income. Not surprisingly, contrary to the common view that people are inherently lazy, most people want to contribute work of some kind, somehow. Too often economists and political philosophers assume that work is just a cost or burden, compensated more or less by pay. But of course opportunities for getting good-quality work are highly unequal. That this is so is not an immutable law of nature, but a changeable feature of societies as they have developed. So, while this book is mostly concerned with money, we should remember that concerns about economic justice go beyond this, to what work people are allowed and required to do.

Precisely because of this variable quality and because no society can survive without work, working is seen sometimes as a *duty* – something people should do even if they don't enjoy it, so that they don't free-ride on the labour of others – and sometimes as a *benefit or opportunity* – enabling us to use and develop our capacities and gain self-respect, something that everyone should have the chance to enjoy. Much economic theory can't handle such important complexities, but we need to face up to them in thinking about work in a future society.

But why does this division of labour into good and bad jobs exist in the first place, so that some have jobs that are skilled, demanding and interesting while others' jobs are tedious, unskilled and perhaps unpleasant? Again, let's imagine a household or team. There are many different kinds of task that need doing, some skilled and absorbing, some unskilled and tedious, but some members hog all the better tasks, leaving the unskilled and boring ones to others. The others would probably resent this inequality. They would complain about what is, in effect, a *qualitative* contributive injustice. If the group monopolising the more interesting tasks then claimed that it should be better rewarded because its work was more skilled, that would no doubt heighten the others' sense of injustice; but even if they got the same pay, the situation would still probably be regarded as grossly unfair. In a democratic team or household, the members are likely to argue that the nice and the boring or unpleasant tasks should be shared out as far as possible.

But while these issues are common sources of argument in teams and households, we rarely worry about the huge differences in the quality of work that people are allowed to do in the economy at large. We don't often hear people complaining in that context that some are able to monopolise interesting, fulfilling work while others are left with boring and maybe unpleasant work. The former are just regarded as more deserving or lucky.

There is one partial exception to this – where the inequality is linked to gender or racial inequality. We do hear objections – quite rightly – to the fact that men and white people are hugely over-represented in the better jobs and women and black people over-represented in inferior jobs. What the critics are generally calling for is a situation where men and women, or people of different colour and ethnicity, are proportionally represented across the board, so that about 50% of top jobs go to women; or, if people from ethnic minorities make up, say, 10% of the population, then we should expect them to constitute roughly that percentage of workers at all levels.

But let's imagine that such a state of affairs had been achieved. Though it would be a fairer society than the one we now have, there would *still* be qualitative inequalities in the kind of work that people did. Some would still be hogging the best work, while others would be left with middling or inferior work. It would just be that none of the different kinds of work would be associated with individuals' race or gender. That might seem fair: surely equal opportunity would have been achieved, because gender and race wouldn't be making any difference to where people ended up? But, as Gomberg argues, it would just be discrimination-free competition for opportunities that were decidedly unequal.[24]

What gets overlooked in the standard view is the *structural* nature of these inequalities. The particular structure producing the inequalities here is *the unequal division of labour*. I don't mean the division between different areas of work, like transport, food production, education or retailing. Rather, I mean the division of labour *within* any such area between better- and worse-quality jobs. If all the skilled and interesting tasks are bundled into a subset of all the jobs, while middling-skilled tasks are bundled up into other jobs and low-skilled and unpleasant tasks are bundled into yet others, then there can't be equality of opportunity because the opportunities are unequal. If the proportions of such jobs are, say, 20:60:20 respectively, then only 20% of workers can have good jobs, 60% will get middling jobs and the remaining 20% will get bad jobs. Though it is widely taken for granted (not only by ordinary people, but by many philosophers and social scientists who should know better), the unequal division of labour is a major source of inequality and social divisions, ensuring that some will have fulfilling and highly regarded working lives – and *at the expense of others*.

This is commonly justified by arguing that because success in getting a good job and upward social mobility is possible for some individuals, success must be possible for all individuals simultaneously. But of course it can't be, because there aren't enough good jobs to go round. It's that fallacy of composition again. Indeed, under these conditions it is in the interest of any particular jobseeker that *others should fail* to find high-quality employment.[25]

What we so easily overlook is that once there is an unequal division of labour, the contributions that individuals can make *can only be unequal, regardless of any difference in their merit*. And if they are then paid according to their unequal contributions, it becomes clear that the resulting pay inequalities are just indirect effects of the unequal division of labour. The most skilled workers, those indispensable to firms, can demand higher pay. And management, faced with surviving against competition and keeping down costs, is driven to minimise the number of people who need skills training and to shift any unskilled tasks away from them and give them to cheaper workers. So the division of labour becomes more unequal still.

In this way, while we often hold strong views about contributive justice in some limited spheres, like work teams or the home, there is little concern about it in the economy as a whole. Yet the kind of work – paid or unpaid – that people do has a huge effect on the kind of people they become and the quality of their lives. It's about time we took this seriously.

Two objections

Identifying the unequal division of labour as a source of injustice implies, of course, that work of different qualities should be more equally shared. But isn't this hopelessly idealistic? Anyway, don't the differences in the quality of work that people do simply reflect differences in intelligence and effort? And doesn't the division of labour make for economic efficiency, from which, supposedly, we all benefit? Let's look at these objections.

Isn't the unequal division of labour a reflection of differences in ability and effort?

In 1776, in *The Wealth of Nations*, Adam Smith famously analysed the benefits of division of labour through his example of the pin factory. Splitting the manufacture into 18 different operations, carried out repetitively and covered by about 10 workers, allowed them to produce over 48,000 pins per day, whereas if each worker had to do all 18 operations on each pin from start to finish before moving on to the next they would scarcely have produced 20 a day. But though he celebrated the extraordinary benefits of this kind of division of labour in terms of productivity, Smith later commented on the human cost:

> The man whose whole life is spent performing a few
> simple operations . . . has no occasion to exert his
> understanding . . . He naturally loses, therefore, the
> habit of such exertion, and generally becomes as stupid
> and ignorant as it is possible for a human creature to
> become.[26]

In his book *The Moral Economy of Labor*, James Murphy cites empirical research on the relation between the intellectual capacities of workers and the complexity of the work they do that showed that over a 10-year period the intelligence of workers doing complex jobs developed, while that of workers doing simple and repetitive work deteriorated. Further, as Smith feared, there is evidence that 'Workers in mindless jobs not only undermine their capacity for the enjoyment of complex activities at work but also their capacity for the enjoyment of complex activities during leisure.'[27] As Murphy adds, while workers are increasingly protected from harm to their physical capacities, they are not protected from harm to their mental capacities.

Smith didn't see the jobs people do as a reflection of their intelligence, but rather the reverse:

> The difference of natural talents in different men is, in
> reality, much less than we are aware of; and the very
> different genius which appears to distinguish men of
> different professions, when grown up in maturity, is not
> upon many occasions so much the cause, as the effect
> of the division of labour. The difference between the
> most dissimilar characters, between a philosopher and a
> common street porter, for example, seems to arise not so
> much from nature, as from habit, custom, and education.[28]

In other words, he thought the unequal division of labour accounted for most of the differences in ability of workers in different jobs. But how could this be? Don't differences in intelligence, ability and aspirations between people show up long before they reach the age of finding a job?

The answer is that the differences result from a process that operates between generations, from parent to child. Take a child whose parents are in low-paid, low-status jobs like labouring or cleaning. They have not only little money or security but little status, indeed they may be looked down upon by others. They may not be able to afford books, holidays or meals out. Their jobs are ones in which there is little or no power to make decisions. Theirs is not to reason why, but just to do what the boss says. Speaking out is risky.

Now think of a child whose parents are professionals – say, doctors – highly paid, and doing responsible, skilled work with lots of status. The people they know are also likely to be in similar positions. So a child not only has economic advantages – holidays abroad, books, the possibility of expensive hobbies like skiing – but becomes accustomed to seeing their parents and other adults go off to do responsible, professional work and get plenty of respect from others. Their parents have power and can take decisions, and are expected to use reasoning in their jobs. Talking at dinner about current affairs comes more easily when you have a job with some executive power that involves decision making. It's much easier to talk in an authoritative way about such things if you've been brought up by people whose position in the division of labour gives them authority.

Research by Leon Feinstein on children's cognitive capacities shows that these develop more slowly in low social-class children than in high social-class children, so that by age 10 (120 months), the brightest of low social-class children at 22 months are overtaken by the weakest of high social-class children. The score at 22 months predicts educational qualifications at age 26 and is related to family background. The children of educated or wealthy parents who scored poorly in the early tests had a tendency to catch up; whereas children of worse-off parents who scored poorly were extremely unlikely to catch up. Feinstein found no evidence that entry into schooling reverses this pattern.[29] Not surprisingly, social mobility in all major capitalist countries, especially the most unequal ones, is low.[30]

The effect of the unequal division of labour on these differences is indirect, shaping the next generation's expectations by shaping the circumstances and behaviour of their parents. Working-class lives, characterised by lack of power, are prefigured in the relatively authoritarian character of much working-class childrearing, which tends to set clear disciplinary limits without defending them through elaborate justifications; again, theirs is not to reason why. Children are also expected to amuse themselves, rather than to interact with adults. (Yes, these are generalisations, and there are many exceptions, but this is what researchers on the topic have found.) By contrast, middle-class parenting places great stress on reasoning, education and self-development and on talking to adults,[31] and for middle-class children this prefigures lives of working in occupations where people are allowed to use their reasoning powers and take decisions, and where they can deal with professionals and managers as equals.

Not surprisingly, working-class and middle-class children tend to acquire different dispositions, expectations and aspirations, and so feel comfortable with different roles and situations. When they enter the labour market they are generally already prepared for the kinds of roles they are likely to get and the kinds of behaviours that will be expected of them. There will be some relation between individual ability and effort and what they get in economic rewards, but ability and effort are themselves influenced by the unequal division of labour and other sources of inequality in society, so we should focus our attention on those, and on their effects on the shaping of individuals. Although these acquired dispositions can be changed in later life, it's a slow and difficult process, one that depends on repeated practice at new behaviours. Not surprisingly, where people from working-class backgrounds are upwardly mobile they often say that they still don't feel they quite fit into their new role and fear that one day they will be 'found out'.

So our upbringing – shaped by our parents' position in the unequal division of labour – has a significant influence on our aspirations and what we regard as attainable; it shapes what is familiar and, hence, what we feel comfortable with. Even our degree of motivation may be shaped by the lottery of birth into an unequal society: middle- or upper-class young people have more and better opportunities than their working-class counterparts, and motivation and aspirations are likely to vary correspondingly, though there will always be exceptions, for a host of possible reasons. But in general it is much harder to see yourself going to university when no one you know has been to one, than it is for someone brought up in a family where it has been the norm. And if there are only a tiny number of job vacancies – and then mainly for dead-end jobs – is it worth making an effort? (If you have never been into a Jobcentre and looked at the jobs on offer, I recommend it.)

It's because motivation, aspirations and dispositions are so influenced by circumstances beyond our control in early life that some eminent political philosophers who have written on economic justice discount them in considering what people should get.[32] I don't wish to discount them altogether, for even from within the massively unequal constraints and opportunities in which each of us grows up there is some room to make a difference. At any rate, like Adam Smith, we should see through the illusion that differences in the quality of jobs and what they require or allow people to do are a reflection of innate differences in intelligence.[33] But there's another common objection to my line of argument.

Isn't an unequal division of labour necessary for efficiency?

Wouldn't defining jobs with a mix of tasks that required different levels of skill be inefficient? Isn't it more efficient to get people to specialise in just one thing? If everybody in an organisation did some skilled work, surely that would be more costly because everyone, rather than just a subset of workers, would have to be trained to do it.

This response confuses two things that are separable: the division of tasks – different steps in making something, packaging it, selling it, dealing with the paperwork and accounts and so on – and different jobs. We can have division of the tasks involved in a job simply by getting workers to rotate among the different tasks, whether this is done on a daily, weekly or monthly basis. Yes, each worker would need to be trained to do a wider range of tasks, but it would avoid the contributive injustice of a minority hogging the best tasks. It would also provide more variety, less boredom, more understanding of the different work tasks involved in the organisation and, hence, better communication within the organisation – and probably better morale and social cohesion because workers would be more equal and better able to understand each other's situation. While there are costs involved in moving workers between tasks, there are also costs in forgoing the advantages of multi-skilled workers who have some understanding of how their work at any given time relates to the work of others and who can thus deal better with problems of coordination. The lack of competitiveness of many traditional western manufacturing firms compared to Japanese firms owed much to the former's excessive specialisation of workers, which meant that few understood how different tasks fitted together, so that product quality was poor and coordination problems were endemic.[34]

It would, in any case, be naïve to imagine that the unequal division of labour is merely a product of the pursuit of efficiencies; it is also a product of the struggles of those in relatively powerful positions to hoard good-quality tasks for themselves while offloading low-quality tasks onto others, and thereby to elevate their own status.[35] The history of professions and skill and demarcation disputes bears witness to this.

But aren't there some kinds of highly skilled specialist jobs that need to be full time if their occupants are to reach a sufficiently accomplished level? You probably wouldn't want to rely on the services of a part-time brain surgeon. And perhaps the best musicians and scientists wouldn't be as good as they are if they had been prevented from investing huge amounts of time in their vocations by the need to do more mundane things. But even these people might benefit from a few days of different work now and again. Yet, while we might want to make a concession for such cases, many skilled tasks could be done reasonably efficiently and well if more people were trained to work within a system of rotating tasks. But it's not just a matter of efficiency: we should think of the benefits to everyone of being able to use and develop their skills and to gain the satisfaction and recognition that goes with this.

The unequal division of labour has become so familiar that we take it for granted, as if it were simply natural or optimal, and we mistake its consequences in terms of unequal skills and abilities as its justifications. It's then only too easy to assume that the inequalities in pay that are associated with the unequal division of labour are deserved. This is perhaps the most common and serious flaw in not only popular but also academic thinking about inequality.

Such a division of labour creates *interdependently* unequal positions: *one person can do a job that is interesting and satisfying for most of their life only if the more boring tasks are done by others.* It might seem idealistic to say that we need to have jobs that involve a much more equal mix of skill levels and qualities if everyone is to have a reasonable chance of realising their potential, because it's so different from the modern world of work that we've become used to, and so we may resist this conclusion. This would be like refusing to believe in human-made global warming because its implications for how we should live are inconvenient. It is inconvenient, especially for those in more fortunate positions (including academics!), but that doesn't make it any less true. It's a prime cause of unfair economic inequality.

New Labour and the rich

There were elements of the belief in a just world in Britain's New Labour, at least as regards the rich and the middle classes. In the 2001 general election campaign, to the consternation of Old Labour supporters, Prime Minister Tony Blair said on television that he wasn't concerned about the gap between rich and poor. In March 2005, in another interview, Blair attempted to qualify his position:

> What I meant by that was not that I don't care about the gap, so much as I don't care if there are people who earn a lot of money. They are not my concern. I do care about people who are without opportunity, disadvantaged and poor. We've got to lift those people but we don't necessarily do that by hammering the people who are successful.[36]

Note the avoidance of the words 'wealthy' or 'rich' (which might be taken to include those who inherit wealth or have other sources of unearned income) and the use of 'people who earn a lot of money' and 'successful', thus exploiting the ambiguity of 'earn' and evading the question of whether having 'a lot of money' and being successful are synonymous. 'People who are successful' cleverly by-passes the issue of whether those who get a lot of money deserve it. It encourages us to accept and admire the rich and not to wonder whether they deserve their wealth. Who could be against or begrudge success? Surely only the envious, resentful about their own 'failure'!

Blair's statement that the successful are 'not his concern' avoids acknowledging any interdependence between wealth and poverty. To be sure, he doesn't say the poor are poor because they lack merit – which of course would have been risky in electoral terms – but because they lack opportunity and are disadvantaged. He could always rely on the Conservative press to do the dirty work of blaming people on low incomes for their poverty. According to the New Labour rhetoric, the unemployed needed to be 'helped back to work', but in practice this meant being disciplined – put under surveillance and required to train for non-existent jobs. At the same time the 'successful' were not said to be 'advantaged' by having monopolised opportunities and used the ownership of assets to siphon off unearned income from others. Blair acknowledged 'disadvantage' but not advantage. New Labour therefore appeared both sympathetic to the poor and generous and unresentful towards the successful (as if raising taxes would be 'hammering' them). With a deft populist gesture, he was able to duck questions of economic justice.

Don't markets ensure that people get paid what they deserve?

It seems obvious: in a market for, say, pizzas, customers will be willing to pay more for the best pizzas than for mediocre ones. So the superior work done by the workers in the first case will be better rewarded. The implication is clear: if you want to be better paid, produce a better product. And if some producers are more efficient – so each worker can produce more pizzas per hour – then they'll be able to make more profit, so the market will reward efficient workers, and less-efficient producers will either have to catch up or go out of business. So markets encourage and reward both good-quality work and efficiency.

If only things were that simple.

First, it's naïve to imagine that the quality of the service or product is reflected in workers' wages, not least because what you pay for a product or service is usually different from what those who produce it get. Often we have little idea of who gets what share of the money that we hand over. A pair of shoes may cost us £50, but how is this split up across the producers and subcontractors, the distributors, managers, accountants and retailers, not to mention shareholders and creditors? Even if we cared, it would be hard to find out, particularly where what we buy comes from a global production network.[37] But in any case we are usually interested only in whether the products on sale are good value for money, not what workers deserve. A partial exception to this is the Fairtrade movement, which has the will and resources to make sure producers as well as distributors and managers get paid a living wage. This may matter to at least some consumers.

Ethical consumption and workers' pay

In all buying, consider first, what condition of existence you cause in the production of what you buy; secondly, whether the sum you have paid is just to the producer, and in due proportion, lodged in his hands. (John Ruskin, 1862)[38]

As it's difficult for consumers to know how much the workers are paid, a simpler way of ensuring that their pay is adequate is to impose a legal minimum wage, possibly a global or globally differentiated one.

Nor should we assume that what employers pay their workers necessarily has much to do with whether they consider them to be deserving. True, within some organisations the better employees may get promoted, or they may be able to use the labour market to get more pay. (Or the 'better' workers, 'those who can go the extra mile', may be those who have the least domestic work to do – another cause of gender inequality.) But generally, employers pay what they have to pay to get particular kinds of workers; competition and the bottom line remind them to take a hard-headed, instrumental approach to pay. Some workers may be better paid simply because they're scarcer, especially if their employer doesn't want the costs of having to replace them if they get a better offer elsewhere. If the supply of skilled workers increases, their pay can be bid down, as the declining pay of graduates shows. Skill and scarcity don't always go together, so skill and pay don't always either. What's more, better-quality goods and services are not always the product of greater effort and merit; they may just reflect different technology or materials.

Similarly, differences in productivity (output per worker) may have nothing to do with merit or how hard people work. In some lines of business there is great scope for the use and development of technology, so that each worker can produce a great deal, and improve their productivity still more as new technology comes in. Many processes in industrialised agriculture and manufacturing are like this. But in other sectors, like teaching and care work, it's very difficult to increase productivity without reducing the quality of the service; indeed, productivity is clearly a problematic criterion in such cases. Consequently these kinds of inherently labour-intensive, static-productivity work tend to be expensive, even though those who do the work tend to be on low pay. Many are funded by taxation, and so resistance to raising taxes puts downward pressure on their pay.[39] Yet they may be doing jobs that enhance their clients' or patients' quality of life; their work is unquestionably socially useful – which is more than can be said for that of many in the financial sector.

At base, the relationship between what people get and what they deserve or merit is weak simply because markets are governed by profit, not by criteria of what workers deserve. What is profitable need have little to do with effort and merit. You may work hard at something that helps others, such as care work, but get little for it. If you sell something that others need and can pay a good price for, then you may do well, whether it involves huge amounts of work or little. Or your employer may get the benefit, not you.

We might like to believe otherwise – that we live in a world where effort and merit are rewarded and lack of effort is not; but this works only up to a point, within the constraints of job shortages and the unequal division of labour and its effects in making people unequal – not to mention the effects of discrimination on the basis of race and gender.

I have a surprising ally in arguing this, a leading neoliberal intellectual: Friedrich Hayek, the economist who inspired Margaret

Thatcher. This is what he wrote regarding the relation between what people deserve and what they get:

> It certainly is important in the market order . . . that the individuals believe that their well being depends primarily on their own efforts and decisions. Indeed, few circumstances will do more to make a person energetic and efficient than the belief that it depends chiefly on him whether he will reach the goals he has set himself ... But it leads no doubt also to an exaggerated confidence in the truth of this generalization ... It is therefore a real dilemma to what extent we ought to encourage in the young the belief that when they really try they will succeed, or should rather emphasize that inevitably some unworthy will succeed and some worthy will fail ... whether ... large numbers will tolerate actual differences in rewards which will be based only partly on achievement and partly *on mere chance*.[40]

Hayek was at least honest in admitting that he was tempted to be dishonest with the young. For him, while the weakness of the relationship between merit and reward was unfortunate, he set more store on the ability of markets to coordinate the activities of millions of people, and to encourage a 'discovery process', where people try out new products on the market and see if the public is willing to buy them. These are indeed important virtues of product markets, but they have nothing to do with economic justice. Interestingly, while neoliberal theorists are happy to say that market outcomes have little to do with merit, neoliberal politicians certainly are not, and pretend that the market rewards merit.[41]

Yet, even then, in so far as achievement and effort do make a difference, Hayek overlooked the effects of job shortages and the unequal division of labour in *restricting* achievement such that only a minority can be 'high achievers'. Further, it's these things, along with other forms of discrimination – and not simply 'luck' – that also shape people's life chances.

What about inequalities of gender, race, sexuality, disability?

Some of the most glaring inequalities in society hinge on these differences. Men dominate the most advantageous positions, while women are concentrated at the bottom and in the middle. Many minority ethnic groups are concentrated in low-income work and under-represented at higher levels. School catchment areas are strongly differentiated by race. People with disabilities are restricted by the ignorance and prejudice of others and by presumptions that the world need be designed only to suit the able-bodied, and so on. Lesbian and gay people may be subject to homophobia, while heterosexuals enjoy what Pierre Bourdieu called 'the profit of normality'. Any of these may have a major impact on people, depending on what it is we are explaining. For example, when it comes to explaining differences in life chances, gender or disability may be even more important than economic class.

These are all *unfair* inequalities, based primarily on various forms of prejudice and discrimination. The discrimination doesn't always have to be intentional. It may be just the product of the way institutions have evolved; failure to design buildings to suit wheelchair users was probably not intended to exclude them, but it creates barriers nevertheless.

Each axis of inequality is likely to intersect with some of the other axes, including the economic inequalities that are the focus of this book. So an upper-class man benefits not only from his class advantages, but from his gender advantages; the converse applies to working-class women. Ethnic divisions may sometimes cut across the other divisions, but may, alternatively, reinforce and be reinforced by them. Sometimes one source of disadvantage may push people into another kind of disadvantaged position: for example, although girls do better in education than boys, they may end up on a lower position than men with the same or even inferior qualifications because of sexism in the workplace and home.

But there are also differences between these sources of inequality and the ones I have been discussing in this book. While gender and race inequalities are produced primarily by sexism and racism, class differences would persist even if the upper and middle classes were nice and respectful to the working class. The unequal distribution of property and the unequal division of labour would be largely unaffected. Class prejudice is common, but it's more a *response to* economic inequalities than a cause of them. By contrast, the ending of sexism and racism would have a major impact on gender and race inequalities.

But inequalities of gender and race may often result not just from prejudice, but from more structural features. Some groups may be trapped in poor areas less by prejudice against them than by their inability to afford better housing. The three key things that give these inequalities of race and gender a structural character are again the unequal division of labour and inequalities in pay, and property ownership.

In this book, I'm mainly concerned with what generates economic inequality, especially what enriches those at the top. It would be an enormous step forward if we could overcome inequalities of gender, race, sexuality and disability, so that these kinds of difference did not advantage some at the expense of others. But it could still be a highly unequal society, with an unequal division of labour, unequal pay and unequal ownership of assets that allowed some to live off unearned income at the expense of others. There would be inequalities, but not ones of gender, ethnicity, sexuality and disability.

Competitive forces will take advantage of any inequalities they can. If a certain minority ethnic group is in a weak position in the labour market because of racism, it may be especially exploitable by firms needing cheap labour. But if there were no such groups, capitalism as a whole would still cope: there are plenty of other ways of making a profit. However, employers do need *workers* (of whatever gender or race and so on), and they do need control over the means of production. Capitalism is not dependent for its very existence on these other sources of inequality, but it does depend on controlling the means of production.

This is why equal opportunity policies are usually quite good on gender, race, age, sexuality, religion and disability, but silent on economic class. Every time firms advertise new jobs they create new positions in the unequal division of labour, even as they attempt to ensure that competition for these unequal positions is discrimination free. While 'enlightened' employers may at least claim to worry about sexism and the like, they don't even pretend to challenge structural class differences.[42]

Neoliberals – New Labour, for example – can appear quite progressive about gender, race, sexuality, disability and condemn those who discriminate against people on these grounds. Unsurprisingly, the elephant in the room is economic inequalities or class differences. Though it never admits it, neoliberalism is a political-economic movement that seeks to legitimise widening economic inequalities and defend rentier interests above all others. Rentiers can live off others regardless of their gender, race, sexuality and so on.

Money talks!

In markets, reasons or arguments to do with fairness or justice don't matter; they're irrelevant. If you're buying a car, the seller doesn't need you to justify why you need one; if you've got the money, you can have it. Your money does the talking.

When people at work lobby for more pay, whether individually or as a union, they may sincerely believe that they deserve more; but what they want from the employer is not expressions of how deserving they are, but more money. If they just get more praise but no extra money, they're unlikely to be satisfied; praise is cheap. Equally, the employers do not have to get into arguments about what their workers deserve in order to set rates of pay, as long as the workers accept them. Sometimes they say they would concede the workers' arguments 'in an ideal world', but that in the current context they simply cannot afford to pay what is being demanded; competitors would undercut them and threaten the survival of the firm. It's a matter of market survival, power and scarcity.

It's not that competitive markets are necessarily immoral, rather that they are *amoral*; they simply don't operate on the basis of moral ideas about what is fair or just or ethical, unless they are regulated to make them so, for example, through minimum wage legislation. Sometimes they may produce outcomes that seem fair, but if so, it's by accident rather than design.

In a market system, outcomes are primarily products of power, usually in the form of scarcity; those who have something that's scarce in relation to the demand for it can command a higher price. So what you get depends on what you have, and what you have determines what you need to do to get an income.[43] If you have assets like land or buildings that others need, you can get rent. If you have spare money you can get interest. If you have enough money to buy shares in a firm you can get dividends and speculate on the stock market. If all you have is your ability to work, then you have to find someone to employ you. If you have skills and expertise that are wanted by others who have money to pay for them, you will be able to get more than others.

The Tea Party again: 'you are not entitled to my income'

This is another popular Tea Party slogan, and we're now in a position to take it apart, though as we'll see there could be a twist in the tail. It reflects a wildly fantasist notion that all tax is theft, and that what we can do in our jobs has nothing to do with our teachers and parents, nor with the commons in the shape of natural endowments, means of production, infrastructure, public education and services like waste collection and emergency services, the legal system, inherited scientific, cultural and practical knowledge and so on, and nothing to do with all the other people who maintain and develop the commons. It is based on the myth of the self-sufficient individual.

Even if your income is earned – that is, conditional on doing work that contributes to the provision of goods and services – there is no way you could do what you do if you hadn't been able to receive transfers and hence support from others, or rely on the commons – from drains to police services. Far from being self-reliant individuals, those who use the slogan are the would-be free-riders. In paying tax they are paying for some of what they have been given.

Also, as we've just seen, what we can get in the market for our work doesn't necessarily reflect our contribution, or how hard we work, or even how skilled we are. It's primarily an effect of our relative scarcity and power.

Here's the twist in the tail, though. Much of what people – including Tea Party members – 'freely' pay out as rent and as interest on debt to rentiers, together with the profit they produce for their employer, *is* unearned; the recipients of these payments are the ones that the slogan should be addressed to.

ELEVEN

The myth of the level playing field

> People with advantages are loath to believe that they just happen to be people with advantages. (C. Wright Mills, 1956)[44]

Privileged people born into rich families, like Tony Blair, David Cameron and Boris Johnson, love to gush about meritocracy, 'aspiration' and hard work so as to distract attention from their privilege. Margaret Thatcher loved to play up her humble grocer's daughter origins, while keeping silent on the benefits of marrying a millionaire ex-public school boy who funded her training as a barrister and bought two houses for them, one of them in Chelsea.

When people think about markets, they usually focus on individual transactions and contracts, ignoring the social context and the history of the situation, or who is doing the transactions; and they usually focus on markets for products, not job markets. There are just buyers and sellers of apples or oranges, who freely agree to contract with one another; if they can agree on a price, the buyer hands over the money for the goods. They're free adults freely exchanging, and so it looks like a level playing field. Even if the seller is richer than the buyer, that hardly seems relevant to understanding how markets work. And what's true of the market for apples and oranges must be true of all markets, mustn't it? Economics textbooks invariably start with such stories.

But if it's a job market, this picture is likely to be seriously misleading. As we've already seen, young jobseekers enter the labour market already unequal, as an indirect result of the effects of the unequal division of labour on their parents. The two most important facts in sociology are, first, that we are all profoundly shaped by our social environments, and second, that we don't get to choose our parents or the environment in which our early, most formative years are spent.

To be sure, some children will do better or worse than their parents, perhaps because they are more or less able or motivated than them. Some will be luckier in relation to the local educational system and labour market they encounter: some will grow up in major cities with diverse job opportunities, some in small towns with a limited and declining range of jobs. Social mobility is far more limited than politicians would like us to believe – and the bigger the distance between the top and bottom, the less social mobility there is.[45]

In the UK, a survey produced for the Prime Minister's office found that the chances of a child born into a middle-class family getting a middle-class job are 15 times those of a child born into a working-class family in Britain and comparable societies.[46] Someone born into a fortunate position might like to think that if they'd been brought up in poverty they would have fought their way up. But it's not only that such moves are rare; what they fail to realise is that if they had been born into such a different situation, they would have become a different person and been unlikely to have acquired the confidence, sense of entitlement and ways of talking that play well in elite circles.

It's not envy to say this; it's simply a matter of acknowledging the effect of inherited, unchosen inequalities on people's life chances. The same point is widely recognised in political philosophy. As the eminent philosopher John Rawls put it in the gendered language of his day:

> No-one deserves his place in the distribution of native endowments, any more than one deserves one's initial starting place in society. The assertion that a man deserves the superior character that enables him to make the effort to cultivate his abilities is equally problematic; for his character depends in large part upon fortunate family and social circumstances for which he can claim no credit.[47]

To be sure, fortunate circumstances are not the monopoly of the well-off, and there are strengths as well as disadvantages in more ordinary upbringings, though that doesn't mean the advantages and disadvantages are evenly distributed: we should beware of a spurious egalitarianism, which, anxious not to be seen as disparaging anyone, denies that inequalities injure anyone – thereby making it seem less important to reduce them.

The playing field slopes steeply.

I started off Part Two with a number of questions, including *do we get what we deserve?* Instead of answering that directly, I tackled a different question: *what determines what we get?* There are many different determinants, but in working through them I hope I've also answered the first question, because it implies that the answer is 'not usually, because so many of the determinants of our income have nothing to do with what we deserve'. And even those that do appear to do so, such as our skills and qualifications, have a lot to do with the position we are born into within an already unequal society. It's still important to consider whether people do deserve their income, and indeed what people ought to get in an ideal society; but dealing first with what actually in practice determines incomes stops us prematurely jumping to the conclusion that people simply get what they deserve.

Unless we recognise the determinants of unequal incomes, we are doomed to misunderstand the nature of economic inequalities in our society and to imagine that we – the rich included – live in a just economic world. As long as that understanding is not challenged, people are likely to object to any major equalisation of distribution on the grounds that this would not be fair because some contribute more complex and responsible labour than others, and hence deserve more. The idea that we are well on the way to having a meritocratic society – that is, one in which the most able and hard-working rise to the top – is a myth; social mobility is limited and weaker than in the post-war boom. Unless there is a rise in the number of places at the top, for every move up the social scale there has to be a move downwards, and those at the top are best at protecting their advantages. When politicians talk about social mobility they keep quiet about this.

Just one more point before we come back to the rich. Actually, it's just as well that we don't have to say more about the issue of 'what we deserve', as it's a can of worms – one that has kept philosophers happily preoccupied for decades, if not centuries. It's not only that there are many different ways of measuring what philosophers call 'desert' (hours worked? effort? quality of work? productivity?; usefulness of the product to the user?),[48] but also that we use the word 'deserve' in diverse ways (for example, when we say a baby deserves care we just mean that it *needs* care, not that it's done something worthy of reward). Need is another criterion for assessing what people should get and be allowed to do. After all, we accept that some people *should* get transfers, because they *need* them and are too young, old, disabled or ill to work.

We don't have to take a stand on how exactly to measure desert in order to argue that asset-based unearned income is *undeserved* – a product of power rather than ethically justified. Quite simply, it's something for nothing, and it's unrelated to need. Imagine that you are a tenant farmer, renting land from a landowner at the same rent as other tenants, and each producing crops for sale. It might be hard to say how much income you deserve for what you produce and sell from the fields you rent, in relation to the amount received by other tenants on the same property. But the difficulty in making *that* judgement in no way makes it difficult to assess whether the rent you all pay is deserved by the landowner. The land was already there, so it's clearly something for nothing.

And it would be strange to argue that we 'deserve' a division of labour that denies so many people the chance to do something worthwhile, or that the people of the rich countries 'deserve' the highly developed commons that they have inherited.

PART THREE

How the rich got richer: their part in the crisis

What have the rich got to do with the economic crisis? A great deal. Like the resurgence of the rich, the roots of the current crisis go back to the 1970s. And they are both associated with the growing dominance of the financial sector, or 'financialisation' as it's sometimes called. In fact, the rise of the rich is an integral feature of the crisis, just as it was of the Great Depression in the early part of the 20th century. But there's also a big difference: this time, many of the rich have not only got richer in the build-up to the crisis but – except for some short-term losses – *after* it too. Compared to their predecessors in the 1920s and 1930s, who then lost out, they are having a good crisis. Capitalism's most successful decades in Europe and the US – the 1950s and 1960s – were also the period when the share of national income cornered by the rich was at its lowest. As we'll see, this was no accident.

The main arguments so far apply to any phase of the history of capitalism, and whether they are right or wrong doesn't hinge on whether capitalism is in a boom or a crisis. But while unearned income based on control of assets has always been a problem, it's grown steadily over the last 40 years. Financialisation represents 'the revenge of the rentier' after being side-lined during the mid-20th century. They're active rather than passive rentiers – part of the so-called working rich – ever seeking out new ways of extracting wealth from the economic system through rent-seeking. Financialisation has been both cause and consequence of a shift from wealth creation to wealth extraction and, with that, a shift of wealth to the rich.

All this can easily get overlooked in accounting for the crisis. It's common to suppose that our current economic problems just go back a few years and result simply from irresponsible behaviour in the financial sector as it mismanaged risk on a spectacular scale. But although there has certainly been extraordinary irresponsibility, mismanagement, irrational exuberance, not to mention greed and indeed criminality, the basic causes go back decades, and they weren't all to do with finance. The problems are not merely technical, to be fixed by an engineering approach that takes for granted the legitimacy and rationality of the basic institutions and practices and merely identifies malfunctions. The crisis is also a product of economic injustice. To understand it requires more than the usual narrative of who did what in a sequence of financial innovation and euphoria followed by disaster: we need to identify the basic mechanisms of wealth extraction that are involved.

TWELVE

The roots of the crisis

There are scores of different accounts of the origins of the crisis. The causes are complex, and different experts give different emphasis to them. Many of the elements are mutually reinforcing so it's often hard to say what came first:[1] but I will at least provide a sketch of the main elements and processes, highlighting the role of the rich.

The crisis was not just a result of the malignant growth of the financial sector alone, but of the interaction between it and the so-called 'real economy'. So it's important to begin by clarifying this relationship.

Finance and 'the real economy'

A capitalist economy needs not only producers of goods and services for sale, but a financial sector. When people talk about 'the real economy', they mean the part that produces and distributes goods and services, as opposed to the financial sector. But the terminology is awkward because the financial sector is no less real. Nor is it dispensable; it is absolutely necessary for the production of goods and services for sale. Provided we remember this, we can go along with the usual crude terminology. The trouble is, necessary though the financial sector is, it can also do things that have a devastating effect on the real economy, as we are now discovering. Finance has come to dominate rather than serve the productive sector of the economy. As Ann Pettifor puts it:

> like a parasite the finance sector invades otherwise healthy economic bodies, rich and poor, and manipulates these to generate greater returns (interest and rent) for the finance sector itself. By doing so, it has weakened, and is

weakening these host bodies. This includes individuals, from students to home-owners to pensioners.[2]

Its activities can seem dauntingly obscure and complex, and its technical language bizarre, but it affects the lives of every one of us. We need to open it up to public scrutiny and understand what it does – not only because we depend on it for loans and mortgages and entrust it with banking our pay and savings, but because we are having to bail out failed banks and rescue the system from itself. The sector has failed spectacularly, but ordinary people are picking up the bill. The damage to the economy as a whole is likely to last for over a decade, indeed a generation, according to Andrew Haldane at the Bank of England.[3]

Our economy needs a financial sector to perform certain important functions. When people describe these, they generally say what it *should* do. When the sector is under attack, it's these functions that its defenders appeal to, as if they described what it *actually* does. But these can be two different things.

Bearing this in mind, here are the most commonly cited 'functions' of the financial sector:

- *providing services* such as safeguarding deposits, providing financial advice, and managing funds in order to maximise their gains;
- *providing credit* to enterprises and households;
- *acting as intermediaries* between lenders and borrowers by taking deposits and providing loans, and between buyers and sellers of financial assets such as shares, bonds and other financial products. In particular, the sector is supposed to use the deposits of savers as a base for investing in economic development;
- *facilitating transactions* – for example by buying and selling currencies – thereby facilitating movements of goods, people and capital across borders. It includes facilitating mergers and acquisitions of companies;
- *managing risk*, estimating and distributing it, providing insurance and using financial instruments to reduce exposure to risk.

Another function, often overlooked, is:

- *managing the creation of money and how it enters the economy* so that it fosters the creation of wealth and meeting of other social goals.

By these means, the financial sector is supposed to facilitate the smooth functioning of the economy, enhancing allocational efficiency[4] (the allocation of resources among competing ends) by moving unused or underused assets to where they can be deployed more effectively. In so doing, it ought to contribute to economic development, more as servant than master, but it is now absolutely clear that the roles have been reversed.

All the activities involve real costs in gathering and managing information, assessing risk, communicating with clients, accounting and so on. While financial institutions must at least cover these costs in what they charge for their services, they also expect to make a margin. In the majority of cases, the organisations that perform these and other functions do so as a means to private gain, including making money for shareholders. They of course seek to maximise the difference between what they offer in interest on deposits and the interest that they charge on loans ('the interest margin'), and the difference between what they pay for assets such as shares and bonds and what they sell them for ('the buy/sell margin'). What they get is what they can, and there is plenty of scope for getting good margins. Particularly through interest and other debt charges, the sector draws a large rentier income from its control of assets and its licence to create credit money.[5] Furthermore, intermediary functions provide extensive scope for 'value-skimming': 'investors' pay experts in banks, brokers, fund managers, lawyers and other specialists, who are in a position to exploit their superior knowledge relative to clients and skim significant gains for themselves.

As well as providing financial services for clients, financial institutions strategically buy and sell assets themselves, using their own funds to make profits; this is variously called 'proprietary trading' or 'investing', or indeed speculating. Wishful thinkers, inspired by Adam Smith's homely tale of how butchers, bakers and brewers could produce beneficial effects for all in pursuing their self-interest in markets (because it is in their interest to keep their customers happy), assume that this cannot be a problem. But then Smith's petty traders were not corporate magnates or rentiers or bankers, well positioned to extract unearned income and speculate on asset bubbles. (Actually, he was well aware of the tendency of competition to lead to the formation of monopolies, and the dangers therein.) Competition among the banks is weak: it's difficult for new banks to set up as competitors because of lack of access to a network of branches and the high costs of securing the IT equipment and traders needed to take part in big-time investment banking. Given their degree of monopoly, it's not in their interest to compete by driving down interest rates and charges to borrowers.

The financial sector is clearly no longer acting as the facilitator of the productive economy; but even though it has failed spectacularly, there's more to the crisis than finance, and we need to address its origins before dealing with recent events.

Origins

These go back to the end of the post-war boom. This was a 'productionist capitalism' in which big companies engaged in continual investment in production and distribution, often with long time horizons, prioritising long-term profitability rather than short-term gains. Of course, it needed a financial sector, but 'financialisation' hadn't been heard of. Bank credit was regulated to keep interest rates down and inhibit asset inflation. Building societies in the UK and Savings and Loans in the US could only lend out existing savings deposited with them. Wages and salaries rose in line with increases in productivity, so by and large employees enjoyed the fruits of economic development. That this happened owed much to trade union pressure, which prevented owners holding back pay and taking all the gains for themselves.[6] But in fact it also helped employers by ensuring that demand was continually raised as workers' pay rose.

To varying degrees in different countries, electoral support for social democracy ensured public investment, and economic security for households. Shareholders had limited impact on firms, as large institutional shareholders like pension funds had yet to emerge and wield influence, and so managers were allowed to concentrate on the nitty-gritty of their businesses, using their specialist knowledge of their products and markets. Real interest rates were low, indeed close to zero. When, in 1957, UK Prime Minister Harold Macmillan was moved to say that 'most of our people have never had it so good', rentiers had never had it so bad, though they were far from extinct.

From boom to bubble

In the late 1960s and 1970s, rates of profit in this productionist capitalism in the established industrial economies began to fall, mainly as a result of the development of a more global economy.[7] Particularly with the rise of East Asian producers, productive capacity grew and competition intensified and squeezed profits. A procession of manufacturing plants in Europe and North America shifted 'offshore' to the newly industrialising countries, to take advantage of cheap, highly exploitable labour and permissive employment legislation, enabling them to escape from organised labour. Technological change in the digital age also disproportionately hit traditional skilled manual workers in the middle of the income distribution. As unemployment in the old industrialised countries rose, increases in real wages slowed down. In turn, this slowed the growth of consumer demand, again making profitable production harder than before. Yet labour productivity – output per worker – continued to rise, so 'jobless growth' predominated. Figure 12.1 shows what happened in the world's largest economy, the US, after 1959.

As Tom Palley, who produced the graph, comments, it shows 'how wages of US production and non-supervisory workers (who constitute over 80 percent of employment) have become detached from productivity growth during the era of financialisation'. In fact, as many commentators have noted, wages and salaries have stagnated in the US for 40 years while the gains have been concentrated in the top 10% of the income spectrum, and, within that, overwhelmingly at the top; the top 0.01% increased their share by a factor of 9, from 0.2% to 1.8%.[8]

In the UK the divergence between pay and productivity started later, in the 1990s, and was less dramatic but still marked(Figure 12.2). Again,

Figure 12.1: Productivity and hourly compensation of production and non-supervisory workers in the US, 1959–2005

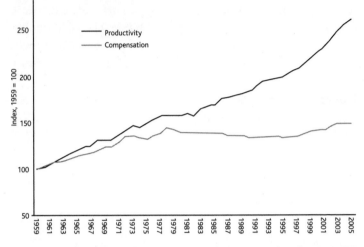

Source: Palley, T. (2007) 'Financialization: what it is and why it matters', Working Paper 525, Washington D.C.: Levy Economics Institute.

only the pay of those at or near the top of the income distribution kept up with economic growth. The weakening of trade unions and employment protection has hit those in the bottom half of the income distribution hardest; the decline in trade union membership correlates with the rising income shares of the top 1%.[9] In so far as there has been an expansion of employment, it is because a larger proportion of jobs are part time, and low paid.[10] Some argue that recent technological change has favoured higher-paid workers who have the necessary skills, but, as the exhaustive analyses of French economist Thomas Piketty show, if this were the case one would expect wage shares across the top 10% or 20% to have increased, when in fact increases have been heavily concentrated in the top 1%.[11] And when we look at the sectors in which the rich are concentrated – finance and real estate – it is clear that the 'earnings' of many of 'the working rich' come from interest, rent-seeking and value-skimming, albeit paid out as salaries and share options. Particularly between 2000 and 2008, an increasing share of growth was taken as profit by

Figure 12.2: UK trends in hourly earnings and labour productivity, 1970–2010

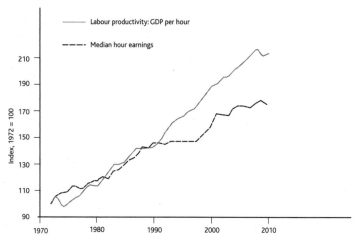

Source: Resolution Foundation (2012) *Gaining from growth: The final report of the Commission on Living Standards*, p 24

owners and shareholders, contributing further to the divergence of wages and productivity growth.[12]

Several studies have revealed similar if not quite so dramatic patterns in a large number of countries:

- In a study of 13 western capitalist countries, John Peters found that while workers achieved a 4% growth in real wages in the 1970s, growth in real wages from 1980 to 2005 was less than 1%, though those employed in the financial sector did better. In the 1970s and 1980s the wage share of national income in these countries peaked at 78%, but then declined to 63% in 2005 while income from profits, stock dividends, interest and rents rose.[13]

- Tali Kristal's 2009 study of labour's share of national income in 16 capitalist democracies arrived at 'an unequivocal conclusion. Since the early 1980s there has been a large and persistent decline in labor's share of national income in most capitalist democracies. The growth of productivity has expanded total income, but in many countries average real wages and fringe benefits have increased more slowly than labor productivity. Meanwhile, income growth has occurred mainly in capitalists' profits, sharply increasing capital's share.'[14]

- The United Nations Conference on Trade and Development (UNCTAD) commented: 'In developed countries, the share of labour income declined, falling by 5 percentage points or more between 1980 and 2006–2007 – just before the global financial crisis – in Australia, Belgium, Finland, France, the Netherlands, Norway, Sweden, the United Kingdom and the United States, and by 10 points or more in Austria, Germany, Ireland, New Zealand and Portugal. In several major economies (including France, Germany, Italy and the United States), a significant proportion of the decline in the share of wages had already occurred between 1980 and 1995. This appears to have been linked to a departure from the post-war social consensus, when wage increases closely followed productivity gains.'[15]

- The International Labour Organization (ILO) found that between the early 1990s and 2007, labour's share of income fell in 51 out of the 73 countries for which data was available. More specifically, labour's share of value added fell by 13% in Latin America, 10% in Asia and the Pacific and 9% in high-income countries. The gap between the top and bottom 10% of waged and salaried workers increased in 70% of countries in this survey.[16]

- Both UNCTAD and the ILO show that in most developed countries, especially English-speaking ones, income from capital gains (unearned income) has gone increasingly to the rich.[17]

- Reports from the International Monetary Fund (IMF), the Organization for Economic Cooperation and Development (OECD) and Oxfam also show a widening of inequalities in most countries, with the rich pulling away from the rest.[18]

Underpinning the economic growth and stability of the post-war boom was the Bretton Woods agreement of 1944, which restricted international movements of capital, limited trade imbalances so that each country's imports and exports did not diverge too much and fixed exchange rates between key national currencies and allowed governments to set interest rates. In effect, it replaced the previous rule by bankers over the movement of capital with rule by governments, so that national economies became more closed. No longer could rentiers move money round the world because 'they think that the degree of leftism in one country looks for the time being to be greater than somewhere else', as Keynes put it.[19] In the absence of this threat, governments could form social contracts with business and workers that regulated their respective shares, rights and responsibilities.

By 1971, the system had ceased to favour a US economy burdened by a growing trade deficit. Under pressure from the financial sector, President Nixon unilaterally ended the agreement and liberalised credit creation and the movement of capital. Globalisation of production and trade was complemented by globalisation of capital and the creation of credit money. This made it easier for 'investors' to pursue the best returns across the world and run away from organised labour and high taxes. They could expand and extend their speculative trading of stocks, bonds and currencies to financial markets around the world. It strengthened the whip hand of the financial sector and weakened the power of governments to control interest rates and credit creation, including their power to encourage real investment and full employment. As hosts to the dominant centres of financialisation, the US and British governments backed this shift to a rentier capitalism.[20]

In 1973 the oil-producing countries restricted oil supply in retaliation for US support for Israel in the Yom Kippur War. This resulted in a rise in energy costs that led to a major crisis, with soaring inflation and declining profits. Inflation reduced the real rate of interest, favouring debtors; debt payments become less onerous if the currency you have to pay them in is losing value fast. For a while, with a still-strong labour movement, many workers could continue to win wage rises to keep up with inflation but, as unemployment rose in the old industrialised countries, the post-war balance of power between capital and organised labour crumbled as deindustrialisation hit union membership. At the end of the decade, leaders like Margaret Thatcher and Ronald Reagan seized the moment to attack the unions and weaken employment legislation. In effect they declared class war on organised labour, which was blamed for the high inflation. In both the US and the UK, the governments raised interest rates, making their currencies strong and hence making business difficult for export industry, as it drove up the prices of exports relative to those of goods from other countries. This caused unprecedented loss of jobs, particularly in manufacturing, where unions were strongest, hitting older industrial communities. To major British businesses this was a price worth paying, and their extensive overseas interests meant that even if they temporarily lost business in the UK they had other sources of profit. For the financial sector, low inflation and high interest rates were good news, enhancing the profitability of financial assets in the 1980s. They also pushed up the cost of borrowing by the public sector, subjecting the welfare state to more pressure. These changes amounted to a shift in power not only from labour to employers, but also from both to rentiers, and indeed from the state to finance. Worse, they increased Third World debt. Bringing down inflation shifted the balance of power back from debtors to creditors, and flows of money from debtors in both the industrialised and developing countries increased.

The 1970s versus now

To read the tabloid newspapers, or listen to neoliberal politicians, one might think the 1970s in Britain were a time of unrelenting misery, when the country was run by 'union barons', paralysed by strikes and power cuts ('the winter of discontent'), with rubbish piling up on the streets and bodies piling up in morgues (because grave-diggers were on strike), while inflation was rampant. Thank goodness things are not like that any more.

Well, I was there, and bearing in mind that there were 3,652 days in the 1970s, and that the power cuts and other disruptions lasted only a small number of days, and then only in some parts of the country, this is somewhat misleading. True, some of the union leaders were a bit abrasive, and sometimes backward as regards gender equality, but at least they were elected, unlike 'barons' – or company bosses.

But the important thing is that in the 1970s ordinary people enjoyed increasing real wages and salaries, sharing in economic growth, even in the period when inflation reached double figures. The financial sector was not out of control. Students received maintenance grants and didn't pay tuition fees; it's hard to imagine now, but they could leave college debt-free. What's more, they and other young people could expect to go on to get a job. Unemployment reached a low of 2.6% in 1974 and remained below 1.5 million for the rest of the decade. Under neoliberalism, things have been reversed; inflation has come down, but unemployment increased to above 2 million for most of the 1980s and 1990s, peaking at almost 3.3 million in 1986. And real incomes have *fallen* since 2000 for most of the bottom 90%.

I was tempted to say that rise in real incomes in the 1970s was in spite of the strikes and union power, but of course, without strong union support, working people would certainly not have maintained their share of national wealth. True, the 1970s were not a golden age; union pay bargaining would have been better if it had been coordinated at a national level, as in Sweden, with all unions together with government deciding simultaneously each year on pay deals, in the light of economic conditions. But, despite the oil crisis and the recession in 1973–75, and the three months of 'discontent' in 1978–79, things got better for most people over the decade.

And we didn't need food banks.

Meanwhile the financial sector swelled enormously. Before the 1970s debts owed to UK banking had grown roughly in line with the growth of the economy – at about 50% of GDP. But since then they have soared to over 500% of GDP.[21] You might think that ramping up their lending so dramatically would necessitate expanding their capital base to protect themselves against the increased risk, but exactly the opposite happened; deregulation allowed them to reduce their capital base and increase risk. Those who owned shares in banks could tap into this growing source of unearned income. Up until the 1970s their returns were similar to those from shares in non-finance companies (less than 10% per year), but from then on they rose to well over 20%. That the banks chose to hand over so much of their enormous profits to shareholders at a time when they needed to build up their capital base speaks volumes about the irrationality of shareholder capitalism.

In the 1980s, governments began to extol the virtues of 'flexible labour markets', a brilliant euphemism for reduced protection, bargaining power and security for workers and a race-to-the-bottom for cheaper labour. In this new environment, slow growth of wages and salaries meant that aggregate demand for goods and services also grew more slowly, making it harder for companies to make a profit from investment in new capacity and products. Two things reduced or postponed the damage; first, the rise in women's employment, which increased household income for many, and second, the dramatic expansion of consumer debt, particularly mortgages and credit cards, although eventually this depressed demand and consumption because the borrowers had to pay off the interest. Low-income families took on the most debt in relation to their income. In the UK in 2006 those earning less than £10,000 a year had average debts of £20,316, a figure that was on average more than three times their annual income.[22]

In this environment, many firms that were struggling to get good returns on productive investment sought out opportunities for 'investment' in finance, which relied more on interest, rent, value-skimming and speculation; the profit rates of financial institutions soared and capital flowed into the sector. In 2004 General Motors made 80% of its profits from its financial division, and Ford made much of its profits from its.[23]

To the extent that firms could undertake profitable productive investment they could almost always fund it internally from retained profits without going to the financial sector for funds. Indeed capital was accumulating in greater volumes than could be used productively, given the sluggish demand. Business was so successful in holding down wages relative to profits that it created a barrier to selling its output; its success in disciplining labour was to become part of its undoing! In geographer and political economist David Harvey's terms, surplus capital switched from the 'primary circuit' of investment in goods and services to the 'secondary circuit' of investment in property and other assets.[24] Here, rates of interest on government bonds and returns on shares were often double those of real investment, reaching levels unprecedented in the 20th century.[25] So, excess capital generated in the productive sectors flowed into the financial and property sectors, inflating the value of assets and enhancing rentier power. As Doug Henwood commented, in the US, 'Far from turning to Wall Street for outside finance, nonfinancial firms have been stuffing Wall Street's pockets with money.'[26] On top of this, ordinary savers, faced with declining state pensions, were encouraged to buy 'investment' products that they could offset against tax and take out private pensions. It was mainly the better-off workers who could afford to do this. Pension funds, mutual funds and banks 'invested' this growing flow of money on their behalf in financial securities. This of course gave them a stake in the expansion of the sector.[27]

Capitalism has always depended on the movement of capital from low-profit ventures into high-profit ones. It's all part of the process of creative destruction that has fuelled the incredible economic growth of the last 250 years. Yet, in the new financialised capitalism, the creativity lay not in long-term investment in goods and services, as it had done in productionist capitalism, but in finding ways of outsourcing activities to cheap labour providers, in sweating existing assets for more income, speculating on price differences in different places and price movements and engaging in tax avoidance and creative accounting. Though finding cheaper labour is often claimed to increase efficiency, it just reduces the amount of demand in the economy because workers have less to spend. Efficiency increases require reorganisation of the ways of doing things so as to increase output per worker, and it is this that accounts for capitalism's success, not cutting wage bills and making people poorer.

As a result of these developments, inequalities widened in almost every industrialised country: top salaries rocketed and the rich cornered much of the growth in income via dividends on shares and capital gains.[28] Meanwhile the taxes they paid fell, and benefits for lower-income people were reduced. The justification for this was that letting the rich get richer would allow more wealth to be created; dividing the pie up more unequally, it was claimed, would allow the pie to grow faster, benefitting everyone. But the opposite happened. Whereas the world economy grew in per capita terms at over 3% during the 1960s and 1970s, it grew at only 1.4% after 1980.[29]

Driven partly by the rise of big institutional 'investors' such as pension funds, insurance companies and mutual funds, the shareholder value movement took off, seeking to make companies distribute more of their profits to shareholders. In France and the US, dividends paid out rose from 30% of profits in the 1970s to 60% by the end of the century.[30] Companies that failed to deliver found their share values falling, making them ripe for takeover by managers who would more effectively serve the interests of shareholders and extract more value from the firms. Long-term investment strategies that deferred gains became liabilities. Companies had to post good results in every quarter. Aggressive cost cutting – including job cutting – took priority over long-term investment. Wealth extraction outweighed long-term wealth creation. In the US, it was only the top 2% who had a significant share of this non-wage income.[31] Whatever the consequences, the shareholders had to be fed.

The shareholder value movement changed the nature of the firms. Instead of coherent groups of activities required for producing particular goods and services for profit, companies came to be treated as bundles of assets to be bought, dismembered and sold off in pieces, in whatever way delivered short-term profits for shareholders. It's tempting to liken the situation to a protection racket in which those who do not pay their protectors enough face the threat of being taken over by other, more demanding protectors. The difference is that some of the protectors are on the inside, top managers whose remuneration packages are heavily weighted with shares and share options – that is, options to buy shares at a future date at a predetermined price – and so they have similar interests to the external protectors.

'The dumbest idea in the world'

Pressure on BP management to cut costs in order to deliver shareholder value is alleged to have led BP to skimp on vital safety measures at the well that blew up in the Gulf of Mexico Deepwater Horizon oil spill. Saving $1 million a day on safety and research and development ended up costing the company's shareholders $100 billion for the clean-up.[32]

Jack Welch, the former General Electric chief, who is thought to have coined the term 'shareholder value' in 1981, finally acknowledged the error of his ways in 2009, saying: 'On the face of it, shareholder value is the dumbest idea in the world . . . Your main constituencies are your employees, your customers and your products.'[33]

Extraordinarily, in this new regime, it made sense for firms to avoid building up accessible cash reserves. Whereas this had been seen as prudent in productionist capitalism, it came to be seen as an invitation for corporate raiders to wrest control of companies so as to plunder their reserves. So reserves had to be reduced or made to look less inviting. One way of doing this was for companies to use them to buy back their own shares. This not only enabled them to reward management with shares, but pushed up the price of the shares by making them scarcer and reduced the amount of tax to be paid on dividends. Of course, while this appeased the shareholders and indulged top managers, it did nothing to improve the productivity and products of the firm. General Motors spent $20.4 billion on share buy-backs between 1986 and 2002.[34] According to William Tabb, between 1997 and 2008 even high-tech Microsoft, IBM and Intel spent more on buy-backs than on research and development.[35] As economist Mariana Mazzucato put it:

> Fortune 500 companies [the top biggest corporations in the US] have spent $3 trillion in the last decade on buying back their stock. Such value extraction has funnelled money away from areas that can increase long-term growth – for example research and staff development – to areas that only increase the inequality between the 1% (whose rewards are linked to stock price movements) and the 99% (whose rewards are linked to investments in the productive economy). Value extraction is rewarded over value creation.[36]

Another way of minimising or offsetting reserves was for companies to 'load up with debt' by borrowing, often to fund speculation or takeover bids of other companies, or again to buy back their own shares. This has the added attraction of providing a way of reducing corporation taxes, because the interest on the debt can be offset against tax.[37]

The spectacle of major firms sacrificing long-term investment so as to produce short-term profits for absentee owners, and taking on debt unnecessarily, highlights the irrationality of financialised capitalism. From the point of view of financial capital, it is crucial to be able to withdraw quickly from any 'investment' and shift to a more profitable one; hence 'the fetish of liquidity' as Keynes called it. The difference between real investment and merely financial 'investment' has rarely been clearer.

So firms in the so-called real economy or non-finance sector found themselves trapped. Faced on the one side with limited profit opportunities from production, and on the other with pressure from shareholders to deliver in the short term, businesses looked increasingly to make gains from other sources.[38] Top management became focused on finding whatever ways it could to push up stock prices so that its shares and share options could be sold or realised at maximum personal gain – again, a task made easier by deregulation.[39] Top executives no longer needed expert knowledge of the products and services they managed; rather, they needed to know how to extract maximum gains for shareholders. If they didn't, they would be replaced by more aggressive managers who would do the job.

Surplus capital floods the system

The financial crisis is not merely a result of an increase in the supply of exotic and potentially dangerous financial instruments. It was also driven by an expansion of demand for them – 'a growing "wall of money" chasing yield'[40] – from spare cash seeking 'investments', at a time when productive investment outlets have been choked by overcapacity and slow growth in demand. As we've seen, one source of this surplus capital looking for outlets was non-finance companies, switching into financial investment. A second source was so-called sovereign wealth funds held by governments, such as China and Saudi Arabia, that had large trade surpluses to 'invest'. They account for 1.5% of the world's total private wealth, equal to the share of the world's billionaires.[41] They too faced limited opportunities for profitable productive investment, so much of their activity has been rent-seeking – for example, buying up land in Africa in anticipation of future commercial exploitation, or property in the US in the expectation of price inflation.

A third source was the growth of private funded pensions. According to Julie Froud and co-researchers, the annual flow of funds into life assurance and pension funds in the UK in the mid-1990s was roughly equal in value to productive investment by all industrial and commercial companies! – only it didn't fund that investment but merely inflated share values.[42] Employees' pension and other savings or 'investments' provided feedstock for the big institutional investors that, thanks to deregulation, could be 'invested' not only in shares and bonds but in riskier financial instruments too. Neoliberal governments were only too happy to back this, as it enabled them to reduce commitments to state pensions. In the US, Britain, France and Germany, 'investors' in shares were given tax breaks so that, in effect, they got a discount on the market price. This was a state-subsidised form of rentiership; those who could take advantage of such schemes not only got access to unearned income but cut their tax contributions at the same time! And of course they were likely to be already comfortably off.[43] It also meant that the most direct means of remedying the surplus of capital – devaluing it – became politically difficult, because such pensions depend on the continued overvaluation of capital.

A fourth source of surplus capital was the rich themselves. Their ballooning incomes and dramatic reductions in top rates of tax created a problem for them: what to do with their spare cash. While there are limits to how many things anyone can actually consume, there are no limits to how much money and assets – or wealth – they can acquire. A few, like Bill Gates, George Soros and Warren Buffett, have given significant amounts away in philanthropic ventures.[44] But most sought to 'reinvest' their spare money in property and finance, whether because of greed, desire to get the highest 'score' among their peers or lack of imagination regarding what else they might do with it. So their vast surpluses seek still more outlets in which they can store their wealth and maximise returns. The demand for more securities to 'invest' in encouraged the financial sector to create ever more financial products that would deliver 'yield'.[45] This it did by relaxing standards and increasing risks – most infamously in the case of sub-prime mortgages. In the US, tax cuts for the rich in the 1980s and 1990s also fuelled the flow of funds to buy junk bonds from companies that were raising cash to buy out other companies.

Deregulation of banks allowed them to shift beyond the traditional 'retail' business in which they took in households' and firms' deposits and lent money out to others. Increasingly they used their other resources to speculate and deliver shareholder value by leveraging – borrowing money cheaply in money markets in order to make bigger 'investments' (bets on the value of financial assets). As we saw in Chapter Seven, leverage massively increases the gains that can be made in speculative activity – but also the losses if it fails. As long as the value of financial assets was inflating, this was extraordinarily lucrative, particularly for those whose pay was tied to the profit made through bonuses or fixed shares of profits ('the comp ratio'); no wonder they imagined they were masters of the universe. But, as leverage rose to over 1:30 in some banks, even a small percentage of failures in their 'investments' could land them in deep trouble. And it did, only they could rely on 'socialism for bankers' to rescue them: governments, recognising that the banks were too big to fail, or too interconnected to the rest of the economy, had guaranteed retail deposits.[46] This of course means that taxpayers pick up the bill for protecting their own deposits and rescuing failing banks. So leverage was key to how the banks privatised the gains from using other people's money to take risks and managed to socialise the losses, leaving ordinary taxpayers to pick up the bill.

And it was the financial sector that ran up the biggest debts. Although neoliberal politicians now like to blame the debt mountain on profligate consumer and government borrowing, so as to provide an excuse for cutting public spending, the financial sector itself was the main debt growth sector, as a result of loans between different financial organisations.[47]

You might think that creating ever greater volumes of credit money would cause inflation. It did, only not in the prices of consumer goods but in asset values, especially property values – the kind of inflation neoliberals love. It increases the wealth of asset holders relative to the asset-poor, who experience wage stagnation and debt deflation.[48] As long as the bubbles are growing, banks lend out more and get still more interest. In John Merryman's words:

> What the people in charge came to understand is that lots of money can be created, without causing general inflation, if it can be largely kept out of the regular economy. While a lot is loaned back into the economy, much is cycled within the banking system. All that 'liquidity,' as derivatives, securities, off balance sheet vehicles, etc, is mostly just chips in the casino. It is a very delicate balancing act of enormous notational wealth, that amounts to a large tumor on the real economy.[49]

Putting everything up for sale

One of the hallmarks of financialisation is the spread of the practice of selling off anything that is believed to be able to produce a predictable income stream in order to get cash now.[50] It could be hospital car-parking charges, mortgage repayments, film royalties, dividends, student rents or student loans.

This process of value extraction is coupled with a key instrument in financialisation: 'securitisation'. This, broadly speaking, is the practice of bundling up loans – typically mortgages, credit card debt or car loans – and, using 'special purpose vehicles' (SPVs), selling them on as an asset that promises to yield an income from the interest payments. The SPVs are legally separately owned from the financial institutions that set them up and usually based in tax havens so they can be used to hide debt. The seller not only in effect gets some of that future income immediately, but is able to lend anew, having sold off the risk and removed it from their balance sheet. Combining hundreds of loans from different places and sources is supposed to reduce risk, provided the risks of individual defaults are not correlated (though, given the far-reaching effects of business cycles on borrowers' finances, it's quite likely that an increase in defaults in one place will be accompanied by defaults elsewhere). Selling on risk is supposed to disperse its effects, but it doesn't reduce the original risk of borrowers defaulting. Indeed, offloading risk to others reduces the ability of lenders to monitor risk, and the need to do so, and hence encourages more risk taking. Actually though, as Ewald Engelen and associates show, contrary to the stories of risk dispersal, risk on derivatives was highly concentrated. In 2010, the notional value of derivatives held by commercial banks in the US was $212.8 trillion.'Of the 1,030 US commercial banks that submitted information on their derivatives exposure, the top five claimed 97% of this notional value.'[51] In this situation, the risk ended up being held by taxpayers, because banks of this size were too big to fail and had to be bailed out. For all the hubris and macho talk about 'risk management' to be found on the websites of the financial sector and in the textbooks teaching its practices, prudence and long-term perspectives were dumped in favour of quick gains and offloaded risk.

Deregulation allowed the buyers of the securities to use them as collateral for borrowing, so streams of interest payments on loans supposedly backed by collateral in the shape of houses were themselves used as collateral by holders of these asset-backed securities for borrowing. In turn, with the money they borrowed they could buy still more securities – further sources of unearned income – and generally engage in more speculation on their changing market values. In such ways finance built its infamous house of cards. As Marx put it, 'interest-bearing capital generally is the mother of all crazy forms'.[52]

Once they had exhausted the market for mortgages among the middle classes, and then securitised the debt, US mortgage companies moved into the sub-prime market by luring low-income households with teaser rates that soon gave way to usurious rates of interest. Having pocketed the commission and fees, they securitised these high-risk, high-interest loans too. So the ability to lay off risk through securitisation induced highly irresponsible, predatory lending and short-term 'investment'. Crucial in all this was what economists call 'information asymmetry'. When most people take their car to the garage for a service, they know much less about what needs doing than do the mechanics, so they can easily be taken advantage of. And dodgy second-hand car dealers with cars that they suspect are developing a serious fault may be tempted to hide this from buyers and get rid of it as fast as possible. Equally, with securitisation, dodgy mortgages can be quickly passed on.

Bundling up hundreds of these sub-prime loans into 'asset-based securities' and then, in turn, slicing, dicing and bundling these up into 'collateralised debt obligations' (CDOs) produced instruments of baffling complexity – and opacity.[53] Enormous simulation models were run on supercomputers to estimate their risk. To be sure, they had to be approved by credit rating agencies – actually, private firms given licences – but here it has to be said that the police force was on the side of the crooks; since the agencies were paid by the institutions they were supposed to rate, and sometimes had a stake in them, it was in their interest to give an AAA rating to almost anything. Yes, it seems not just outrageous but scarcely credible, yet it is symptomatic of the unaccountable power of the sector.

No doubt the buyers of the securities knew this but did nothing about it because they, or any others exposed to the risk, assumed they had covered themselves by buying 'Credit Default Swaps' (CDSs) to protect themselves. In effect, they paid a fee to banks to guarantee the securitised loans, should they fail – a kind of insurance, you could say. But this in turn encouraged the feeling that it was safe to buy still more CDOs. Worse, up to an estimated 80% of the market for CDSs involved clients who were not themselves exposed to the relevant credit risks ('naked' CDSs, as they're known in the game)! In other words, it's like everyone in your road taking out insurance against your house burning – in effect taking a bet that it actually would, and hence having an interest in it doing so! This goes directly against a fundamental principle of insurance – that you can only insure what you own. *Financial Times* journalist Wolfgang Münchau's comment on naked CDSs was: 'There is not one social or economic benefit. Even hardened speculators agree on this point … the case for banning them is about as a strong as that for banning bank robberies.'[54]

Those who correctly predicted that the value of the securitised mortgages would collapse, such as billionaire hedge fund manager John Paulson, made a fortune betting on this. In 2008 he got $3.7 billion. He was involved in helping the investment banking firm Goldman Sachs put together one of the very same securitised mortgage packages that he was betting against. Goldman Sachs reportedly sold the package to investors without telling them about Paulson's involvement in choosing the mortgages that made up the package, some of them extremely toxic.[55]

The nominal value of CDO and CDS contracts rocketed to more than global GDP; such was the optimism of the financial elite that defaults wouldn't happen on a major scale. In the UK, the nominal value of Barclays and Royal Bank of Scotland's (RBS) CDSs was £2.4 trillion each in 2008 – roughly four times total UK government annual spending. Not surprisingly, when the housing bubble burst, defaults soared and the house of cards collapsed; institutions like Lehman Brothers, AIG and Icelandic banks that sold the CDSs couldn't pay out, went out of business or were bailed out by taxpayers.

It's easy to see all this just in terms of money and risk, as the outcome of innumerable 'innovations' each of which seemed a clever wheeze at the time but cumulatively and unwittingly built a pile of debt that would sooner or later collapse. It illustrates how what seems rational to individual agents in the short run can spell eventual doom for the collectivity. But there is also more to it than that. No matter how many times debts are bundled up and sold on in various guises of Byzantine complexity, at base they depend on a social relation of wealth extraction in which mainly low- or middle-income borrowers provide unearned income in the form of interest payments to the rich. Ironically, some of those who had entrusted their savings to pension funds were unknowingly funding 'investment' in the anything-but-secure securities.

Privatisation and the neoliberal 'strategic deficit' plan

Cutting taxes on the rich reduces the revenue available to governments for the state sector, and high interest rates increase borrowing costs for governments. This has the effect of putting governments in what George W. Bush approvingly called 'a fiscal straitjacket'. He liked the idea because it provides governments with arguments for cutting state spending by privatising services.[56] We see a similar phenomenon now in Britain as the government uses the deficit as an excuse for cutting the public sector and for further privatisation. And when governments switch from taxing the rich to borrowing from them, this is a double gain for the rich. Squeezing the welfare state also weakens labour and keeps wages down. Whether as lenders or employers, the rich win either way.

One of the peculiarities of political discourse is the habit of drawing a distinction between tax-funded and privately provided services that are apparently provided by private sector 'investment', as if that meant we didn't have to pay for them! Sometimes the excuse is made that in the latter case we at least have a choice over what happens to our money, but in practice, with utilities and basic services, we have little alternative, and we don't get to choose whether we want to subsidise shareholders. Tax-funded investment is not conditional on providing unearned income for shareholders; much privately funded investment is. Privately funded 'investment' consists primarily in buying an existing set of assets that will deliver revenue. James Meek has it right when he argues that ordinary people end up paying 'private taxes' to companies for privatised services:

> [What] makes water and roads and airports valuable to an investor foreign or otherwise, is the people who have no choice but to use them. We have no choice but to pay the price the tollkeepers charge. We are a human revenue stream; we are being made tenants in our own land, defined by the string of private fees we pay to exist here.[57]

In turn, privatisation allows taxes to be cut further. In the UK, water bills have gone up by nearly twice as much as inflation since privatisation, and energy costs and train fares have soared, the latter by 17% in real terms.[58] The net effect is that instead of taxing the rich and the well-off, we pay them to deliver services and borrow from them to fund the deficit. With tax-funded public assets the burden of supporting them is borne by better-off taxpayers. When these assets are sold off to private operators, the fees do not generally vary according to the user's income, so the better-off benefit and low-income households face proportionately bigger bills. The privatisation of public utilities has given their operators a monopolistic power to milk ordinary citizens so as to provide their shareholders with unearned income.

Hence, though they may pretend otherwise, a colossal deficit is not such bad news for neoliberal governments: it provides them with an excuse for cutting welfare spending and public investment and selling off public assets that are likely to provide safe streams of income – effectively rent – for private companies. Indeed these were policies which the International Monetary Fund (IMF) and World Bank pushed as a condition of support for economies in trouble. When the debtor is in difficulty, the creditor can force the debtor to sell off their assets. This practice of dispossession has been going on for millennia.

Bond markets: vigilantes, bogeymen and banks

> Thank Heaven for the bond markets. They protect us all from the in-built fiscal excesses of democratic politics. (Charles Rowley, Professor of Economics at George Mason University in the US)[59]

> State bonds are nothing but the price of a share in the annual tax yield. (Rudolf Hilferding, 1910)[60]

Bonds used to be a relatively safe and boring kind of financial investment, but with the growth in recent decades of a secondary market in bonds (second-hand bonds) they've become a key game in casino capitalism. Just as shares are bought not just for the dividends they yield, but for speculating on their changing market values on the stock market, so bonds are bought not just for the interest they pay but for speculative gain. The rise of the bond markets has helped to enrich the top 1%, who hold most of the bonds held by households,[61] and also the banks, pension funds and other financial organisations that hold the rest. In 2011, the global bond market was worth $100 trillion (£62 trillion).[62] Its growth has greatly enhanced the power of the rich over governments.

Bonds are just a form of interest-bearing debt, and therefore a source of unearned income. They are a kind of IOU: a 10-year bond at 5% interest is a promise to pay the holder that rate of interest for 10 years and then return the principal. They are not just things or assets; they involve a social relation between borrower (the issuer of the bonds – usually a large company, local authority or government) and lender.

Like most forms of debt, bonds tend to transfer wealth upwards to the rich; in the case of public debt they divert tax payments into funding interest payments to the rich. This is how rentiers like it: cut taxes to the rich so they can lend to the government by buying bonds funded by 'the little people' who pay tax. (Leona Helmsley, an American real estate millionaire heiress nicknamed The Queen of Mean, who was convicted of tax evasion, was reported to have said: 'We don't pay taxes. Only the little people pay taxes …'[63]) But the fortunate 40% may also benefit a little, if unknowingly, in so far as some of their savings are 'invested' in bonds by pension funds, though most will pay out more interest than they receive over their lifetime. Unwittingly they help such institutions to discipline governments that borrow from them. But the flip side is that, politically, this means that the financial institutions responsible for 'investing' their savings cannot be allowed to fail.

An assured rate of interest of 5% on a 10-year bond is pretty good, assuming that the rate of inflation is lower – the kind of investment the rich used to favour to support themselves in retirement. But active rentiers compete endlessly for the highest gain at each moment by continually moving their funds between whichever financial markets seem to offer most. It's now rare for bondholders to hang on to their bonds for the full duration of the bond, and most prefer to play the bond market continually; indeed, on average, bonds are held for about a month. In the 1980s the growth of leveraged buyouts funded by bonds – often called 'junk bonds' – boosted the market. So too did the spread of capitalisation of streams of income of diverse sorts, as these were used by organisations to finance new issues of bonds.

Bonds issued by governments ('public' or 'sovereign' debt) have usually been regarded as the safest, because governments can supposedly just raise taxes in order to pay debts, and so bondholders looking for a secure place to store their wealth buy such bonds even though the rate of interest is low. But when weak economies perceived to be at risk try to raise money by issuing bonds, the interest rates get driven up, as we've seen in southern Europe. In 2013, rates of interest on Greek bonds were four to five times those on UK bonds.[64] This is the familiar story of usury: those who are least able to pay interest are expected to pay the most. High rates reflect not only risk but power. What's more, it's become clear since 2007 that holders of bonds issued by states that get into difficulties will be bailed out, so it's increasingly the taxpayers who hold the risk.

The value of bonds on the secondary market is strongly influenced by fluctuations in the economic environment, so bondholders are highly sensitive to changing economic conditions and policies. Clearly, for those buying new bonds, a high interest rate (relative to the risk of default) is attractive, but existing bondholders don't want to see interest rates in the economy at large rising, for that devalues their assets relative to other outlets for speculation. Here's why: a bondholder might be getting 5% interest on their 10-year £10,000 bond, that is, £500 per year, but if interest rates in the wider economy then rise, say to 6%, their 'investment' will be sub-optimal. In the secondary market, buyers will be interested only in buying such bonds at less than their face value, in order to offset their lacklustre rate of interest. The face value of the bond would have to be discounted to £8,333, so that the £500 fixed payment equalled a 6% yield for the buyer. On the other hand, if interest rates generally fall, say to 4%, then the value of the bond with a 5% interest rate will be increased, for it will obviously be attractive to 'investors' and sell for more – in fact it would be worth £12,500.

Creditors always like inflation to be kept low so that the interest they receive doesn't lose value too much. Governments need to be able to convince bondholders that they can do this, but they just tell voters that low inflation is good news for everyone. It is, in so far as it means that our money isn't losing value so fast; certainly, runaway inflation of the kind experienced in the mid-1970s, when rates exceeded 10% per year, is not sustainable. But a modest rate of inflation is generally conducive to economic growth, while choking off inflation altogether stifles growth. And of course inflation is good for debtors because it reduces the value of their debts.

Countries that become dependent on borrowing on the bond markets – mostly from large domestic and foreign banks, pension funds and insurance companies – can find themselves in a vulnerable position if they do not meet bondholders' preferences regarding economic management, let alone if they are at risk of defaulting. For example, in 1993 in the US when the Clinton administration introduced new legislation to greatly expand healthcare without properly funding it ('HillaryCare'), long-term interest rates began to rise. The 10-year rate on US Treasury bonds touched 8% in 1994. The consequent threat of a credit crunch in the business sector, and higher mortgage rates for prospective home buyers, generated enough political opposition to stop it going through Congress.[65] Bondholders – sometimes dramatised as 'bond market vigilantes' – can simply bid up interest rates or refuse to lend anew. As James Carville, lead strategist for US President Bill Clinton famously commented, 'I used to think that if there was reincarnation, I wanted to come back as the President or the Pope. But now I want to be the bond market: you can intimidate anyone.'[66] Now, the same credit rating agencies that got things so wrong in rating credit derivatives mark down the credit ratings of countries that refuse to embrace austerity: in the euro-crisis, they drove the cost of borrowing for Greece, Ireland and Portugal, and then Italy, up to unsustainable levels, forcing their governments to think the unthinkable.[67] On 'Black Friday' (13 January 2012), Standard and Poor's downgraded the credit rating of nine European countries, prompting complaints that Europe's future was being determined by American private credit rating agencies. This was another way in which politics was being determined by private business, overriding democracy. Higher interest rates meant that more taxpayers' money was diverted from the public sector into bondholders' pockets. What is more, the downgrading of government bonds had a contagious effect on the perceived riskiness of other investments in those countries.

But Paul Krugman suggests another interpretation: just as parents may find it useful to invoke a bogeyman to discipline their children, so governments can take advantage of the threat of upsetting the bond markets (and credit rating agencies) to justify policies that might not actually upset them or that they don't actually demand, and then use them as scapegoat. (In fact they regularly invoke 'the markets' as if they were a force of nature that had to be obeyed. See box 'Beware "the markets"'.) Governments can claim that bondholders demand policies of austerity and privatisation in return for extending credit, even if they don't.[68] Bondholders may realise that cutting spending is likely to make default more likely, not less, so arguably it's not in their self-interest to demand austerity. Ireland has taken massive doses of austerity, inducing an inevitable slump, without reducing its risk of default or making bondholders any happier.

Beware 'the markets': the angry gods must be appeased!

Announcing a programme of £6 billion worth of public sector spending cuts, the UK's new Conservative Chancellor of the Exchequer claimed: 'This early, determined action has earned us credibility in international markets. It has meant that our promise to deal decisively with the deficit has been listened to' (George Osborne, 2010).[69]

'The markets demand cuts, privatisations, a smaller state.' Hearing such talk, one might reasonably wonder how something like 'a market' can demand anything. Who or what are 'the markets'?

Often they're the bond markets, but that doesn't tell us much, for we need to know who the key actors are. As we've seen, they're major financial institutions; including the very ones whose bailouts have worsened the credit risk of the governments that rescued them and hence that need to borrow from them. So 'the markets' is a useful euphemism for concealing the identity of powerful, sometimes familiar, financial institutions. Often it's accompanied by another useful decoy term – 'investor'. One regularly hears financial sector spokespersons, usually just calling themselves 'economists', explain things in homely terms of what an 'investor' would do in a given situation, as if buying government bonds were the sort of thing that ordinary people do. Even before the crisis, there was a tacit understanding in both the financial sector and government that 'markets' and 'investors' were the appropriate terms to use, not Goldman Sachs, Barclays or Deutsche Bank. This of course presents the class interests of rentiers as no different from the general interests of the wider population.

And the term 'markets' has still more possibilities. It's a way of avoiding attributing responsibility to anyone or anything – as if there were no agents actually buying and selling. When Margaret Thatcher said 'you can't buck the market' she invoked a powerful force to which we must submit – only it will actually be better for us if we do submit, for supposedly, the market is a miraculous thing that brings outcomes superior to any that planners or politicians could devise.

The economic crisis is a threat to the big bondholders as well as the borrowers. Greek public debt, for example, is mostly held by French, German, US and Greek banks, so the threat of default also threatens the likes of Société Générale, Deutsche Bank and so on, and this in turn frightens their governments, who don't want them to fail. As Mervyn King, the then Governor of the Bank of England, so aptly put it, 'banks are global in life, but national in death'.[70] The banks, pension funds and insurance houses that dominate the bond markets are also the same institutions that fuelled property bubbles in Greece, Ireland and Spain that later contributed hugely to their economic crises. As always, behind any debt relation, there's a story of how the unequal relationship arose in the first place. The people of those countries, who are accused of living beyond their means, who are now suffering, are saving not their countries but their irresponsible, predatory creditors, who so confidently claimed that they had devised financial instruments that could effectively manage risk. The 'rescue plans' are not for the Greeks or Irish, but for the banks.

As with the bondholder bogeyman ruse, governments can use the claim that people's savings depend on the survival of banks to justify bailing them out in the event of failure. In the Irish case, the government claimed that this was why it was necessary to bail out the Anglo-Irish Bank (AIB). In 2012 Irish banks used state funding to pay €18 billion to bondholders in AIB and four other banks that were bailed out, with a further €17 billion to come in 2013.[71]

However, according to research by David Malone, out of 80 bondholders of Irish debt, only 7 deal with pensions or operate as a cooperative savings institution, and these tend to have smaller holdings. Many of them are foreign banks, some of them privately held banks managing the assets of foreign, super-rich individuals – not pension funds or high street banks holding people's savings. An example is the EFG Bank of Luxembourg, part of the European

Financial Group, which is the third-largest private bank group in Switzerland. Managing over €7.5 trillion in assets, it is 40% owned by Mr Spiro Latsis, son of a Greek shipping magnate and ranked 51st in the list of the world's billionaires in 2006. His personal fortune is estimated to be about $9 billion.[72] So the Irish public has been making sacrifices to ensure that such creditors do not lose out on their 'risk taking'. Another key bondholder heavily exposed to Irish debt is the RBS, now 84% publicly owned, and so the UK government has an interest in the Irish people bailing out their banks. The steep rise in public debt since the crisis, and hence dependence on bondholders, is partly a result of the public having to pay to bail out banks that are bondholders!

As in all usury, when things go wrong, the lenders, and those who have an interest in their survival, try to discipline the failing borrower. So, in the Greek debt crisis the so-called 'troika' of lenders – the European Central Bank, the European Commission and the IMF – set conditions for rescuing Greece, including 'massive layoffs in the civil service, the dismantling of social protection and social services, reduction of social budgets, increase in indirect taxes such as VAT, the lowering of the minimum wage'.[73] In September 2012 the troika considered requiring the Greeks to work a six-day week (they already work longer hours than Germans), and later a proposal for withdrawing state support for Greek islands with populations of less than 150. These remind one of 'debt peonage', and invite accusation that the debt is 'odious' in so far as it derives from agreements made behind the backs of voters and against their will.[74] As Paul Jay puts it, the debtor governments' obligation to the bondholders is absolute, but their duty to their own citizens is relative. By 2013, Greece had 27% unemployment, 60% youth unemployment, a drop of 25% in GDP and a 40% reduction in family income. Meanwhile, its debt burden *increased* – from 120% of GDP in 2010 to almost 180% in 2013![75] To be sure, the Greek government had failed to collect taxes for years, but, as usual, all the blame for the crisis was laid at the debtor's door.

But there's another twist to the story. When, in the Greek debt crisis, German Chancellor Angela Merkel called upon the banks to 'take a haircut', that is, to write down the value of their bonds by 50%, the banks procrastinated because some, like Goldman Sachs, had taken out insurance in the form of CDSs on the Greeks defaulting, so they stood to gain more from a default than a rescue![76] So the banks were in a heads-we-win-tails-you-lose situation.

Thinking of such situations in terms of usury helps us to put debt relations in their context and to take note of how they evolved. As is abundantly clear in the European debt crisis, many of the same major financial institutions that have promoted asset bubbles and the crisis are now, as bondholders, extracting, via governments, unearned income from taxpayers, particularly those who are the victims of the crisis. As the ancient critiques said, usury allows the strong – and nowadays, the too-big-to-fail – to take advantage of the weak. But in addition, in contemporary rentier capitalism, our dependence on banks makes many of us have a stake in the success of the rentiers.

Shuffling ownership: the market for companies

> Over the past twenty five years, giant companies in the UK and USA have spent as much or more on buying other companies as on fixed capital investment ... (Savage and Williams, 2008)[77]

For firms struggling to increase their sales revenue in the face of sluggish demand, taking over other companies provides a way of buying revenue. Traditionally, mergers and acquisitions happened between firms in complementary lines of business, where it made technical and logistical sense to combine operations; in the 1980s the development of information technology brought many communications and computer firms together to profit from their synergies. In financialised capitalism this productionist logic gives way to mergers and acquisitions driven mainly by the pursuit of new sources of rentier income. Just how important mergers and acquisitions were can be seen from the fact that from 1980 to 1998 the amount of cash applied to acquiring financial assets in the US equalled 70% of the sum spent on productive investment, and in the UK, for 1980–96, it equalled more than 80% of that amount.[78] 'Serial acquiring' is primarily a centralisation of wealth extraction, with debatable benefits in terms of wealth creation in the wider economy.

Adding insult to injury was the rise of 'the leveraged buyout', a practice so monstrous in its parasitism that it's a wonder it's legal. Here, the would-be buyer borrows vast sums, often through issuing junk bonds (with tax deduction on the debt), to buy out a company – *and then loads them up with debt to pay for the buyout.* In some cases, this has reduced corporation tax payments to zero – a direct subsidy to parasitic rentiers. The bought-out company then has to cut costs – and often the workforce – in order to fund the junk bonds. This was a prime cause of the 'downsizing' of companies in the 1980s and 1990s. So there was a direct link between the rise in unearned income going to the tiny minority who could afford to buy such bonds and the loss of earned incomes of those workers who were displaced following leveraged buyouts.[79]

Imagine you have worked for years in a business that is then subjected to a leveraged buyout. Without consulting you, the firm's absentee owners have sold the business to a private equity company that has borrowed tens or hundreds of millions to buy out the company, saddling your organisation with the debt repayments, putting your own job and those of others in the organisation in jeopardy. Almost certainly the private equity company has also raided your pension fund. Those who kept their jobs would effectively be working in part just to pay off those unwanted debts. In fact such debts would be 'odious' debts, because the workers would be responsible for paying debts imposed over their heads.

As one of the most successful football clubs in the world, Manchester United was making a substantial profit and free of debt in 2005, and was able to buy some of the world's best players. It did so as a public company, with shareholders. Then the Glazer brothers, a US private equity company, made an offer of £790 million, which the directors accepted, and took the club private.[80] They didn't buy it simply from their existing reserves but instead borrowed ('leveraged') £525 million. They then saddled the club with paying off the debt, using the club's assets as collateral. In 2007–10, the club had to pay £130 million just in interest. By early 2012 this had reached £500 million, without reducing the debt much. Not surprisingly, purchases of new players were hit and the club began to lose ground to more generously funded clubs. Investment in players took second place to maximising the amount pumped out to the club's creditors.[81]

In 2010, the bailed-out RBS lent £7 billion to the American food giant Kraft for its £11.9 billion takeover of Cadbury's. Kraft had a history of hostile takeovers and asset stripping. The main beneficiaries were the hedge funds that bought shares prior to the deal, and Cadbury's shareholders.[82] As a commentator from the International Union of Foodworkers (IUF) notes:

> it is hugely relevant to question the meaning of 'investment' in a world where 'investment banks' have no stake in the companies on the receiving end of the deals, when 'investors' buy and sell shares with a perspective which has been compressed from years to days and even minutes, and when pension funds ostensibly acting on behalf of employees' long term interests are increasingly indistinguishable from traders motivated solely to increase their assets under management. The only group with a long-term investment in the future of their workplaces, it would appear, is the workers who build the businesses. The Cadbury deal shows just how few cards they hold – and what has to change.[83]

Kraft later broke promises to the government and workers about employment guarantees.

Leveraged buyouts are particularly worrying where they involve private companies providing public utilities. These are popular targets, as they are effectively monopolies and promise a reliable stream of income – 'human revenue', to use James Meek's term again – to borrow against. In 2008, 11 water and electricity companies, including Thames Water, Wales & West Utilities and Electricity North West, borrowed tens of billions via securitisations.[84] As a result, consumers now face rising bills to cover the debt repayments.

The irony is that the employees' pension funds, 'invested' in such deals, provide a major source of gains for the rich and super-rich, often indirectly putting those very employees' jobs at risk from post-takeover cost-cutting to deliver more shareholder value. Some firms were bought and sold several times by different private equity firms, and in some cases were made to take on still more loans to fund dividends.[85]

Financialised capitalism appears to have enacted the illusions of mainstream economics, in which buying and selling, rather than production, are seen as primary: as if wealth could be endlessly created just by lending and buying and selling existing and future assets: as if continually shifting to more profitable sources of revenue could be a substitute for real investment in goods and services; as if shareholder pressure for unearned income and an overactive market for corporate control would ensure economic development. It's extraordinarily naïve to imagine that a hyperactive market for the control of companies will ensure that those companies will produce better products with greater efficiency.

Even from the standpoint of the mainstream, the financial sector can no longer take refuge in a markets-are-always-right line. *Financial Times* economics editor Martin Wolf puts it clearly enough:

> A market works well if, and only if, decision-makers
> confront the consequences of their decisions. This is not
> – and probably cannot be – the case in finance: certainly,
> people now sit on fortunes earned in activities that have
> led to unprecedented rescues and the worst recession
> since the 1930s.[86]

Arm's-length lending, with the risks on one side borne by the borrower and on the other passed on through securitisation, allows the lender to escape the consequences of their decisions on lending.

THIRTEEN

Key winners

Who were the main beneficiaries of the rise of finance? Some have attracted considerable publicity and scrutiny, while others have largely escaped it.

Intermediaries: the anonymous rich

Around the world every year an astronomical number of transactions take place in the financial sector. While the majority may be automated, the more customised ones provide rich pickings for intermediaries in financial and legal institutions who provide the services necessary for conducting them for fees and commission. The intermediaries are an essential part of the financial ecology and make up the majority of the working rich in the financial sector. Flourishing from being near a big till where they can engage in value-skimming and assisting active rentiership, they are a key group of beneficiaries of financialisation. The more trading – or churning – of assets they can facilitate, the greater their income; not surprisingly, they encourage transactions rather than wait for custom. Managers of funds on behalf of clients such as pension funds can take advantage of their superior market knowledge to corner a significant share of the gains for themselves and to charge high fees. Trading of customised financial products such as credit derivatives 'over the counter' – that is, one-to-one between buyer and seller rather than in a competitive market trading more transparent standardised products with many buyers and sellers – heightens the information asymmetry in favour of sellers and the opportunity for them to extract rents. Carrying out mergers and acquisitions is an especially lucrative line of business, with fees averaging 1.5% of deal value. Vodafone's takeover of Mannesman yielded $640 million in fees for intermediaries.[87] These fee revenues are typically concentrated at the top. In Goldman Sachs, around 8% of net revenue was claimed by partners who made up about 1% of the firm's 25,000 workforce, receiving bonuses of nearly $7 million in 2005. Then there is the support force of public relations people, consultants, marketing experts, lawyers, creative accountants and tax avoidance experts, all of whom are in a strong position to reap large rewards.

In the financial sector in Britain, the number of intermediaries has been estimated at 15,000.[88] These largely anonymous members of the so-called working rich far outnumber chief executive officers (CEOs) and senior executive directors (c.600), let alone footballers and celebrities.

CEOs' pay: because they can

> You have to realise: if I had been paid 50 per cent more, I would not have done it better. If I had been paid 50 per cent less, then I would not have done it worse. (Jeroen van der Veer, former Chief Executive, Royal Dutch Shell)[89]

> OK. If I am being honest with you then yes, let's whisper it, but the truth of the matter is that all of us are overpaid. There is nothing magical about what we do. Anybody can do it. (Allen Wheat, Chief Executive of the giant investment bank Credit Suisse First Boston, 1998)[90]

> If you've made a lot of money, it's really just a matter of keeping score. (H.L. Hunt, Texan oil millionaire)[91]

CEOs are only a minority of the rich and super-rich, but they are very much figureheads and subject to public scrutiny, though not public accountability. CEO pay has risen 127 times faster than worker pay over the last 30 years. In 2005, the average CEO was paid nearly 300 times as much as the average worker, whereas in the post-war boom they were paid 'only' 24 times as much.[92] In the financial crash CEO remuneration fell in 2009 to just (!) 185 times that of the average worker.

Predictably, the banking sector has been more extreme.

> In 1989, the CEOs of the seven largest banks in the US earned [sic] an average of $2.8 million, almost a hundred times the annual income of the average US household. In the same year, the CEOs of the largest four UK banks earned [sic] £453,000, fifty times average UK household income. . . . Yet by 2007, at the height of the financial sector boom, CEO pay at the largest US banks had risen nearly tenfold to $26 million, more than five hundred times US household income, while among the UK's largest banks it had risen by an almost identical factor to reach £4.3 million, 230 times UK household income in that year.[93]

The trend has continued. In the US, Ron Johnson, CEO of J.C. Penney (department stores) topped the list in 2012 with $53.3 million – 1,795 times the average industry worker's pay of $29,688. Seven other CEOs got over 1,000 times average pay.[94]

How did this happen? Are these increases a reflection of an extraordinary improvement in the contribution of CEOs to the performance of their firms over the last 50 years? Is a CEO on 1,000 times as much as a worker adding 1,000 times more value to the company? They're often claimed to be exceptional individuals, but are they so much more exceptional than their more modestly – but still amply – paid predecessors in the post-war boom? Unsurprisingly, the answer is no: researchers have found little or no relation between pay and performance. For shareholders the key performance index is dividends and share prices. These have certainly risen in recent decades, but, as we saw, that's because the value of shares has been inflated by surplus capital from pensions and other sources feeding into the stock market. Increases in revenue that reflect an economic upswing can also easily be claimed as products of CEOs' contributions. But even where there is a correlation, the evidence shows that it's usually accidental. There's inevitably a time lag between a CEO's decisions and their effects, so new CEOs are likely to be rewarded for their predecessors' contributions, if any. Either way, almost by definition, management is in a position to take credit for the achievements of others, and for windfalls. Further, like today's star footballers and musicians compared to those of yesteryear, the growth of the market allows them to extract more economic rent.

Stories of greed, 'rewards for failure' and 'golden parachutes' are a staple of the media. In 2008, Aubrey McClendon of Chesapeake Energy cleared $112.5 million in a year when the company's stock fell by 40%.[95] Rumblings have been heard at some shareholders' meetings about CEO pay, and many commentators long for a 'shareholder spring' in which arrogant, overpaid CEOs are humbled. As usual, they completely fail to question the legitimacy of shareholding itself, mistaking it for a major source of real investment by deserving risk takers. But aside from that, even on its own terms, as long as CEOs deliver or appear to deliver increases in the value of their company's shares, why should shareholders complain if the CEO benefits too? In giant firms, the value of their pay is small compared to the total value of all their shares and employees' wages. Julie Froud and fellow researchers argue that CEOs basically engage in value-skimming, calling it a victimless crime, on the grounds that their greed doesn't significantly hurt any one individual.[96] This is hardly a justification, of course.

CEO pay has not only rocketed but changed in composition, with stock options and retirement benefits accounting for an increasing proportion of pay, the former rising in US top companies from 8% of pay in 1990 to two-thirds in 2001.[97] The official rationale for this was that it aligns CEOs' interests with those of shareholders. In practice this encouraged them to engage in short-term manipulation of accounts to push up share prices, to allow executives to cash out (sell) at inflated prices.[98] Comparing the US unfavourably to Germany, where shareholder value has had limited effect, William Tabb writes: 'The use of stock options to encourage executives to maximize shareholder value weakened American capitalism to an incalculably dramatic extent.'[99]

CEOs need to be well networked in order to know what the best deals are and to convince 'investors' that their companies will be successful. But they also need their contacts and friends – usually executives from other companies – to serve on the remuneration committees that decide on their pay. CEOs are primarily concerned with how their pay or 'compensation' [sic] compares to that of other CEOs.[100] All this creates a ratchet effect that continually drives up pay. It's laughable to suppose that remuneration committees bring any legitimacy to pay setting; they are a simply a means by which the rich can help each other to get richer.

Arguably though, there is at least a soft force holding them back – public outrage. This varies between countries according to their history and culture, and has retreated over time: Anglo-Saxon societies tend to be more accepting of such pay rates than continental European societies, which in turn are more tolerant than Japan, though they are catching up. As the rich get richer, and those immediately below them try to keep up, the inequalities become normalised. Typically, CEOs tough out the objections for the few days that they are raised, and the issue is forgotten until the next year, when it can happen all over again. Significantly, executive pay has continued to rise – indeed soar – *after* the crash, despite the public outcry. In 2011–12 pay and benefits of business executives in the top FTSE 100 companies rose by 27% to an average of £4 million each.[101] Commentators from across the political spectrum agree that CEO pay has had little to do with performance and everything to do with economic rent and power.[102]

Bank bonuses: 'Heads I win, tails you lose'

If there's one thing that has inflamed public outrage at the banking crisis more than any other, it's bankers' bonuses. Their recipients appeared to inhabit a different world from the rest of society, oblivious to the wider crisis that they helped to produce, making arrogant claims about their alleged star qualities as wealth creators that distinguished them from ordinary mortals. They certainly appear to be good at pursuing their self-interest; there is no reason to doubt their competitiveness and speed of thought, even if they lack wisdom, ethics or understanding of the wider situation. Why would they need the latter anyway, as long as they're making money?

Of course, the bonuses went only to a tiny proportion of bank employees at the top – executives, traders, salespeople, wealth managers and specialists in arranging mergers and acquisitions and new issues of shares (initial public offerings) for companies. Within these elites the proportion of total pay in the form of bonuses generally increases from 40% for juniors to 80% at the top for seniors. In addition to pay denoted as bonuses, senior members of financial institutions are in many cases paid a ratio of net revenues (the 'compensation ratio'), which encourages them to leverage deals as much as possible so as to maximise those revenues and boost their 'compensation' – thereby also magnifying risk.[103]

In 2006, the year before the crash, Goldman Sachs paid out $16.5 billion in 'compensation', an average of roughly $623,418 per employee. It was a year in which the leading employees could expect to get $20 million to $25 million each, with some traders who booked big profits getting as much as $50 million each.[104] *But after the crash, the bonuses continued.* In 2010–11 financial sector bonuses in the UK totalled £14 billion, having risen by 58% since 2000–01.[105] In 2010 more than a hundred employees of the bailed-out RBS received more than £1 million each, with total bonuses totalling £1 billion, even though the bank reported losses of £1.1 billion in the same year![106] Similarly, our old friend Goldman Sachs received $10 billion of state assistance and paid out $15.4 billion (£9.6 billion, or £269,000 per employee) in 2010.[107] Citigroup and Merrill Lynch lost $54 billion, paid out nearly $9 billion in bonuses and then received state bailouts totalling $55 billion.

The rewards for failure represented two fingers waved at the public. As New York State Attorney General Andrew Cuomo put it, 'when the banks did well their employees were paid well. When the banks did poorly their employees were paid well. And when the banks did very poorly, they were bailed out by taxpayers and their employees were still paid well.'[108] Only recently have any banks started to introduce mechanisms for clawing back bonuses in cases of individuals who can be linked to losses.[109] But star employees have even been given 'retention bonuses' and 'multiple year guaranteed bonuses'. Oxymorons? Yes!

But the problem is worse than one of rewards for failure, for the system encourages the very behaviour that gets banks into trouble through excessive risk taking. Yes, the recipients are almost certainly greedy, unprincipled and ruthlessly competitive, but it's the way the financial system is currently configured that invites this behaviour.

In an excellent paper, James Crotty argues that the 'rainmakers' (as the recipients of bank bonuses are known in the US) make money by speculating on the upside of bubbles, in the knowledge that the bonuses will continue in the downturn.[110] They can make most profit by borrowing millions to make bigger bets – in other words, by leveraging – and by extending more loans to the public, both of which substantially increase the exposure of their institutions to risk. Leveraging to buy assets pushes up asset prices, which pushes up the value of collateral, which allows more borrowing, and so on, until it all goes into reverse. The bigger the risks they take, the higher their bonuses. When a bubble bursts, the paper value of the asset evaporates but the value of the bonuses (which is calculated on the basis of this paper value) does not; it remains a claim on real goods and services.

Ratings agencies, in the pay of the organisations whose products they rated, and often 'investing' in them, had no incentive to reveal the build-up of risk. And worse, the calculation of the bonuses themselves took no account of the riskiness of the deals. For example, traders made bonuses for selling insurance on derivatives whose risks were seriously underestimated. As they had no incentive to estimate the risk, they didn't do so. And since those at the top of the companies, who of course had the most influence, also had the biggest personal stake in the bonus system, they had the biggest incentive to push their firms into high-risk strategies that maximised bonuses in the boom. Instead of hedging risk, they increased it.

In short: bubbles + leverage + bonuses = disaster.

Why are banks so resistant to cutting bonuses, especially when these reduce the amounts available to distribute to shareholders? Surely one would think they would attract new entrants into the market who would undercut the big players, and floods of new recruits offering to do the same work as the rainmakers for slightly smaller bonuses? Briefly, the answers (again, following James Crotty) are:

1. The bosses have a personal interest in retaining bonuses.

2. They would lose their star rainmakers to competitors, and even though an industry-wide cap on bonuses might be possible in principle, in practice, they have little incentive to secure one.

3. There is surprisingly little competition between the big banks to lower their fees and rates. Financialisation has produced a centralisation of ownership in the sector. There are very few big banks and the heavy investments in information technology and in developing networks that are needed to compete make it difficult for new firms to enter the market. With the bankruptcies and mergers that followed the crash, the concentration of ownership in financial services actually *increased*. Already too big to fail, they have for the most part become bigger.

4. Even though, predictably, thousands of able graduates want to get in on the bonanza, those in the institutions who select them have no interest in diluting their own gains. Also, new recruits first have to serve an apprenticeship doing smaller deals before they are deemed skilled enough to make big deals, and again, their mentors have no interest in allowing their juniors to undercut them in doing the same work for less.

For all these reasons, the rainmakers are positioned within a system that yields enormous economic rents from creating, buying and selling financial products that are mostly claims on the wealth produced by others.

It is not only radicals who have concluded that the bonus system is one of institutionalised wealth extraction: Keynesians like Paul Krugman, respectable financial journals like the *Financial Times* and the *Wall Street Journal*, and insiders like Andrew Haldane, Executive Director of Financial Stability for the Bank of England, and Jean-Claude Trichet, then President of the European Central Bank, have said as much. Here are some examples:

From the *Financial Times*:

> By paying huge bonuses on the basis of short-term performance when negative bonuses are impossible, banks create huge incentives to disguise risk-taking as value creation. Moreover, if bankers are rewarded for

pursuing risky strategies that appear highly profitable for an extended period and then blow up, it is others who pay the costs.[111]

Trichet:

> Over time the creation and assumption of *financial risk* became the core activity of financial markets. At some point, the financial system seemed to be no longer there primarily to hedge existing risks, but more and more to create its own.[112]

Haldane:

> The banking industry [like the car industry] is also a pollutant. Systemic risk is a noxious by-product. Banking benefits those producing and consuming financial services – the private benefits for bank employees, depositors, borrowers and investors. But it also risks endangering innocent bystanders within the wider economy – the social costs to the general public from banking crises.[113]

Martin Wolf, again at the *Financial Times*, summarised the situation thus:

> Financial systems are important servants of the economy, but poor masters. A large part of the activity of the financial sector seems to be a machine to transfer income and wealth from outsiders to insiders, while increasing the fragility of the economy as a whole.... Banks are rent-extractors – and uncompetitive ones at that.[114]

Wolf also asked: 'Can we afford our financial system?' His response was unequivocal: 'The answer is no.' I agree. Its wealth is not only mostly parasitic but achieved at the cost of destabilising whole economies. It's both unjust and dysfunctional.

Stratospheric incomes

In 2006 the 25 highest-paid hedge fund managers in the US made $14 billion, three times the combined salaries of New York City's 80,000 school teachers. Yet economists struggle to demonstrate any benefit to society from the activities of the hedge funds.[115]

The Campaign for America's Future commented:

> Hedge fund operators' management fees are taxed as capital gains, for example – for money they're earning, not investing – which allows them to pay just 15% on their income. Million-dollar households make 42% of their income, on average, from capital gains at these ultra-low rates today. The portion of 'their' income that isn't being taxed at the 15% rate is subject to the official top marginal tax rate of 35% under the Bush tax cuts – and that's before the loopholes kick in.[116]

The City: the goose that laid the golden egg or the cuckoo in the nest?

> The people of Goldman Sachs are among the most productive in the world. (Lloyd Blankfein, Goldman Sachs chief executive, November 2009)[117]

> Let me thank you first for the scale of the contribution you make to the British economy – the £50 billion of income, 4 per cent of national output, and the one million jobs that arise. (Gordon Brown, Chancellor of the Exchequer, 2004 Mansion House speech to the financial sector)[118]

> [W]e have seen renewed worries that London's prominence and the wealth it attracts and generates may be distorting the broader economy possibly adding to social tensions – that it may be more a cuckoo in the nest

than a golden goose. (Sir John Gieve, Deputy Governor
of the Bank of England, 26 March 2007)[119]

In Britain, rentiers and their political servants and sycophants are
apt to warn against regulating the financial sector for fear of 'killing
the goose that laid the golden egg'. Has not the sector delivered
spectacular growth, becoming the most dynamic sector of the
economy? It would surely be madness to restrict it.

Amazingly, two years *after* the financial crash in 2007, Gordon
Brown's successor, Alistair Darling, addressing the same audience at
the Mansion House, said: 'The City of London and other financial
centres such as Edinburgh and Leeds, remain an immense asset to
our country. The financial sector makes up 8 per cent of our national
economy.'

It would be naïve to imagine that measures of the contribution
of the financial sector were reliable. Measuring this depends on
deciding on whether financial activities just involve a redistribution
of existing income, or are productive. Is interest such a transfer or
a reflection of a productive contribution? As we saw, mainstream
economists might argue that transfers enhance allocational efficiency,
though we have already dealt with the weaknesses of that argument
in mistaking profitability and success in rent-seeking for economic
development. As researcher Brett Christophers has shown, on some
systems of measurement, the City's contribution would come out as
negative, on others, positive, and to widely varying degrees.[120] Over
the last 40 years, the financial sector worldwide has used its political
muscle to change how its economic contribution was categorised so
that what were formerly transfers now count as 'productive'.

No less than the Bank of England's Andrew Haldane and his
colleague Vasileios Madouros argue that the financial sector has
grossly overvalued its contribution to the UK economy.[121] The sector
often claims that it contributes by bearing risk, but, as the authors
note, bearing risk, for example buying a bond, does not contribute
anything productive; it is not a value-adding activity. *Managing* or
assessing risk – for example, checking that borrowers are creditworthy
and that the lender is not dangerously exposed – is necessary and
indirectly productive. But increasing risk taking – constructing a

house of cards of credit on a small and fragile asset base – is certainly not. The extraordinary profits made before the crash were the result of increased risk taking, and not reflections of productive contribution; in the end they resulted in crashing the economy. As the authors put it: 'If risk-making were a value-adding activity, Russian roulette players would contribute disproportionately to global welfare.'

What's more, banks that are too big to fail do *not* bear risk: the public does. And the scale of the bailouts has outweighed the gains made in the sector before the crash. Haldane and Madouros estimate that for the 25 largest global banks, the average annual subsidy between 2007 and 2010 was hundreds of billions of dollars, and possibly – according to the IMF – over $1 trillion.

Another insider, Adair Turner, Chair of the UK Financial Services Authority, described some activities of the financial sector as 'socially useless'.[122] The Manchester CRESC team commented: 'In its present form, finance is a pro-cyclical activity with limited job-creating capacity and a proven ability to disrupt the economy at great cost to the taxpayer.... Banking delivers little social value and instead operates "for itself".'[123]

As regards employment, the financial sector accounts for only 6.5% of UK employment and has remained static since the 1990s. It provided 6.8% of government tax receipts, while manufacturing, widely dismissed as of marginal importance in the new economy, provided 13.4%. The financial sector has been highly active in helping clients to avoid tax; in so doing it has taken fat commissions for reducing the state's income. And junk products such as payment protection insurance are examples of activities with negative value. The sector has also drawn many of the most able members of the workforce away from more productive activities. More generally, the sector has damaged economies by encouraging the switch from investment in productive uses to speculative, rent-seeking outlets. If the sector is supposed to be so important for growth, isn't it interesting that the sector was much smaller in the post-war boom?

All this means that the view of the City of London (and other major financial centres) as engines of their national economies is fundamentally flawed. The City likes to portray itself as the saviour of the UK economy, helping the south-east of England boom while subsidising the 'backward' regions of the north and west. But, given the financial sector's concentration in London and its success in privatising gains and socialising losses, it's the rest of the country that has had to bail out the City, while its rescuers have lost out. In geographical terms, the majority of the country's population cannot afford to continue to transfer wealth to the metropolis.[124]

Martin Wolf of the *Financial Times* was equally robust in his condemnation of the financial sector: 'The UK has a strategic nightmare: it has a strong comparative advantage in the world's most irresponsible industry.' The influence of the sector, with its 'light-touch' approach, was 'surely malign'. Echoing John Gieve's less-appealing avian metaphor, he wrote that Britain needs to ask itself a 'painful question: how should the country manage the cuckoo sitting in its nest?'[125] Given that financial capital can extract wealth from other economies than those in which it is resident, it is possible that some parts of the UK may indeed share some of the benefits of this global wealth extraction. In so far as this is true, or governments believe it is, financial institutions may win concessions from the host government by threatening to move elsewhere.

Marx's favoured metaphor was not the cuckoo, but the parasite, a metaphor taken up by a range of other commentators: 'Usury centralises money wealth ... It does not alter the mode of production, but attaches itself as a parasite and makes it miserable. It sucks its blood, kills its nerve, and compels reproduction to proceed under even more disheartening conditions.'[126] Michael Hudson adds that the smart parasite takes control of the brain of the host organism and makes the host believe that it is performing an important and beneficial function.[127] A more polite term for it is 'cognitive capture'. Alistair Darling's craven response to the financial sector even after the crash – and the similar responses of most leading British politicians since then – illustrates the phenomenon perfectly.

Bailouts: socialism for the rich

Gore Vidal, the late American writer, once described US capitalism as 'free enterprise for the poor and socialism for the rich'. That was in 1969, but how much more true it is now.

When the banks deemed too big to fail were bailed out by the public, their creditors and shareholders were also protected in the process; the rentiers were rescued from the consequences of their own excess. The tough rhetoric of compete or die, rule by the market and freedom from the state was quickly forgotten, as states came to the rescue. And they were bailed out with scarcely any strings attached. The rationale was that they were so strongly connected to the rest of the economy, indeed global economy, that failure could not be countenanced. Given that banks are global in life, but national in death, they could hold governments to ransom: too much of the economy relied on credit from them, and the pensions and other savings of the fortunate 40% were tied to the fortunes of the financial sector. The shift from public to private pensions put pensions at the mercy of the booms and slumps of the financial markets. By putting their eggs in many baskets (some, like hedge funds, high risk; others, like government bonds of European countries, supposedly safe) pension funds thought they were secure. Pension funds and insurance houses that had protected themselves by buying CDSs found that the banks that sold them couldn't afford to honour them in the event of default. In September 2008, global private pensions dropped in value by 20% in one week.[128]

Northern Rock on the rocks

In the UK, the first bank to fail and be bailed out – to the tune of £27 billion – was Northern Rock, which had led the way in over-lending on mortgages and securitisation. Commenting on the former chairman Matt Ridley's views, George Monbiot writes:

> As chairman of Northern Rock, he was responsible, according to the Treasury select committee, for the 'high-risk, reckless business strategy' which caused the first run on a British bank since 1878 ... Before he became chairman, a position he appears to have inherited from his father, Matt Ridley was one of this country's fiercest exponents of laissez-faire capitalism. He described government as 'a self-seeking flea on the backs of the more productive people of this world ... governments do not run countries, they parasitise them. ...'

> What did the talented Mr Ridley learn from this experience? The square root of nothing. He went on to publish a book in which he excoriated the regulation of business by the state's 'parasitic bureaucracy' and claimed that the market system makes self-interest 'thoroughly virtuous'.
>
> Having done his best to bankrupt the blood-sucking state, he returned to his family seat at Blagdon Hall, set in 15 square miles of farmland, where the Ridleys live – non-parasitically of course – on rents from their tenants, hand-outs from the Common Agricultural Policy and fees from the estate's opencast coal mines. No one has been uncouth enough to mention the idea that he might be surcharged for part of the £400m loss Northern Rock has inflicted on the parasitic taxpayer. It's not the 1% who have to carry the costs of their cock-ups.[129]

Estimates of the size of the UK bank bailout range between £289 billion and £550 billion – or nearly £10,000 for every British resident – exceeding the £203 billion of tax that the sector paid in the five years up to 2006–07.[130] These costs are around 1% of gross domestic product in the UK. By the end of 2009 the total value of bailouts in the US, UK and euro area equalled $14 trillion, or almost a quarter of the world's gross domestic product.[131]

But the impact on the wider real economy in terms of recession is still more serious. As Andrew Haldane said:

> [T]hese direct fiscal costs are almost certainly an underestimate of the damage to the wider economy which has resulted from the crisis – the true social costs of crisis. World output in 2009 is expected to have been around 6.5% lower than its counterfactual path in the absence of crisis. In the UK, the equivalent output loss is around 10%.[132]

He estimates the present value of expected future economic losses due to the crisis at between $60 trillion and $200 trillion for the world economy. Ireland's economy – one of the hardest hit – contracted by 7.5% in 2009.[133]

The bailouts amount to a massive transfer of debts from the private to the public sector – and a subsidy for the rentiers: bankers' debt became sovereign or national debt. Governments raided the public purse to lend money at rock-bottom rates of interest to banks, which then used it to lend back at higher interest, through buying government bonds paying 4% or 5% or consumer credit paying 12–18%.[134] Governments took toxic assets off banks and insured them, and created money to buy other financial assets from them ('quantitative easing'). The banks used the opportunity to 'deleverage', that is, pay off debts and build up reserves, while of course keeping themselves in the manner to which they were accustomed as regards pay and bonuses. They failed to increase their already low level of lending for productive investment by businesses. Meanwhile, aggregate demand was depressed by austerity policies, rising unemployment and people cutting back on spending to pay off their debts. From the point of view of economic regeneration, the bailouts were about as successful as 'pushing on a string'.[135]

Governments that had to fund substantial bailouts put themselves at risk. Stagnant or shrinking economies also mean increased government debt, because revenues from taxes decline and welfare expenditure goes up as unemployment rises, all of which increase the risk of default. When this predictably resulted in a worsening of the credit rating of those countries, the financial elite demanded more cuts, particularly cuts borne by ordinary taxpayers. When the parasite got sick through over-gorging, the host organism fed it some more, so it could lend us back our own money at interest.

Now it has become clear that major banks are too big to fail, they have still less incentive to act prudently, as they are seen as a safe risk by other companies – indeed they can raise credit more easily than banks that are small enough to fail! When the rewards of acting in an anti-social way are greater than the penalties for doing so, this is called 'moral hazard'. According to Mervyn King, the 'massive support extended to the banking sector around the world ... has created possibly the biggest moral hazard in history'.[136]

Champions of free enterprise, who had campaigned against state regulation and poured scorn on the public sector and welfare state, were happy to pocket state subsidies on a hitherto unseen scale.

Contrite they were not. Losing none of their brazenness, they then lobbied fiercely and mostly successfully against state regulation of the sector, so that they could continue to live the adolescent dream of unconditionally supported autonomy.

The bailout is itself a huge transfer of wealth from the majority of society to those at the top. If the financial sector were to pay for the damage it has done throughout the economy and put its house in order, we could say that the situation was merely one of malfunctioning and repair, but since the victims have had to bail out the perpetrators, who remain free to repeat the crime, it's also a straightforward injustice. After all the puffed-up, self-congratulatory talk from the financial sector of expertise in 'risk management', it was ordinary people who had to pick up the tab.

Doom loops

The surge in government demand for credit to cover the direct costs of propping up the financial system and the indirect costs of growing unemployment, underemployment, and diminishing tax receipts has helped, with more than a little irony, to put highly lucrative new business the way of many of the financial institutions that had to be rescued by the state in the first place.[137]

When banks know they are too big to fail and that governments will always bail them out, they are likely to take bigger risks threatening bigger crises, which will need even bigger bailouts, which makes them take bigger risks still ...

The extraordinary cost of bailing out banks weakens government finances, and so when they need to borrow from banks, the banks insist on higher interest rates to protect themselves against the risk of governments defaulting, though this of course weakens state finances still further; and if that threatens banks lending to them, they will need bailing out ...

So when governments rescued the banks from going under, the rescued threatened to drown the rescuers; who then needed rescuing by the rescued, who then ...

As Benjamin Kunkel comments:

> A far simpler and more effective monetary policy would
> have been for the government to print a new batch of
> money, distribute an equal amount to everyone, then sit
> back and watch as stagnant economies were stirred to life
> by the spending and debts were paid down and eroded
> by temporarily higher inflation. The inconceivability of
> such a policy is a mark not of any impracticability, but
> of the capture of governments by a financial oligarchy.[138]

This has happened before:

> It is certainly a tragically comical situation that the
> financiers who have landed the British people in this
> gigantic muddle should decide who should bear the
> burden, the dictatorship of the capitalist with a vengeance.
> (Beatrice Webb (1858–1943) English sociologist,
> economist and reformer)[139]

FOURTEEN

Summing up: the crisis and the return of the rentier

> None of us can thrive in a nation divided between a small number of people receiving an ever larger share of the nation's income and wealth, and everyone else receiving a declining share. (Robert Reich)[140]

> You never want to let a serious crisis go to waste ... it's an opportunity to do things you could not do before. (Rahm Emanuel, White House Chief of Staff, 2008)[141]

The return of the rich over the last 40 years has been the return of the active rentier, including the working rich who are in positions of power such that they can siphon off wealth produced by others, whether in their own organisations or elsewhere. Rentier shares of national income increased significantly in most industrialised countries since the 1980s.[142]

In the UK, the trend has been particularly marked in the property sector. In the 2000s, lending to the commercial property sector grew by 3.5 times (this includes the development, buying, selling and renting of property but excludes the construction of new buildings) while lending to all non-finance sectors (including construction) lagged slightly behind growth of GDP. In the process, lending to commercial property rose from being 60% less than lending to productive sectors to being 50% more. Lending by the later-to-fail RBS and Lloyds TSB accounted for half of this. This fuelled a commercial property bubble: after the financial crisis property values plummeted, putting the loans against them at risk. By 2007, 79% of

British bank lending was on property (houses and businesses) and to other financial institutions for trading – particularly on derivatives based on property loans.[143] From 1996 to 2008, lending to businesses for productive investment declined. When the bubble burst in 2008, commercial property prices fell by 26.4%.[144]

In 2006, according to the Office of National Statistics, the biggest contribution to economic growth over the previous 15 years had come from the letting of dwellings, where the 'value' supposedly 'created' had risen by 120%, to reach £45 billion per year. Rentiers mistake wealth extraction for wealth creation: as the *Guardian* journalist Patrick Collinson put it:

> In modern Britain, it seems, putting up the rent is somehow regarded as economic growth. The US dominates in technology, Germany makes millions of cars, Japan still makes consumer electronics. Britain produces buy-to-let landlords. How our competitors must envy our economic success.[145]

The size and profitability of the financial and property sectors surged relative to the non-financial sector, though there was some blurring of the line between the two sectors as non-finance companies also sought gains through financial products. The growing stranglehold of the shareholder-value regime, the enfeeblement of organised labour under competition from cheap labour overseas and political attacks at home and the resulting stagnation of consumer demand have made their contributions to the crisis too. Executives and key workers were able to take advantage of weakened labour to take a bigger share of their firms' revenue. A bloated financial sector has created a succession of bubbles, and skimmed off wealth in the process. This victory of capital over labour, and of creditors over debtors, has produced a contradiction: in restricting aggregate demand, it constrains profitable productive investment and growth.

Of course finance has a vital role to play as a servant to the economy, in oiling the wheels of business, in arranging credit and dealing with risk, but it can easily become the master and make the rest of the economy its servant. The occupational hazard of finance is that in seeking to make money out of money through lending, value-skimming and speculating, it focuses on wealth extraction and loses sight of the necessity of wealth creation in goods and services. In the bubble that preceded the crisis, bank lending to productive businesses declined from 30% to 10% as lending to other financial institutions and the property market grew.[146] The financial sector's control of financial assets – ultimately, claims on the labour and products of others – means that, unless it is strongly regulated it can dominate governments to serve its interests. Mainstream economics, with its obsession with idealised models of markets and its evasion of the difference between earned and unearned income, is complicit in this.

In effect, there has been a temporary victory of money (exchange-value) over goods and services (use-values), though it can only ever be a temporary victory because the value of money ultimately depends on people producing goods and services. Wealth extraction through interest-bearing credit has far outstripped the capacity of wealth creation through productive investment to repay the debts.

The growth of consumer debt and its normalisation, whether in the form of mortgages, credit card debt, student debt or other loans, has a disempowering effect on an increasing proportion of the population. Whereas workers can go on strike, organising collectively to stop production and hit their employers where it hurts most, what can debtors do? With the exception of indebted students, they do not have a collective identity or defensive organisation – they are just individuals. If the debtors default on repayments, then they risk having their homes repossessed or having to declare themselves bankrupt.

Absurdly, the UK Coalition government claims that the crisis is the product of excessive state spending by the previous Labour government. This is contradicted by the global character of the crisis, and by the evidence on borrowing, *especially* in the UK, where financial sector debt is seven times the size of public debt, and where total debt almost equals ten times GDP.[147] So the government, aided by a compliant press and a feeble, craven opposition, has set up the public sector as scapegoat for the crisis. But it has been innocent bystanders, the 99%, but especially those on low to middling incomes, who have been told that 'we' must reduce 'our debt' and tighten our belts. Not only have real wages dropped but public sector cuts have led to job losses, particularly affecting women, while benefits for the unemployed, the disabled and people on low incomes have been drastically cut. Austerity for the masses and ultra-cheap bailout loans and quantitative easing for the banks mean another massive dollop of unearned income for the rentiers. As Adair Turner – again, a more candid member of the financial establishment – put it:

> British citizens will be burdened for many years with either higher taxes or cuts in public services – because of an economic crisis whose origins lay in the financial system, a crisis cooked up in trading rooms where not just a few but many people earned annual bonuses equal to a lifetime's earnings of some of those now suffering the consequences. (Turner, 2009)[148]

PART FOUR

Rule by the rich, for the rich

We may have democracy, or we may have wealth concentrated in the hands of a few, but we can't have both. (Justice Brandeis)[1]

Wealth, as Mr Hobbes said, is power. (Adam Smith)[2]

Though it's rarely acknowledged, while we may still live in democracies, they're increasingly overshadowed by the rule of the rich – or 'plutocracy'. (Some call it oligarchy – rule by the few, but this fails to highlight their wealth.) As the economic power of the rich has grown, so has their political power. Yes, everyone still has the vote,[3] but it's the rich who dominate politics.

How has this happened? How has the plutocracy, particularly the financial elite, been able to get away with crashing major economies, while maintaining their power and making others pay for its mistakes? In the UK, they've got away with it by blaming the public sector, the previous Labour government, and penalising and stigmatising those who have least to do with the crisis – the unemployed and other people on benefits. Remarkably, despite being key players in the most serious economic crisis for 80 years, the City of London and Wall Street have effectively seen off any threats to their power, and deepened their grip on politics. How come they seem to control everything when no one voted for them?

In this part, we look at how this power works, how it flows between governments, companies, lobbyists, think-tanks and other organisations, and how it uses tax havens as power bases. We then go from the ugly – corruption, crime and the muzzling of the watchdogs – to the apparently benign – philanthropy. We end with some views from the plutocracy regarding how they might continue their domination of economics and politics.

FIFTEEN

How the rule of the rich works

It's tempting to imagine there must be some kind of conspiracy among the rich that has enabled them to become so dominant. But there's no stable, coherent organisation, governed from a centre. Still, even rich individuals, acting on their own, have disproportionate political power. Modern plutocracy is just a set of ever-shifting alliances among rich organisations and individuals whose interests overlap sufficiently for them to find it useful to cooperate from time to time, as well as compete.[4] Capitalism is too dynamic, fractious and anarchic for membership of the plutocracy to be fixed or for it to develop much organisation. As Marx said of capitalists, the key players are 'hostile brothers'. Opportunism is the norm, plus a shared presumption of the impossibility of disinterested behaviour, excused by a quasi-religious belief in the miracle of 'efficient markets', as Hywel Williams observed.[5] The infiltration and capture of the state by the rich has been a piecemeal process, with roots going back decades.

The most obvious manifestations of plutocracy are political donations and lobbying by business, the overlapping social and corporate networks and mutual courtship of top politicians and the rich, and the wealth and elite origins of politicians themselves (at the time of writing there are 18 millionaires in Britain's cabinet, and a handful schooled at Eton). Less visible is the offshore world of tax havens, which allow the rich to escape the rules that apply to the rest of us. But the rule of the rich has still deeper foundations in the very *structure* of capitalism that enable them to dominate politics.

Silent power

As long as the commanding heights of the economy are controlled by a minority who do whatever yields them the highest profits, then, since governments need to support the economy in order to keep up employment and standards of living so as to retain electoral support, they need to keep the owners and controllers of big business sweet so that they will continue to invest. This is true of capitalism in both booms and crises. *Even without any lobbying or political donations, those who control major businesses would still be in a dominant position.* To varying degrees this structural source of power may be restrained by strong labour organisation, though globally mobile capital can easily escape it. But at times like now, when labour is relatively weak and the rich are resurgent, this structural power is unrestrained, indeed it's protected and encouraged by governments.

There couldn't be a clearer manifestation of this structural dominance than the forced public bailout of banks deemed too big to fail, while their bosses escaped any serious penalties and continued to pay themselves millions. At root, the financial sector has enormous structural power simply because of its wealth, control of our money and influence on the economy. In an economy that's not only capitalist but financialised, policies must suit creditors – inflation must be minimised and capital must be as mobile as possible. As Doug Henwood puts it, 'Public debt is a powerful way of assuring that the state remains safely in capital's hands. The higher a government's debts, the more it must please its bankers.' They can always move their money to somewhere else.[6] And as we'll see, tax havens mean that there invariably is somewhere more favourable for them.

On top of this, they are ideally positioned to take advantage of elite education and control of the media, and the control of knowledge that goes with these. These support their symbolic power: they have the best start in life and so tend to capture the best opportunities, so it is easy for them and others to imagine that they must be special people, meritocrats rather than plutocrats. In the UK, Tony Blair, David Cameron and Boris Johnson[7] are prominent captives of this delusion, though it spreads downwards too. As Pierre Bourdieu put it: 'all power owes part of its efficacy – and not the least important part – to misrecognition of the mechanisms on which it is based'.[8]

Despite their considerable structural power, the plutocracy have not relied wholly upon it, but stepped up efforts to bend politics to their interests, especially where the crisis has brought their legitimacy into question.

Political donations: cash for policies

It would be naïve to imagine that rich individuals and big businesses made political donations to parties purely out of admiration of their principles. They donate primarily in order to buy influence and to further their self-interest. They want some bang for their buck, not only to get their favoured party elected (donations always go up before elections) but to get the right policies. It is massively undemocratic: in effect, behind the scenes it's thousands of votes for a few who can get the ear of politicians, some of whom may be looking for lucrative directorships in the companies that lobby them. A quarter of the top 1,000 individuals on the Sunday Times Rich List in 2012 had donated a total of £83.6 million to political parties. As Tony Benn said, the wallet trumps the ballot.

The UK caps the amount that anyone can give to a political party, but big donors can get round this by routing donations via family members and companies. By these means, Sir Anthony Bamford and his family and companies donated nearly £4 million to the Conservative Party between 2001 and 2010. Top of the list of donors is Lord Irvine Laidlaw and companies, who donated over £6 million in that period.[9] Those who donate more than £50,000 to the Conservative Party join 'the Leader's Group', which entitles them to meet the party leader and other senior politicians at dinners and attend receptions and key political events. This group includes 57 individuals from the financial sector.[10]

Not surprisingly, given the return of the rich and the rise of finance from a supporting to a dominant role, political funding has both grown and changed in composition. Formerly the Tory party got most of its money from membership dues and local fundraising. Now it gets most from business. Financial sector donations have taken the lead, doubling under Cameron's leadership, to make up 50.8% of party funding,[11] with 27% coming from hedge funds and private equity.[12] In 2008, 77% of Boris Johnson's London mayoral campaign was funded by hedge funds and private equity firms. Are you surprised that Johnson is an opponent of regulation for the City?[13]

Things have changed for Labour, too. Where it once got 90% of its income from trade unions, under New Labour, this fell to 30% by 2001 as Tony Blair and allies managed to win over corporate donors by distancing themselves from Labour's working-class origins and ingratiating themselves with the rich.[14] Between 2001 and 2008, private equity bosses Sir Ronnie Cohen and Nigel Doughty contributed £1.8 million and £1 million respectively to Labour, the former Goldman Sachs partner John Aisbitt gave £750,000 and hedge fund executive William Bollinger gave £510,000. As Robert Peston commented: 'Tony Blair decided it was preferable for Labour to be financially dependent on wealthy individuals than on the party's trade union founders; but both forms of dependence can create conflicts of interest in the formulation of policy.'[15]

In the early years of New Labour a third of its highest-value donors were given government jobs of various types, and, as with Tory donors, many were given peerages or knighthoods. (The rich tend to be interested in symbolic capital as well as financial capital.) Things changed when the financial crash came and Labour lost power, and its corporate and individual donors fell away. In 2010, Labour's biggest donor, John Mills, owner of a shopping channel, gave Labour £1.65 million in his company's shares.[16] By 2013, only about 3% of donations to Labour came from companies, and 7% from individuals, though this is likely to rise before elections – if the party can persuade the plutocracy that it won't threaten them.

The union vote has of course been controversial: members of the 15 trade unions affiliated to the Labour Party pay a small sum each month (about 66p each in the biggest such union, UNITE), unless they opt out of doing so. (Those people who work for companies that give money to political parties – usually the Conservatives – can't opt out or have any say over donations, despite their contribution to the wealth from which the donations are made.) In 2012, £3 million of UNITE's £7 million political fund went to Labour in affiliation fees. In return, the union has a major influence in the election of Labour leaders. But, as the *Guardian*'s Aditya Chakrabortty points out, when it comes to policies, there's a difference from Tory donors here: whereas the big funders of the Tory party expect and usually get favours, the 15 trade unions that provide Labour with much of its funds get neoliberal policies that reduce the power of working people and allow the rich to take more.[17] Such is New Labour's embrace of the neoliberal agenda. At the time of writing, the Labour leadership is proposing to switch to an opt-in system that would be likely to slash the amount it receives from unions, though it would improve the democratic credentials of the funding.

In the US, things are bigger, of course – and worse, though at least they're a bit more transparent.[18] In the 2012 election each candidate spent more than $1 billion! Over 40% of donations to political parties in the US come from the top 0.01%.[19] In 2014 in the US, limits on individual donations for each election were raised from $123,000 to $3.6 million.[20] Both parties are funded by major companies secure in the knowledge that their sponsees will be compliant. After all, their targets have similar business interests: in 2011, the wealth list of the richest 50 Congress members was topped by Michael McCaul's $294 million, with Randy Neugebauer at 50th having a paltry $6 million. Mitt Romney, the Republican candidate, 'worth' at least $250 million, made his money through private equity, organising leveraged buyouts. His top five donors were all Wall Street banks. Meanwhile Barack Obama got $700,000 from each of Microsoft and Google and just over $1 million from Goldman Sachs.[21] Small hope, then, of getting any serious regulation of banks or of information technology monopolies.[22] Obama is reported also to have got $884,000 from oil and gas companies in the run-up to the 2008 election. The leading climate change denier in Senate, James Inhofe, was funded to the tune of half a million dollars over five years by fossil fuel energy companies, particularly Koch Industries, involved in oil, gas, minerals, timber and chemicals.[23] The Koch brothers also fund the lunatic fringe of the Republicans, the Tea Party. Amid all the noise of the last US election, candidates were eerily silent about climate change. This is plutocracy at its most brazen.

Charles Ferguson argues that in the United States both main parties are heavily funded by major companies, so that they both adopt similar neoliberal economic policies and differ significantly only on social issues.[24] Things are not so different in the UK, where both main parties are in thrall to the City and compete for the endorsement of Rupert Murdoch and other media oligarchs. What kind of democracy is this?

Fat cats in the snow: the World Economic Forum (WEF) at Davos

This is the place to be seen if you're super-rich or seeking to ingratiate yourself with them and influence them. The WEF is an invitation-only organisation comprising '1,000 of the world's top corporations, global enterprises usually with more than US$ 5 billion in turnover'.[25]

It describes itself as an 'independent international organization committed to improving the state of the world by engaging business, political, academic and other leaders of society to shape global, regional and industry agendas'.

But as Elizabeth Leafloor says: 'In practice, world leaders of business, banking, and politics gather *behind closed doors* and cement plans to benefit their interests while publicly celebrating their opportunistic solutions as global salvation.'[26] It's a forum for facilitating rent-seeking.

Each year we are treated to the nauseating spectacle of the super-rich and their hangers-on at Davos in the Swiss Alps, pretending to save the world while siphoning off more wealth from it. Over five days of 'pomp and platitude', 2,500 business executives, bankers, politicians, press and a handful of academics and charities jet and helicopter in to expand their contacts and look for opportunities. Discussing world problems like global warming, and even inequality, helps to present the plutocracy as benevolent prophets on the mountainside. Having a few sessions open to the media, and inviting some major charities and academics, helps to provide it with some legitimacy. Organisations like Oxfam, torn between doing so and legitimising the event and missing the chance to highlight the situation of the poor and powerless in the gaze of the world's press, opt for attending.

Forty heads of state attended Davos 2014. It's now become a venue for side meetings to address major geopolitical issues – like the Syrian crisis. Evidently a global plutocrats' forum is seen as an appropriate setting for them; at least business interests will be represented. (Well, plutocrat politicians are there anyway, so why not make global diplomacy come to them?) And business has major interests in wars, particularly resource wars, as was so clear in Halliburton's, G4S's and other companies' involvement in the Iraq war. Meanwhile, the governed are kept at bay through massive security.

Noam Chomsky contrasts the WEF with the alternative World Social Forum:

> The dominant propaganda systems have appropriated the term 'globalization' to refer to the specific version of international economic integration that they favor, which privileges the rights of investors and lenders, those of people being incidental. In accord with this usage, those who favor a different form of international integration, which privileges the rights of human beings, become 'anti-globalist.' This is simply vulgar propaganda . . . Take the World Social Forum, called 'anti-globalization' in the propaganda system – which happens to include the media, the educated classes, etc., with rare exceptions. The WSF is a paradigm example of globalization. It is a gathering of huge numbers of people from all over the world, from just about every corner of life one can think of, apart from the extremely narrow highly privileged elites who meet at the competing World Economic Forum, and are called 'pro-globalization' by the propaganda system.

Singer Bono had it right when he called Davos 'fat cats in the snow'.

The lattice of influence

The plutocracy makes use of a dense lattice of relationships between businesses, trade and professional organisations, think-tanks, lobbying firms, politicians, political party researchers and special advisors to politicians. Their members not only network with one another but shift between these organisations. Whether it's from business to lobbying and political posts, or politics to directorships and lobbying, each move expands their inside knowledge and connections, and their lobbying power. And of course, in addition to the lines of influence and career moves there are flows of money. Unprincipled and careerist politicians are easily seduced by promises of lucrative consultancies and positions. Predictably, the incestuousness of the lattice and its dominance by rich individuals and private businesses has a narrowing effect on their view of the world, pushing the experience of ordinary citizens into the background. In 2013–14 the UK government pressed ahead with a Bill facilitating secret lobbying by big business while restricting charities, campaigning groups and NGOs lobbying in the run-up to elections – another victory for plutocracy over democracy.

When ordinary people lobby politicians, it's generally about some matter or policy that they care deeply about: schools, planning, health services, the environment or issues of justice and fairness. Where business is concerned, lobbying is directed towards making more money, whether it's about tax or getting public sector contracts or generally seeking to steer policy in directions that increase its income. While many firms do their own lobbying, dedicated lobbying firms have become a £2 billion industry in UK. These work for private companies and rich individuals and are allowed by UK legislation to be extremely secretive about their identity and how much they provide.[27] Unlike campaigning organisations like Greenpeace that do lobbying, they conceal their sources of income and do not depend on donations from ordinary people.

Arguably, as Charles Ferguson claims, the main effect of lobbying comes not through the arguments it presents but from the lure for politicians of a lucrative job in the corporate sector when they leave government.[28] And how tempting it must seem after the grind, conflict, public scrutiny and unimpressive pay of a political career. But politicians under the spell of the plutocracy are not necessarily corrupt and swayed only by money or personal interest. They may already sincerely believe in the just world myth, and that the private sector is always better than the public sector. They may imagine that every financial 'investment' supports a real investment, that the financial sector is the new engine of capitalism, that what is good for the City/Wall Street is good for the UK/US, and that, despite the embarrassing stall of the crisis, it just needs a few minor tweaks

246

to power us forward again. The true believers may just regard their payments from business as rewards for already having a correct view of the world, and see political donations just as a means to defend this view in the next election. And it's not surprising that they hold these beliefs and still get elected, for the myths are pervasive and shared by many others – a product of a neoliberal capitalist worldview that has consolidated over nearly 40 years.

Private health companies have for years been pressuring New Labour and the ConDem coalition to privatise healthcare services in the National Health Service (NHS), so that the NHS becomes little more than a public façade for a host of private health companies. United Health UK, a branch of a US multinational private health firm, employed a political insider Simon Stevens and former health policy advisor to Tony Blair as its UK vice-president. Alan Milburn, Secretary of State for Health for New Labour, and a key driver of Private Finance Initiative deals on hospitals, became a paid advisor to Bridgenorth Capital, a private equity firm involved in financing private health services, and had links with Alliance Medical, Match Group, Medica and the Robinia Care Group. Patricia Hewitt, former Labour Health Secretary, became an advisor to Boots, the pharmacy company, and was paid £55,000 by Cinven, which bought 25 private hospitals from BUPA, the private health insurance company; she also joined the board of BUPA for another £52,000 for attending 10 board meetings a year – all while remaining a Member of Parliament. Former Health Minister Lord Warner is a non-executive chairman of UK Health Gateway, and also works as an advisor to Xansa and Byotrol, which also sell to the NHS. And the list goes on.[29]

Lynton Crosby, David Cameron's chief election strategist, is also a lobbyist working for a number of powerful clients, including private health companies, the tobacco industry and fossil fuel companies. In late 2010 he advised the health companies on how to exploit the 'failings' of the NHS, shortly before the government announced a new policy – unmentioned in its election manifesto – extending the privatisation of the service. In 2012, cuts (or rather, 'efficiency savings') of £20 billion to the NHS by 2015 were announced,[30] and a public campaign of broadcasting the failings of NHS hospitals was launched to try to weaken the loyalty of the British public to the NHS and ease the way for further privatisation. Having initially supported a plan to make plain packaging of cigarettes compulsory, Cameron later rejected it. The Coalition government also announced major tax breaks for gas fracking firms looking to operate in the UK. Fossil fuel energy companies have made sure that plenty of high-ranking politicians have financial interests in their businesses and, not surprisingly, low-carbon energy policies have been tokenistic at best.[31] One of the firms already prospecting in the UK was a subsidiary of a Crosby client. The Conservative Party denied any conflict of interest in Crosby's appointment and, in a way, it was right; as one would expect in a plutocracy, business and government interests are already in harmony.

Political capital for economic capital

Former Prime Minister Tony Blair – estimated wealth £70 million – has played an active lobbying role for companies since resigning as an MP.

As one of his former advisors, Geoff Mulgan, observes, 'Blair received a reputed £3.5 million a year as an advisor to JP Morgan, £0.5 million advising Zurich Financial, £1 million advising Kuwait, and an undisclosed sum advising private equity firm Khosla Ventures.... we can be safe in assuming that they weren't paying for his expertise in designing financial products.'[32] He has also advised the Kuwaiti royal family and the Kazakhstan dictatorship[33], and earns up to £250,000 per speaking engagement.

Although Blair is not mentioned in the following observation by Matthew Yglesias, it fits him perfectly:

> If you leave office held in high esteem by the Davos set, there are any number of European Commission or IMF or whatnot gigs that you might be eligible for even if you're absolutely despised by your fellow countrymen. Indeed, in some ways being absolutely despised would be a plus. The ultimate demonstration of solidarity to the 'international community' would be to do what the international community [that is, the plutocracy]

wants even in the face of massive resistance from your domestic political constituency.[34]

Not surprisingly, given the risks presented by the crisis, the financial sector is the most active lobbyist of government. The Bureau of Investigative Journalism discovered 129 organisations engaging in some form of lobbying for the finance sector in 2011, with over 800 people employed directly and at a cost of £92.8 million. Lobbyists include in-house bank staff, public affairs consultancies, industry body representatives, law firms and management consultants. They could rely on finding sympathetic ears in government: 'Some 124 peers, equivalent to 16% of the House of Lords, have direct financial links with financial services firms. On Lords committees scrutinising last year's budget, peers who were paid by finance firms formed the majority.'[35] The City of London Corporation, representing the financial sector, called in public relations and lobbying firm Quiller to do 'high profile, intensive crisis and reputation management'. Quiller is run by George Bridges, old Etonian, Oxford graduate and friend of George Osborne, and 2006 campaign director of the Conservative Party.

Mervyn King, outgoing Governor of the Bank of England, said this to the Treasury Select Committee in 2013: 'It's also important that banks don't leave conversations with the supervisors [that is, financial regulators] and feel that the next step is to telephone Number 11 [the Chancellor's official home] or even Number 10 Downing Street, and lobby officials or politicians to put pressure on the supervisors to back down on their judgements.' Pressed for detail, he said: 'There were certainly calls made to Number 11 and even in some cases to Number 10 to try and put pressure on supervisors to modify, "be more reasonable", in their judgements.'[36]

It was revealed that the four leading UK accountancy firms had provided MPs, political party offices and government departments with staff and consultants for free – a neat way of influencing policy without money being handed over. For instance, in 2009, 'George Osborne and then shadow minister MP Greg Hands received support from Deloitte in the form of "services and advice" provided in connection with a report that informed the Tories' March 2010 energy paper "Rebuilding Security" in which they promised, if elected, to reform taxation and licensing to promote offshore oil and gas development.'[37]

Among the important policy changes won by finance lobbyists in Whitehall and Westminster were:

- the slashing of UK corporation tax and taxes on banks' overseas branches, after a lobbying barrage by the City of London Corporation, the British Bankers' Association (BBA) and the Association of British Insurers. The reform will save the finance industry billions;
- the neutering of a national not-for-profit pension scheme launching in October that was supposed to benefit millions of low-paid and temporary workers;
- the killing of government plans for a new corporate super-watchdog to police quoted companies.[38]

The Reverend Stephen Green was employed by HSBC bank from 1992, becoming executive director of investment banking there from 2005, at the time of its drug-money laundering. He was made Lord Green of Hurstpierpoint, enabling him to sit in the House of Lords, where he became the unelected Minister of State for Trade and Investment in 2011, advising George Osborne, and a member of the cabinet committee on banking reform.[39] He has played a key role in encouraging companies to participate in the design of government policy. One innovation is the pairing of 80 or so top companies with key ministers, who have to meet them whenever they request it. There were 698 of these 'buddies' meetings in the first 18 months of the scheme.[40] Not surprisingly, the government does what the various finance, energy, food, pharmaceuticals and media companies want.

In 2013 it was learned that the government's subsidy policy for gas-burning power stations was being designed by an executive of ESB, a company that builds such power stations.[41] As George Monbiot argues, such developments go beyond lobbying, allowing companies to displace democratic processes and implant their own agendas in the heart of government.[42]

According to the Sunlight Foundation, the top twenty
banks and banking associations met with just three
agencies – the Treasury, the Federal Reserve, and the
Commodity Futures Trading Commission – an average
of 12.5 times per week, for a total of 1,298 meetings over
two-year period from July 2010 to July 2012. JP Morgan
Chase and Goldman Sachs alone met with those agencies
356 times. That's 114 more times than all the financial
reform groups combined.[43]

Think-tanks are another player in the lattice of influence, though,
despite carefully cultivated appearances, many differ little from
lobbying firms. Because the rich tend to be right wing and can out-
fund others, right-wing think-tanks predominate. They're typically
secretive about who funds them: that they 'rely on donations of
individuals and companies' is about all they'll reveal. Take the website
of Policy Exchange, a highly influential right-wing think-tank: it
fails to identify where it gets its money from, though it does say
'We are extremely proud of our independence. We do not accept
commissions or any public money.'[44] 'Independent' in think-tank-
speak means *dependent on rich individuals and companies who do not
want their identities made public*. It does acknowledge that there is one
supporting organisation called American Friends of Policy Exchange,
'a completely independent organisation that works across the political
spectrum'. Well, given the narrowing of the political spectrum
under neoliberalism, that's hardly impressive; it wants to influence
whoever has or is likely to get power, and it is confident that it can
succeed, whatever party is elected. It reassures anyone interested that
American Friends of Policy Exchange has full tax exemption status
under 501(c)3 of the Internal Revenue Code and is able to receive
tax-deductible donations.[45] Although such think-tanks are secretive
about funding you can get an impression of the revolving-door
phenomenon and their class position by looking up the profiles of
their key staff on their websites and what they have done previously
– often working for politicians, and having an Oxford degree.

Above all, think-tanks seek access to power by presenting
themselves as supposedly independent seekers of truth. In the US,

the billionaire Koch brothers – climate change deniers and owners of many polluting industries – are among the funders of the 'State Policy Network' with an $83 million network of right-wing think-tanks across every US state. Their spokespeople get presented as neutral 'experts' in the media. In the UK, the BBC's *Newsnight* often introduces representatives of right-wing think-tanks like the neoliberal Institute of Economic Affairs (IEA) as 'economists', while any members of left-wing think-tanks who get in are introduced as coming from 'left-leaning' organisations.[46] British American Tobacco paid the IEA £30,000 for opposing plain packaging of cigarettes. Standard Life Healthcare, now part of the private health firm PruHealth, lobbied for more 'insurance-based private funding' in the health service through the pro-market think-tank Reform. The Prudential, the insurance giant behind PruHealth, paid Reform £67,500 in 2012.[47]

Of course, many who work in think-tanks do have good intentions of making the world a better place, but in addition to the constraints of keeping funders happy, there is *realpolitik* to deal with too: if they want a hearing in policy circles they have to speak the language and negotiate the favoured framings and assumptions of their intended audience. Their careers depend on it.

The infiltration and capture of the state by the plutocracy has been a walkover rather than a struggle: politicians have fallen over themselves to invite them in, often under the pretext that successful business people have special skills not found in the public sector. The doors were flung wide open for them without the need of a Trojan horse. The political class is either from the rich class or in awe of it, and out of touch with the majority of voters. A statistical study of political influence in the US shows that senators, especially Republicans but also Democrats, are influenced overwhelmingly by the rich, only slightly by the middle classes and not at all by the bottom 30%.[48] In Britain, New Labour strategist Peter Mandelson infamously declared the party 'intensely relaxed about people getting filthy rich as long as they pay their taxes'. Of course, the qualification was quickly forgotten. Now even the suggestion of a 50% marginal tax on incomes above £150,000 brings a wave of condemnations as 'the politics of envy', penalising 'wealth creators' and driving them abroad. It's never been in doubt that the Conservatives were the political wing of the rich class, but the other major parties have become similarly obsequious to the rich.

SIXTEEN

Hiding it

> Where the labourers and artisans are accustomed to work for low wages, and to retain but a small part of the fruits of their labour, it is difficult for them, even in a free government, to better their condition, or conspire among themselves to heighten their wages. But even where they are accustomed to a more plentiful way of life, it is easy for the rich, in an arbitrary government, to conspire against them, and throw the whole burthen of the taxes on their shoulders. (David Hume, philosopher, and friend of Adam Smith, 1752)[49]

Tax havens, where many of the rich hide their wealth, are a major component of plutocracy.[50] They are not just places that happen to have low taxes, but *secrecy jurisdictions* in which financial wealth can be *hidden*. They conceal who owns this wealth, how much they own and where it comes from. The owners may be individuals, banks, corporations, drug cartels, the mafia or arms dealers, but their identities are hidden by front or 'shell' companies and 'offshore trusts'. According to research by ActionAid, in 2011, 98 of the top 100 companies listed on London's stock exchange used tax havens, with 4,492 of their overseas companies located in subsidiaries.[51] This doesn't mean that the money actually stays there, for once its original sources have been concealed it can be recirculated, usually back to major financial centres, to be 'invested'; but the ownership of that money is vested in anonymous companies registered offshore.

The Tax Justice Network estimates that in July 2012 at least US$21 trillion – and possibly as much as US$32 trillion – was hidden in tax havens by the world's wealthiest people. Such figures do not include 'the vast amount of wealth held in the form of real estate, superyachts, works of art and even racehorses that is "owned" by secretive offshore companies, trusts and foundations. An estimated c. $250 billion is lost in taxes each year by governments by wealthy individuals holding assets offshore.'[52]

Tax havens enable companies not only to avoid tax but to escape regulation of their activities, so they can do offshore what is illegal onshore. They provide a means for banks to hide their most risky, indeed reckless, activities off their balance sheets and avoid reserve requirements and other regulations. This is how the Northern Rock bank – bailed out by the UK government at a cost of £850 billion – concealed the risks it took. According to researchers Ronen Palan, Richard Murphy and Christian Chavagneux, half of all international bank lending is conducted via tax havens, and a majority of hedge funds are based in them.[53] The top four British banks had 1,649 subsidiaries in tax havens in 2011, including more than 300 offshore 'vehicles' for their own use, and many more for their customers.[54] This makes it extraordinarily difficult for regulators to monitor and discipline them – even if they wanted to. They have therefore played a major role in the financial crisis, and continue to pose a threat.

Such shell companies or trusts can be set up on a matter of days, sometimes simply by filling in online forms, or instantly, over the phone in some cases, thereby allowing transactions arranged in New York, London or wherever to be booked offshore, where they can escape taxes and regulations that would otherwise apply. No goods need flow through or be made in the havens. They just provide companies with legal identities that are bound by the havens' own, generally minimal rules, plus the vital ingredient of secrecy (or 'confidentiality', as they prefer to call it). Companies registered in tax havens are protected from scrutiny by stringent secrecy laws that are upheld by local officials firmly in the pocket of financial interests. In Switzerland it's a crime, punishable by prison, to break bank secrecy. The fact that such a company might be owned and run by, say, a British or German bank or multinational doesn't stop it being a separate legal entity. The tax havens can provide 'nominee directors' for the offshore companies to help hide their identities. Charging for such services is the basis of many tax havens' economies. The British Virgin Islands, for example, with a population of less than 25,000, is host to over 800,000 companies. There are examples of single buildings in tax havens providing the address of more than 1,000 companies.

Tax havens include not only exotic locations like the Cayman Islands or Mauritius but metropolitan financial centres such as the City of London and Zurich, and countries like Ireland, Luxembourg and Switzerland; some argue that the US and UK themselves and several other leading economies could be included.[55] 'Offshore' jurisdictions may actually be onshore, like the City, or the US states of Delaware, Nevada and Wyoming; most of the Fortune 500 top companies are registered in Delaware. According to the Tax Justice Network, in Nevada, there are no capital gains, gift tax, personal income tax and inheritance tax. In Wyoming, there are no corporate taxes, inventory taxes, unitary taxes, gift taxes, estate taxes, personal income taxes, franchise taxes and inheritance taxes.'[56]

Wherever they are located, tax havens operate not as distant, isolated enclaves but as highly connected elements of plutocratic networks. They are not minor aberrations or sideshows but integral parts of the neoliberal global economy, constructed with the connivance and sometimes the encouragement of the most powerful governments in the world. Just as Guantanamo Bay both is and is not part of the US, allowing the US government to do things it can't legally do on its own territory, tax havens have the protection and support of the major countries that sponsor them, but sufficient independence for their sponsors to claim that they are not their responsibility and hence are beyond their control.

The UK's tax haven network is the biggest of all, accounting for nearly half the 73 jurisdictions listed in the Financial Secrecy Index.[57] Nicholas Shaxson describes it as a spider's web with concentric rings of havens. There's an inner ring of 'Crown Dependencies': Jersey, Guernsey and the Isle of Man, then another ring of 'Overseas Territories' such as Bermuda, the Cayman Islands, Gibraltar, the British Virgin Islands, the Turks and Caicos Islands and Montserrat, and then an outer ring including Hong Kong and Singapore. Jersey alone has more than £400 billion stashed in offshore trusts. With zero tax for corporate profits of foreign firms, 'respectable' companies like Barclays, Marks and Spencer and ITV set up offshore trusts there.

The havens channel money, cleansed of evidence of its original source, to other centres, particularly the City of London, often by complex routes.

The City of London, or 'The Square Mile', arguably the largest financial centre in the world, is also the home of a unique local authority, known as the City of London Corporation. Unlike ordinary local authorities, it's not just its 9,000 or so residents who are able to vote in its elections but the companies located within it; indeed, they get votes proportional to their number of employees and together can easily outvote the residents! Thus, according to Shaxson, companies including foreign firms such as Goldman Sachs and the Bank of China can vote in these elections, though naturally their employees have no say in how they vote. The Corporation has funds of over £1.3 billion. Although it's officially charged with promoting and protecting the City's financial services sector at home and abroad, it is highly secretive about its own finances, although it did reveal in 2012 that it spent £12.8 million on 'City representation'. It operates as a hugely powerful lobbying agency for financial interests.[58] Uniquely, it has an official, known as the 'remembrancer', with an annual budget of £6 million, who is allowed to sit in the House of Commons and vet legislation to protect the interests of the City.[59] The Corporation has been immensely successful in its mission, though it got a helping hand in 1996 from Tony Blair, who reversed the Labour Party's long-standing opposition to it and endorsed and extended its power.[60]

The position of the City at the centre of the UK's tax haven network is reflected in the webpage of Mark Boleat, the Corporation's current Policy and Resources Committee chair and chief lobbyist: it tells us that he was born in Jersey, was formerly a member of the Gibraltar Financial Services Commission and currently has non-executive positions that include the States of Jersey Development Company and Chair of the Channel Islands Competition and Regulatory Authorities.[61]

'Transfer pricing' – or 'mis-pricing' – is another key to the havens' existence. Multinational companies can play off countries against each other to minimise tax by rigging their accounts. They can shift profits across borders to where taxes are lowest, minimising their declared profits where taxes are relatively high – even if those places are also where they do most business. Let's say a company does much of its business in country A, where profits are relatively highly taxed. It then:

1. sets up an operation in country B, a tax haven;
2. gets the branch in B to bill the branch in A for some service rendered. The amount B charges A should be enough to push up A's costs so that it has no profit to tax, or as little as it reckons it can get away with without attracting too much scrutiny;
3. result: the profits are safely transferred to B, where they largely escape tax.

In 2012 Starbucks admitted that its British sales revenue was $398 million, but paid no corporation tax on this, because it channelled revenue to other countries. For example, it paid royalties, which were deductible from taxable income, to a unit in the Netherlands, appearing as costs to the UK operations. When this came under fire from the public, the company graciously deigned to make a 'voluntary' payment of £20 million to the British government over two years – and without any discussion from the British tax authorities.[62]

In 2011, Amazon, with its European headquarters located in Luxembourg, reported $11.6 billion in European revenue (equivalent to €8.9 billion at the time of writing), but posted a relatively miniscule after-tax profit of €20 million on those sales and thus paid tax worth only about €8 million. So, effectively, its tax rate was just over 0.1% of its sales![63]

Like all companies and other organisations, these businesses depend on a workforce and a customer-base that is educated, a health system that keeps their workers healthy and a public infrastructure, including a legal system. While the little people pay their taxes for all these things and more, many incredibly wealthy companies free-ride on them.

The double Irish and the Dutch sandwich

Google's sixth 'core value' is: 'Do the right thing: don't be evil. Honesty and Integrity in all we do. Our business practices are beyond reproach. We make money by doing good things.'[64]

Google cut its taxes by US$3.1 billion, using a technique that moves most of its foreign profits through Ireland and the Netherlands to Bermuda. These strategies, known to lawyers as the double Irish and the Dutch sandwich, helped Google to reduce its overseas tax rate to 2.4%.[65]

Margaret Hodge, who chairs the UK parliament's Public Accounts Committee, took Google's UK Vice-President, Matt Brittin, to task over this: 'You are a company that says you "do no evil". And I think that you do do evil.' Hodge, who has repeatedly challenged rich and irresponsible business leaders, was condemned by the Treasury for 'grandstanding' and scaring off foreign investment.[66]

Transfer pricing is a business in itself: in 2009, accountancy firm Ernst & Young employed 900 staff just on working out transfer pricing packages to sell to companies.[67] Many major multinationals each employ hundreds of lawyers and accountants to work out ever more ingenious ways of avoiding tax. Yet at the time, the UK's tax authority, Her Majesty's Revenue and Customs (HMRC), employed only 600 workers to check the affairs of 700 companies, and only about 100 of those deal with tax avoidance. In 2011, its budget was cut by £3 billion. But then, back in 2005 Gordon Brown, the Chancellor of the Exchequer, had obsequiously reassured the Confederation of British Industry that the government would apply 'not just a light touch, but a limited touch' to financial regulation, and to tax too. He went on to reassure his audience that he rejected the old assumption that business, unregulated, will invariably act irresponsibly.[68] In so doing he was joining in the beggar-thy-neighbour game of trying to attract companies from overseas to come to the UK. HMRC was then making job cuts of 25,000. This was completely false economy, for in 2008 its so-called 'large business service recovered 92 times its costs', while 'the "special investigations section" fighting the most complex avoidance cases had yielded 450 times its costs'.[69] Even so, the plutocracy successfully disarmed or evaded the fiscal police.

When defending their practices, companies using tax havens to avoid or evade tax typically use two excuses. One is that their practices are 'not illegal'. You might think that means that what they're doing is legal. But that's not necessarily the case: it may just mean that the practices have not yet been tested in a court of law. And so many avoidance and evasion schemes are being devised by teams of expert accountants that it's hard for any legal system to keep up with them. 'Avoidance' is not illegal, 'evasion' is illegal, but when the systems are deliberately opaque, it's hard to tell which category they fit, though avoidance certainly goes against the spirit of the law. The second myth is that corporations have a duty to avoid tax in order to meet their obligation to maximise shareholder value. But there is no such obligation in law.

Tax havens compete with one another to attract the rich and their wealth, creating a race to the bottom ('tax competition') that continually pressures other countries to lower their own taxes, or at least those that most affect the rich. Escaping financial regulations also creates a race to the bottom to deregulate onshore economies. Rates of corporation tax have fallen across the rich countries since the 1970s. Companies that hide activities offshore can undercut those companies that actually do pay their tax; those that do pay may complain but, not surprisingly, many decide that if they can't beat them, they may as well join them. This of course means that either 'the little people' have to pay more tax, or their governments cut spending on the welfare support that guarantees them some security and public services. We see both responses across Europe and in the US. Hence, billionaire Warren Buffett's complaint that his secretary pays more tax than he does.

Tax havens haemorrhage money from developing countries too, not only by allowing multinationals operating in such countries to avoid tax, but by allowing dictators and corrupt local elites to hide money offshore, often money that was given as aid for development – though the lenders might not mind if it's hidden in their own secret subsidiaries. Lost tax revenues far exceed overseas aid, so before people point to the failures of aid, they need to look at illicit flows of capital. In the UK in 2012, the Commonwealth Development Corporation, the private-sector arm of the government's aid programme, routed nearly half of its investments in developing countries through Mauritius, the Cayman Islands, Luxembourg, Guernsey, Jersey and Vanuatu.[70] Investigators at the Global Financial Integrity Unit (GFIU) estimated that developing countries lost $859 billion in 2010 tax evasion, crime, corruption and other illicit activity.[71] Contrary to the usual assumption, Africa is a net creditor to the global economy. Oxfam estimates that tax havens are depriving the world of £100 billion in lost revenue – lower than the GFIU figure, but enough to end extreme poverty in the world twice over.[72]

Banks and drug money

The UK's HSBC bank laundered billions for South American drug cartels and for Iran by using tax havens. While it paid a fine (or 'settlement') of £1.25 billion ($1.9 billion) to the US – not to the UK, which failed to investigate – the bank escaped criminal convictions, prompting the charge that bank bosses were too big to jail. In the US, Wachovia, a subsidiary of the Wells Fargo Bank, admitted to laundering more than $378 billion for Mexican drug gangs. At the same time it got $8 billion in tax breaks.[73]

Every now and then, governments make threatening noises about secrecy jurisdictions, vowing to force them to make their business transparent. This would be a formidable task, because unless there were a clamp-down on all havens simultaneously, money would just move to those that escaped. A vast amount of political and economic clout is invested in their continued secrecy and operation. And even where (supposedly) onshore governments do have some leverage, as the UK does over its tax haven network, they can always use the half-truth of the independence of the havens to excuse their failure to do anything about them. But it's also precisely because the havens belong to networks involving the great financial and corporate centres of the world that governments in such centres have a perverse incentive to allow the arrangements to continue. The City of London, itself a tax haven at the centre of the UK network, so lavishly praised by the government before the crash for being the most dynamic sector in the economy, benefits hugely from the inflows of extracted wealth from the other havens.

But then, what would you expect from a government that, like so many, had been captured by a plutocratic elite?

The Prime Minister's father: a tax avoidance specialist

David Cameron's father, Ian Cameron, moved from stockbroking (that is, serving rentiers) into organising tax avoidance while Cameron junior was at Eton. By setting up companies in Panama, Jersey and Geneva in which to hide his own wealth and that of rich clients, he and his clients avoided paying UK taxes. In both 2012 and 2013, Cameron junior began claiming that he would get tough on tax avoidance, though nothing of any substance has resulted from this. Cameron senior left £2.74 million in his will, of which his son got £300,000. How much in addition is held offshore is unclear, though in 2009 Ian Cameron's wealth was estimated at £10 million by the Sunday Times Rich List. He was chair of Close International Asset management, a multimillion-pound investment fund based in Jersey; a senior director of Blairmore Holdings Inc, registered in Panama City and currently worth £25 million; and also a shareholder in Blairmore Asset Management, based in Geneva.[74] (Blairmore was the name of the family's former home in Scotland.)

> 'I do not think it is fair any longer to refer to any of the overseas territories or Crown dependencies as tax havens.' (David Cameron, 10 September 2013 in response to a question in the House of Commons about tax havens)[75]

In 2009, Lord Myners, the government minister charged with stopping corporate tax avoidance, was found to be part-time chair of an offshore company that avoided over £100 million a year in taxes.[76] Lord Blencathra, a former Conservative minister with close links to the government, is simultaneously sitting as a peer in the House of Lords and lobbying on behalf of a Caribbean tax haven. Despite being paid by the Cayman Islands government to represent the interests of its financial services industry, he is able to vote on UK legislation affecting the territory.[77] The Cayman Islands are estimated to be home to 70% of the world's hedge fund registrations.

In September 2012, having given £2.6 million to the Conservative Party, Lord Fink, the then party treasurer and hedge fund boss, lobbied for lower company tax so that the UK could compete with tax havens. Fink is also a director of three firms that have a subsidiary or parent company in the Cayman Islands, Luxembourg and Guernsey. This is not unusual: 67 other peers and MPs have interests in tax havens. Lord Fink argued: 'I don't see why the UK should not compete for jobs that at present are going to the Cayman Islands. I lobbied George Osborne [Chancellor of the Exchequer] when the Tories were in opposition. I have long felt that the British government loses jobs to tax havens by allowing the Revenue to have these rather archaic rules [that is, that businesses should actually pay their taxes]'.[78] (Actually, even if he really did care about jobs, it's very unlikely that they would go to the Cayman Islands – population 57,000.) 'If you want to be a successful business and attract invisible earnings to the UK, you have to be based offshore.'[79] While Lord Fink clearly wanted Britain to become a tax haven, he meant this only for the rich; the rest who pay taxes would remain firmly onshore. Someone has to bail out the banks and pay for education, health, local authorities, the legal system, defence and social services, after all.

Lord Fink's words did not go unheeded: having cut the UK corporation tax to 21% in December 2012 (it was 28% in 2010), George Osborne, the Chancellor of the Exchequer, cut the tax paid by UK multinationals on profit attributed to offshore arms that make loans to other units to 5.75% in January 2013, thereby making it even more worthwhile to shift income to tax havens![80] In March 2013, he publicly denounced aggressive tax avoidance as 'morally repugnant'.[81]

The world of offshore, and hiding one's wealth in trusts, is so far from the experience of ordinary people that it's not surprising that it's hardly an election issue. But high-profile cases of major companies like Starbucks, Apple, Amazon and Google paying miniscule amounts of tax in some of the countries where their sales are biggest have forced the issue into the news. When complaints about tax havens rise, governments can pretend to deplore them too, and promise to take action, while continuing to support them under the table. Researchers Palan, Murphy and Chavagneux describe tax havens as 'a massive organized attempt by the richest and most powerful to take advantage of collective goods on a scale rarely seen'.[82] They are another means by which the rich free-ride on the rest of us, enjoying the benefits of public spending funded by taxes that we, the little people, pay. They undermine attempts to regulate banking so as to protect customers. They support plutocracy over democracy.

From the UK's Centre for Economics and Business Research

'In an age of financial market liberalisation, more sophisticated financial products and easier access to wealth management services, high-income individuals can now tap into new means of reducing their tax burden. Income Tax has essentially become a voluntary tax, where individuals can opt-out by utilising financial products.'[83]

The report opposed the plan to raise the top rate of income tax in the UK to 50%.

SEVENTEEN

Legal corruption: above the law or making the law?

> When plunder becomes a way of life for a group of men living in society, they create for themselves, in the course of time, a legal system that authorizes it and a moral code that glorifies it. (Frédéric Bastiat, French writer and economist)[84]

> It is not wisdom, but Authority that makes a law. (Thomas Hobbes)[85]

Insider dealing; laundering drug money; evading sanctions against rogue states; taking over companies to load them up with debt, and raiding their pension funds; designing products that were doomed to fail in order to bet on them failing, or taking insurance out on other businesses' products failing, and helping to undermine them so as to cash in; mis-selling mortgages and payment protection insurance (mostly useless but very profitable); credit rating agencies having a financial interest in the companies they are rating; fixing interest rates on interbank lending so as to conceal banks' true position and maximise profits; engaging in trades that would make short-term gains while undermining long-term growth; forcing small business borrowers out of business so as to get their property and sell it ...

Are these practices criminal? Many are not actually illegal, amazing though it may seem, and hence not officially criminal, though we might regard them as such. In the case of tax, avoidance is not illegal, but evasion is illegal; or as former Chancellor of the Exchequer Denis Healey put it, the difference is 'the thickness of a prison wall'. It's hard to tell when business is allowed so much secrecy. (Interestingly, though, many important models in mainstream economic theory assume that people have perfect information.) New and evermore ingenious ways of avoiding or evading tax are continually being dreamt up by teams of experts, many of them in major accountancy and audit firms, indeed this is a competitive strategy. My colleague Bob Jessop calls it 'criminnovation'.[86]

That many of these practices are not illegal speaks volumes about the capture of the state and the regulatory system by the financial sector. Daniel Kaufmann, President of the Revenue Watch Institute and a former Director at the World Bank speaks of 'legal corruption'. This refers to

> efforts by companies and individuals to shape law or policies to their advantage, often done quasi-legally, via campaign finance, lobbying or exchange of favors to politicians, regulators and other government officials. It is dealings between venal politicians and powerful financial and industrial executives. In its more extreme form, legal corruption can lead to control of entire states, through the phenomenon dubbed 'state capture,' and result in enormous losses for societies.[87]

In democracies in the shadow of plutocracy, it would be naïve to suppose that the law is impartial. Since the 1980s, governments have been persuaded by a succession of different interests in the financial sector to deregulate finance, to allow free mobility of capital, to pull down the safety walls between high street banking and investment or casino banking, and to allow all manner of risky financial products to be traded. But there was always also re-regulation, only in favour of the big players. Lawyers have profited handsomely from drafting secrecy rules that tax havens use to protect the businesses they hide.

All this has happened in piecemeal fashion – again with no conspiracy or central organisation. At first it all looked unproblematic, in fact, the sector boomed: deregulation appeared to work. There were a few crises, but nothing to come close to 2007. The impressive expansion of the sector's revenue seemed to justify everything.

In the US, Michael Hudson comments,

> Predatory finance has concentrated wealth and used it to buy control of governments and their regulatory agencies. It even has taken over the Justice Department and the courts, so that financial fraud in America has been decriminalized. Bank lobbyists back the campaigns of politicians committed to deregulating banking and its major clients (real estate, natural resources and monopolies). So there is no regulation of outright criminal behavior even by the largest banks such as Citicorp and Bank of America where fraud was concentrated.[88]

The City's and Wall Street's escape from the threat of serious restructuring is a function not only of their control of the commanding heights of the economy and their colonisation of the polity and the networks influencing policy, but also of their success in constructing a *story* of success – in which, whatever the turmoil of the crisis, the sector remained vital to the future as the powerhouse of their respective economies. Beginning in the 1980s, the financial sector built up a narrative celebrating the success of 'free markets' and the 'masters of the universe' – the CEOs, 'rainmakers', star traders and fund managers – who knew how to play them. Endlessly replayed and embellished in the media, from news programmes to Hollywood films, the narrative became part of popular culture. Even if it was often more tolerated than celebrated, the greed, arrogance and brashness of it all were seen as compensated for by the benefits it supposedly brought to economies. Even if what the confident men in shirts and red braces, standing in front of the rows of computer monitors, were saying sounded dubious, or simply went over people's heads, it was assumed that their specialist expertise couldn't be challenged.

The counterpoint in the narratives was always manufacturing, sneeringly called 'metal-bashing' and the like, backward and just so last century; the future lay in the arcane world of finance, intelligible only to exceptionally clever people, whose dazzling success would produce wealth that benefitted all. But in the UK, the sector actually employs many fewer people than does manufacturing, its numbers have flat-lined for two decades and it pays less tax.[89] And, mediocre though British manufacturing's performance has been, it has never saddled the country with a bill of the magnitude of that created by finance.

In academia, economists, at least mainstream ones, provided justifications for deregulation by reference to the theory of 'efficient markets', a bizarre theory based on if-pigs-could-fly assumptions in which financial markets correctly assess all relevant information, correctly estimate risk and allocate resources, provided the state does not interfere.[90] Some of their theories were put into practice in the construction of financial markets, so, rather than being external academic observers, some economists were part of the game and making money for major financial businesses. In the US, certain leading mainstream economists, as true believers, traded on the symbolic capital of their academic credentials and moved between university posts, jobs with major financial institutions and positions as regulators and government advisors – Alan Greenspan, Glenn Hubbard, Larry Summers, Frederic Mishkin and Laura Tyson. The revolving doors were spinning. No wonder mainstream economists have been mouse-like in their criticism of the financial system, as they had been important players in it. As Phil Mirowski has shown, they had too much investment – financial as well as intellectual – in the system to repudiate it; blunting the critical knives was a way of protecting their own discipline.[91] But then, it was hardly surprising that the growth of business schools in universities and the shift of economics departments into them – itself one of the most obvious indications of the infection of universities by neoliberalism – would push them into the embrace of business. And why should economists who believe in the primacy and universality of self-interest let truth get in the way of pursuing it?[92] Those who think academics should help businesses should draw a lesson from their role in the crisis.

Over the last four decades, successive UK governments have been mesmerised by the financial sector, fêting it as the shiny new engine of the UK economy. A string of top politicians from both main parties gushed over its achievements. In a speech before the financial crisis, Prime Minister Tony Blair obligingly complained about *over-regulation* of finance: 'Something is seriously awry ... when the Financial Services Authority [FSA] that was established to provide clear guidelines and rules for the financial services sector and protect the customer against the fraudulent, is seen as hugely inhibiting of efficient business by perfectly respectable companies that have never defrauded anyone.'[93]

Actually, the FSA – more of a lapdog than a watchdog – failed miserably in holding back the construction of the house of cards; it was both ill-equipped in terms of expertise and reluctant to investigate and prosecute.[94]

So extensive has been the capture of the state, that even after the crash, the deepest recession for 80 years and a succession of scandals, the political classes still regard the financial sector as the golden goose, merely in need of better care. Even in opposition, New Labour remains anxious to reassure us – or the City – that finance will be in safe hands. But then, at the same time as leader Ed Miliband was giving speeches distinguishing 'predators' in the financial sector from 'producers', New Labour was courting a donation of £1 million from tax exile and property tycoon Andrew Rosenfeld.[95]

Saving 'our' City

One way of ducking questions of legality, let alone ethics, is to argue that if we don't take advantage of these opportunities, others will, to our cost (the everybody's-doing-it defence): if practice x is not allowed in the City, *we* will lose out to *them* – Wall Street, or Frankfurt, wherever they still allow it. Apart from the blatantly unethical character of the response, it's important to ask who 'we' is here. Actually, it's not most of us who can take advantage of these 'opportunities', but certain elements of the financial elite, and although they like to claim that we share the same interests, we don't, for as we saw, the City is more cuckoo-in-the-nest than golden goose. To be sure, our savings and pensions are an important source of funds for the sector, but the very notion that the City is 'ours' needs to be questioned.[96]

The lack of criminal prosecutions is extraordinary. Where charges are brought, say for fraud, the usual practice is for the bank to get an out-of-court settlement – a cheap way of avoiding admitting criminal liability. Michael Hudson comments again:

> Nearly every large Wall Street bank has paid large sums of money to settle fraud cases without admitting criminal liability for their huge gains. So no banker has gone to jail. The top executives know that if they are convicted of billions of dollars of fraud, their banks will pay a fraction of this amount, not themselves. So the bank still makes a bundle even after paying the nominal fine, letting the culprits keep their salaries, bonuses and stock options for writing junk mortgages and operating in a manner that would have sent them to jail back in the 1980s.[97]

But the UK is notably softer on financial crime. It was US investigators who brought the involvement of British banks in the Libor interest-rate rigging and money-laundering scandals to light, so that they have paid more in fines to the US than the UK. In the case of the highly profitable but mostly worthless payment protection insurance deceitfully (mis-)sold to UK borrowers, the total that banks will have to pay back reached an estimated £16 billion in 2013.[98]

Too big to jail; *or* One rule for the rich and ...

Fred Goodwin, former boss of the failed RBS, bailed out by UK taxpayers at a cost of £45 billion, merely lost his knighthood and had his pension cut from £703,000 to £342,500 per year. As Michael Meacher points out, the standard penalty for a burglar who stole one ten millionth of this – £4,500 – would be jail, normally for four years.[99] Nine thousand jobs have subsequently been lost at RBS.

Nicholas Robinson, an electrical engineering student with no criminal record, was jailed for six months for stealing bottles of water worth £3.50 during the riots in London in August 2011. While the UK government has yet to prosecute any bankers, it immediately set up 24-hour courts to try those arrested in the riots.

Is it the culture?

A common response in the media is to bemoan greed and the get-rich-quick character of the 'culture' of the financial sector, which many celebrated or at least tolerated in the financial boom, and to wonder whether and how banking can be made more ethical. To be sure, greed has become rampant and it is indeed shocking that so many leading figures in the sector scarcely seem to know what ethics is, so imbued are they with self-righteousness, entitlement and arrogance, or when the occasion demands it, faux-humility and protestations of helplessness.

Financial sadism

In 2012, Greg Smith, Head of Equity Derivatives at Goldman Sachs, resigned in disgust at the growth of a culture in which clients were called 'muppets' and the prime concern of the company was to maximise what it could take from them, regardless of whether the products benefitted them, and employees enthused about 'ripping their eyeballs out'.[100]

But the problem is not just negligent or reckless individuals, or cocaine-fuelled traders, ever seeking to rout competitors and clients, but *the 'criminogenic environment' of the financial system*.[101] Tax havens, for example, are deliberately constructed with the covert patronage of the UK, US and other major governments, and though their main purpose is to help the rich and corporations to hide wealth and dodge tax, they are also a safe refuge for drug money, illegal arms-trade cash and the harvests of fraud. To ignore this environment is to miss the elephant in the room – the structure of the system itself, and the sector's capture of the regulatory system, so that what would otherwise be defined as illegal is not. Yes, there is a problem with the very 'culture' of the financial system. It comes from the financial pressures and opportunities that make such behaviour probable. Deregulated, neoliberal finance actively encourages malpractice. In volatile, fiercely competitive financial markets, with constant pressure for short-term gains that deliver shareholder value, ruthlessness, including aggressive tax avoidance and/or evasion, is essential for success, at both corporate and individual level.

Hormonal traders

The financial sector is and has always been male dominated, macho and mean, but it is becoming more so. Since the crisis, a new drug of choice, after cocaine, has emerged among financial executives and traders wanting to be alpha males: testosterone. Several clinics that used to offer it as treatment for impotence are now providing it to traders wanting to stay aggressive, confident and decisive throughout their 12-hour working days.[102] This of course makes them even more likely to take extreme risks and act irresponsibly and unethically.

Worrying about ethics and wider consequences would mean playing the sucker and losing out to rivals. In the upper reaches of the financial sector, and particularly in investment banking, the system attracts the ethically challenged and moulds individuals to be still more selfish and myopic. The wider social costs of their private actions simply don't come into the equation. This is why media handwringing about ethics rather than the system itself must have many members of the financial sector privately rolling their eyes – or smirking. The fact that banks are too big to fail, so that they can privatise gains and offload losses (and boost their credit rating as a result), is a systemic problem, not one of rogue traders or arrogant CEOs, or indeed merely of bonuses. While all advanced economies need a financial sector, there is always a risk that it will change from servant to master, and the more that making money out of money – especially through claims on future wealth – is detached from the real economy and deregulated, the more likely this is to happen.

Warm bath or icy waters?

In advertising to ordinary consumers, the banking industry goes to great lengths to hide its self-serving character by making lavish TV commercials in which ordinary but attractive people do life-affirming things, like starting families and decorating their new houses, helping their communities and embracing their ethnic others in striking expressions of public joy and warmth. (Try putting 'Halifax advert videos' in your search engine.) Who knew that the generous 'gift' of a 25-year mortgage at 5% interest could bring such joy? Nothing could be further from the reality of global finance, where 'the icy waters of egotistical calculation', as Marx and Engels called it, hold sway.[103]

In addition to the pressures and huge incentives to make profit by any means possible, a little-noted feature of the culture of the financial sector is not just the arrogance but the ignorance of so many of its senior members, though of course the two are related. It was not only that bosses had limited understanding of their most exotic products, but something more general: a kind of 'money-illusion', in which getting more money – that is, bigger claims on the wealth produced by others – is mistaken for creating wealth. They deceived themselves as well as others.[104]

To acknowledge the importance of the criminogenic environment and the hopelessly limited ways of thinking available to people is not to excuse individuals. It's not a case of responsibility lying with *either* individuals *or* the system; *both* deserve our anger and concern. And there have been whistle-blowers and conscientious objectors. But individuals are easier to identify than complex systems, so the popular media, congenitally impatient, seek individual scapegoats and ignore the system, which of course suits the financial elite fine, for it leaves its enabling structure intact.

Don't blame Adam

The wise and virtuous man is at all times willing that his own private interest should be sacrificed to the public interest of his own particular order or society. (Adam Smith)[105]

Adam Smith is not only the founder of economics but one of our most misrepresented thinkers, regularly invoked as a one-eyed apologist for the pursuit of self-interest, or even selfishness, by both the Right and the Left. Anyone who actually reads his work can see this is grossly unfair.

Poachers as gamekeepers

At the height of the crisis it was easy to imagine that, given the catastrophic malfunctioning of the financial sector, it would be rigorously investigated and radically disciplined and restructured by the state. Many have offered diagnoses and a few have called 'foul!', but scarcely any senior figures have been prosecuted, and the remedies have been superficial and limited.

As the crisis in Europe deepened, democratically elected leaders in Italy and Greece were replaced by so-called 'technocrats'. The word makes it seem that all that had to be dealt with was technical, engineering problems, not issues of political economic power, so it was supposedly legitimate for politicians to hand over to technical experts for a while, for the politicians were both ignorant of the financial system's working and too biased by political ties to do what was necessary. Hudson describes it as 'a scientific sounding euphemism for bank lobbyists'.[106] In effect, the technocrats protected the rule of the rich from the threat of democratic reaction.

Goldman Sachs' European reach

In a famous article on Goldman Sachs in *Rolling Stone*, Matt Taibbi wrote: 'The world's most powerful investment bank is a great vampire squid wrapped around the face of humanity, relentlessly jamming its blood funnel into anything that smells like money.'[107]

It also ensured that it was represented far and wide in politics. In the US, Goldman Sachs men Robert Rubin and Hank Paulson both served periods of office as Treasury Secretary.[108] But it has also had extensive influence in Europe. Here are just some of the more prominent examples, mostly from 2011:

Mario Monti – the 'technocrat' – was imposed as Prime Minister of Italy in 2011 in place of the absurd but democratically elected Silvio Berlusconi. Previously, in 1995 Monti had been appointed by Berlusconi to the European Commission, where he was involved in regulating competition and mergers and acquisitions. He later chaired an Italian

Treasury Committee on the financial sector. Given his strategic importance, Goldman Sachs invited him to be an international advisor, and, of course, lobbyist.

Italian banker Mario Draghi's posts have included President of the European Central Bank in 2011 and Managing Director of the Italian central bank, and he was a member of the World Bank, interspersed and overlapping with positions at Goldman Sachs. Like Monti, he has an American PhD in mainstream economics. He was involved in the controversy over attempts by the Italian and Greek governments, aided by Goldman Sachs, to conceal the extent of their public debt by using complex derivatives. Hiding this debt was crucial for Greece's being allowed to join the euro in 2001, and for this Goldman Sachs got $300 million. It was assisted by the head of the Greek central bank, Luke Papademos, who was later appointed Prime Minister. On the Greek side, another former Goldman Sachs employee, Petros Christodoulou, Head of Greece's debt management agency, was also alleged to be involved.

Peter Sutherland, Attorney General of Ireland in the 1980s and another former EU Competition Commissioner, is now non-executive chairman of Goldman Sachs' UK-based broker-dealer arm, Goldman Sachs International; until its collapse and nationalisation he was also a non-executive director of RBS.

Belgian Karel van Miert, former EU Competition Commissioner, was an advisor to Goldman Sachs. So was Otmar Issing, former board member of Germany's Bundesbank, economic advisor to Angela Merkel, and one of the creators of the euro.[109] Antonio Borges, former head of the International Monetary Fund's European division, was previously vice-chairman of Goldman Sachs International. Since 1985, three European commissioners for competition have been Goldman Sachs men.

In the UK, Lord Griffiths is another international advisor to Goldman Sachs, and Vice-Chairman of Goldman Sachs International. He is a director of Times International Holdings Limited, former professor at the London School of Economics, former Dean at City University Business School, and was a director of the Bank of England from 1983 to 1985.

Between 1985 and 1990, he was the head of Prime Minister Margaret Thatcher's Policy Unit, where he 'was a chief architect of the government's privatization and deregulation programs'. In 2009, following a record-breaking $22 billion that was given out to Goldman Sachs executives and leadership in payment and bonuses, Lord Griffiths told a British audience that they should 'tolerate the inequality as a way to achieve greater prosperity for all'.[110]

In 2013, Mark Carney, a Canadian and former Goldman Sachs man, became the new Governor of the Bank of England.

In recognition of its achievements, Goldman Sachs won the 2013 Public Eye's Jury Naming and Shaming award.[111]

The financial sector was remarkably successful in policing itself, and hence in minimising change. In the UK, the Bischoff and Wigley official reports on the crisis were overwhelmingly written by City insiders, who used the opportunity to replay the story of the City as golden goose, and hence deserving support. Bischoff was a former Chair of Citigroup, and Wigley, European Chair of Merrill Lynch. Likewise the anodyne 'Independent [sic] Commission on Banking'.[112] Even when Northern Rock and the RBS were nationalised, the threat of democratic influence that might steer the banks towards funding real investment was blocked by elite City figures in the newly established United Kingdom Financial Investments. Where previously they sought to 'create' value for private shareholders, they now did this for taxpayers as shareholders, with the goal of re-privatising the banks in future. Meanwhile, in Europe, the financial elite dominated economic policy, and politicians from each country, anxious to defend 'their banks', complied with the demands of creditors, at the expense of the wider public and the public sector.

In the US, Barack Obama came to power in 2009, two years after the start of the crash. With several banks taken into public ownership and the sector on the back foot, there was an opportunity for some radical measures, but instead of appointing any economists who had been critical of the financial sector, he appointed several insiders to key government posts. The biggest cheese was Larry Summers as

Director of the National Economic Council. As Charles Ferguson explains,[113] Summers has an interesting record: a Harvard economics professor and sometime Harvard President, and a former Chief Economist at the World Bank, he

- advocated cutting corporation tax and unemployment insurance;
- supported (while at the World Bank) the idea of rich nations exporting pollution to poor countries on the grounds that thinly populated African countries were 'underpolluted';
- denied anthropogenic climate change and resource limits;
- suggested women were inferior to men at scientific reasoning (for which he later apologised);
- actively promoted the deregulation of derivatives that turned out to be toxic (those that Harvard 'invested' in while he was President dropped in value by $1 billion dollars[114]), and endorsed the removal of barriers between retail and investment banking;
- lobbied energetically for a range of financial businesses to which he gave lavishly paid speeches; in 2008 he made $1.7 million from 31 speaking engagements (Goldman Sachs paid him $135,000 for one speech);
- before his appointment by Obama worked one day a week at a hedge fund for over $5 million a year, while holding his chair at Harvard.

Ferguson estimates that he made $20 million from hedge funds and investment banks. Predictably he opposed sanctions on bankers and restrictions on their income, and advocated tax cuts rather than infrastructure investment to kick-start growth.

Bastions of propriety or tax dodgers' attack dogs?

Accountants and auditors tend to be portrayed in popular culture as boring and nerdy, but utterly sound individuals. External auditors of public organisations and small firms may be feared but respected.

But when it comes to the big four companies that dominate accountancy and auditing for global capital – KPMG, PricewaterhouseCoopers (PwC),

Deloitte Touche Tohmatsu, and Ernst and Young, we encounter a different world. And I don't mean their much-publicised 'promotion of the arts, academic chairs, and even institutes of ethics'.[115] I mean their secret activities. Each of them has a major presence in all of the major tax havens, and many of the minor ones. All of them actively promote these secrecy jurisdictions and profit from developing and selling aggressive tax-avoidance schemes or 'products' for clients: a perfect example of value-skimming. The Tax Justice Network reports that the US Senate Permanent Subcommittee on Investigation (SPS) found that some of these products were almost certainly illegal. It also found that KPMG may have made at least US$180 million from the sale of some such schemes and that collectively the schemes it sold had probably cost the US Treasury up to US$85 billion in lost revenue. KPMG was heavily fined as a result. All of the big four have been involved in dealings that were subsequently ruled illegal or unacceptable by the SPS or the UK's Tax Tribunal or the European Court of Justice.

PwC's international operations are hidden behind an obscure company in London that claims to have no income but that operates its global website. In 2012 it was fined £1.4 million, for 'very serious' misconduct over its audit of JP Morgan Securities. The fine was described as 'the greatest penalty ever administered to a professional accountancy firm in the UK'. PwC was then worth £2.4 billion.[116]

Yet all this hasn't stopped the big four spinning the revolving doors of government, seconding staff to key departments, including, in the UK, the Treasury, HMRC and also to party policy teams. New Labour has been advised by Chris Wales of PwC (and formerly of Goldman Sachs) and of the partly business-funded Oxford Centre for Business Taxation.[117]

In May 2014, the board of HMRC included a former senior partner of KPMG and a former senior member of Arthur Andersen and Co, a major accountancy firm that was broken up in 2002 and taken over by the big four after being found guilty of criminal charges relating to the firm's handling of the auditing of Enron. Another member of the board was a tax partner of PwC for 25 years.[118] Of course, they could be using their experience of working on the other side for the public good. It would be nice to think so.

In a battle with bankers in 1832, Andrew Jackson, the 7th US President, told a delegation of bankers: 'You are a den of vipers and thieves. I intend to rout you out, and by the eternal God, I will rout you out.'[119] One might have hoped that this would have happened after the crash of 2007–08, but it didn't. In Britain, researchers from CRESC ask 'what other industry enjoys near limitless state guarantees, brushes aside financial scandals, polices itself and places itself under the protection of Westminster elites?'[120] Parliament is crawling with corporate lobbyists, advisors and 'researchers'. We cannot afford to leave the financial sector in the hands of those with an interest in not fixing it.

Rigging the system

Big business may not yet run the world, but it's getting there by rigging the rules of the global economy in its own interests. A key step is through new trade pacts that allow multinational corporations to escape many of the regulations and restrictions that national governments try to impose on them. Trade treaties are complicated, dry and technical, and rarely get more than a few reports in the less-read business sections of newspapers, but two new ones being developed in 2013 should set alarm bells ringing. These are the Trans-Pacific Pact (TPP), involving 12 nations round the Pacific Rim,[121] and the Transatlantic Trade and Investment Partnership (TTIP) involving the US and 28 European Union states. Together they account for 60% of global output.

They seek to establish one set of regulations and standards within their respective areas for multinationals. While they will no doubt be justified as 'cutting red tape', their aim is to maximise the economic and political power of international business by minimising government restrictions on their operations, whether they are for protecting public health, employment conditions or the environment, or simply for allowing governments to control their economies. The most likely – and intended – outcome is a race to the bottom in standards. The treaties also look set to extend corporations' intellectual property rights, preventing individuals and other companies, including smaller businesses across the world, from benefiting from their innovations without paying them rent. As we saw in Parts One and Two, companies themselves typically benefit from countless freely available innovations of the commons, yet their powers to privatise their own innovations are being extended. Policies voted for in democracies across the world to ensure affordable medicines, to block genetically modified crops and the sale of inadequately tested drugs and to protect food standards or internet freedom are under threat.

But how can it be that the governments involved in the treaties are giving away power to corporations, so that their electorates have even less influence on their economies? The answer is that the pacts are being developed in secret, largely by corporate lawyers and technocrats, with massive influence from business lobbyists. Effectively they're corporate wish-lists. They're undemocratic in the manner of their conception and anti-democratic in their content.

> Access to drafts of the TPP chapters is shielded from the general public. Members of the US Congress are only able to view selected portions of treaty-related documents in highly restrictive conditions and under strict supervision. It has been previously revealed that only three individuals in each TPP nation have access to the full text of the agreement, while 600 'trade advisers' – lobbyists guarding the interests of large US corporations such as Chevron, Halliburton, Monsanto and Walmart – are granted privileged access to crucial sections of the treaty text.[122]

In Australia the government refused the Senate access to the secret text of the trade deal it was negotiating in Singapore, saying it would be made public only after it had been signed. Similarly, TTIP negotiations have been proceeding largely in secrecy, with all the important information withheld from the public and any democratic debate. Significantly, Wikileaks has been the main source of information about them. While the European Commission has held just 8 meetings with civil society groups about the TTIP, it has had 119 with corporations and their lobbyists.

These trade pacts seek to augment the intellectual property of companies, prolonging patents beyond 20 years, enabling them to extract more rent for longer from 'their' products. Internet service providers will be required to filter and block content – thereby giving companies control over users' use of 'their' products, stopping sharing or reverse engineering and adaptation. Tim Berners-Lee, the inventor of the internet, may have said 'this is for everyone', but some major companies want to privatise and control it for their own interests. Julian Assange of Wikileaks comments:

> If instituted, the TPP's intellectual property regime would trample over individual rights and free expression, as well as ride roughshod over the intellectual and creative commons. If you read, write, publish, think, listen, dance, sing or invent; if you farm or consume food; if you're ill now or might one day be ill, the TPP has you in its crosshairs.[123]

Most alarming of all are the 'investor–state dispute settlement' mechanisms: these allow big corporations to sue governments before secretive arbitration panels composed of corporate lawyers, bypassing domestic courts and overriding the will of parliaments![124] These mechanisms are already being used by a Swedish nuclear company contesting the German decision, following the Fukushima disaster, to end its reliance on nuclear power. In Australia the Philip Morris tobacco company is suing the government for attempting to make plain packaging compulsory. In Argentina, in the financial crisis, the government responded to popular anger about rising costs of living by freezing energy and water prices, only to find itself hit by over 40 law suits issued by the private companies involved, and had to pay $1.15 billion in compensation.[125] Developing countries, already weak relative to multinationals, stand to lose still more power.

In the case of *Occidental Petroleum vs Ecuador*:

Occidental faces a range of allegations in Ecuador in relation to abuses of the country's human rights, social and environmental laws. The corporation was found to have breached contract terms in relation to a share transfer deal, as a result of which its contract was cancelled. Occidental immediately retaliated by filing a billion dollar ICSID [International Centre for the Settlement of Investment Disputes] claim. In October 2012 the Ecuadorian state was ordered to pay $1.7 billion plus interest in compensation, the equivalent of fifteen years worth of social welfare payments for the country. The Ecuadorian government is attempting to appeal the ruling.[126]

Once multinationals can sue national governments, even the threat of such legal action can block democratically supported legislation that limits their power.

Of course, whenever information about these initiatives leaks out to the public, the public relations line is that the treaties will help growth and investment and yield thousands of new jobs. Precedents such as the North American Free Trade Agreement have done no such thing. The goal of corporations is to maximise profit for their shareholders, not create jobs, and although they may sometimes do this, unless demand for their products is growing very fast, they generally increase profits by *reducing* what they spend on employing people. As usual, we are told that what's good for big business is good for us, but as business has switched to rent-seeking and weakening democratic control of its operations, that is less true than ever. It is time to end the rule of the rich.

EIGHTEEN

What about philanthropy?

We need philanthropy to lessen hostility towards the rich. (Tony Blair)[127]

When I give food to the poor, they call me a saint. When I ask why they are poor, they call me a communist. (Hélder Câmara, former Roman Catholic archbishop in Brazil)[128]

Philanthropists are not only rich, but generous and benevolent too, so how could anyone complain? But where do philanthropists get their money from, and are those sources legitimate? That's the most basic question to ask of philanthropy, but although I've been answering it in this book, it's rarely asked, perhaps because it seems churlish. But even if we leave aside the question of the origins of the donors' wealth, there are other problems with philanthropy, and they have everything to do with the rule of the rich.

Charity or justice?

Charitable giving in response to one-off disasters, such as for victims of earthquakes, is different from charity responding to persistent and unjust inequalities, for unless the injustice is challenged it merely provides a way of making it less intolerable, and therefore more durable. The work of some charities, such as Oxfam or Christian Aid, is partly directed against injustice and neglect – at the causes and not merely the symptoms of problems, as in their campaigns against tariffs that discriminate against poor countries and favour rich ones;

and of course some, like Amnesty International, are overwhelmingly concerned with justice.

To be sure, the plight of the recipient may be seen as a matter of concern, but philanthropy tends to treat it as a misfortune rather than as the outcome of social structures and processes. Philanthropy depoliticises not only because it involves individuals rather than the state, but because it so often ignores the social, economic and political origins of suffering. It's better at dealing with the pathologies associated with poverty than with poverty itself. And some philanthropy is directed towards quite different ends, like supporting elite universities like Oxford, Cambridge and Harvard. Yes, in some cases, the money may pay for some bursaries for a few students from low-income families, thereby providing the institutions with a useful defence against accusations of elitism, but it not only brings prestige to the donor but also reinforces the hierarchy of educational institutions. The poorest universities, attended by students from low- and middle-income families, get nothing. Similarly, donations to art galleries are a common form of 'philanthropy' that supports elite culture.

Philanthropy sets up a divide between the dynamic, 'successful', generous and usually well-publicised benefactor and the poor, helpless recipients, who, of course, ought to be grateful, while observers admire and applaud from the side lines. It presupposes rather than challenges inequalities; indeed, by treating them as an opportunity for benevolence it makes them appear less problematic. All's well and fair because, look how generous the rich are!

Benevolent acts within such relations may cause humiliation, particularly where they draw attention to the recipients' lack and do not remove the sources of the problem. Getting justice is an *entitlement*, one that recognises the dignity of the individual as an equal, and does not treat them as a pitiable, unfortunate inferior, dependent on the generosity of others. 'We don't want your charity: we want justice', is an old but fair response.

What's in it for the donor?

Most charitable gifts from ordinary donors, who frequently give a larger proportion of their income than do much richer people,[129] are offered anonymously. Philanthropy differs in that philanthropists generally want their name or company brand all over their gifts; the universities and arts foundations they donate to are expected to name something after them. One of Tony Blair's ventures is officially called The Tony Blair Faith Foundation. An added bonus in many countries is tax relief on charitable giving. In the US the top 1% get 38% tax relief on charitable giving.

For the rich and super-rich, already sated with personal consumption, philanthropy offers a different kind of capital from money, but one that legitimises their wealth: *symbolic capital* in the form of a legacy that evokes admiration. Peter Buffett, disillusioned son of billionaire philanthropist Warren Buffett, comments:

> As more lives and communities are destroyed by the system that creates vast amounts of wealth for the few, the more heroic it sounds to 'give back.' It's what I would call 'conscience laundering' – feeling better about accumulating more than any one person could possibly need to live on by sprinkling a little around as an act of charity.[130]

And having one's name or company brand attached to a good cause is good public relations; you don't even have to declare how much you've given; for companies it buys an aura of 'corporate social responsibility'. At the annual World Economic Forum in Davos, the super-rich gather to be seen at the sessions on philanthropy, and bathe in the glow of benevolence.

Philanthropists don't just want to give money and allow the recipients to use it as they see fit; they want to have some control over how it's used, because, let's face it, the rich, being so clever and successful, know best. And they consider their wealth, whatever its origins, as theirs to use as they wish. Instead of funding programmes run by participants and experts on the basis of their local knowledge, the philanthropists' donations generally come with strings attached, and often dollops of arrogance. In Tony Blair's words:

the best philanthropy is not just about giving money but giving leadership. The best philanthropists bring the gifts that made them successful – the drive, the determination, the refusal to accept something can't be done if it needs to be – into their philanthropy. It is creative not passive; it seeks to disrupt not follow conventional thinking. It steps into areas Government is too fearful or too risk adverse to go. It uses technology and its power to change the world in innovative ways. It is visionary, seeing the connections, the trends, the patterns that others don't.[131]

Heroic indeed. So Mr Blair – sycophant of the super-rich, friend of Murdoch, Gaddafi and Berlusconi, and poodle of George Bush, whose disastrous 'judgement' led the UK into war in Iraq – knows best. And as he once put it, 'I only know what I believe.'[132] Hence his preference for policy-based 'evidence'. The philanthropists bless others not only with their money but with the gift of their special skills and insights. No need for tiresome democratic procedures, for local knowledge and specialist expertise,[133] or transparency and accountability to others; the paymaster calls the tune – and the publicity.

Buffett junior coined the term 'Philanthropic Colonialism' for this:

People (including me) who had very little knowledge of a particular place would think that they could solve a local problem. Whether it involved farming methods, education practices, job training or business development, over and over I would hear people discuss transplanting what worked in one setting directly into another with little regard for culture, geography or societal norms.[134]

'Philanthrocapitalism'

This has become a buzzword for an approach to philanthropy that uses profit-seeking business thinking and market methods to achieve its goals. Michael Edwards, a researcher on philanthropy, quotes Kurt Hoffman, director of the Shell Foundation: 'Charities have failed for decades to deliver . . . do we want to continue with the status quo or apply some fresh, inherently efficient [sic] and potentially very effective thinking to find new solutions?'[135] Goals have to be simple and measurable so that they can be monitored, though it's possible to include non-financial goals, such as numbers of vaccinations. This again tends to encourage meeting those targets even where the local context throws up other more important things to do. (Many of us are familiar with the harm that such simplistic thinking can do in the public sector.) These methods may indeed work well for selling better widgets at a lower price, but they are likely to be detrimental when applied to complex problems of social and political inequality. Here's Peter Buffett again: 'business principles are trumpeted as an important element to add to the philanthropic sector. I now hear people ask, "what's the R.O.I.?" when it comes to alleviating human suffering, as if return on investment were the only measure of success.'[136]

As Edwards argues, philanthropy and philanthrocapitalism tend to target symptoms and fail to get to their roots. He writes: 'The reason is pretty obvious: Systemic change involves social movements, politics and government, which these experiments generally ignore.'[137] Major economic inequalities are not just 'resource gaps' but are grounded in the unequal power between classes, ethnic groups or men and women. Structural problems require structural solutions. For example, rural poverty in developing countries is rarely something that can be resolved just by, say, introducing genetically modified seeds for crops (though that certainly suits the multinationals that produce them), but typically requires changes to land rights, patriarchal social structures and credit and distribution systems. Microfinance at low interest may in some cases be helpful for poor communities, but it can and has on occasion served as a Trojan horse for large banks to siphon off wealth from poor people.[138]

Social problems are inherently political, and hence responses to them are likely to be contested in the target societies, but neoliberal philanthropy attempts to ignore such politics and seek technical, managerial and market solutions, though of course these are far from politically neutral. As Edwards puts it:

> The function of markets is to facilitate exchange, not
> to negotiate solutions democratically. Markets work

according to supply and demand, not solidarity or fairness or the satisfaction of human rights. They utilize competition, not the co-operation and collaboration that build successful social movements and strong alliances for change. They measure success against a clear bottom line which is easy to evaluate but absent from pretty much every situation in which non-profits work. And to succeed in the marketplace you need to exert a high degree of control over supply chains and other variables, which is the opposite of empowering others for independent action. Importing markets into the very domain in which people seek to challenge their distributional failures is deeply ill-conceived.[139]

Philanthropy distorts

Even if they give close to home, precisely because they're at the top, philanthropists' understanding of life at the bottom tends to be limited. Yet because of their power, non-governmental organisations seeking help have to adjust their goals to appeal to major benefactors – a phenomenon called 'mission drift'. Philanthropists tend to go for high-visibility, appealing projects rather than hidden but necessary changes.

An investigation of the Bill and Melinda Gates Foundations' project on AIDS by the *Los Angeles Times*[140] found that while it had indeed saved lives it also distorted local health services' work:

• By pouring most contributions into the fight against such high-profile killers as AIDS, Gates grantees have increased the demand for specially trained, higher-paid clinicians, diverting staff from basic care. The resulting staff shortages have abandoned many children of AIDS survivors to more common killers: birth sepsis, diarrhea and asphyxia.

• The focus on a few diseases has shortchanged basic needs such as nutrition and transportation, undermining the effectiveness of the foundation's grants. Many AIDS patients have so little food that they vomit their free AIDS pills. For lack of bus fare, others cannot get to clinics that offer lifesaving treatment.

• Gates-funded vaccination programs have instructed caregivers to ignore – even discourage patients from discussing – ailments that the vaccinations cannot prevent. This is especially harmful in outposts where a visit to a clinic for a shot is the only contact some villagers have with healthcare providers for years.

The *Los Angeles Times* report cites many examples from Africa where philanthropic interventions had serious disruptive effects on local health systems, diverting resources from what was most needed to the programmes that were being supported. In many cases, the prime cause of sickness and death is hunger, as a result of poverty.

Philanthropy vs. democracy

Philanthropists may also fund think-tanks and political campaigns. Even if you approve of the particular political positions they support, it still leaves the more basic problem: the ability of the rich to buy political influence. Instead of collectives, local or national or transnational, dealing in a democratic way with problems that affect them, the rich philanthropist outsider – a beneficiary of unearned income based on control of assets – steps in and by-passes democracy, while the recipients are positioned as passive and dependent on the discretion of the rich. Even where philanthropists consult them, their voice becomes a discretionary gift, when it should be their entitlement as persons of equal worth. According to Edwards, the Bill and Melinda Gates Foundation, the largest funder of global public health after the US and UK governments, 'has a board of three family members plus Warren Buffet'.[141] It is not accountable to the public.

It is not that philanthropy never does any good: sometimes it does. But too often the prior question of the legitimacy of the philanthropist's wealth is ignored. If the rich were taxed as they were during the post-war boom, or prevented from getting their unearned income in the first place, the use of that wealth could be democratically determined.

No society can exist without giving, simply because no one is self-sufficient and everyone is dependent on care by others at some time in their lives. In human history, 'gift relations', where people work and provide for one another, reciprocating gifts over time where they can, are arguably the most common form of economic relationship.[142] One of the deprivations and sources of shame caused by poverty is the inability to afford to give to loved ones. But, as inequalities widen and wealth concentrates at the top, instead of multiple flows of small gifts between people who are roughly equal, we get something radically different: a monopoly – or 'monoculture', as Edwards calls it – of funding by a tiny number of unaccountable individuals. Even if their actions are not self-interested, they are self-directed. Rather than depend on the preferences of would-be philanthropic saviours, we need to have democratically funded and accountable systems drawing upon the most appropriate expertise and local knowledge. Poverty is a problem of the maldistribution of productive resources and purchasing power. The rich are part of that problem, not the solution. Philanthropy is a way in which the rich can gain some legitimacy while retaining control over vast resources. It's an arm of plutocracy, not a negation of it.

NINETEEN

Class: don't mention the war!

'Plutonomy': for rich eyes only

Combining plutocracy with economy, 'plutonomy' was a term coined in 2005–06 by Ajay Kapur of Citigroup, a major US financial group bailed out by the American people in 2008 after sustaining huge losses in the crash. It was introduced in a series of reports, the last of which was called *The Plutonomy Symposium – Rising Tides Lifting Yachts*.[143] It was sent only to Citigroup's wealthiest customers, but leaked to the press. It claims that the US, Canada, UK and Australia are the only plutonomies; much of continental Europe and Japan, which haven't experienced such major upturns in wealth controlled by the rich, are 'the Egalitarian Bunch'.

According to the report, plutonomies have three key characteristics:

1. They are all created by 'disruptive technology-driven productivity gains, creative financial innovation, capitalist friendly cooperative governments, immigrants … the rule of law and patenting inventions. Often these wealth waves involve great complexity exploited best by the rich and educated of the time.'

2. There is no 'average' consumer in Plutonomies. There is only the rich 'and everyone else'. The rich account for a disproportionate chunk of the economy, while the non-rich account for 'surprisingly small bites of the national pie'.

Kapur estimates that in 2005, the richest 20% may have been responsible for 60% of total spending.

> 3. Plutonomies are likely to grow in the future, fed by capitalist-friendly governments, more technology-driven productivity and globalisation.

Democracy is potentially a threat:

> Perhaps the most immediate challenge to Plutonomy comes from the political process. Ultimately, the rise in income and wealth inequality to some extent is an economic disenfranchisement of the masses to the benefit of the few. However in democracies this is rarely tolerated forever. One of the key forces helping plutonomists over the last 20 years has been the rise in the profit share – the flip side of the fall in the wage share in GDP… However, labor has, relatively speaking, lost out. We see the biggest threat to plutonomy as coming from a rise in political demands to reduce income inequality, spread the wealth more evenly, and challenge forces such as globalization which have benefited profit and wealth growth.

Nonetheless:

> Our own view is that the rich are likely to keep getting even richer, and enjoy an even greater share of the wealth pie over the coming years.

And again,

> RISKS – WHAT COULD GO WRONG? **Our whole plutonomy thesis is based on the idea that the rich will keep getting richer**. *This thesis is not without its risks.* For example, **a policy error** leading to asset deflation, would likely damage plutonomy. Furthermore, the **rising**

wealth gap between the rich and poor will **probably at some point lead to a political backlash.** Whilst the rich are getting a greater share of the wealth, and the poor a lesser share, *political enfranchisement remains as was* – **one person, one vote** (in the plutonomies). At some point it is likely that labor will fight back against the rising profit share of the rich and there will be **a political backlash** against the rising wealth of the rich. This could be felt **through higher taxation on the rich** (or *indirectly* through higher **corporate taxes/ regulation**) or through trying to **protect indigenous** [home-grown] **laborers**, in a push-back on globalization – either *anti-immigration, or protectionism*. **We don't see this happening yet, though there are signs of rising political tensions**. However *we are* keeping a close eye on developments. (Emphases in the original)[144]

What's the most serious threat to democracy? Extremist groups? Terrorists? No. It's the plutocracy, stupid.

Denial and acquiescence

I began this book with a quote from Warren Buffett: 'There's class warfare, all right, but it's my class, the rich class, that's making war, and we're winning.' This is a truly surprising comment, not only because it comes from one of the richest people in the world, but because he dared to mention not only 'class', but 'class warfare', and further, to admit that 'the rich class' had started it. It was mirrored later by an Occupy banner saying 'Class war – they [the 1%] started it'.

We're not used to thinking of the rich initiating 'class war', because, Buffett apart, the rich normally pretend that only the Left initiates class wars, out of envy and greed, just as strikes are invariably portrayed as being started by labour, never provoked by employers. Like 'class struggle', it's associated with Marxism, with tiny groups of true believers who saw the class struggle as either constantly in process or just about to break out, even though little could be further from the minds of most working people. For many, it conjures up images of male manual workers striking and picketing. As a result, anyone who accuses the plutocracy of waging class war is met with faux-shock and dismissed as divisive and dangerous, just trying to stir up trouble. Clay Bennett's cartoon of a plane trailing a banner saying 'stop the class war' while dropping bombs at the same time summed it up.[145] As another Occupy poster put it, 'Why is it only "class warfare" when we fight back?'.

Margaret Thatcher strove to represent class as a communist concept. Yet she was the complete class warrior. In the 1980s she put into practice a plan, devised by Nicholas Ridley and leaked in 1978, to provoke and defeat strikes by organised labour, particularly in mining. You can read it on the Margaret Thatcher Foundation website.[146] The rest is history.

When Tony Blair said 'the class war is over', he meant we should accept the victory of the rich. For they, unlike their predecessors (often their parents), are supposedly merely 'middle class' and 'successful', even though they are in the upper reaches of the top 1%. Never mind unearned income and the unequal division of labour, job shortages or the lottery of birth in a highly unequal society: class is reduced to a matter of character and effort. Another way of avoiding acknowledging the working class while dividing them was to bang on about 'hard-working families', flattering those who were lucky enough to have jobs, as if they were better people than those who don't. Now the Conservatives counterpose 'hard-working people' and 'strivers' to 'skivers'.

It's as if class were purely an outmoded prejudice, having nothing to do with real and growing inequalities. At worst, where once talk of different classes was accepted as referring to something – to groups with similar economic and political interests that are in certain ways opposed to other such groups – it now, for many, refers to nothing except the speaker; it merely brands them as a socialist or 'Marxist', Old Labour, living in the past. They cannot possibly be talking *about* something, and can therefore be refused a hearing. Yet class remains the elephant in the room.

Political parties know that to win elections they have to win over those in the middle of the income spectrum, and so, as Seamus Milne says, UK politicians are increasingly following the US practice of referring only to the middle class, never the working class or the upper class.[147] There is just the middle class and those 'on benefits' positioned as parasitic on the rest – an incapable, hopeless residue. Meanwhile, the middle class are invited to identify with those above them, not below. At least in the US, 'liberals' like Robert Reich and Elizabeth Warren increasingly seek to highlight the declining living standards of the middle class and counterpose them to the rich and super-rich.

The lived experience of class is a complex matter, in which life-shaping inequalities are met with mixtures of embarrassment, denial, self-justification and congratulation, defiance, resentment, deference and condescension.[148] But recent years have seen an ever more brazen form of what sociologist Pierre Bourdieu called 'class racism', directed at 'chavs', 'trailer trash', 'scroungers' and so on. Though it has become unacceptable to use racist language, at least in official public discourse, it's open house for similar derogatory language and a visceral hatred for those on low incomes and/or benefits. Indeed, there is a case in the UK for arguing that the white working class have come to be seen in racialised terms.[149] 'They' are condemned even before they speak, immediately slotted into comedy and tabloid stereotypes, evoking either ridicule or sneers, fear and disgust, their words rendered only as confirmation of their inferiority and incorrigibility. In this way, they are treated as objects, and denied the status of fellow citizens who deserve a hearing and an understanding of the context in which they live.

The welfare state is no longer presented as a mark of a civilised society, providing a system of universal mutual support based on need, and from which the vast majority have benefitted, but as a burden. 'Welfare' is now coming to be used in the UK in the American pejorative sense, as something the inadequate are 'on', at the expense of the rest of us.[150] This is a kind of class war waged by the Right at the level of the meaning of words.

But the remarkable thing about the return of the rich is the lack of overt resistance, indeed the strange acceptance of austerity policies for the 90%, even after lower- and middle-income groups have seen years of declining real wages and benefits and erosion of public services. Many of those on low incomes have voted, against their own interests, for parties that protect and further plutocracy, the Tea Party in the US being the most striking example. Whipping up hostility to the poor, to immigrants, refugees and asylum seekers all helps to distract attention from the rich. Research in Britain and the US on attitudes to those at the bottom shows that some of those most hostile to them are themselves at the bottom.[151] So support for such parties continues as they blame the welfare state and those supported by it for a crisis very much associated with the return of the rich and their pursuit of ways of extracting wealth. In Britain, a government packed full of upper-class ministers must scarcely be able to believe its luck in deflecting public anger away from the rich of the financial sector and towards those groups least able to defend themselves. In the US, a political class of millionaires fights for big business while retaining popular support through crass populism. Opposition parties, fearful of offending big business, and particularly finance, offer at best slightly less harsh remedies.

Getting things in proportion

UK tax expert Richard Murphy estimates tax avoidance (not illegal) at £25 billion and tax evasion (illegal) at £70 billion, or combined, £260 million per day. That's over 260 times estimated benefit fraud.[152]

The rich class are winning the war on the economic front partly because they have been winning it in popular culture. The 1960s may have seen the end of traditional overt snobbery and working-class deference, but these have been replaced by a form of spurious egalitarianism that, via endless talk of social mobility, equal opportunities and meritocracy, denies the extent and effects of major inequalities in people's circumstances and life-chances. British public school[153] educated politicians like Blair and Cameron get away with it by avoiding any shows of attachment to high culture that might seem snobbish or dated (grouse shooting, for example) and pretending to be just middle class rather than upper class. In the US, it's long been the case that you can get away with excessive wealth if you have a middle-class demeanour; now the British, even the monarchy, are learning.[154] This reluctance even to name the working class is an insult to working-class pride and dignity. Where the working class were portrayed mostly respectfully in films and TV in the 1970s, they are now ridiculed and slurred.[155] TV programmes like the Jerry Springer and the Jeremy Kyle shows, *Wife Swap*, *Benefits Street*, *From Ladettes to Ladies* and *We Pay Your Benefits* provide a regular diet of poverty porn – of public humiliation in 'the theatre of cruelty', as Phil Mirowski calls it.[156] They reaffirm viewers' sense of superiority, offering them a safe zone of snobbery, schadenfreude and self-righteousness. And they keep their audiences' contempt focused downwards, blaming the effects of structural inequality on personal failings, or 'lifestyle choice', while, out of sight, the rich get richer.

PART FIVE

Ill-gotten and ill-spent: from consumption to CO_2

There are still more reasons why we can't afford the rich. Here we look at how they spend their money, and how this affects others and the planet. There is not only the obscenity of wasteful expenditure in a world in which 721 million people – a third of them children – have to live on less than $1.25 a day.[1] Excess has come to be defined as the key to a good life, so millions seek ever greater and more unsustainable consumption. But actually it is unlikely to improve their well-being. The plundering of the earth's resources cannot continue; above all, our insatiable appetite for fossil fuels is driving global warming. The effects are already impacting on populations across the world, threatening our environment, food systems and futures.

Stopping global warming is the biggest challenge modern society has had to face, and it's clear that few want to face it, least of all those who have the biggest stake in the status quo and can protect themselves from its worst effects – the rich. But it also is incompatible with capitalism itself, for capitalism depends on endless growth and we have already far outstripped the capacity of the planet to cope. For wealthy countries, growth is producing more problems than solutions.

Part Five explores these issues.

TWENTY

Spending it

There were 104 billionaires in Britain in 2014.[2] What could you buy with £1 billion? You could pick up 50 luxury mansions at £20 million each. A private jet? The Gulfstream G550 range of jets are priced at £28–£44 million each, so you could buy not just one but a fleet. You could spend over £100 million on a supersized luxury yacht, or have your own IMAX theatre for £1.18 million. Like Formula 1 supremo Bernie Ecclestone, you could spend £30 million on your daughter's wedding. And you could blow a few million on hiring a leading pop star to sing at your birthday party. Then there are small luxuries: the Bornrich website advertised a £437,000, jewel-studded iPad case, a £3.5 million diamond-encrusted dress and shoes for £312,000.[3] Or you could treat yourself to the most expensive cocktail ever, at £35,000 a throw; indeed, you could have one a day for 78 years.[4] Like US presidential candidate Mitt Romney, you could have a car elevator installed in your house for a mere $55,000. You could stay at the best hotels, perhaps the iconic Burj Al Arab in Dubai at £1,188–£2,716 per night. It sounds a ruinous price, but if you were a sterling billionaire you could afford to stay in one of its most expensive suites every night for nearly 1,000 years.

So the super-rich are faced with a problem: what can they buy that they can actually use? As H.L. Hunt, the Texan millionaire, once said, 'You can only sleep in one bed at a time. You can only wear one suit at a time. You can only drive one automobile at a time. And you can only eat one meal at a time.'[5] How many times a year might they use a luxury yacht? Even if they decided just to buy, say, four luxury mansions, one yacht and one jet, a billionaire would still have over £700 million left to spend. What sense would there be in spending on things they would scarcely use, except to make a statement to the world of their disproportionate wealth? No wonder they recycle most of their money into financial investment that will store and add to their mostly unspendable income. They could go in for symbolic profits, through philanthropy; though less wasteful, this still means that the wealth they have extracted is put beyond democratic control. When they've already got all the things they could possibly buy and use, and the sheer wastefulness of their consumption finally dawns on them, then pure money for money's sake and their 'score' or position in the league tables of the super-rich are all that's left to strive for. Even those with just a few millions may find it difficult to spend all their money on things they can make use of.

Wasteful consumption also means wasteful production. *Producing extremely expensive things that will rarely be used or are nothing more than signifiers of opulence is a waste of time, energy and precious materials, and worse, a waste of human labour.* In the language of mainstream economics, though it's not the sort of thing economists of that stripe would ever say, it's a flagrant 'misallocation of resources'. The Burj Al Arab hotel, at over 1,000 feet high, is part of a huge development built on land reclaimed from the sea and including luxury apartments and lagoons. It's a monumental waste of resources, and a huge addition to Dubai's already bloated CO_2 emissions. Expensive, iconic buildings have been erected before, of course, but at least some, like cathedrals and sports stadia, benefit the wider population. The Burj caters purely to the vanities of the rich.

Luxury spending by the rich can trump the basic needs of people on lower incomes. It drives up house prices in major cities, making it difficult for low- and even middle-income people to afford to live in them, as has happened in London for many years.[6] Worse, luxury spending on second or third homes may mean that local people who need to be there all the year are priced out by those who will spend only a few weeks there. Something similar is happening on a global scale, where food production in poor countries is being replaced by production of biofuels for rich consumers, exacerbating the global food crisis. Through their spending, the rich can command the labour and products of vastly more people than can others. In so doing they divert workers from producing goods and services for ordinary people, and into producing luxuries for the rich. *They distort economies.*

Watch where you moor your yacht!

In case you missed it, the November 2012 issue of *Mediterranean Berths and Marinas* had the headlines 'The Taxman Clouds the Mediterranean Sun: a Look at the Challenges Facing Owners [sic] Taxes in Cyprus, Italy and Spain' and 'Why Berths Aren't Big Enough' – an article on the problem posed by increasingly large luxury yachts, and illustrated by a picture of one 162.5 metres in length. On top of that, there's now a shortage of berths in the western Mediterranean. Regardless of whether the tide is rising or falling, it's lifting yacht sales.

In the same journal Phil Berman, of US-based Multihull, also helpfully suggests: 'If you buy outside the EU and corporately flag it in a non-EU country you are not an EU owner. That's what most people do. Registration in somewhere like the Cayman Islands, or closer to home Gibraltar, means that a European can buy a €3 million yacht built in Italy or France and completely avoid value added tax.'[7]

Of course, ports and marinas are concerned that raising taxes will drive away the yachts and their owners, hitting local businesses; but then, if all the Mediterranean countries raised their taxes and closed the loopholes, the rich would have either to pay up or stay out of the Med. Alternatively, one could just tax away or block their sources or unearned income in the first place. This might result in a lot of luxury yachts being sold off by owners who couldn't afford to keep them. No doubt they could be adapted for trips for the public and put to more intensive use.

When we think about how much money people should get, we are actually considering how big their claims on the labour of others should be, relative to those of others. In the modern global economy, though we rarely think of it, each of us relies on thousands of other workers to produce the goods and services we consume, be they garment workers in the Philippines, assemblers of electronic goods in China, banana growers in St Lucia or call centre workers in India – or, indeed, shop assistants, dentists, garage mechanics and bar staff in our local town. As we saw in Part Two, the inequalities at the international level derive mainly from inequalities in the level of development of 'the forces of production'; workers in countries like India or Thailand get much less for supplying westerners with goods than western producers get from selling stuff to them, because they have had different economic histories, usually with colonial domination and unequal exchanges going back centuries.

The rich may claim that their wealth trickles down as they spend it, thereby creating jobs – after all, those mansions and yachts need looking after. But the lower propensity of the rich to spend their money on goods and services – largely because they have more than they can use – means that relying on luxury consumption is an inferior way of generating jobs. In the UK, £1 billion could provide 45,896 people with the median wage (£21,788), most of which they would spend on goods and services, creating far more jobs than would a billionaire who might spend only 10% of it. Instead of crumbs from the table, glossed as 'trickle down', you would have a much larger injection of spending throughout the economy.

Conspicuous consumption and hidden work

In Britain, many people like to visit 'stately homes' and admire the lavish grounds and buildings. Often the booklets describing their history will say that the house was built by the first Earl of X, the west wing by his son, while another descendant laid out the grounds with the lake and the avenue.

Of course, none of them did any such thing. What they did was pay for others to do the work. As Raymond Williams so powerfully demonstrated in *The Country and the City*, the celebrated 'great families' that 'go back centuries' owe their prominence and assets to the unacknowledged labour of hundreds of unrecorded workers (whose families also went back centuries), who produced the house and grounds and serviced their exorbitant lifestyle. In addition, many more workers from further afield, some of them slaves, including those in colonial plantations and mines, toiled to produce the wealth appropriated by the owner. Impressive though they may be, stately homes are monuments to exploitation and unearned income, and consumption levels far beyond the reach of those

> who worked to sustain them. They are grotesquely out of proportion with what one household working on its own could develop and manage.[8]
>
> Owners and CEOs of contemporary firms are similarly wont to claim responsibility for what their workers have done. Today the vertical class relations of 'upstairs and downstairs' may have mostly been displaced horizontally to different parts of the city or of the world, but they continue in new forms.

It was the aristocrat economist Keynes who identified the tendency of the rich to spend a smaller proportion of their incomes than the rest of the population. But he didn't try to justify it by claiming that they would fund productive investment instead of spending on consumer goods. He saw that wages and salaries are not just a cost but a source of revenue. If people can't afford to buy more consumer goods, it won't be profitable to produce more, so there will be a lack of outlets for productive investment. Then, of course, there will be more incentives to switch to 'investing' in existing assets and claims on the future incomes of others. Increased inequality is actually dysfunctional for capitalism.

There's another way in which the spending of the rich, and indeed some of the merely affluent, is likely to be dysfunctional: through their employment of *servant labour*. By this I mean employing people to do things they can actually do themselves. Most people are perfectly capable of making their own bed and cleaning the bathroom, and the efficiency gains of getting a specialist bed maker or cleaner to do it are minimal. When servants became scarce in Britain in the early 20th century, giving rise to 'the servant problem', some aristocrats wondered who would empty their chamber pots. The answer, of course, too awful to consider, was the rich themselves. If the employers are no good at doing these things themselves they've obviously been spoilt or are suffering from learnt helplessness, like that induced by patriarchy – 'the men-just-can't-cook syndrome'. (Clearly, it's different if the employer is too old or disabled to do it themselves.)

By contrast, most of us have little expertise in car mechanics, medicine or plumbing, and it would take us years to learn about such things and get hold of the necessary equipment so that we could self-service, and even then it wouldn't be worth it because most of the time we wouldn't need to use those skills. It's far more efficient to have specialised mechanics, doctors and plumbers to do it continually for hundreds of people. The first kind of division of labour is economically irrational, the second, rational, because it saves time all round.[9] So servant labour lacks an economic rationale. And being paid to do something for someone that they could equally well do themselves lacks the dignity of doing something for them that they couldn't do or couldn't do as well. It results from a power imbalance: economic inequalities are so great that the rich can afford to get the poor and needy to do things they are capable of doing themselves. This is why the proportion of workers who are doing servant labour, like cleaners, chauffeurs and nannies, is greatest where economic inequalities are greatest; hence you get more servant labour in California, Rio or London than you do in Denmark or Japan.

Alternatively, the rich may claim that employing servants means more time in which to do their own more valuable work. (Actually, many employers of servant workers use the extra time it gives them for leisure.[10]) Their work may indeed be more valuable, but as we saw in Chapter Nine, that's thanks to the unequal division of labour and their occupation of a privileged place within it; employing servants just adds to the contributive injustice. And it doesn't remove the unequal contributions of men and women to domestic work, merely shifting it from unpaid work by women to low-paid work usually also done by women. Some may claim that their working hours are so long that they don't have time to do these mundane self-servicing tasks; but a limit on working hours would mean that such work would be shared between more people, so the benefits and costs of work would be spread more equally. Elite workaholism – monopolising the best work and restricting the number of other people who can do it – is a form of contributive injustice. The combination of people who are rich but time poor and others who are time rich but money poor is also a major irrationality of modern economies. Of course, a servant job is better than no job, and those who employ them often claim they are doing good in providing them with employment, but this is making a virtue of an inequality that forces people with little money into servile work. It doesn't tackle the underlying problem of wide inequalities.

Emulation, envy and vanity

In capitalist culture, money is widely taken as a measure of personal worth: the size of your salary, your budget, the price of your house, car, clothes, mobile phone or watch signal your status to others. A 5-year-old second-hand car may be half the price of a new one, but, if well maintained, the difference in its performance, comfort and reliability is minimal. Yet many are willing to pay the extra for a new one just for the recognition it brings among others for whom such things matter. In his celebrated book, *The Theory of the Leisure Class*, Thorstein Veblen claimed that the rich consume not merely to meet their needs but to make a statement – a 'provocative distinction' that sets them apart from others.[11] Hence the childish competition over who has the biggest yacht, the most expensive watches, the most palatial houses, the biggest private jet(s) – or, at the bottom of the hierarchy, the most expensive trainers. At every level, owning such objects is a way of saying 'we're as good as you – or better'.

I remember watching a TV programme about the lives of travelling salesmen (and they were all men), whose long hours on motorways were passed by monitoring the cars that overtook them, and those they overtook themselves. They didn't mind being overtaken by someone who had a more expensive model than their own, but were annoyed if they were overtaken by someone driving a cheaper model, seeing this as a sign of disrespect, a threat to the pecking order. The minute differences of trim and model number represented status differences that had a ridiculously inflated significance for them.

Pathetic though such craving for status relative to others may seem, it reminds us of the fact that we are deeply social beings, needing the acceptance and recognition of at least some others so as to feel adequate and maintain a sense of self-respect and esteem, though that can easily get diverted into a desire to be envied, so that others feel inadequate in comparison. The American jibe 'if you're so clever how come you ain't rich?' sums up this capitalist consumer culture. As I showed in Part Two, structural economic inequalities prevent many people from contributing fully to society and being able to enjoy the recognition and sense of worth that comes from that. So it's not surprising that many see consumption – retail therapy – as a way of compensating. Yes, many things we buy may enhance our lives too, enabling us to do things we couldn't do otherwise – from mobile phones, online videos and musical instruments, to meals out and visits to the cinema. That's not the issue, this is not an argument for the hair shirt. Nor am I denying that capitalist competition has brought us many of these innovations; it clearly has. The problem here is the pursuit of goods primarily for status.

Status seeking: anti-social or just pointless

Thomas Frank, in *Pity the Billionaire*, cites a recommendation in *Trader Monthly* (a magazine for financial sector traders) that a $300,000 record turntable is 'a huge middle finger to everyone who enters your home'.[12] Nice. Status competition through conspicuous consumption is ultimately anti-social.

As Tim Jackson the ecological economist says, we're 'being persuaded to spend money we don't have on things we don't need, to create impressions that won't last, on people we don't care about'.[13]

Large inequalities, and the constant need of firms to sell us stuff, mean that it is easy to keep the customer dissatisfied. In the 18th century, Adam Smith recognised that this pursuit of goods for the distinction and envy they are imagined to bring helped to drive the emerging commercial economy. It still does: Juliet Schor reports that in the US, 'Since 1990, inflation-adjusted per-person expenditures have risen 300 percent for furniture and household goods, 80 percent for apparel, and 15–20 percent for vehicles, housing, and food.'[14] Clothes, for example, are now bought far more frequently: 'In 1991 Americans bought an average of thirty-four dresses, pairs of pants, sweaters, shirts, underwear, and other items. In 1996 that number had risen to forty-one. By 2007 per person consumption had soared to sixty-seven items.'[15] This is just a part of a wider picture of growing consumption – and waste, as more products end up in landfill. In the

UK, it has been recently estimated that 15 million tonnes of food are wasted every year, nearly half of it by households.[16]

As the rich grow richer, the tendency of those with less to want to emulate them is likely to become stronger. The growth of celebrity culture is in part a celebration of their conspicuous consumption. Veblen argued that each income group tended to aspire to consume at the level of the one above it. The more unequal a society is, the greater the amount of status envy and sense of relative deprivation among many of those on low and middling incomes. Tawney referred to 'the moral humiliation that gross contrasts of wealth and economic power necessarily produce'.[17] As he also said, in order to respect each other for what we are, we must cease to respect each other for what we earn. Wanting to emulate luxury consumption in order to win status is completely different from wanting to emulate achievements or virtues, like being able to cook well or produce work of a high standard, or make others happy.

But Smith also saw envying wealth and pursuing status through consumption as misguided, since it reflected a distorted view of the worth of people: 'This disposition to admire, and almost to worship, the rich and the powerful, and to despise, or, at least, to neglect, persons of poor and mean condition … is … the great and most universal cause of the corruption of our moral sentiments.'[18]

We still have these double standards: prison for those found guilty of welfare benefit fraud, mere disapproval or small fines arrived at through gentlemen's agreements for major tax avoidance or evasion. They are central to neoliberal culture.

It is a mistake to envy the rich. Envy of their excessive consumption only encourages emulation. And using control of assets to extract wealth that others have created is hardly worthy of envy. It's unjust and dysfunctional.

The well-being argument

It would be a mistake to assume that rising consumption in already rich countries is necessarily a sign of progress. Research on well-being and happiness shows that beyond a certain level of income, further increases in wealth have little impact on well-being.[19] Above this threshold, health and security, social cohesiveness and trust, being able to contribute and getting recognition for it, and having friends, make more difference. Capitalism may be good for producing economic growth, but the ever-increasing pace of life and demands of employment increase stress and make it difficult for many to care for loved ones, sustain relationships and relax and recover.

Richard Layard, a leading researcher on happiness, estimates that across the world this threshold income lies at about $20,000 or £16,230.[20] Of course, it depends a lot on the cost of living and the number of dependants we have. Most people in rich countries are already above this level, so that consuming even more goods produces only short-lived satisfaction. The buzz from a new car or electronic gizmo soon wears off. Above the threshold, further increases are likely to depend on other things than more money. The new field of 'happiness research' provides abundant evidence of this. Happiness levels have flat-lined for 40 years in the UK and the US, while incomes have continued to rise.[21] In Europe there are have been only small increases in happiness. To be sure, there are substantial minorities – growing in the recession – of people with incomes below the threshold, and for whom more money would definitely improve their lives significantly. Indeed, anxiety about making ends meet can put relationships under stress, and cause shame and mental illness. So redistribution of income and power from the rich and affluent to those on low incomes would produce an overall net improvement in well-being.

Richard Wilkinson and Kate Pickett's influential book, *The Spirit Level*, also shows that insatiable acquisitiveness is not the route to well-being. Rather than rely just on people's own assessments of their happiness, it looks at data on things like life expectancy, health, violence, crime, education, trust and social mobility.[22] Again, they find that once average incomes in countries reach a certain point, further increases make little difference to well-being as measured by indicators of these things. What *does* make a difference to well-being in rich countries is the degree of inequality: the more equal of the rich societies tend to score better than the others on a wide range of indicators of well-being, from life expectancy and health, to low crime rates, high educational performance, social mobility and social trust, as Figure 20.1 shows.[23] What is more, even the affluent do better in more equal societies. So the well-being of someone on £100,000 a year in a more equal society like Sweden or Japan is likely to be higher than that of someone on the same income in the US or UK. The precise reasons for this are likely to be complex, but in so far as feelings of self-worth depend on comparisons with others, and trust in others decreases with social distance from them, people in more equal societies tend to be happier.

Trust and happiness

'Trust is a major determinant of happiness in a society. Levels of trust vary widely between countries. The percentage of people who say "Most people can be trusted" is only 30 per cent of people in the U.K. and U.S., compared to 60 per cent some 40 years ago. But in Scandinavia the level is still over 60 per cent, and these are the happiest countries too.'[24]

Figure 20.1: Health and social problems are worse in more unequal countries

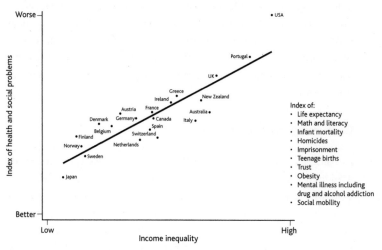

Source: Wilkinson, R. and Pickett, K. (2009) *The spirit level*, London: Allen Lane

Happiness research shows that whether people are happy tends to depend first on what they're used to, and on how they compare to others – on habituation and social comparison, in other words.[25] The habituation effect is like a ratchet: as income rises, so too do our ideas about what we need in order to be happy – except that beyond the threshold we don't actually gain much.

Children's well-being

A UNICEF report in 2007 comparing child well-being in 21 rich countries showed it to be generally better in the more equal societies. The UK and US did particularly badly, coming 21st and 20th, respectively. The Netherlands and Sweden were 1st and 2nd. An update in 2013 covering 29 countries again showed the more equal countries in the top part of the table, with the UK at 16th and the US at 26th, three places above Romania. The country 'scores' were derived from data on material well-being, health and safety, educational well-being, family and peer relationships, behaviours and risks and subjective well-being.[26]

The implication of all this is that *a levelling-down of the incomes of the rich and well-off need not involve a levelling-down of well-being*; more frugal ways of life could be as good or better, though our attachment to high-consumption lifestyles would make this hard to appreciate, at least in the short run. As we'll see later, this may become a necessity, not an option.

Consuming the planet

According to Juliet Schor, 'From 1980 to 2005, the weight of materials used to produce a dollar of GDP fell about 30 percent on a worldwide basis, or 1.2 percent a year. Because output grew more, there was a 45% [*sic*] increase in materials use overall.'[27] The reduction in weight per dollar is an overestimate because a lot of production was shifted out of the US to producers in other countries, particularly China. The effects of lower material content have been swamped by growth. Similarly with energy: energy expended per dollar of GDP in the US has fallen by a half since 1975, but energy demand has increased by

40%. The rate of use of materials has already overshot the ecological capacity of the globe, with the rich countries far in the lead: it's been estimated by the Global Footprint Network that if everyone in the world consumed at the level of US citizens, it would require five earths to support them sustainably, or three earths at European levels of consumption.[28]

Like most electronic goods, mobile phones – now numbering several billion worldwide – contain small amounts of toxic substances such as mercury, lead, arsenic and cadmium. Millions of phones and other gizmos are discarded every year, to be replaced by 'upgraded' models. Those that end up in landfill sites will take over 1,000 years to rot down, leaking toxic substances into water sources. Recycling electronic goods – often done in poor countries – is itself hazardous, for both those who do it and the environment. Unless made to do so, as in the EU, producers of the devices don't have to pay for the recycling costs or compensate anyone for the environmental damage that follows.[29] These costs – or 'externalities' as economists call them – are not external to societies or the planet. They eventually have to be paid by others, especially future generations, either in money or in an inferior environment, and sometimes in illness.

No 'away'

Last spring I visited the beautiful Isle of Eigg, in Scotland, with a population of just 80 or so. The islanders are exceptionally environmentally aware and not only generate their own electricity from solar, wind and hydro, but minimise waste products by emphasising reuse and recycling. And one can see the sense of this: on such a tiny island, it's only too clear that there's nowhere to throw away rubbish – plastics, dead fridges or cars and other non-degradable stuff. What was a benefit becomes a burden. You could just ship the waste off the island to be dumped somewhere else, but of course, even if you could afford to do that it merely shifts the problem. Whatever you buy there, you find yourself asking, what will I do with it when it's finished?

There's a more general, indeed global, problem here: the costs of disposing of or recycling stuff need to be considered at the time of manufacture and purchase and borne by those involved rather than third parties. This, after all, is the polluter-pays principle.

The disposable plastic spoon epitomises the absurdity of undervaluing nature by treating resources as worth only what it costs us to extract and use them (Figure 20.2). Economic competition may improve efficiencies in the use of labour and any given amount of materials and energy, but if the sources of those materials and energy are non-renewable, then we are just plundering the earth with ever-greater speed. Optimists may believe that we will discover new reserves and, with new technologies, new resources. We may do, but that will probably just mean more despoliation. We've already seen how compound interest mounts up, but with compound growth of resource use, the effects are not merely figures on balance sheets indicating ballooning debts, but vast holes in the ground, pollution and environmental destruction. It's unsustainable.

Figure 20.2: 'Just wash the spoon'

Source: http://posters-for-good.tumblr.com/post/13199697341/just-wash-the-spoon

Key environmental impacts include soil erosion, deforestation, water salinisation, accumulation of insecticides and pesticides, particulates in the air, tropospheric (lower atmosphere) ozone pollution, stratospheric ozone loss, toxic chemical waste, heavy metals, asbestos, nuclear waste, rapid biodiversity loss (marine as well as terrestrial), acidification of the oceans, hormone discharges into the water supply, endangered fish stocks and, of course, climate change (of which more later).[30] No wonder some environmental scientists believe that the pace at which we are transforming the earth – land, sea and atmosphere – warrants the designation of a new geological period, 'the anthropocene'.

As the native American saying goes, 'When the last tree has been cut down, the last fish caught, the last river poisoned, only then will we realize that one cannot eat money.'

More on yachts

From George Monbiot:

[T]here's a strong correlation between global warming and wealth. I've been taking a look at a few super-yachts, as I'll need somewhere to entertain Labour ministers in the style to which they are accustomed. First I went through the plans for Royal Falcon Fleet's RFF135, but when I discovered that it burns only 750 litres of fuel per hour I realised that it wasn't going to impress Lord Mandelson.[31] I might raise half an eyebrow in Brighton with the Overmarine Mangusta 105, which sucks up 850 litres per hour. But the raft that's really caught my eye is made by Wally Yachts in Monaco. The WallyPower 118 (which gives total wallies a sensation of power) consumes 3,400 litres per hour when travelling at 60 knots. That's nearly a litre per second. Another way of putting it is 31 litres per kilometre.

Of course, to make a real splash I'll have to shell out on teak and mahogany fittings, carry a few jetskis and a mini-submarine, ferry my guests to the marina by private plane and helicopter, offer them bluefin tuna sushi and beluga caviar, and drive the beast so fast that I mash up half the marine life of the Mediterranean. As the owner of one of these yachts I'll do more damage to the biosphere in 10 minutes than most Africans inflict in a lifetime. Now we're burning, baby.[32]

But what about climate change? Isn't that a product of over-consumption too? It is, but to deal with it we need to put it into a bigger framework that includes but extends beyond the rich.

TWENTY-ONE

The twist in the tail: global warming trumps everything

As Shamus Kahn observes, the rich think of themselves as 'a collection of talented individuals who have a unique capacity to navigate our world', rather than as dependent on occupying positions in the economy from which they can extract more wealth than they contribute.[33] They are not free-floating individuals but occupants of positions within economic relations between different groups or classes. Their fortunes are made through these relations with others – as employers with employees, shareholders with claims on the wealth produced by employees, landlords with tenants, lenders with borrowers, sellers with buyers. The first four of these relations are invariably unequal, and the last often unequal too. To understand how the rich come to be rich, we had to identify these relations. Economics is relational. Sometimes it's a positive-sum game, sometimes a zero- or negative-sum game.

Following these connections meant confronting basic features of capitalism, particularly the control by a minority of key assets like technology, land, property and finance. Of course, there are and have been different kinds of capitalism; much depends on how it's regulated, particularly how far labour, consumers and the environment are protected through the state and civil society. In the neoliberal version of capitalism that has developed over the last 40 years, the injustices of capitalism's wealth extraction processes have grown, and their irrational and dysfunctional character has resulted in the worst economic crash for 80 years. The UK and the US have led the way, but most other developed countries have followed, some more closely than others, from Ireland to Turkey, to South Korea and New Zealand. Meanwhile the International Monetary Fund and the

World Bank have imposed neoliberal policies on developing countries and former Soviet Bloc countries as a condition of support, forcing them to privatise, reduce labour protection and taxes, and open their borders to multinational companies. Despite the economic crisis, neoliberalism stumbles on, zombie-like, creating more asset bubbles and protecting the rich by imposing austerity on the least-powerful.[34]

At various points we have encountered other problematic features of our capitalist global economic order: the unequal division of labour, which gives good-quality work to some at the expense of meaningful work for others; unequal exchange between countries with different levels of development; and wasteful consumption. All of these things are related to the rich, but also to things beyond them. So, inevitably, the critique of the return of the rich is also a critique of capitalism.

There have been many other critiques of capitalism since its birth: as exploitative and unjust; as irrational, contradictory and crisis prone; as a rat race that leads to burn-out, selfishness, loss of meaning in life and loneliness; as a source of economic insecurity and poverty amid plenty; and as environmentally damaging, threatening the future of the planet. This book is meant to supplement, not supplant, these other critiques. While they all hit home to some degree, this doesn't mean that capitalism hasn't also brought significant benefits, compared to what went before – most strikingly, unprecedented technological change and, in many cases, substantial improvements in several aspects of the quality of life.

Yet the return of the rich needs to be seen not only in the context of capitalism, but in an even bigger picture. Despite the appalling damage done by neoliberalism, in the long run, the biggest threat to our futures is climate change, driven by capitalism's dependence on compound growth. This has to be addressed now, not postponed to a day when the economic crisis has been resolved in some fashion.

Global warming: the basics

The vast majority of scientists who have devoted their lives to studying climate and its effects are agreed not only that rapid global warming is occurring but that it results from human activities that emit greenhouse gases, especially carbon dioxide. Yet the tiny numbers of climate change sceptics have been given enormous publicity – and many of them financial support from energy and other companies. Some of the sources of greenhouse gases are direct, like exhaust from cars and power stations; others, like increasing methane emissions from livestock as meat consumption grows, are indirect.

We've already seen 0.85 degrees Celsius of global warming since 1880.[35] That may not seem much, but the rise in temperatures over land is higher than this; the oceans take longer to warm up, though marine life and chemistry is already being radically affected. Yes, climate is never static anyway, but overall, the rate of warming is much faster than at any time in the earth's history. In the Arctic, where summer ice has shrunk by a third, it means that the amount of solar energy reflected back by ice is reduced, and is absorbed by the darker seas instead. In the tundra of northern Siberia, Canada and Alaska, the thawing of the permafrost is releasing methane – a much more powerful, though shorter-lived, greenhouse gas than CO_2 – from the soil into the atmosphere.[36] In these ways, global warming is in danger of becoming self-fuelling, and out of control.

Like compound interest, CO_2 emissions caused by human activity have grown exponentially. They can stay in the atmosphere for more than a century before they are reabsorbed by plants and the oceans. At present, the planet's oceans and terrestrial ecosystems can absorb only about half of the CO_2 emissions we are producing, and the tropical rainforests, which are key 'sinks' or re-absorbers of CO_2, are still being cut down relentlessly. Even since the 1990s, the period in which the phenomenon of global warming has become widely known, growth in emissions has not slowed up. In 2013, CO_2 levels in the earth's atmosphere exceeded 400 parts per million. The last time this happened was more than 3 million years ago, when the Arctic was ice free and sea level was up to 40 metres higher than now.[37] It will take a long time for enough land ice in Greenland and Antarctica to melt and raise sea levels to the same extent, but small rises are already threatening low-lying areas like Bangladesh, and of course most of the world's densely populated areas are low lying.

We can also expect more frequent extreme weather events and destruction of people, property and crops. Even New York, where subways and basements were flooded by Hurricane Sandy in 2012, is at risk. Typhoon Haiyan, possibly the worst in recorded history, laid waste to huge areas of the Philippines in 2013, killing thousands and leaving millions homeless. This event made it all too clear that extreme weather can sweep devastating tidal surges across low-lying and often populous coasts. The combination of global warming and such events is truly disturbing: droughts, deforestation and desertification (already happening in Spain, parts of Africa and California), increased extinctions of species and loss of biodiversity, food shortages, deaths from heat exhaustion, and mass migrations of people. By 2009, according to the Global Humanitarian Forum report *The Anatomy of a Silent Crisis*, hundreds of thousands of deaths had been caused by global warming, and many millions more people were negatively affected.[38] Under these conditions we can expect political tensions to rise, and some think 'resource wars' will become common.[39]

Many climate scientists fear that even a 1 degree Celsius warming is risky, but the more optimistic figure of 2 degrees Celsius as the maximum that we can risk has been widely touted in political discussions, though this is very much a politically acceptable figure. Without rapid action, the world could warm by 4–6 degrees Celsius by the end of the century.

If we are to stop global warming, we need to cut emissions startlingly quickly. Even if we stopped completely today, time lags in the effects of past emissions on climate would mean that temperatures would continue to rise another half a degree, taking us to 1.4 degrees Celsius higher than temperatures before industrialisation. The longer we leave taking action, the bigger the problem will get. Mike Berners-Lee and Duncan Clark calculate that if we are to have even just a 50% chance of keeping below the 2 degrees Celsius target we have to reduce emissions to little more than the 1850 figures by the end of this century.

But who should take responsibility for such action? Naturally, those most dependent on fossil fuels are most reluctant to do anything. The usual story we hear about greenhouse gases and climate change goes like this: For many years, the old industrialised countries were the prime culprits in causing global warming, but now they've been overtaken by China, which is building dozens of new coal-fired power stations (the dirtiest kind of fossil-fuel energy source) every year, so that's where we should point the finger. *What is almost always overlooked in the media and by politicians is that emissions of CO_2 stay in the atmosphere for many decades, even centuries.* So a large proportion of the greenhouse gases that are currently causing global warming have been there for a very long time. For older people like me this means that some of the carbon emissions that we were unknowingly responsible for when we were young are still in the atmosphere, contributing to global warming today. Even if I were to become completely carbon neutral for the rest of my life, I would not be able to offset those emissions. It also means that the old industrial countries like the UK, Germany and the US have a much bigger responsibility than their annual footprints indicate. The US's cumulative emissions since 1750 are roughly four times those of China, even though China's annual emissions now exceed those of the US.[40] In effect, the western industrial powers and Japan owe the rest of the world a huge debt – or damages. And while you can simply write off financial debts from balance sheets, you can't write off billions of tonnes of CO_2 in the atmosphere.

Stephen Pacala, the director of the Princeton Environmental Institute, has estimated that 80% of the emissions in the atmosphere come from old industrialised countries, which make up about 20% of the world's population. Blaming China as the main offender is wrong not only because it's a late industrialiser: it's also wrong because a substantial part of China's emissions total should actually be attributed to the rich countries, as it derives from manufacturing goods for those countries; further, China still has relatively low emissions per person – 6 tonnes per person, compared with the US's 18 tonnes. (The average world level is 4.9 tonnes per person.)

And, if we care about climate justice, it's emissions per capita that matter, rather than per country, for, as Pacala argues, the biggest emitters tend to be the affluent, whether they live in rich or poor countries. Pacala claims that the world's 500 million richest people (about €100,000 income per person or more), *just 7% of the world's population, were responsible for 50% of all greenhouse gas emissions in the world.*[41]

Energy slaves

The US accounts for one-third of global wealth, 22 per cent of world energy consumption and one quarter of total carbon emissions. Its population is only 5 per cent of the world's total. Each American has, it is calculated, 150 'energy slaves' working 24 hours a day to support this scale of energy use. (John Urry)[42]

The bottom 50% of the world's population, by contrast, are too poor to emit much; in fact so low are their emissions that they could benefit significantly from economic development before their emissions became a problem. And such development could substantially improve their life expectancy and well-being without much impact on carbon footprints.

Is it possible to have a reasonable level of development without excessive carbon emissions? Pacala estimates that as long as incomes across the world were capped at $40,000 per person, CO_2 in the atmosphere could be stabilised. While this is probably one of the more optimistic outlooks, researchers Julia Steinberger and Timmons Roberts found that some countries actually combine long life expectancy and a high score on the UN Human Development Index (HDI) with low carbon emissions that would be sustainable if replicated across the globe. What's more, as technology becomes less carbon intensive, this combination becomes possible for more countries. So there is some evidence that well-being *can* be decoupled from high carbon emissions. Just as well-being doesn't require great wealth, the good news about climate change is that nor need well-being cost the earth.

But there's no sign of this good news in the most affluent countries, which have several times larger emissions than countries like Costa Rica, Vietnam and Uruguay, but are only slightly better in terms of the HDI and life expectancy.[43] Incomes in the US are higher than in Japan or Spain, but the US is no better than them in terms of the HDI, even though its emissions per person are twice those of Japan and three times those of Spain or France. So both well-being and carbon emissions have got a lot to do with ways of living. One billion pounds spent on basic health services and education has a bigger impact on human well-being than £1 billion spent on air travel.

As the rich get richer, their carbon emissions increase, though at a declining rate. This is partly because the more money people have, the more of it they save or 'invest'. In addition, price and emissions aren't always strongly related: while a luxury meal might cost 20 times as much as a basic meal, the carbon emissions are unlikely to be so many times greater. Still, within rich countries, high-income groups are responsible for substantially higher emissions than the rest of the populace, particularly as a result of their higher mobility, especially air flights. It's been estimated that in the US a three-person household on $100,000 a year – hardly rich – has roughly twice the carbon footprint of a three-person household on $30,000 a year.[44] Yet, in global terms, even less well-off people in rich countries have large carbon footprints, mainly because they live in highly developed societies dependent on fossil fuels.

Climate scientists differ on just *how* fast we need to cut emissions, indeed on whether we have already passed a point of no return, but they all agree that the longer we leave it, the harder it will get. We certainly can't afford the carbon footprints of the rich, as they exceed their global allowance by so much more than others. True, many less wealthy than them also need to cut their emissions, direct and indirect, but it would be unreasonable to expect them to reduce their carbon footprints while the rich carry on as now.

So what would be an effective and fair global response aimed at stopping global warming?

Contraction and convergence

This is the name of an approach proposed by the Global Commons Institute.[45] The idea is to move towards a situation in which all nations have the same emissions per person (convergence) while contracting them to a level which is sustainable (Figure 21.1). So a country with 5% of the world's population should be allowed no more than 5% of this global sustainable level. This would require those nations that currently have emissions per person above this target – rich countries – to make reductions proportionate to the amount by which they exceed it. At the same time, those nations that are currently below the target – poor countries – would be able to increase their emissions up to that level. So countries with very high individual emissions would have to make the most rapid reductions. Both the required rates of convergence and the degree of overall contraction can be adjusted, depending on estimates of the risks of runaway climate change and on international negotiations.[46]

Figure 21.1: Contraction and convergence

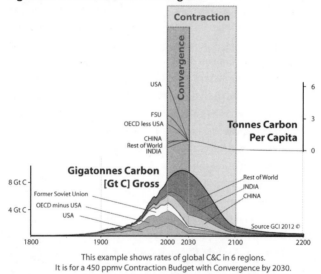

This example shows rates of global C&C in 6 regions.
It is for a 450 ppmv Contraction Budget with Convergence by 2030.

Source: Global Commons Institute, http://www.gci.org.uk/

This proposal scores well in terms of simplicity, though of course it would take an international agreement to implement it. It would put an end to the current situation where some countries are endangering the futures of others by pumping out unsustainable levels of greenhouse gases. Although it seems fair, it actually lets the old industrialised countries off lightly, for their vast historical accumulated emissions are ignored. Of course, this is not how those countries would see it, indeed they would be likely to complain that they were having to make the biggest sacrifices. But then, according to the polluter-pays principle, that's exactly what they should do.

The earth is finite. We cannot go on living in a way that would need three planets to sustain it. The industrial revolution that has swept round the world in the last three centuries took no account of this. Capitalism refuses any finite limits and its culture cannot accept the idea that we might have enough in terms of material goods; we must always have more. Soviet communism, as polluting as capitalism, thought it could triumph over nature in its race to industrialise. Another way must be found.

The diabolical double crisis

From much of this book so far, or at least until the last chapter, you may have got the following implicit answer to the big question of what we should do in the wake of the neoliberal crisis: given that the rise of the rich and the related slowdown in the growth of ordinary people's wages and salaries have, together, stalled the global economy, slowing the growth of demand and restricting opportunities for profitable productive investment, we should cut off or tax the rich's sources of unearned income and redistribute wealth downwards. This would boost demand and allow economic growth to resume, for those on lower incomes would spend all or most of their new, additional income on goods and services. This is what ended the Great Depression and led to the post-war boom, though post-war reconstruction also provided a major investment outlet. In other words, redistribution plus growth is the answer.

That *would* be the big message, were it not for something far more important for our future: *such a policy would accelerate global warming, indeed it would make runaway global warming and its dire consequences inevitable.* This is indeed a colossal inconvenient truth. Particularly now, when austerity policies are clearly worsening the economic crisis, growth seems the obvious answer. So, for the financial crisis, growth is a big part of the solution; but from the point of view of the climate crisis, it's the problem, at least for the richer societies. We are therefore in a *diabolical double crisis* in which remedying one crisis in the obvious way will only make the other worse. This is the twist in the tail.

Perhaps, though, there is a way out?

Green growth?

One superficially attractive alternative is 'green growth', a scenario in which we switch to a low-carbon but continuously growing economy, so that we still enjoy what we think of as a good life based on ever-increasing consumption but without burning fossil fuels. Its attractions are greater than its plausibility.

The only way capitalism could be greened would be by 'decoupling' economic growth from growth in greenhouse gas emissions. However, as Tim Jackson has demonstrated, such an outcome is highly unlikely. True, as we've already seen, energy and carbon intensities per unit of output have declined: the 'energy intensity' of each unit of output is 33% lower now than in 1970, globally. But this improvement has been more than offset by the economic growth during that period,[47] such that CO_2 from fossil fuels increased by 80% from 1970 to 2007 and by 40% since 1990, and grew at 3% per year between 2000 and 2007. What's more, this growth has occurred during a long period of stagnation of wages and salaries, and hence relatively slow growth of aggregate demand. Capitalist recovery would make the possibility of carbon reduction even more remote. Frankly, capitalism is incompatible with saving the planet. Capitalism is addicted to growth and goes into crisis if it cannot grow. That is why it has been so dynamic and transformative. Workers always have to produce not only enough to provide for their own pay and all the other costs of production and distribution, they also have to produce enough to provide for owners of businesses, shareholders, landowners, money-lenders, speculators and value-skimmers. At the same time fierce competition between companies to maximise profit pressures firms into producing more with a given number of employees. If they can't keep up with rivals, they go out of business. A capitalist economy in which consumption, particularly of energy, levels off and 'enough is enough' is an impossibility.

Green growth in the rich countries of the world is a pipe dream. The idea that once we get over the financial crisis and annual compound growth resumes at 2–3% per annum we can decarbonise the economy is absurd. Carbon-capture technology is still in the experimental phase. 'Geoengineering' projects, such as cloud seeding or putting giant reflectors in space or fertilising the oceans to absorb more CO_2 are hugely risky, and only encourage governments to stall on CO_2 reduction.

So is there another way out of the double crisis?

Reduced consumption: sufficiency?

For the rich countries at least, not growth but zero growth or even 'de-growth' are likely to be the only feasible ways of cutting greenhouse gases fast enough to stop runaway global warming, and that of course would mean more modest consumption, including reduced mobility, particularly for the rich and well-off. We certainly can't afford the rich, for environmental as well as economic and social justice reasons. But where environmental matters are concerned, those with excessive carbon footprints extend below the rich to include many of us in the rich countries.

This may horrify some. Hasn't one of the most sobering effects of the current economic recession been the prospect that our children are unlikely to enjoy the opportunities in terms of work and consumption that their parents have enjoyed? And let's acknowledge a further twist: the older and middling-to-better-off members of the population have already enjoyed things like cheap air travel and come to think of seeing the world as something both normal and within their grasp, indeed as an entitlement. Every day we are encouraged to book holidays in far-flung places. And it would be ridiculous to deny that such travel has enriched people's lives. How can those who have enjoyed such things now kick down the ladder and say that young people and those with less money should not aspire to them too?[48] There's no getting away from this dilemma. It seems grossly unfair to the latter group, but we have long been living beyond our carbon means. Certainly we need to raise the incomes of the poorest in the rich countries and support growth in poor countries, but if we want to stand any chance of stopping global warming, rich countries have to consume less, starting with the richest – the least green of all. Hence the necessity of contraction and convergence.

We are told by politicians that globalisation is the future – ever-increasing integration of different economies, more imports and exports, more travel, both freight and passenger. The total distance travelled by all the parts in a computer or car may be equivalent to the distance from the earth to the moon. The politicians are wrong: *de-globalisation* is necessary for a sustainable future. Unless and until we can devise low-carbon forms of travel, which means, in effect, an alternative to petroleum-based fuel, there will have to be much less of it, and much more local production. And in more localised economies we are much less likely to harm the environment because any damage and waste are less likely to be out of sight and mind.

A new geography

Cutting back on travel – both freight and passenger, including commuting – would change the geography of our societies, both within and between countries. We're used to having a small number of huge factories and warehouses supplying millions of people, sometimes in several countries. Where once every rich country had its electronics and car producers, now there are a few multinationals serving whole continents. This global geography is very much dependent on cheap – wastefully cheap – fossil fuels, especially oil.

As John Urry puts it, 'there is no Plan B to replace the oil that accounts for at least 95 per cent of current transportation energy'.[49] So, in the absence of some miraculous invention of a low-carbon form of energy, whether we like it or not, future generations may have to accept much-reduced mobility. This would mean developing a new, more localised geography of production and distribution, so that far more of what we consumed was produced in our regions, or at least our own countries. It's absurd for British people to eat onions from Chile and apples from New Zealand. It's also absurd to grow carrots in Scotland, ship them to a distribution centre in the south of England, and then ship them back to Scottish consumers.[50]

Reducing transport and shortening supply chains in turn would mean more job variety at the local level and away from the metropolis, because lots of areas would have activities that used to be carried out centrally or overseas.[51] Some things might be more expensive, in consequence, though much better environmentally.

There is a much more positive side to this, though. Bearing in mind the well-being threshold, above which increases in wealth have not brought greater happiness and well-being, a levelling down from the top, combined with a levelling up for those at the bottom, need not mean poorer lives. Indeed, it could improve them by bringing the benefits of living in more equal societies – having more in common with others and greater trust, and more willingness to support collectively provided education and health services. Privatising such services erodes the sense of the public good and of public service in which, through helping others, we help ourselves; we can flourish best together. It means greater equality of opportunity because children do not grow up in grossly unequal circumstances. We need contraction and convergence *within* countries in terms of wealth as well as between them in terms of greenhouse gas emissions.

Reducing our carbon footprints isn't only a matter of using less energy to heat our homes by improving insulation or finding lower-carbon forms of travel – our 'direct' emissions, as they're sometimes called – for these only make up a small minority of our CO_2 emissions. The bulk of the emissions for which we are responsible are 'indirect' – they arise from the production and distribution of all the other goods and services we use, from the internet through to the food we eat and public sector goods like education.

Take food, for example. The rich countries have high-carbon diets, thanks, in particular, to their taste for large quantities of meat. Animal products are a less efficient and more polluting source of calories than are vegetable products and grains because animals consume a lot of energy just to keep alive. Worst of all is beef. According to Juliet Schor, the average US beef diet emits the equivalent in greenhouse gases (not only CO_2 but methane) of 1,800 miles of driving. Vegetarian or low-meat diets are much greener. The carbon footprint of the average 4 ounce cheeseburger is 2.5kg of CO_2 but for a veggieburger it's only

1kg.[52] A steak is equivalent to 25 bananas in terms of CO_2.[53] Meat consumption is now growing fast in countries that have traditionally not eaten much meat, such as China and India; sadly, it seems to be seen as a mark of progress.

There's another inconvenient fact. It's been found that where people reduce their direct carbon emissions, they tend to use their savings to buy more goods, thereby increasing their indirect emissions![54] So they may even unwittingly increase their emissions by improving their home insulation. The problem is that in rich countries it's difficult to reduce your carbon footprint by much, for while we can do things like installing energy-saving light bulbs and better insulation in our homes, it's not within our power to reduce many of our indirect emissions.

You could try assessing your carbon footprint by using one of the many carbon footprint calculators available on the internet.[55] When you've put in your data and worked out your current footprint, try doing it again with some changes – maybe no air flights, or doing without a car, or eating less meat. Going without these may sound drastic enough, but you'll probably find it would reduce your emissions by only a quarter, or a maybe a third. Even if you got an electric car, the electricity would probably be generated by burning fossil fuels. It would certainly be a big step forward if we could all reduce our emissions by a quarter, but beyond that things become much more difficult if we want to live in a similar way to how we do now. What do we do about the carbon emitted in the production of our washing machines, televisions, computers and in the fertilisers used to grow our food, and in moving so many of these things from distant places?

To reduce our indirect emissions we have to change the way energy is produced in the first place. This depends on corporations rather than individual households. Energy corporations are amongst the biggest companies in the world and, given our dependence on them, they have tremendous economic – and political – power. Take the case of BP, which temporarily identified itself as 'Beyond Petroleum' in 2000. It's the fifth-largest company in the world. It constitutes 9% of the capital on the London Stock Exchange and its shares form one sixth of the invested value of pension funds in the UK,[56] so inevitably the government is likely to assume that what is good for BP is good for British pension holders. On its website BP offers visitors an energy (carbon footprint) calculator.[57] It thereby encourages them to think that reducing carbon emissions is just an issue for us as individuals, rather than for the likes of BP, as if it just passively responded to whatever consumers demanded. James Marriot calculates that the carbon footprint of BP's production and distribution processes and its products is twice that of the UK.[58] BP is massively investing in the extraction of oil from bitumen ('tar sands') in Canada, an extraordinarily energy-intensive and polluting technology. The cartoon by Robert Mankoff in Figure 21.2, originally published in *The New Yorker*, hits the nail on the head.

Figure 21.2: 'Unprecedented opportunities for profit'

"And so, while the end-of-the-world scenario will be rife with unimaginable horrors, we believe that the pre-end period will be filled with unprecedented opportunities for profit."

Whatever they may say, the last thing energy companies want to see is declining demand for energy. Of course, strictly speaking it's not fossil fuels that they are ultimately most committed to, but profit; if they could make more money out of low-carbon energy production, then they would switch to that – not because it's greener but in order to increase profits. But for the time being they are heavily committed to fossil fuels. According to Thomas Jones, if we are to meet the 2 degrees Celsius target, '80% of the vast quantities of fossil fuel reserves held as assets by publicly listed companies will lose all their value, and the huge sums currently being expended on finding new reserves will all be wasted: result, financial meltdown (again)'.[59] Rather than see the shrinkage of Arctic ice as a calamity caused by burning fossil fuels, energy companies are treating it as an opportunity for getting access to new oil fields, while keeping quiet about how this will further accelerate global warming.

Of course, every one of us has a responsibility to address climate change, but, as we've seen, beyond a certain level it is very hard for us to do so, given our dependence on external energy systems that rely principally on fossil fuels. Responsibility lies heavily with business, especially in the energy sector. BP and other energy producers can be confident that in so far as domestic consumers do reduce their direct energy consumption, the reductions will be small and probably offset by increases in their indirect energy consumption.

So the problem is not one of fossil fuels running out; indeed it would be better if they did, and quickly, but new reserves are being discovered and brought into production. Fossil-fuel companies are already borrowing against revenue from future extraction, and their creditors are banking on it. As Berners-Lee and Clark so rightly say, if our need for fossil fuels is an addiction, the addicts are being told to stop while the dealers are getting government support![60]

Yet challenging big business is the last thing neoliberal governments want to do, for they are its servant and defender. One of the features of the neoliberal era is the attempt by governments to make individuals responsible for providing for themselves where previously the state did this. It's clearest in attempts to reduce state provision of education and health and to blame the unemployed for job shortages. Some sociologists, never afraid of coining an ugly word, call this 'responsibilisation'. Treating our response to global warming as one of individuals becoming more responsible in their choices is entirely consistent with this. In this way, governments can avoid blame if things don't work out at the same time as they not only avoid challenging big business but deliver new customers to them through privatisation. Focusing purely on individual consumers depoliticises things.

Although many neoliberal politicians dismiss global warming as fiction, it's hard to believe that they really believe the vast weight of scientific research is mistaken. Philip Mirowski has researched neoliberal think-tanks and argues that – contrary to appearances, particularly their tendency to deny climate change – neoliberals actually have a strategy for dealing with it. This strategy has three parts:

1. deny climate change;[61]
2. advocate carbon markets, in which permissions to emit CO_2 can be traded;
3. invest in 'geoengineering' to weaken and reverse global warming and its effects. This might include cloud seeding, adding chemicals to the ocean to stimulate CO_2 absorption, or capturing CO_2 and storing it underground, or putting mirrors in space to reflect back sunlight, and so on.[62]

This may indeed be the strategy, but, as Mirowski points out, it's madness. Each element of it is flawed, though the first two are straightforward bits of deceit. First, the neoliberals know damned well that global warming is happening and that it's the result of over two centuries of fossil-fuel burning. But, in order to buy time, they deny its existence or say it's nothing to do with human action, just as tobacco companies knew that smoking was a health hazard and yet denied it so that they could continue to profit from it. And attacking scientists, especially where they come up with inconvenient truths, is always a good populist ploy.

Second, they advocate carbon markets *because they know they don't work*. The idea is that the government sells permissions to businesses to emit carbon. Those involved in sectors that can reduce their emissions will profit from doing so because they can sell some of their permissions to others who can't or won't. By progressively restricting the total number of permissions, the government can reduce emissions, and do so in a way that is responsive to the different needs of different businesses. But the business sector can easily prevent it reducing emissions: aside from the sheer political might of major energy companies, they also hold much of the technical information that the regulator needs in order to run the system, so they can protect themselves, and even make profit out of it, especially by constructing derivatives related to the carbon price – another financialisation opportunity. Not surprisingly, experiments with such markets in Europe, the US and New Zealand to restrict emissions have failed miserably. But they appeal to mainstream economists, trained to think in terms of economic models rather than real political economic processes, and they are a good way of buying more time for capitalism.

Third, there's the long-term neoliberal solution of geoengineering. Technological optimists will always say the history of capitalism has been one of unpredicted inventions and innovations, some of them, like the internet, of vast consequence; so don't worry, something will turn up.[63] The dangers of creating unwanted side-effects by meddling with highly complex and interdependent systems of climate and the ecology, including the chemistry and life of the oceans, are huge. Nevertheless, having learnt nothing from over two centuries of imagining that we can always dominate nature, there are research projects in progress on geoengineering, and a feverish scramble for patents on technologies; the profit has to be the main thing, of course. The neoliberal dream is a world whose population is held to ransom by a few geoengineering companies that control the climate.

Some of the projects are funded by billionaires, such as Bill Gates and Richard Branson. Branson, self-publicist and head of the Virgin group of companies, was reported to have said: 'If we could come up with a geo-engineering answer to this problem, then Copenhagen wouldn't be necessary. We could carry on flying our planes and driving our cars.'[64] (Branson, appropriately enough, lives on an island in the Virgin Islands, avoiding UK taxes.) So banking on geoengineering also encourages complacency about our current fossil-fuel-addicted economies and lifestyles. Branson's imagined world is a bizarre one in which one part of capitalism freely burns still more carbon while another part mitigates its effects, both of them regulated by profit.

But if capitalist-driven growth continues, global warming may get to the stage that even those who don't want it are forced, in desperation, to turn to geoengineering. Rich nations and rich communities within them will be the most able to take the heat, and turn away those trying to flee drought, floods and loss of livelihoods. This again is madness.

Where does the problem of the rich come into this?

Reading this, you might be wondering whether the problem of the rich is a distraction from dealing with something far worse – global warming? No; on the contrary.

Those who think the problem of the rich might divert us from saving the planet are in danger of ignoring a key barrier. Through overproduction of debt, and rent-seeking, the businesses that sustain the rich are mortgaging our future and that of the planet. Brazil is clearing its forests to generate hard currency to pay foreign debts.[65] Through their interests in fossil fuels and in growth, and through their domination of politics, they are worsening the problem. Far from it being a diversion, stopping this economic dependency is a major part of what's necessary for stopping global warming. And of course, the social justice arguments remain, whether global warming continues or stops. But, as we've seen, replacing our neoliberal capitalism with a more productive and less unequal capitalism is not the answer.

We also can't expect the majority in the rich countries to make a sacrifice when the rich minority escape doing so. Hervé Kempf puts the point well:

> But would we limit our waste and try to change our life-style while the Fat Cats, up there, continue to luxuriate in their air-conditioned SUVs and their villas with swimming pools? No. The only way you and I will agree to consume less material and less energy is if the material consumption – and consequently the income – of the oligarchy is severely reduced.[66]

No one likes to be the sucker, making sacrifices so that others can carry on as usual. Just as I'd be happy to pay more taxes if those who are paid more than me pay proportionately more, but not otherwise, so sacrifices in consumption need to be geared to ability to make them.

We need to combine the critique of the rich with green critiques of capitalism, so that we can develop alternatives. A green, sustainable economy that will appeal to people needs economic justice, radically improved life chances for those at the bottom and strengthened democracy. Clearly, radically different ways of living are needed.

CONCLUSIONS

TWENTY-TWO

So what now?

We can't go on as we are now. That's the most important point. If we are to create more equal and just societies that are environmentally sustainable, it's clear not only that we can't afford the rich, but that we can't afford to perpetuate an economic system predicated on inequality and endless compound growth. The dream of 'green growth', with capitalism delivering sustainability, is like selling guns to promote peace. We need an economy that can function on the basis of *enough*, instead of insatiable acquisitiveness. Much more equal societies are desirable in themselves for allowing all to develop their capacities and to develop a sense of the public good, and of mutual respect, solidarity and care; but that's impossible if we are constantly pressured to compete in the rat race for positions that are themselves very unequal. Nor can we expect some to accept more modest levels of consumption if others are free to consume more than their share of what the planet can cope with. George W. Bush's response to global warming was to say: 'The American way of life is not up for negotiations. Period.' But an American way of life for everyone in the world would require an estimated five planets to support it. We can't afford that.

So there's also an environmental argument for equality: no one has the right to more of the earth's resources, including its capacity to re-absorb CO_2, than the total of those resources divided by the world's population (the principle underlying contraction and convergence). It's imperative for preventing runaway global warming and an ever more hostile environment for human and other life, but it also means much greater equality within and between nations.

Back to basics

Crises are opportunities. The neoliberals are seizing the opportunity to push down wages, dismantle the welfare state, allow corporations to dictate policy and push up profits still more. To offer a genuine alternative we need to go back to basics. It is no good just trying to oppose the status quo on its own limited ground, answering only the questions that it poses. If we did that, then at best we might slowly emerge from the economic crisis in a decade or two to find that our quality of life was no better and the planet was even more damaged. Even though radical change is needed in the financial sector, on its own that's nowhere near up to the task of tackling our diabolical double crisis of economy and environment. Even though it's tempting to say 'it's pay-back time', just (!) redistributing economic and political power back to the majority would not change the game enough to allow us to flourish in future.

Contrary to neoliberalism, economies are supposed to serve societies, not vice versa. As Aristotle argued, money is a means to an end, not an end in itself; it is madness to devote our lives to accumulating money.[1] But under capitalism, what Aristotle regarded as an aberration becomes a necessity: capitalists survive by accumulating money, and go out of business if they don't, and they employ their workers only as long as they make this accumulation possible. We should remember Robert and Edward Skidelsky's analogy of the two people who are wandering around lost, but each of whose main concern is not to find the place they were meant to be going to, but just to be in front of the other, regardless of where they're going. That's what capitalism is like: never mind where we're going, as long as capitalists are in profit. It obscures the point of economic activity: provisioning to enable us to live well – and, we can now add, in a way that is sustainable, so that future generations are not faced with a deteriorating environment and a world riven by forced migration and resource wars.

Hence the need to confront a wider range of issues than the mainstream debate is prepared to consider. How can we organise economic life in ways that are *fair, conducive to well-being, and sustainable?* We are social beings: that means we are unavoidably dependent on each other in a host of ways, whatever kind of society we live in. That dependence can take mutually beneficial, life-enhancing forms, or oppressive, zero-sum, exploitative forms. How can we replace the latter with the former?

Shibboleths like 'competition is always good' need to be challenged. Yes, it can sometimes raise the general standard of practice and encourage innovation, but it can also lead to a race to the bottom – cutting wages, cutting taxes to attract the rich, closing firms without putting anything in their place, offloading costs onto others, including dumping waste in countries where the law is too weak to stop it, and increasing inequalities.

Likewise 'economic efficiency'. Of course it's usually good to do things 'efficiently', though often that's confused with cost savings achieved through cutting pay. Labour-saving technology like information technology has *not* enabled reductions in working hours, because the greater the competition between organisations, the more likely it is to mean that we just have to do more in the same working day. A microwave oven may save you time at home, allowing you to do other things as you wish, but in a fast-food restaurant it just means each worker has to produce more meals in a given time. We have always to ask: efficient for whom? Does it give us more time, or just speed up the treadmill? And as the case of the disposable plastic spoon reminds us, what is 'cost-effective' in money terms can be an absurdly wasteful and polluting use of resources. In the public sector, much cost cutting in the name of 'efficiency' merely reduces service quality and distracts services from their core purposes, so that schools teach to the test and hospitals reduce patient care and send patients home too early so as to free up beds. It encourages vacuous nonsense from management about 'leveraging our skillsets to meet the challenge of competition going forward', and suchlike, eroding professionals' commitments to doing what is best for clients, patients and students, and other workers' desire to do their job well. It can produce stress, disaffection and burn-out in workers – too busy to care for themselves and family or to have time for friends. We have to weigh all these things up in the different spheres of economic life and limit and regulate competition accordingly.

All this means questioning our whole way of life and what well-being and wealth are. What is consumption for? What is really 'development'? Many development economists have already argued that GDP is pretty useless as a measure of development. Real development means creating circumstances that allow everyone simultaneously to be able to have and do the things necessary for a good life: having enough food, shelter and health services; having security and freedom from threat and violence, including sexual violence; being able to develop their capacities through education and access to a range of activities; being able to participate in political decisions that affect them and having free speech and conscience; being able to care for others and be cared for; being able to have respect and interact with others without coercion, exploitation, stigma or neglect; and so on.

I'm referring here to 'the capabilities approach', pioneered by Amartya Sen, the Indian economist and philosopher, and Martha Nussbaum, the American philosopher, as a way of thinking about well-being and development.[2] Economic resources and measures are not ends in themselves, just a means to the end of living well. Well-being requires not only the elimination of avoidable suffering[3] but enabling people to be active and make the most of their potential so that they can *flourish*. Individuals may decide to forgo some of these opportunities if they so wish, but the important thing is that they should be *available* for all *simultaneously*. Greater equality does not mean more uniformity. On the contrary, as Tawney argued, it enables everyone, and not just a few, to get the chance to use and develop their particular, individual abilities, so that greater equality is conducive to greater variety. And, as he put it, 'Though an ideal of an equal distribution of material wealth may continue to elude us, it is necessary, nevertheless, to make haste towards it, not because such wealth is the most important of man's treasures, but to prove that it is not.'[4]

Even in developed societies, access to all these 'capabilities' is not open to all: long-term job shortages mean long-term unemployment for some, while the unequal division of labour means that for those who can get work, its quality varies considerably, enabling some to use and develop their capacities, while for others it offers no more than a wage. Women are still expected to be primarily responsible for housework, and they suffer discrimination in the labour market, even though in many countries their educational qualifications are better than men's. And in some developing countries their access to education is limited. Removing barriers to education for women is empowering and unleashes a huge reservoir of capacities. It also tends to reduce family size and slow down population growth. So, while resources are needed to create capabilities, the changes needed are not just economic, but involve reorganising how we live and do things, and altering the balance of power in society.

Contrary to mainstream economics' miserable, demeaning view of individuals as purely self-interested − an attitude that our neoliberal societies actually foster − it's common for people to want to contribute to society and help and be useful to others, and to appreciate and feel inspired by the contributions of others, even where they don't benefit from them personally. One of the harms of job shortages is that they make the unemployed feel useless and unable to contribute and participate. This is a key cause of depression. (It's also why retirement is a peak time of depression.) A truly developed society is one that makes it possible for all to contribute what they can.

The neoliberal dream of a society of self-reliant individuals, able to avoid any dependence on others beyond what they can pay for, is absurd and deceitful. Those who regard themselves as wholly independent, perhaps because they have taken out private health insurance and a private pension, are deluding themselves; they are still dependent on others, but through having the financial power to be so, rather than because those others agree that they need it. There is nothing wrong with transfers of wealth between people, where they're for supporting those unable to work, such as children, the sick or elderly. The problem is when transfers are based merely on control of assets that others need but lack − so that they provide owners with unearned income, at the expense of those less well off. Neoliberalism doesn't just redistribute wealth from the 99% to the 1%. The neoliberal attack on the welfare state cuts back democratically regulated transfers of income based on needs, and expands flows of unearned income based on control of assets, pushing people from the generous arms of the former into the grasping claws of the latter.

It shrinks the humane part of our economy and diverts wealth to an economy based on power. Transfers based on the agreement of others to provide certain kinds of a support as an entitlement, a right, are the mark of a civilised society, as opposed to a society of all against all, in which those who can get to control the most assets win at the expense of others, simply because they can.

This means that care work must be valued in itself, rather than as an inconvenient interruption to employment. Child benefit and benefits for carers should be as normal as wages. It's central to all societies, so employment shouldn't be the only route to an income. At present, universal benefits for such things are frequently attacked for giving taxpayers' money to well-off parents or pensioners. But the problem here is not the universal benefit, but the prior inequalities. With major reductions in inequality, the problem becomes unimportant.

Actually, neoliberalism does *not* produce self-sufficient individuals. In 'freeing' them from democratically controlled support via the local and central state, it produces new forms of dependency for the majority: indebtedness – isolated individuals dependent on those who control money, those who will 'support' them only if they provide their creditors with unearned income in the form of interest. Within organisations, replacement of any element of democracy with managerialism ('leadership') reduces employees' autonomy and encourages them to compete with each other in order to win management approval. We need each other, but we don't need the dependence of the rich on our wealth production. Further, neoliberalism increases nations' dependence on borrowing from the rich instead of taxing them to make them contribute.

When a country switches from providing its students with grants to giving them loans, which it then sells off to private business, it doesn't free those students from dependence and make them self-reliant. It just means that instead of being temporarily dependent on a state that has supported them from birth and to which they will continue to pay taxes throughout their lives, they become dependent for decades on private lenders who have previously done nothing for them and who just want to extract as much interest as they can. It's another switch from democratically regulated transfers of income based upon need to payments of unearned income to those who control money. Similarly, when people switch from renting a house from the state to buying one, they become more, not less dependent; while the 'rent' they pay to the state need only pay for construction and repairs, their mortgage repayments make them dependent for decades on private creators of credit money seeking interest.

Nature must be valued not as a mass of resources that we can simply exploit one by one according to separate myopic calculations of costs and revenues and opportunities foregone, but as whole ecosystems in an interconnected planet, in which things have value beyond advantages that they happen to bring us in terms of money. *Price is not value; it's just one, very limited, one-dimensional way of assessing something that's multi-dimensional.* The idea of pricing individual species by creating ownership rights in them may be a way in which private corporations can enrich themselves by charging for what was formerly free, but it is an absurd way to value things that are always dependent on immensely complex webs of relationships that make up the world's ecosystems, or 'the biosphere'. Nature needs respect and a sense of wonder, not plunder. Often environmental battles are portrayed as between hard-headed, basic economic needs and soft-headed, nerdy concerns about butterflies or rare spiders and the like. But actually they are about how we, as part of immensely complex, interdependent ecosystems, and utterly dependent on them, act within them and change them. Our global division of human labour allows people in each locality to ignore the consequences of the exploitation of resources from distant places, on which they depend. Unless regulated to do so, markets don't have to provide information about such things. Neoliberal economists claim that market prices give us all the information we need. They don't, and never will.

Nature provides things like soils, water, fish and plants for free, but it makes no sense to regard them as free to be used without limit, regardless of the health of the biosphere. Nature doesn't respond to the signals of the market. Capitalist firms live or die according to whether they make profit, not whether they meet social or environmental goals. There may be some cases where pricing resources may help to regulate their use, but markets for things like forest products and fish can also speed up rather than stop their extinction. Blanket arguments for markets as the solution to everything – or alternatively, as the source of all evils – are too simplistic. But where markets are allowed, they have to be regulated to stop exploitation of labour and unsustainable practices, and to protect biodiversity.

Yet, in addition to that still rather instrumental view of our environment, we should not forget its beauty and richness. Being able to appreciate and enjoy it is an important part of well-being, and we should not apologise for these values simply because they don't fit with a narrow economic perspective. As Ruskin said, 'there is no wealth but life'.[5]

Steps

How do we change all this for the better, to make societies fairer, supportive of well-being and environmentally sustainable? It's time for some proposals. If many of my suggestions seem drastic, that's because, in the face of the diabolical double crisis of economy and environment, they need to be. They are far from a complete list. But many of them would have to be combined for each to be effective. They are not a manifesto or a programme, just *some* of the things I suggest need to be done – a contribution to an urgent debate, already going on in some quarters, but which I hope others will join. In Britain, the Green Party's Green New Deal is currently probably the nearest thing to it.

In keeping with the main argument of this book, we need not only to tax the rich and redistribute wealth back to the rest, but to cut back their sources of unearned income in the first place.

First, rent. The most obvious way to stop private owners from extracting rent (beyond covering construction and maintenance costs) from others is to nationalise land and minerals, so that rent comes under democratic control, or for the state to tax ground rent through a land-value tax. Those who are horrified by the idea of land nationalisation need to be reminded that it need not prevent people owning buildings and benefitting from improving them and the land; it's just a matter of recovering for society the gains made from the privatisation of nature and space itself. Although state-controlled rents are likely to be much lower than private rents they can still be set higher in the more sought-after areas than in less-popular areas.

This would allow rent to serve its 'allocational' function, ensuring that users who most need to locate in a given area can do so. And in much more equal societies, differences in what land and property users are willing to pay will reflect mainly differences in their needs and wants rather than differences in income. However, under international law, nationalisation of land would require compensation of landowners (in effect, compensating them for the loss of the benefit of providing a disservice to tenants), whereas states are free to charge whatever taxes they like. A land-value tax has been favoured on the Right as well as the Left: in the US, it was advocated by the capitalist reformer Henry George. It would, he argued, stop landowners siphoning profits from enterprises in the form of rent and thereby holding back development. In the 18th century, it was supported by Adam Smith. Even Chicago economist Milton Friedman, a key figure in the rise of neoliberalism, described it as 'the least bad tax'.[6] Of course, neoliberal politicians ignore this, as their parties rely on the votes and financial support of property-owning classes and rentiers, so instead they *encourage* rent as a source of income. It's no surprise that the powerful invoke economic theories only in so far as they suit them.

Other kinds of private rent extraction – for example, by monopolies, often through intellectual property, should also be more tightly regulated. This means instituting a regime that limits who can secure copyright and patent, and for what period, so as to balance the public good with the need to reward and support innovators. The struggle to stop the control of the internet by private companies is a particularly important new battle.

Wanting to change property rights may set alarm bells ringing for many. But the goal is not to destroy property but to protect it and to prevent those who rely on earned income or transfers from being ripped off by those who use property to extract rent. It's to ensure that people can have secure homes that they can control and care for, whether they own them or rent them from mutual associations or the state, where rents can be democratically controlled. In the latter cases, there are possibilities for devolving control to tenants. And let's remember that neoliberalism has already changed property rights by stealth and power – allowing private companies to privatise more and more of the commons and offloading the property that private banks no longer find profitable – toxic assets – onto the public.

Second, interest and credit money. Interest, especially at high rates, is the problem, not credit. Credit provides a way of facilitating development and making sure money is put to use, rather than lying idle. But it should not be used as a device by which the rich can take advantage of the rest. The most important function of credit should be to fund productive investments and projects. The risk of lending should be shared by the lender and the borrower, so that if the project being funded fails, the lender is responsible for part of the losses. This motivates banks to form closer and better-informed relationships with borrowers. Lending for consumption and purchase of assets should be secondary and much more tightly regulated than now, so that it doesn't fuel asset bubbles: rapidly increasing the amount house-buyers can borrow merely pushes up house prices without creating any new wealth, and transfers wealth from the asset-poor to the asset-rich. Borrowing for house purchase, for example, should be supported on a mutual basis, where, in effect, members pool risks and banks can lend only what they have. Chronic house-price inflation, caused by a combination of housing shortages and excess credit, must be stopped by building state and mutual housing and regulating credit for private housing; it could establish stricter eco-housing standards, following the precedent of the post-war years in the UK, where building standards of state housing bettered those of private housing.

The flip side of this is that savers – who of course need not be investors in any meaningful sense – should expect no more than a zero real rate of interest on their savings so that they just retain their value. Only if they use their savings to invest productively is there any justification for a bigger return.

As we saw, the creation of credit money by private banks allows them to extract wealth. Creating credit money is a good idea if it's used primarily for productive investment, if the deadweight costs of interest are minimised and if it's accountable. But private banks have proved to be lamentable at funding productive investment and over-lend on existing property and financial assets, causing asset bubbles and excessive debt. Better to spend new money into the economy than to lend it at interest, and to control the creation of money by private banks too.

The neoliberal orthodoxy, backed by mainstream economics, is that governments are inferior investors to private investors: governments, it's claimed, tend to create too much credit money and cause inflation, lack the skills to make investment decisions and allow political considerations to influence decisions. The neoliberals couldn't be more wrong.[7] If we are to support productive investment in ethical and environmentally sustainable businesses, national and regional and specialist banks are needed whose remits restrict them accordingly. Such banks would need to work closely with businesses to share knowledge of what real investment is needed. And why, in democratic societies with a much more equal distribution of income and no element of plutocracy, would it be wrong for political considerations to influence decisions? Under neoliberalism, the political interests of the rich are masked as merely economic considerations, but there's nothing apolitical about cutting top rates of tax, cutting tax-evasion investigators, allowing private utilities companies to siphon off public money to shareholders and supporting asset inflation.

Third, profit from the ownership of businesses. The problem here is that even though the businesses may be productive, the people who produce the goods and services – the employees – have no say in how the money brought in by the sale of those goods and services is used. The output and the revenue belong to the company owners – even though they may be no *more* than owners and do no work for the business. In the standard business model, bizarrely, they or absentee shareholders are the sole stakeholders. Even if they are working capitalists, managing the business as well as owning it, there is no good reason why they should have exclusive control and rights over the business, while their employees have none. And how outrageous that owners whose profits depend on their workers should be able unilaterally to close businesses if it suits them. Democracy stops at the workplace door, at present. With the tyranny of the shareholder value movement over the last 40 years, this absurdity has worsened. It is essential that this situation is reversed, both as a matter of justice and to ensure that workers' interests are aligned with those of their organisation. We need to assert the rights of

351

workers (including employee managers) as key stakeholders, although, particularly in businesses with captive markets, it's also important to have user representation too. Company accounts and those of public organisations need to be made public and to be sufficiently detailed for people to be able to make judgements on what is happening to them. Organisations over a certain size, say 20 employees, should be obliged to have worker representation and part-ownership, so that workers can jointly formulate business plans.

There are many different models for cooperatives,[8] but they tend to work best in networks including mutual banks and other complementary organisations in which know-how can be shared and new products and services developed. Beyond such networks committed to this form of organisation, it is important that shares are not transferable to outsiders. The stock market is dysfunctional and unjust. Making shares tradable exposes business to uncommitted 'investors' interested only in wealth extraction. There is no reason why outsiders should be able to buy and sell access to streams of unearned income from controlling and speculating on assets, and without contributing to any work or real investment in the companies in which they have shares. Having a market in company ownership is supposed to allow companies to be controlled by those who can manage them best, but what does 'best' mean here? We are still waiting for 'the euthanasia of the rentier' that Keynes called for.

This need not eliminate all competition in the markets for goods and services and, hence, the scope for users to take their custom elsewhere. Competing worker-controlled firms, with influence from committed banks holding shares in them, having to sink or swim in markets for their products, would have an interest in efficiency and in having the best managers they could find. And such businesses could still merge, split or make alliances if they found it made sense to do so; the lack of a stock market needn't mean a frozen economic system.

While worker-owned enterprises would still compete for consumers' custom, they would hardly be likely to sacrifice themselves in order to do so; they would not, for example, sack themselves so that they could be replaced by workers in a cheap-labour country! Even if they chose to make some sacrifices, they would have the dignity of deciding for themselves rather than having them imposed under pressure from responsibility-free absentee owners. Instead of choosing the low-road strategy of cutting pay, training and conditions, they would have an interest in choosing the high road of long-term innovation and upskilling.

Markets, regulated to be servants rather than masters, are often the best way of coordinating users and producers. For many products (not virtually all, as the neoliberals imagine) markets can marshal the local knowledge and wants of countless producers and consumers – a task beyond the powers of any agency trying to control production across the whole economy. Further, by allowing competition among producers, markets encourage a 'discovery process' in which new products can be tried out. But, as neoliberals fail to acknowledge, the producers in the markets needn't be capitalist organisations. We don't always have to choose between capitalist firms and the central state.

But sometimes we do need local or central-state control, albeit with worker and user representation. For both efficiency and social justice reasons, some, like railways, education and health, are best if provided by publicly accountable state monopolies. In the UK the National Health Service – the crowning glory of the post-war welfare state – is currently being destroyed not only by stealth cuts in state funding (£20 billion over five years), covert privatisation and an orchestrated campaign of bad news, but by new legislation that forces hospitals to stop cooperating where their strengths are complementary and instead to offer services to competitive tender from private health service companies. In such cases, enforcing competition adds significant costs of tendering and legal services for making contracts and dealing with litigation; it allows private providers to siphon off taxpayers' money to shareholders, and to cherry-pick the more profitable patients and leave the state and voluntary sectors with the rest. No wonder the US private healthcare system is one of the most expensive in the developed countries, and the NHS one of the cheapest.[9] For similar reasons, many formerly state-owned businesses that have been privatised, particularly in energy and water supply, will need to be renationalised or changed to mutual associations, and to ensure that energy sources become sustainable and not primarily a source of rent.

Finance fit for purpose

Here the changes will have to go far beyond the usual prescriptions of breaking up the big banks so that they are no longer too big to fail, and separating high street banking from speculative 'investment' banking so banks are not able to gamble with ordinary people's money. And it is not enough merely to attack bonuses either; caps on bonuses just result in higher basic salaries and deal with symptoms of the crisis rather than basic causes.

Banks should safeguard deposits, provide financial advice, recycle currently unused money to where it can provide most benefit, provide credit to enterprises and households, facilitate and regulate large transactions, including cross-border flows, and pool and manage risk, not amplify it through securitisation and leveraging. Some current financial practices and products may assist these tasks, for example, hedging against risk; but, unless tightly regulated, they can easily become destabilising and threaten the real economy instead of supporting it. As heterodox economist Ha-Joon Chang says, complex financial products should be allowed only if they can be proved both safe and productive in terms of benefits to society, just as new drugs have to be approved before they can be marketed. This is also in line with the UK Green Party's call for a board of expert financial regulators that is truly independent of financial institutions, instead of stuffed with rentier grandees, like most regulatory boards.[10] The euthanasia of the rentier and the shift from shareholders to employees and users as key stakeholders will also radically reduce the scope for value-skimming on transactions.

Above all, the money supply, which the banks have steadily privatised through digital credit money to provide a source of interest over the last 40 years, should be brought back under public control. Finance, including the creation of public money on a debt-free basis, and public credit must be made democratically accountable so as to ensure that it functions to support a new economy based on securing environmental sustainability and social justice.[11]

A key feature of the neoliberal era has been the freeing up of cross-border flows of capital, so that increasingly rentiers and capitalists can 'invest' anywhere and move money to wherever they can avoid most tax and find the lowest costs, while value-skimmers can profit from the useless churning of financial markets. Restrictions on such flows were a key factor in the post-war boom. If businesses are to be publicly accountable and amenable to influence from democratic governments, their ability to escape national jurisdictions needs to be restricted. Governments would be less susceptible to the blackmail of capital flight at the first sign of anything challenging plutocratic power. But that's also why such controls would need to be introduced instantaneously, rather than gradually.

Neoliberal theory supports free-market principles: 'protectionism' is taboo. Yet, when it suits powerful countries, this is forgotten. Protectionism has been and continues to be a central plank of US and European Union policy – particularly for their heavily subsidised agricultural sectors. Protectionism for us, free trade for everyone else. Poorer countries need to heed not the word of the rich countries but their practice, and protect their infant industries as the rich did, particularly in food, and become more self-sufficient. But as we saw, international trade will have to be reduced anyway to cut carbon emissions.

A crackdown on corporate tax avoidance and tax havens, and tighter regulation of businesses, would boost government tax revenues considerably – with estimates standing at $53 billion in the US, and £4.1 billion in the UK.[12] The introduction of 'country-by-country reporting' would require multinational corporations to disclose their accounts and taxes paid in each of the countries in which they operated, for all the companies they controlled, so that their operations were transparent and open to inspection by governments and the public. There should be no secrecy for companies. They are private only in terms of ownership; they employ, sell to and affect the public, so they should be accountable to it.

A transactions tax, as proposed by Nobel laureate James Tobin, set at a tiny percentage of financial transactions, could both raise considerable sums and benefit economies by reducing incentives for speculation, and hence volatility, and allow governments more control over their economies. As Tobin said, it was intended to 'throw some sand in the wheels of our excessively efficient international money markets'.[13] Stability brings long-term benefits, including a better environment for real long-term investment. Such a tax would fall most heavily on those financial organisations that engaged in high-frequency trading – chiefly 'investment' banks trading on their own account (rather than for clients) and hedge funds. Depending on the rate of tax and the range of transactions it covered, it could yield billions. Tony Dolphin at the Institute of Public Policy Research estimates that a 0.01% transactions tax in the UK could raise £25 billion. Sometimes called 'the Robin Hood tax', it could pay for substantial green investment and for empowering those on low and insecure incomes.[14] Predictably, it is widely opposed by financial interests.

Taxing more and taxing less[15]

> Every person, if possible, ought to enjoy the fruits of his labour, in a full possession of all the necessaries, and many of the conveniencies of life. No one can doubt, but such an equality is most suitable to human nature, and diminishes much less from the *happiness* of the rich than it adds to that of the poor. It also augments the *power of the state*, and makes any extraordinary taxes or impositions be paid with more chearfulness. Where the riches are engrossed by a few, these must contribute very largely to the supplying of the public necessities. But when the riches are dispersed among multitudes, the burthen feels light on every shoulder, and the taxes make not a very sensible difference on any one's way of living.
>
> Add to this, that, where the riches are in few hands, these must enjoy all the power, and will readily conspire to lay the whole burthen on the poor, and oppress them still farther, to the discouragement of all industry. (David Hume, 1752)[16]

'Where else is the money coming from?', you may ask. It should come first from taxing unearned income based on ownership of assets, which means taxing the extraordinary wealth and income of the rich. Most important is a progressive wealth tax, so that the higher reaches of the 1% pay tax on their wealth, with the rate increasing, the richer they are. As Thomas Piketty proposes, this should be *global* (he calls it a 'global capital tax'). This would require two things: first, international agreements, though it could start with the EU and build outwards; and second, financial transparency. The latter is needed to stop wealth being hidden; it's absurd that it's often difficult to find out who owns financial assets, and who is indebted to whom, as happened in the Cypriot financial crisis. And unless we know who owns what, where, then we have little chance of stopping the plutocracy and holding the rich to account. Developing countries, especially, are victims of pillaging in secret. The problems are not technical but political; as Piketty says, in the US, banking data is automatically shared with tax authorities for over 300 million people. Countries, businesses and individuals that refuse to cooperate should be automatically sanctioned.

Second, and again as Piketty proposes, we need an 'exceptional tax' on private capital to pay off national debts, allowing governments to escape the power of bondholders, so that they can fund social expenditure independently and without causing a financial crash. As the private wealth of the richest is much greater than public debt, a progressive tax on their wealth could remove that debt within a year. Capital gains from the rise in value of existing assets should be heavily taxed. Whether local or national, taxes on property should be strongly progressive, so that those with the biggest properties paid the most.

Such taxes could also prevent inequalities between the rich and super-rich and the rest from widening, indeed reduce them (the largest fortunes tend to grow at 6–7% per year);[17] further, they could provide funding for major investment in alternative energy and conservation. More on this shortly. Talk of global taxes may make you think 'in your dreams', but the nightmares of global warming and the growing power of the plutocracy are already reality. Again, radical responses are necessary.

Inheritance taxes on bequests over a certain amount (£20,000? £50,000?) would provide a further way of clawing back masses of mostly unearned income and preventing inequalities from being enlarged by the tendency of the children of the well-off and rich to get large windfalls unrelated to need – or their contribution. Twenty-eight per cent of all wealth in the UK is inherited, but only 13% of people receive a significant inheritance.[18] And, as Piketty shows, the more the wealth of the rich grows, relative to rates of economic growth, the bigger the proportion of income that the rich get in the form of inheritance. Coupled with other forms of redistribution, such a tax could stop huge windfalls but allow *more* people to give and receive a *modest* inheritance, tax free.

Income tax should also be steeply progressive, as it was in many countries in the post-war boom, although, particularly with a wealth tax on the rich, income tax could actually be *cut* for the worst-off and those in the middle in rich countries. VAT – a tax on consumption goods that weighs most heavily on the poorest, as all their income has to go on consumption – could also be cut for necessities, though remain or increase for luxury goods.

Carbon taxes and other green taxes are essential: they would be applied to extractors and users of fossil fuels, tropical hardwoods and rare minerals and other scarce non-renewable resources, and to polluting activities. This of course would mean pushing up taxes on fuel for transport, making air, sea and most road transport more expensive. The road and airline lobbies would of course oppose this, fighting for the right to offload the costs of pollution, including carbon emissions, onto others, but the need for such taxes to cut fossil fuel use is inescapable.

There would be more jobs for tax inspectors, but their main job would be targeting the big, multinational tax avoiders, like Amazon, Google and Starbucks. With tax evasion estimated at £70 billion in the UK,[19] the inspectors would pay for their salaries many times over. Corporate free-riding on ordinary taxpayers must end. In Norway and Finland, the governments require information on everyone's income, net worth and taxes paid, and make that information available to the public. This discourages tax evasion and makes possible a well-informed debate about economic inequality and how much tax people should pay. If the ways in which the rich avoid tax became more transparent they would be exposed to the glare of the public eye. We could find out how much every Tom, Diane and hedge fund manager paid in taxes. People might be concerned about privacy, but, given that pay is dependent on social relations between people

– employees and employers, and sellers and buyers – it's questionable whether it should be.[20] What we get paid depends on what we can get from others, or at least how much they are willing to part with. Yes, the rich might be embarrassed by having their wealth revealed, but so they should, and if some of the world's richest countries can do it, why can't others?

Taxes are just one side of the equation. Government expenditure is the other. Neoliberals love to accuse governments of excessive public spending. Sometimes they're right. The UK government is wasting £100–130 billion on its Trident submarines, its pointless 'independent' nuclear deterrent (actually, it's American controlled). That would pay for the NHS for a year.[21]

Pay and working conditions

> Our merchants and master-manufacturers complain much of the bad effects of high wages in raising the price, and thereby lessening the sale of their goods both at home and abroad. They say nothing concerning the bad effects of high profits. They are silent with regard to the pernicious effects of their own gains. They complain only of those of other people … (Adam Smith)[22]

Apart from these changes, we would need a higher minimum wage, equal to the living wage – that is, sufficient to get people above what is generally agreed by governments to be the poverty line: two thirds of median income.[23] In the UK, as the government prefers not to admit, the majority of people relying on benefits are in households that have someone in employment; clearly, their pay is inadequate. With a living wage and restrictions on usury, loan sharks offering 'easy credit' online would become extinct. At a global level, in low-wage countries a pay increase of just a dollar an hour would boost living standards, increase demand for goods in those countries and yet make only a small difference to the overall cost of export goods.[24] A global minimum wage would not only help the poor but make a major contribution to the convergence and contraction strategy that the world needs.

But we also need either a *maximum* pay rate or a very high top rate of tax of 80% or 90%, like we had in 'The Golden Age' of capitalism, the 1950s and 1960s, when the high-paid did not whinge about needing incentives. As for what that maximum pay or top tax threshold should be, take your pick – £70,000, £100,000, £150,000, £200,000 or …? Remember, though, that individual carbon footprints correlate with income, and even the lowest of these figures tend to be associated with footprints that exceed the planet's capacity to absorb them.

Pensions should be state run and funded through taxes, that is, by transfers between generations. Being democratically regulated, the transfers would be needs-based and donated. It would be up to the electorate to decide how much should go on these transfers. Private pensions, 'invested' in financial securities, by contrast yield asset-based unearned income. They favour the fortunate 40% who can afford to save and use their savings to get interest and speculative profit. A pension is something we all need, so it should be treated on that basis, not on an everyone-for-themselves-and-tough-if-you're-poor basis (or tough if you're a woman with an interrupted employment history). State pensions have been more generous in the past and could be again in the future. Given that private pensions would be threatened by the ending of the shareholder value model, state pensions would need to increase quickly. People could still of course save privately to top up their state pensions, although again, they should not expect to get unearned income (a positive real rate of interest) on their savings unless they used them to fund productive investment.

Shortening the working week would increase the number of jobs and avoid the absurd situation where we have some with plenty of money but no time and others with plenty of time but not enough money. Organisations should not be able to rely on compulsory workaholism, and offloading the costs of the health problems it causes onto individuals and the state.

Benefits for the unemployed and for those with disabilities or ill-health should be enough to allow them to live with dignity and security. Long-term unemployment – overwhelmingly in areas of long-term decline and disinvestment – is likely to damage people, but the primary problem is job shortages, not individual deficiencies. Half of Spain and Greece's youth have not suddenly become lazy since the crisis. Job creation is the main solution. The areas of decline – the Detroits, Liverpools and Middlesbroughs – are also the areas in which there are huge expanses of abandoned and often poisoned land that need to be cleaned up and developed. It is ridiculous to encroach on precious rural land to build houses and shops while this is the case. Most of all, there is much work to be done to build a green economy.

The restoration and improvement of the welfare state for everyone would be a big step towards a humane economy and society. As equality increased it might be possible to build support for a universal basic income to replace most specialised benefits, providing both security and a simplified welfare system.

It will no doubt take a long time to reduce the unequal division of labour, given how deeply embedded it has come to be in our societies. But two things should help. First, democratising ownership and control of enterprises is likely to make it more probable that they would share out good and bad tasks more equally. Or they might vote instead to pay those doing the lower-quality work more than those doing the better-quality work: workers could then have a choice – poor work but good pay versus nice work and more modest pay. In so far as pay is seen as a compensation for the burden of working, this makes sense.[25] Second, reducing inequalities in pay would weaken the financial incentive to strip out the less-skilled and more tedious tasks from the higher-paid jobs and give them to lower-paid workers. However much it might upset our familiar ways of thinking about paid work, a more equal division of labour would offer the chance for more people to develop and use their abilities, to live fuller and richer lives and to work in fairer and more cohesive workplaces.

Going green

We have to leave fossil fuels in the ground, shale gas included, and rapidly develop sustainable energy systems, but also consume less energy through improved domestic insulation and reducing waste. Massive funding is needed for urgent research on renewable energy. As the UK Green Party puts it, we need a 'green army' to make buildings energy efficient and, where possible, partially self-sufficient. This in itself would create thousands of new jobs. But it would be geared to sufficiency rather than everlasting growth. Forests, particularly rainforests, which reabsorb CO_2, must be strictly protected.

For both their own well-being and that of the planet, the better-off in the rich countries need to consume less. At the other end of the spectrum, the 1.3 billion – 18% of the world's population – living on less than $1.25 a day need to be helped out of absolute poverty.[26] Given how late in the day it is for stopping runaway global warming, there simply isn't time to wait decades for alternative energy supplies to build up; shocking though it may seem, the better-off will have to cut their direct and indirect CO_2 emissions by consuming less, and sooner rather than later.

Ballooning 'easy credit' allows people to consume more, earlier, but in the long run it's expensive for borrowers and for the planet, for it requires continuing economic growth to pay off. And it's the upper reaches of the 1% that have the biggest stake in that debt and growth and in controlling economies in their own interests. The rich are also the only ones who can protect themselves to a significant degree from the worst consequences of global warming. That's why people sympathetic to the green cause need to challenge the power of the rich and the way spending and investment are funded.

Going green implies that, rather than worship new things above all, we should value things that are durable and easily maintained and repaired. Being able to repair stuff will become a vital skill. Recycling will need to be stepped up, and to stop non-degradable waste it would be advisable, as far as possible, to prevent it being moved outside localities, so it can't be pushed out of sight and mind.

We cannot achieve change on the speed and scale required to stop global warming without nationalising major energy companies, so as to create a rapid, managed reduction in CO_2 emissions and major investment in renewables. The future of fossil fuels is too important to be left in the hands of companies accountable only to shareholders purely interested in money. At the same time, local and individual initiatives in renewable energy generation must be actively supported. When countries are faced with major emergencies, as all are where climate change is concerned, they can quickly mobilise huge resources, including by sequestering private capital, as they do when they go to war. There is no time to fiddle about, negotiating incentives with companies too powerful and committed to continuing fossil fuel extraction to respond.

The partial return to more locally based economies as long-distance transport was reduced to cut emissions would also stop the race-to-the-bottom tendency. In particular, our dependence on oil for moving people and goods has allowed low-density suburbs and long – inefficient! – commutes, but unless a low-carbon substitute can be found, this legacy will be unsustainable. The decentralisation of activities from major cities, as a remedy for high transport costs, will offer more the chance of working closer to home, and diversify occupational choice in medium and small cities. Low-carbon public transport will have to be not only expanded but improved to make it more reliable and attractive. Cycling solves many local transport needs and, as I can personally testify, it is not only healthy but life enhancing. Local skills banks, social currency networks, shared parenting networks, seed bank networks and housing co-operatives all offer different ways of living in ways that enhance well-being and sustainability. In towns as different as Toronto and Bristol, Brighton and Hove, and Detroit, networks are developing to link local food producers and local consumers, including, in the British cases, hospitals, prisons, schools, nurseries and care homes, to provide visible, accountable, farm-to-plate supply chains, healthy food and local control. Combining support for local organic farmers and reducing the meat content of meals in the public institutions not only lowers CO_2 emissions, but offsets the higher costs of organic production.[27]

Yet this is not a call for parochial, purely inward-looking communities, and certainly not pre-industrial ones. It would be madness to throw away the benefits of modern medicine and communications, for example. Many national and international links, exchanges and movements will still be necessary, and indeed beneficial, but their development needs to be regulated according to criteria of well-being and sustainability.

Some things will become cheaper: with more equal incomes, land tax, new social housing and restrictions on credit, house prices need not rise any faster than prices of other products, so housing costs need not take up an ever-increasing share of our incomes. Reducing the hidden interest charges built into the plastic-card money system could also lower costs. But some things will become more expensive: transport is likely to be one of them, but it's necessary to reduce movement and stimulate the search for low-carbon alternatives. And we would only be able to afford to buy things that were viable to sell while paying those who produced them a living wage. Some consumer goods and services might therefore become more costly, as they would incur a kind of fairtrade premium over the 'free market' price. And quite right too. The whole point of economic activity is to enable people to provision themselves; it's ridiculous to regard forms of economic activity that prevent poverty as 'uneconomic'. Economies are supposed to support people, not vice versa.

Democracy

Finally, and essential for everything else, we have to remove the political as well as the economic dominance of the rich, and rebuild democracy. We should be under no illusions about how difficult this will be. The plutocracy may be a mass of ever-shifting temporary alliances, rather than an organised conspiracy, but it controls the media and mainstream politics, and will fight hard and dirty to maintain its power. The security services can monitor our use of the internet and mobile phones. Energy companies can switch the lights off to hold us to ransom, financial companies control private pensions. Coups are not just things that happen elsewhere. Yet, the plutocracy of the early 20th century was pushed back by democratic political pressure,[28] and our 21st-century plutocracy can be made to retreat too, only it needs to be done more decisively and permanently this time round.

Political donations to parties must be severely limited in size. If we are to have election campaigns fit for democracy rather than plutocracy, then we have to embrace state funding for parties. Elements of proportional representation in countries that currently lack it are needed in order to allow support for minority parties to have an effect. Restoring democracy would require having far stronger restrictions on politicians advising companies and having financial interests in businesses than is currently the case, not only during their terms of office but both immediately before they enter politics and for a period of several years after. Corporate lobbying must be far more strictly controlled and infiltration of the state by corporate representatives reversed.[29]

We cannot afford to allow the mass media to continue to be dominated by privileged elites and corporate interests. At present, winning the approval of media moguls like Rupert Murdoch is a price politicians have to pay so as to get elected. Before coming to power in 1997, Tony Blair flew to Australia in 1995 to ask for Murdoch's support, and later became his friend, and godfather to his daughter. Later, Blair's former aide, Alastair Campbell, alleged that in 2003 Murdoch – a keen supporter of going to war with Iraq in order to get its oil – phoned Blair to urge him not to delay the invasion.[30] Not surprisingly, scarcely a whisper of criticism of the war was allowed in the 175 newspaper titles, covering three continents, that Murdoch then controlled, and this at a time when a substantial proportion of British and Australian people opposed the war. The media empires must be broken up, and the internet 'digital commons' defended from attempts by corporations to control its form and content and harvest our personal data to sell off to others and pass on to government security agencies. One way of democratising the media would be to give everyone a voucher, say for £100, to spend on their favourite not-for-profit media outlet, so as to offset the power of the state and corporations.[31]

Finally, the upside

As I said, this is a contribution to thinking about the present and the future, not a manifesto, and others will spot many gaps and have valuable proposals and criticisms. Nor have I tried to discuss political strategies. And there are many other important kinds of change needed to improve our lives, many of which also require much more equal societies – combating sexism and racism, for example; but my main concern here has been the rich. Change requires action on many fronts. A necessary though not sufficient step if we are to progress is to call the rich to account, expose their income and wealth as largely unearned and their power as undeserved, undemocratic and exploitative. Unless we can get this widely understood and ditch the nonsense about 'wealth creators' and a return to business as usual, we stand no chance of improvement.

In combination, blocking asset-based unearned income, improving needs-based welfare, reducing inequalities in pay, making workers and users key stakeholders in economic organisations, democratising politics and redirecting investment into sustainable energy sources and ways of living could make our lives and those of the next generations so much better. Freed in our daily lives from the treadmill of excessive competition and overwork, and from economic insecurity, able to live with others as equals, neither deferred to nor condescended to, and enjoying a stable climate and caring for our environment rather than conquering it, we could actually start living more and enjoy each other and our extraordinary world. Yes, that's 'utopian', but why would we not want to head in that direction, especially when the alternatives are so appalling?

We truly cannot afford the rich and the systems that support them. They are living beyond our means and those of the planet, and their interests are at odds with those of the 99% and the environment. We must stop supporting them.

Afterword

Left, right, or in the muddle

Many readers – and even more non-readers! – of this book will regard it as 'Left-wing'. 'Pro-99%' or 'pro-planet' might be better, but I don't care how you classify it: I do care whether the arguments are sound, and what the counter-arguments are, if not. The Right normally applies the Left label as a stigmatising term, in order to avoid engaging with the issues raised, yet even leading organisations of the rich and powerful now have to admit that rising inequality and global warming are major problems.

In January 2015, the World Economic Forum, which holds its annual meeting of the super-rich in Davos (see pp 244-5), proclaimed that inequality and climate change were 2015's challenges, and chided those who dismiss concern about inequality as the politics of envy:

> Challenges abound – fundamental institutions and global governance are broken, corruption is pervasive, the rich are becoming richer and the poor poorer, rising middle classes are being squeezed by volatile commodities, inequality is fuelling unrest, climate change and environmental degradation are undermining social and economic development …[1]

Then there's the International Monetary Fund (IMF), a major player in the global debt crisis. Its managing director, Christine Lagarde, said "All will benefit from steps to cut excessive inequality … Our findings suggest that – contrary to conventional wisdom – the benefits of higher income are trickling up, not down."[2] The Organization for Economic Cooperation and Development (OECD), representing rich countries, makes similar points in a report called *In it together: Why less inequality benefits us all.*[3]

Moving from Mammon to God, or his representative, in an eloquent encyclical letter, Pope Francis shocked the political elite with his call to value the earth and its ecology, live within ecological limits and drastically reduce inequality.[4] The letter is informed not only by Catholic theology but also by an extensive review of research on climate, inequality and development. It is also refreshingly direct:

> The earth, our home, is beginning to look more and more like an immense pile of filth. (p 17)

> Humanity is called to recognize the need for changes of lifestyle, production and consumption, in order to combat this [global] warming. (pp 18–19)

> The foreign debt of poor countries has become a way of controlling them … In different ways, developing countries, where the most important reserves of the biosphere are found, continue to fuel the development of richer countries at the cost of their own present and future. The land of the southern poor is rich and mostly unpolluted, yet access to ownership of goods and resources for meeting vital needs is inhibited by a system of commercial relations and ownership which is structurally perverse. (p 38)

And repeatedly the Pope argues that inequality must be addressed at the same time as climate change:

> every ecological approach needs to incorporate a social perspective which takes into account the fundamental rights of the poor and the underprivileged. (pp 68–9)

Exactly.

The rich and super-rich know very well that in the long term rising inequality and climate change are threats, including to their own pockets, but they show little sign of wanting to act on this. Collectively they may recognise it, but individually they certainly don't want to reduce their own power. Although such reports present interesting data and acknowledge some of the dangerous consequences of increased inequality, their explanations avoid the key relationships of power on which the rich depend through their control of the economy. And – apart from the Pope's encyclical – they fail to admit the absurdity of perpetual growth in a finite world.

EUsury: plutocracy trumps democracy

Anyone who doubts the power of the plutocracy and the lengths it will go to enforce its economic regime needs only to observe the saga of Greece and the EU – the very model of modern usury.

Predictably, Greece has been represented as the wayward, overspending, incompetent debtor, needing to be taught a lesson by the successful, prudent and long-suffering creditor. These moralistic reactions reduce the matter to the enforcement of a simple moral rule: debtors should always pay their debt. They ignore what is always key to understanding debt: the wider historical context in which the unequal relation between lender and borrower arises.

Certainly, there has been plenty of incompetence and corruption on the Greek side in recent decades, though it was the Greek elite who were responsible and who gained most from it, sometimes with the active support of major European companies,[5] and external financial bodies, as we saw earlier, in the case of the use of complex derivatives to conceal government debt (pp 209–11 and p 277).[6] From the debts inherited from the military dictatorship, to the blind eye EU leaders turned to Greece's financial position in order to admit it to the Eurozone in 2001, to the wheeling and dealing and cost spirals of the Athens 2004 Olympics, it was not ordinary Greeks who were responsible.

Yet it was also not just a matter of questionable decisions made by individuals, but the wider context of deregulated finance globally. Over-lending by banks precipitated the crisis in 2007, and the banks feared default by Greece would prompt Spain and other bigger debtors to seek relief too, breaking the rule of EUsury.

Particularly for the 50%+ of young Greeks who are unemployed as a result of years of austerity, the debts are 'odious', because they did not agree to take them on; they were imposed on them by others, against their will. And under EUsury, Greece has been forced, against its clearly expressed democratic will, to take on more unpayable debt while imposing further austerity measures that will make it still more unsustainable. Even the IMF belatedly recognised that the debts are unpayable and that the creditors would have to take a 'haircut'.

Although debtors normally subsidise creditors by giving back more than they get, the dominant message of the popular narratives was, as usual, the opposite. Loans to other countries are news: repayments with interest are not. The Greek negotiating team were portrayed as wanting handouts when in fact they were seeking to reduce their dependence. According to the Jubilee Debt Campaign's analysis of official figures, if Greece pays its debts in full, the European Central Bank and its member national banks stand to make between €10 billion and €22 billion profit, while the IMF has already made €2.5 billion of profit out of its loans to Greece since 2010.[7]

In fact, it is not primarily Greece that is getting bailed out but the banks that recklessly lent to them. For years, major banks in the north have lent to southern Europe, allowing it to buy goods from the north. For example, German and French arms companies have been happy to see northern European banks lend money to Greece to buy their products. (Greece spends a greater proportion of its GDP on defence than any other EU nation.[8])

In old-style usury, debtors who could no longer pay their debts were made to give up their property and their freedom, and to work directly for the creditor; they became debt-slaves. Under EUsury, Greece has to accept a fire-sale of €50 billion of its assets to private companies, with half of the revenue to go to a trust fund in Athens supervised by creditors. It's clear that the creditors don't just want paying back, they want Greece's assets. Although Greek rates of pay and state social spending are well below the EU average, the creditors have decided that trade unions need restricting, and support for pensions for people on low incomes reduced. In classic colonial style, the Troika is sending officials to monitor and micro-manage the implementation of the 'deal'. This includes — seriously! — changing rules governing the ownership of pharmacies, the shelf-life of milk, and the weight of loaves sold by bakeries.[9] Quarterly reviews will be conducted to check progress, and automatic spending cuts will be made if there are deviations from the programme.

So the lenders have made it more difficult for Greece to repay its debts. Austerity has shrunk the Greek economy by 29% since 2010, making its debts relatively larger, from 133% of GDP in 2010 to 174% in 2014. Like so many features of our economy it's both unjust and dysfunctional.

It is an extraordinary illustration of the way in which – despite all the talk of shrinking the state and freeing up the market – the heavy hand of the European state is being used to establish the kind of markets and property ownership that meet with the approval of creditors. No wonder the reaction in Greece was "this is a coup". Even the *Financial Times* said 'a bailout on the terms set out in Brussels risks turning the relationship with Greece into one akin to that between a colonial overlord and its vassal.'[10] But financial coups are so much more civilised than military coups. Meanwhile, as it punishes Greece, the European Central Bank attempts to keep recession at bay by e-printing €1.1 trillion in quantitative easing to buy government bonds – a move that is likely to promote asset inflation and benefit the banks and the rich.

After the First World War, Germany was made to pay reparations of $33 billion – a burden that triggered hyperinflation and economic misery for many ordinary German households. At first the US intervened to stagger the payments and provide loans, but after the 1929 crash, it demanded full repayment of the loans. The result was economic decline and unemployment for six million people – fertile ground for the rise of Nazism. (Greece's own neo-Nazi party, Golden Dawn, could benefit from more punishment of the country by its creditors …) After World War Two, lessons were learned: the cancellation of debts and the US's provision of aid under the Marshall Plan enabled Germany's economic recovery. Greece was one of the countries that took part in that debt cancellation. But of course, now, the roles have been reversed, and Germany will not consider acting similarly vis-à-vis Greece.[11]

Although every debt crisis is different, there are plenty of echoes here of an old story: that of the Third World debt crisis and the conditions the World Bank and the IMF attached to its loans to

debtor countries, frequently requiring purchases of goods and services
from the Global North, and forcing them to privatise public assets,
and make deep cuts in public services. As Susan George comments:

> Now it's our turn. Now it's called austerity. Call it what
> you like, but it's the same policy – it's socialise losses,
> privatise profits … [and] this has been pushed to a point
> where, although we began richer than the countries of
> the south … we are really creating now a situation where
> there are desperately poor people in Europe, in Britain,
> in normally wealthy countries.[12]

With breathtaking vindictiveness, when the Greek people voted
'no' (οχι) to the bailout deal, the Troika's response was not to make
concessions but to impose an even harsher deal. Tax expert Richard
Murphy's reaction to the Greek crisis was apt:

> It is a game bankers are playing to show who us who
> is in control.
> It is a ruse to show that debt is above democracy.
> It is a device to show that states must bow to banks.
> It is contrived to show people matter less than money.[13]

Muddle over climate

Faced with the choice of saving capitalism or the planet, governments'
words and actions typically point in different directions.

Back in 2008 Obama's message was: "Time to end the tyranny of
oil; in my administration, the rise of the oceans will begin to slow." Yet
in 2011 a massive expansion of coal mining was allowed in Wyoming,
which of course helps raise sea levels through global warming.[14] Just
how far the tune had changed by 2012 can be seen from this boast:

> Over the last three years, I've directed my administration
> to open up millions of acres for gas and oil exploration
> across 23 different states. We're opening up more than
> 75 percent of our potential oil resources offshore. We've

quadrupled the number of operating rigs to a record high. We've added enough new oil and gas pipeline to encircle the Earth, and then some.... In fact, the problem ... is that we're actually producing so much oil and gas ... that we don't have enough pipeline capacity to transport all of it where it needs to go.[15]

But then in February 2014, he did veto a Bill to construct the Keystone KL pipeline carrying oil from the Canadian tar sand fields to Texan refineries. And in August 2015 he announced a bold plan for 'clean power'. The justification? 'We're still contributing to the problem. Carbon pollution is the biggest driver of climate change.'[16] Just weeks later he went to the Alaskan Arctic to witness the retreat of glaciers first hand - only to approve drilling for oil there.

In the UK, things were not much better: Prime Minister and former PR man David Cameron, who in 2006 hugged huskies in Norway and said he wanted to lead "the greenest government ever", was later reported to have told his aides to "cut the green crap". Now his new government has promised to promote shale gas fracking come what may, and continues its massive subsidies to fossil fuel companies, while cutting a range of pro-environment policies, from the green investment bank to solar subsidies and green taxes.[17]

These contradictory actions are of course not just the result of muddled thinking or duplicity but myopic and craven responses to the powerful contradictory forces of the diabolical double crisis of economy and climate. We have to choose between capitalist growth and the planet: we can't save both.[18]

The future is open

Any how-to-get-rich-quick book will tell you that the key thing is not simply working hard, but getting control of assets that will bring you unearned income. They don't use that terminology of course – as ever the magic word 'investments' conceals it – but that's the standard message. And the evidence supports it: according to the World Wealth Report 2015, those with more than US$1 million in investable assets, excluding their primary residence, collectibles, consumables, and consumer durables, held 26% of their wealth in cash deposits, 27% in shares, 18% in real estate, 17% in fixed income securities (e.g. bonds), and 13% in 'alternative investments' – hedge funds, derivatives, foreign currency, commodities and private equity.[19] In other words, most of their wealth continues to come from and to yield unearned income, and at others' expense.

For the majority of people in much of Europe, continued austerity has been the story, with deficits serving as a spurious justification for cutting the welfare state. But it's good news for rentiers in the UK, whose unearned income has been enlarged in 2015 by additional tax breaks from the new Conservative government.[20] 'Feral finance', as Richard Murphy calls it, continues to call the tune. When central banks e-print money – using 'quantitative easing' – to support the financial sector, it's accepted by the political elite, even though the banks use it to resume their inflation of asset values through lending against existing property and speculation. When quantitative easing is called for to fund real investment for green and social purposes, there are howls of protest. As always, economics is political. The more accurately the economic sources of power are identified, and the more clearly viable alternatives are put forward, the more the powerful will seek to demonise critics. As I write, the UK's political elite, shocked by the election of a new Labour leader who opposes austerity and the rule of finance, has reacted with venom and misrepresentation so extreme it's almost comical.[21] That's not surprising when three-quarters of UK newspaper circulation is controlled by five billionaire tax exiles, with politics to match.[22] What is surprising is that such alternative movements can gain momentum despite this.

So, gloomy though much of this is, there are also reasons to be hopeful.

The future is always open; anti-austerity movements have gained strength in Latin America, southern Europe, and even the UK. The plutocracy's control is looking increasingly precarious. Politics and economies do change. For the sake of the planet, the young and future generations, they must.

Andrew Sayer
September 2015

Notes and sources

Chapter One: Introduction

[1] http://en.wikiquote.org/wiki/Warren_Buffett. In 2013, Buffett was ranked by Forbes as the fourth-richest person in the world.

[2] World Top Incomes Database. See Piketty, T. (2014) *Capital in the 21st century*, Cambridge, MA: Belknap Press, for details and analysis. However, these are figures for pre-tax income, and since taxes on the rich have fallen dramatically in the last 30 years, their post-tax income share has risen more.

[3] In the US between 2002 and 2012 – years spanning the boom and crash – family incomes of the bottom 90% fell by 10.7% and the top 10% experienced increases from 2.7% (the top 10% to 5%) to 76.2% (the top 0.01%). Matthews, D. (2013) 'You're probably making 10 percent less than you were ten years ago. The top 0.01 percent is making 76.2% more', *Washington Post*, 6 December, using data from Piketty and Saez, World Top Incomes Database, http://knowmore.washingtonpost.com/2013/12/06/youre-probably-making-10-percent-less-than-you-were-ten-years-ago-the-top-0-01-percent-is-making-76-2-percent-more/.

[4] Bell, B. and Van Reenen, J. (2010) 'Bankers' pay and extreme wage inequality in the UK', Centre for Economic Performance, London School of Economics.

[5] See Saez, E. (2013) 'Income inequality: evidence and implications', lecture at University of California, Berkeley, 2013, http://www.youtube.com/watch?v=_y7Xtwxd90I.

[6] Inequality Briefing (2014) Briefing 26: 'Almost one third of wealth in the UK is inherited, not earned', 11 April, http://inequalitybriefing.org/brief/briefing-26-almost-one-third-of-wealth-in-the-uk-is-inherited-not-earned.

[7] Oxfam (2015) 'Having it all and wanting more', Oxfam Briefing, 15 January, http://policy-practice.oxfam.org.uk/publications/wealth-having-it-all-and-wanting-more-338125.

[8] Oxfam (2014) 'Working for the few: political capture and economic inequality', 178 Oxfam Briefing Paper, 20 January.

[9] Dorling, D. (2012) *The case for austerity among the rich*, London: Institute of Public Policy Research; Saez, E. (2013) 'Income inequality: evidence and policy implications', http://elsa.berkeley.edu/users/saez/lecture_saez_arrow.pdf.

[10] Dorling, D. (2013) 'Fairness and the changing fortunes of people in Britain', *Journal of the Royal Statistical Society A*, 176(1), 97–128. The income share

of the next 9% rose very slightly over the hundred years. Special thanks to Danny Dorling for directing me to this and several other important data sources.

[11] See Skidelsky, R. and Skidelsky, E. (2013) *How much is enough? Money and the good life*, Harmondsworth: Penguin.

[12] Sources for these estimates are given in Part Five.

[13] Zero Hedge (2011), http://www.zerohedge.com/article/rich-are-about-get-very-very-rich-study-finds-global-millionaire-wealth-set-more-double-2020?utm_source=feedburner&utm_medium=feed&utm_camp aign=Feed%3A+zerohedge%2Ffeed+(zero+hedge+-+on+a+long+enou gh+timeline%2C+th

[14] For example, Orton, M. and Rowlingson, K. (2007) *Public attitudes to inequality*, York: Joseph Rowntree Foundation; Horton, L. and Bamfield, T. (2009) *Understanding attitudes to tackling economic inequality*, York: Joseph Rowntree Foundation; Pahl, R., Rose, D. and Spencer, L. (2007) 'Inequality and quiescence', Institute for Social and Economic Research Working Paper, 22; Osberg, L. and Smeeding, T. (2005) 'Social values for equality and preferences for state intervention in the USA and Europe', Russell Sage Foundation.

[15] Thanks to Mike Norton for the data.

[16] See the Inequality Briefing at: http://inequalitybriefing.org/ and ICM Poll at http://inequalitybriefing.org/files/Inequality_Polling_(Q1-Q2)_-_May_2013.pdf and Office of National Statistics (ONS) 2008/10 Wealth and Assets Survey, chapter 2.

[17] Institute of Fiscal Studies (2012), figure calculated from 'Where do you fit in?' calculator, http://www.ifs.org.uk/wheredoyoufitin/. The figure is adjusted for household size, to take account of differences in expenditure.

[18] Data from the World Top Incomes Database, 2012.

[19] Saez (2013); Freeland, C. (2012) 'The self-destruction of the 1 percent', *New York Times*, 13 October.

[20] Source: http://www.ukpublicspending.co.uk/fed_spending_2015UKbn.

[21] The Bloomberg data shows that billionaires' incomes fluctuate by many millions from day to day, because most of their wealth is held in the form of investments like stock options, whose prices change continually. http://www.bloomberg.com/billionaires/2014-01-03/cya.

[22] Green, D. (2013) 'Should we (and everyone at Davos) worry about extreme wealth?', Oxfam Policy and Practice Blog, http://policy-practice.oxfam.org.uk/blog/2013/01/extreme-wealth.

[23] Forbes, 'The world's billionaires', 2013, http://www.forbes.com/billionaires/list/#tab:overall.

[24] Davies, N. (2003) 'The golden rule that saves the super-rich millions', *Guardian*, 11 April, http://www.theguardian.com/uk/2002/apr/11/politics.economy1.

[25] Sunday Times Rich List, 2013.

[26] Shiller, R. (2012) *Finance and the good society*, Princeton, NJ: Princeton University Press.

[27] There are many competing interpretations of neoliberalism. It's useful to distinguish neoliberalism as an academic theory, led by economists such as Friedrich von Hayek and Milton Friedman, from neoliberalism as a political tendency, where ideas from the theory are drawn on opportunistically, and bent to political ends, often hiding the less palatable elements of the theory, such as its anti-democratic arguments, from the public. The interests of the rich dominate political neoliberalism. Sometimes the term is just used to cover 'everything that's been happening recently', but this misses its specificity and the counter-currents. For those wanting to read more on it, I recommend David Harvey's (2007) *A brief history of neoliberalism*, Oxford: Oxford University Press. Best of all, especially in relation to the crisis, is Philip Mirowski's (2013) *Never let a serious crisis go to waste*, London: Verso.

[28] Sayer, A. (2007) 'Moral economy as critique', *New Political Economy*, 12(2), pp 261–70. Many associate the term 'moral economy' with Edward Thompson's research on regulated markets: (1971) 'The moral economy of the English crowd in the eighteenth century', *Past & Present*, 50, pp 76–136. Thompson saw the moral economy as the opposite of the market economy. See: http://humanitiesunderground.wordpress.com/2012/04/22/the-moral-economics-of-wellbeing/. Unfortunately this historical focus has led many to assume that moral economies ended with capitalism, and that capitalism is not in any sense a moral economy. I and other more recent commentators argue that it is. For examples, Booth, W. (1994) 'On the idea of the moral economy', *American Political Science Review*, 88(3), pp 653–67; Keat, R. (2004) 'Every economy is a moral economy', unpublished manuscript, University of Edinburgh, available at: http://www.russellkeat.net/admin/papers/39.pdf. Michael Sandel's (2012) *What money can't buy*, Harmondsworth: Penguin, is an accessible example of political and moral philosophy's contribution to the study of moral economy. Valuable though such contributions are, they don't give us much purchase on how capitalism works in practice, largely because they take its basic structures as given and focus on very specific practices such as selling human organs. In my view, moral economy becomes more powerful – and more threatening to the powerful – when it questions the basic institutions of capitalism, particularly their property relations. More searching are: John O'Neill's (1997) *The market*, London: Routledge; Alperovitz, G. and Daly, L. (2010) *Unjust deserts*, New York, NY: The New Press; Murphy, L. and Nagel, T. (2005) *The myth of ownership*, Oxford: Oxford University Press; Graeber, D. (2011) *Debt: The first 5000 years*, New York, NY: Melville House Publishing; and Polanyi, K. (1947) *The great transformation*, New York: Basic Books.

[29] Nelson, J.A. (2006) *Economics for humans*, Chicago, IL: University of Chicago Press; Graeber (2011); Brown, M.T. (2010) *Civilizing the economy*, Cambridge: Cambridge University Press.

[30] MacIntyre, A. (1999) *Dependent rational animals*, London: Duckworth.

[31] Sayer, A. (2011) *Why things matter to people: Social science, ethics and values*, Cambridge: Cambridge University Press.

[32] Adam Smith bears no little responsibility for projecting market exchange or barter back into history as universal features of human life, when historical evidence shows that they have been strictly subsidiary in most of human history, and sometimes absent. See Graeber (2011).

[33] Lerner, M.J. (1981) *The belief in a just world: A fundamental delusion*, New York: Plenum.

[34] Horton and Bamfield (2009). See also Unwin, J. (2013) *Why fight poverty?*, London: Publishing Partnership; Kelly, N.J. and Enns, P.K. (2010) 'Inequality and the dynamics of public opinion: the self-reinforcing link between economic inequality and mass preferences', *American Journal of Political Science*, 54(4), pp 855–870; Shildrick, T. and MacDonald, R. (2013) 'Poverty talk: how poor people experiencing poverty deny their poverty and why they blame the poor', *The Sociological Review*, 61, pp 285–303.

[35] Cited in Orton, M. and Rowlingson, K. (2007) 'A problem of riches: towards a new social policy research agenda on the distribution of economic resources', *Journal of Social Policy*, 36(1), 59–77.

Part One

Chapter Two: Three dangerous words: 'earnings', 'investment' and 'wealth'

[1] In his book *The power elite*, C. Wright Mills wrote 'ordinary men, even today, are prone to explain and to justify power and wealth in terms of knowledge and ability' (1956, Oxford: Oxford University Press, p 351).

[2] Wilde, O. (1908) *The picture of Dorian Gray*, Penguin.

[3] Brown, M.T. (2010) *Civilizing the economy: A new economics of provision*, Cambridge: Cambridge University Press. See also Skidelsky and Skidelsky (2012).

[4] Ruskin, J. (2007) *Unto this last*, FQ Classics, p 89.

Chapter Three: Income: earned or unearned?

[5] Some might question whether some things that people get paid to produce, such as cluster bombs or heroin, are 'goods' or have 'use-value' at all. It's a good point, but as it doesn't make any difference to my argument whether one adds a third criterion to cover this or not, I've left it out to keep things simple.

[6] I include accounting, deposit banking and retailing, even though they deal with exchange value and transferring property, on the grounds that any advanced economy needs to make significant use of markets for coordinating the division of labour (Sayer, A. (1995) *Radical political economy: A critique*, Oxford: Blackwell). They need to be strongly regulated, however, if they are not to dominate. 'Earnings' by accountants helping firms to dodge tax

would not come under my definition of work derived from producing use-values.

[7] Thanks to Chris Holden for highlighting this.

[8] United States Census Bureau 2013, http://www.census.gov/newsroom/releases/archives/income_wealth/cb13-165.html.

[9] Hobson, J.A. (1937) *Property and improperty*, London: Gollancz.

[10] Welshman, J. (2006) *Underclass: A history of the excluded, 1880–2000*, London: Hambledon Continuum; see also Shildrick, T., MacDonald, R., Furlong, A., Roden, J. and Crow, R. (2002) *Are 'cultures of worklessness' passed down the generations?*, York: Joseph Rowntree Foundation.

[11] See Inequality Briefing 19: 'Does getting parents into work get children out of poverty?', http://inequalitybriefing.org/brief/briefing-19-does-getting-parents-into-work-get-children-out-of-poverty.

[12] Under the ConDem coalition government, unemployment figures have fallen. This is not so surprising, given (1) the ever more demanding conditions set for getting Jobseeker's Allowance, and the strategy of using these conditions to remove people from the unemployment figures; and (2) that they conceal the increasing proportion of vacancies that are part time or involve zero-hours contracts. In April 2014 there were 1.4 million workers on the latter. The proportion of part-timers in the workforce has also risen in the US in the last 40 years.

[13] Tawney, R.H. (2004) [1920] *The acquisitive society*, Mineola, NY: Harcourt Brace and Howe.

[14] Hudson, M. (2008) http://dandelionsalad.wordpress.com/2008/09/08/'modern-debt-peonage"-economic-democracy-is-turning-into-a-financial-oligarchy/.

Chapter Four: For rent … for what?

[15] Smith, A. (1976) [1776] *The wealth of nations*, ed. E. Cannan, Chicago, IL: University of Chicago Press, Bk I, ch V, p 56.

[16] Paine, T. (1797) *Agrarian justice*, paragraph 11, http://geolib.pair.com/essays/paine.tom/agjst.html.

[17] Churchill, W. (1909) *The people's rights*, ch 4, http://www.wealthandwant.com/docs/Churchill_TPL.html.

[18] Tawney, R.H. (2004) [1920] *The acquisitive society*, Mineola, NY: Harcourt Brace and Howe.

[19] http://www.richest-people.co.uk/duke-of-westminster/.

[20] Mill, J.S. (1965) *Principles of political economy*, in *Collected Works*, ed. J.M. Robson, Toronto: Toronto University Press, vol 3, bk 5, ch 2, sec 6, p 821; and Paine, *Agrarian justice*, para 15.

[21] *Guardian* (2014) 'Empty homes scandal of UK's billionaires row', 1 February.

[22] Stiglitz, J.E. (2012) *The price of inequality*, London: Allen Lane, p 32; see also Kay, J. (2012) 'The monumental folly of rent seeking', *Financial Times*, 20 November, http://www.ft.com/cms/s/0/3c72c7f0-3278-11e2-916a-00144feabdc0.html#axzz34zGZwF7d.

[23] Thompson, G. (2006) 'Prodded by the left: richest man talks equity', *New York Times*, 3 June, http://www.nytimes.com/2006/06/03/world/americas/03slim.html?pagewanted=1&_r=0&ei=5088&en=87ff5ffac4ee12aa&ex=1306987200&partner=rssnyt&emc=rss.

[24] Freeland, C. (2012) *Plutocrats: The rise of the new global super-rich*, London: Allen Lane, p 195.

[25] Giles, C. (2012) 'All that money growing on trees', *Financial Times*, 19 March, http://blogs.ft.com/money-supply/2012/03/19/all-that-money-growing-on-trees/#axzz1peBhsxr6 .

[26] Meek, J. (2012) 'Human revenue stream', *London Review of Books*, 20 March. Thanks to John Allen for this reference. See also Leaver, A. (2013) 'Growth in whose interests?', *Discover Society*, 3, www.discoversociety.org/2013/12/03/growth-in-whose-interests/.

[27] Ferguson, K. *Everything is a remix*. Video, http://www.youtube.com/watch?v=NAKa0AJHhL4. The implications of our debt to existing knowledge are elaborated further in Part Two.

[28] Public Patent Foundation (2011) 'Organic seed v Monsanto', http://www.pubpat.org/monsanto-seed-patents.htm.

[29] 'Patent trolls' are even worse – they patent things invented by others but not yet patented and then threaten small and medium-sized businesses with costly law suits (Bob Jessop, personal communication).

[30] Bamfield, L. and Horton, T. (2009) 'Understanding attitudes to tackling economic inequality', Joseph Rowntree Foundation, http://www.jrf.org.uk/sites/files/jrf/attitudes-tackling-economic-inequality-full.pdf.

[31] BBC News (2012) 'Premier league clubs climb to new highs', 31 May, http://www.bbc.co.uk/news/business-18248540.

[32] Rosen, S. (1981) 'The economics of superstars', *American Economic Review*, 71(5), pp 845–58.

Chapter Five: Interest ... for what?

[33] Keynes, J.M. (1936) [1973] *The general theory of employment, interest and money*, Houndmills, Basingstoke, Macmillan, p 376.

[34] Pettifor, A. (2014) *Just money*, available from Prime Economics, Commonwealth Publication, http://www.primeeconomics.org/?wpsc-product=just-money-how-society-can-break-the-despotic-power-of-finance-2

[35] http://www.thenation.com/article/169760/occupy-20-strike-debt, accessed 16.09.12

[36] Lazzarato, M. (2012) *The making of the indebted man*, Cambridge, MA: MIT Press, p 20.

[37] Cited in Kennedy, M. (2012) *Occupy money*, Gabriola Island, BC, Canada: New Society Publishers, p 23.

[38] And formerly Christianity: 'The rich ruleth over the poor, and the borrower is servant to the lender', Proverbs 22: 7. Graeber, D. (2011) *Debt: The first 5000 years*, New York: Melville House Publishing.

[39] Graeber (2011, p 331) claims that the term 'self-interest' originated in the 17th century through an adaptation of the financial concept of interest.

[40] This apt term is Ann Pettifor's (2006) *The coming first-world debt crisis*, Houndmills, Basingstoke: Palgrave.

[41] McFayden, cited in Coggan, P. (2011) *Paper promises*, London: Allen Lane, p 197.

[42] Hudson, M. (2012) *The bubble and beyond*, Dresden: ISLET.

[43] Thanks to Ruth Wodak for discussions on this point.

[44] Cited in Talabi, S. (2011) 'A Nigerian approach to Islamic banking', *Business Day*, 25 August, http://www.businessdayonline.com/NG/index.php/law/legal-insight/26439-a-nigerian-approach-to-islamic-banking.

[45] Hudson (2012, p 97).

[46] Microfinance, having once aimed to provide loans at minimum interest rates has all too often become simple usury. See Roy, A. 'Who profits from the poor', illustrated video talk for Globalpov, http://mouthbeef.tumblr.com/post/50643246247/mollycrabapple-perhaps-the-best-illustrated#.

[47] The Money Charity (2014) Debt statistics, 12 June, http://themoneycharity.org.uk/debt-statistics/

[48] Kara, S. (2012) 'Bonded labor: tackling the system of slavery in South Asia'. The International Labour Organization estimates a minimum 9.3 million are in forced labour in the Asia-Pacific region, the majority of whom are in debt bondage. See http://www.antislavery.org/english/slavery_today/bonded_labour.aspx.

[49] The Money Charity (2014) 'UK household debt to rocket by 43% in the next 5 years', 2 April, http://themoneycharity.org.uk/uk-household-debt-to-rocket-by-43-in-the-next-five-years/.

[50] Homebase and Dorothy Perkins websites, 13 June 2014

[51] Ferratum, https://www.ferratum.co.uk/; Wonga, https://www.wonga.com/. The usual defence of these rates is that providing small amounts of credit to large numbers of people involves heavy administration costs. The costs may be high, but not that high! A survey by *Which?* in May 2012 found that 60% of borrowers from Wonga used the loans to pay household bills and for essentials like food. Forty-five per cent had to roll over loans at least once: http://www.which.co.uk/news/2012/05/new-which-research-exposes-payday-loan-failings-286258/.

52 Wonga's market value grew from £17 million at the end of 2010 to £384 million in May 2012: 'Wonga: the men who made £50 million from other people's cash woes', *Daily Mirror*, 13 May, http://www.mirror.co.uk/night-copy/wonga-the-men-who-made-50million-830110#ixzz2gUGJGPYw.

53 Certainly, where friendships are involved, many follow Polonius' advice to his son in *Hamlet*: 'Neither a borrower nor a lender be. For loan oft loses both itself and friend' (Shakespeare, *Hamlet*, Act 1, scene 3, 75–77). Even to offer or accept an interest-free loan might be seen as introducing an unwanted, if temporary, dependence and asymmetry into what would otherwise be seen as properly a relationship of equality and generosity. For this reason, people may prefer to borrow impersonally from a bank and pay interest, rather than borrow from a friend at zero interest.

54 David Graeber's term for this asymmetry is 'the logic of hierarchy' (Graeber, 2011). Gift relationships, where 'debts' are not precisely quantified or ever cleared but alternately reciprocated at intervals by each person, thus maintaining the relationship, are the norm in human history. One of the most distinctive, indeed exceptional, features of modern societies is that so many relationships between people are contractual, and hence can be terminated with the meeting of agreed mutual obligations: you did this for me, I paid you the agreed amount, that's the end of our relationship.

55 This contradiction is a secular version of the Old Testament 'Deuteronomic ruling', which caused consternation among theologians and divided Christians for centuries:'Unto a stranger thou mayest lend upon usury; but unto thy brother thou shalt not lend upon usury', Deuteronomy 23: 20. Nelson, B. (1969) *The idea of usury: From tribal brotherhood to universal otherhood*, 2nd edn, Chicago, IL: University of Chicago Press. Psalm 37: 21–22 says, 'The wicked borrow and do not repay, but the righteous give generously, those the Lord blesses will inherit the land, but those he curses will be destroyed.' Religions rarely do consistency.

56 Hodgson, G. (2013) 'Banking, finance and income inequality', Positive Money, https://www.positivemoney.org/publications/banking-finance-and-income-inequality/. While this is interesting, it represents national financial systems as closed rather than part of an international system; it also ignores mechanisms of redistribution from poor to rich that do not depend on the creation of interest-bearing credit money.

57 Henwood, D. (1997) *Wall Street*, London: Verso, p 4.

58 Warren, E. (2007) 'The coming collapse of the middle class', Jefferson Memorial Lecture, University of California, Berkeley, http://www.youtube.com/watch?v=akVL7QY0S8A.

59 Lazzarato, M. (2012) *The making of the indebted man*, Cambridge, MA: MIT Press, p 87.

60 Coggan, P. (2011) *Paper promises*, London: Allen Lane, p 267.

61 Wolf, M. (2010) 'The Fed is right to turn on the tap', *Financial Times*, 9 November.

[62] Turner, A. (2014) 'Creating money – for what purpose?', Lecture, London School of Economics, 24 March, http://www.lse.ac.uk/newsAndMedia/ videoAndAudio/channels/publicLecturesAndEvents/player.aspx?id=2356. See also Steve Keen's lecture at http://www.debtdeflation.com/ blogs/2012/09/22/american-monetary-institute-conference-2012/.

[63] Mellor, M. (2010) *The future of money*, London: Pluto Press. See also Pettifor (2014).

[64] Pettifor (2006); Mellor, M. (2010) *The future of money*, London: Pluto Press; Ryan-Collins, J., Greenham, T., Werner, R. and Jackson, A. (2011) *Where does money come from?* London: New Economics Foundation.

[65] Michael Bulley, 15 November 2014, http://www.guardian. co.uk/commentisfree/2011/nov/15/money-privatised- stealth?INTCMP=SRCH.

[66] Mainstream economists may not know this, but bankers do. Pettifor quotes Paul Sheard, the chief economist of Standard and Poor's, in a note headed 'Repeat After Me: Banks do not Lend out Reserves': 'Banks lend by simultaneously creating a loan asset and a deposit liability on their balance sheet. That is why it is called credit "creation" – credit is created literally out of thin air (or with the stroke of a keyboard). The loan is not created out of reserves. And the loan is not created out of deposits: Loans create deposits, not the other way around' (Pettifor, 2014, p 25).

[67] This means that they don't necessarily wait until they (the bank) first has a certain level of reserves. 'In the real world, banks extend credit, creating deposits in the process, and look for the reserves later' (Alan Holmes Senior Vice President, Federal Reserve Bank of New York (1969), cited by Positive Money at http://www.positivemoney.org.uk/how-banks-create-money/ proof-that-banks-create-money/).

[68] Pettifor (2006), p 56. Geoff Mulgan uses the metaphor of 'predation', but in most cases this is too strong: predators kill their victims rather than just free-ride on them: Mulgan, G. (2013) *The locust and the bee: Predators and creators in capitalism's future*, Princeton, NJ: Princeton University Press.

[69] Ryan-Collins et al (2011).

[70] Pettifor (2006), p 62.

[71] See David Harvey's *Limits to capital* for an analysis of fictitious capital ((1982), London: Verso).

[72] As Hudson comments, 'Finance and banking courses are taught from the perspective of how to obtain interest and asset-price gains through credit creation or by using other peoples' money, not how an economy may best steer savings and credit to achieve the best long-term development.' This of course is equivalent to the difference between financial and real investment. Hudson, M. (2011) 'How economic theory came to ignore the role of debt', Real-World Economics Review Blog, 57, 6 September, https://rwer.wordpress.com/2011/09/06/rwer-issue-57-michael-hudson/.

[73] Ryan-Collins et al (2011), p 50.

[74] In the US, student loan debt now exceeds $1 trillion (Hudson, M. (2012) 'Scenarios for recovery: how to write down the debts and restructure the financial system', http://ineteconomics.org/sites/inet.civicactions.net/files/hudson-michael-berlin-paper.pdf).

[75] Henwood (1997), p 205. Paul Krugman calls the lender 'patient' and the borrower 'impatient'. As Steve Keen comments, this is typical of the way mainstream economists present the lender in better light than the borrower. Keen suggests 'speculator' and 'entrepreneur' instead: http://www.debtdeflation.com/blogs/.

[76] Pettifor (2006), pp 136–7.

[77] Tripp, C. (2006) *Islam and the moral economy*, Cambridge: Cambridge University Press; Pettifor (2006). In practice, the prohibitions on usury in Islamic banking sometimes get compromised, but that doesn't mean the principles aren't defensible. Given that they have to operate in a global neoliberal environment, it's not surprising that their influence is restricted. In the wider world, self-interest rules, but that doesn't mean the moral economic arguments against usury are not good ones. Might – or self-interest – is not necessarily right.

[78] Hudson, M. (2012) *The bubble and beyond*, Dresden: ISLET, p 55. According to Adair Turner, only 15% of UK bank loans go to businesses: Turner (2014).

[79] Hudson (2012), p 55.

[80] Stiglitz, J. (2012), *The price of inequality*, London: Allen Lane, p 191.

[81] See note 77.

Chapter Six: Profit from production

[82] David Schweikart's (2000) *After capitalism*, New York: Rowman & Littlefield Publishers, develops this point well.

[83] There are other kinds of capitalist too: merchant capitalists make money simply by buying and selling without producing, acting as intermediaries between producers and consumers; financial capitalists make money out of lending at interest, and are in effect rentiers.

[84] Applicants to public sector jobs have to convince the employer that they can do the job effectively enough to justify being paid. While the public sector has to work within budgets, neoliberal governments have tried to make public organisations compete in zero-sum games for funds to make them more like the private sector, in the belief that this will make them more efficient and effective. Or, as in health and education, they have allowed capitalist businesses to compete for them.

[85] Strangely, this point is missed by Thomas Piketty (2014) *Capital in the 21st century*, Cambridge, MA: Belknap Press, p 423.

[86] Some readers might be wondering at this point, isn't this like Marx's labour theory of value, and hasn't it been discredited? (By the way, for what it's worth, Adam Smith also had a labour theory of value, though few modern economists who invoke his authority seem to realise it.) Actually, I agree

that Marx's theory of value is flawed, for reasons argued by Gerry Cohen, but my argument is only superficially similar to Marx's, as those who know what it involves will recognise (Cohen, G.A. (1989) *History, labour and freedom*, Oxford: Oxford University Press). It doesn't require us to treat all kinds of labour as reducible to an equivalent, or to treat labour time as the measure of value, though from an ethical standpoint, how much time people spend working is something to consider in terms of what they deserve. All that my argument in this book requires is for us to recognise that the output must be worth more than what it costs to produce it for there to be a profit. You don't have to accept Marx's theory of value to recognise that the systematic generation of profit depends on the production of a surplus. For capitalists, it's what this fetches in money when it's sold that matters.

[87] Marx, K. (1996) [1867] *Capital*, vol I, ch 13, London: Lawrence and Wishart, pp 448–9.

[88] Marx, K. (1998) [1894] *Capital*, vol III, ch 23, London: Lawrence and Wishart, p 545.

[89] Though in several professional occupations, unpaid internships are becoming a precondition of subsequent employment.

[90] As in the case of Apple, highly profitable companies may decide they do not need to pay dividends; their shareholders are nevertheless happy as long as the value of their shares is increasing. Arthur, C. (2012) 'One year on, Apple after Jobs has a new, more ethical flavour', *Guardian*, 5 October.

[91] The secondary market in shares is generally defended as necessary for encouraging people to buy shares in the primary or initial public offering market; 'investors' will be more confident about buying new shares if they know they may be able to profit from a rise in their market price, or offload them if they are dissatisfied with their returns. Given that the secondary market accounts for over 97% of share dealings, this is a classic example of the tail wagging the dog.

[92] Tawney, R.H. (2004) [1920] *The acquisitive society*, Mineola, NY: Harcourt Brace and Howe. See also Murphy, R. (2010) 'The pension problem', *Soundings*, 46, pp 54–63.

[93] Erturk, I., Froud, J., Johal, S., Leaver, A. and Williams, K. (2007) 'Against agency: a positional critique', *Economy and Society*, 36(1), pp 51–77.

[94] Keynes, J.M. (1973) [1936] *A general theory of employment, interest and money*, London: Macmillan. He also included in his recommendation 'the euthanasia of the cumulative oppressive power of the capitalist to exploit the scarcity value of capital'.

[95] Keynes, J.M. (1933) 'National self-sufficiency', *The Yale Review*, 22(4), pp 755–69.

[96] Henwood, D. (1997) *Wall Street*, London: Verso, p 5.

[97] Tawney, R.H. (2004) [1920] *The acquisitive society*, Mineola, NY: Harcourt Brace and Howe.

[98] Adam Smith thought it was justifiable only in special cases.

[99] Andrew Haldane at the Bank of England argues that in view of this, banks inevitably increased risks to maximise shareholder value: 'For shareholders, the sky is the limit but the floor is always just beneath their feet. To maximise shareholder value, therefore, banks need simply to seek bigger and riskier bets.' Haldane, A. (2012) 'The doom loop', *London Review of Books*, 34(4), 23 February, pp 21–2.

[100] On this see Randy Martin's excellent (2007) *The financialisation of everyday life*, Houndmills, Baskingstoke: Palgrave.

[101] Personal share ownership in the UK has *fallen* proportionately in the last 50 years, from 54% of shares on the London Stock Exchange in 1963 to 10% in 2010 (BBC News, 27 January 2010, http://news.bbc.co.uk/1/hi/business/8482601.stm).

[102] Department for Work and Pensions, *Family Resources Survey, 2009–10*, Table 6.7; and Froud, J., Johal, S., Haslam, C. and Williams, K. (2001) 'Accumulation under conditions of inequality', *Review of International Political Economy*, 8(1), pp 66–95.

[103] Langley, P. (2007) 'The uncertain subjects of Anglo-American financialization', *Cultural Critique* 65, pp 66–91.

[104] Engelen, E., Ertürk, I., Froud, J., Johal, S., Leaver, A., Moran, M., Nilsson, A. and Williams, K. (2011) *After the great complacence: Financial crisis and the politics of reform*, Oxford: Oxford University Press.

[105] Froud et al (2001).

Chapter Seven: Other ways to skin a cat

[106] Tabb, W.J. (2012) *The restructuring of capitalism in our time*, New York: Columbia University Press, p 260.

[107] Griffith, M. (2011) 'We must fix it', London: Institute of Public Policy Research.

[108] Cooper, G. (2008) *The origin of financial crises: Central banks, credit bubbles and the efficient market fallacy*, Petersfield: Harriman House.

[109] Meek, J. (2014) 'Where shall we live?', *London Review of Books* 36(1), 9 January.

[110] Dyson, R. (2013) 'Tax threat for buy-to-let', *Telegraph*, 13 December, http://www.telegraph.co.uk/finance/personalfinance/borrowing/10484798/Tax-threat-for-buy-to-let.html.

[111] http://england.shelter.org.uk/campaigns/building_more_affordable_homes/price_check.

[112] Cited in Rowlingson, K. and McKay, G. (2011) *Wealth and the wealthy*, Bristol: Policy Press.

[113] Langley, P. (2007) 'The uncertain subjects of Anglo-American financialization', *Cultural Critique* 65, pp 66–91. Langley adds: 'the value of outstanding buy-to-let mortgages in the United Kingdom rose from £2 billion at the end of 1998 to £47 billion by June 2004.... buy-to-

let property investors in effect lever their investments through mortgage borrowing and rely on the rental payments of their tenants' (p 82).

[114] Engelen et al (2011), p 139.

[115] Savage, M. and Williams, K. (2008) 'Elites: remembered in capitalism and forgotten in social science', *The Sociological Review*, 56(s1), 1–24.

[116] Mill, J.S. (1848) *Principles of political economy with some of their applications to social philosophy*, bk V, ch II: On the general principles of taxation, v 2.28, http://www.econlib.org/library/Mill/mlP64.htm.

[117] Freeland, C. (2012) *Plutocrats: The rise of the new global super-rich*, London: Allen Lane, p 42.

[118] Krugman, P. (2014) 'Why we're in a new gilded age', http://www.nybooks. com/articles/archives/2014/may/08/thomas-piketty-new-gilded-age/; Piketty, T. (2014) *Capital in the 21st century*, Cambridge, MA: Belknap Press. This is what Thomas Piketty and Emmanuel Saez infer from the data, wrongly, in my view (Piketty, T. and Saez, E. (2006) 'The evolution of top incomes: a historical and international perspective', *American Economic Review* 96(2), pp 200–5). In Part Three we'll illustrate the role of the active rentier in the financial crisis.

[119] It can be highly skilled too: the design of financial instruments is a highly technical job, and the 'quants' – top mathematicians employed by financial institutions – became a key factor in their success, though they have little to do with productive investment.

[120] Toynbee, P. and Walker, D. (2008) *Unjust rewards*, London: Granta. The authors do an excellent job in showing not just the excessive rewards, but the extraordinary ignorance of their rich interviewees regarding the lives and pay of ordinary people.

[121] Bell, B. and Van Reenen, J. (2010) 'Bankers' pay and extreme wage inequality in the UK', Centre for Economic Performance, London School of Economics.

[122] Figures from Institute of Fiscal Studies (2008) 'Racing away: inequality and the evolution of top incomes', IFS briefing note 76 (authors: Mike Brewer, Luke Sibieta and Liam Wren-Lewis).

[123] Institute of Fiscal Studies (2008). Apart from income from salary or investments, the remainder of incomes for all groups comes from self-employment and from pensions and other benefits.

[124] de Goede, M. (2005) *Virtue, fortune and faith: A genealogy of finance*, Minneapolis: University of Minnesota Press.

[125] For an example of this kind of bogus claim, see Vincent Amanor-Boadu (2008) 'In defense of speculation', http://www.agmanager.info/marketing/ publications/marketing/InDefenceofSpeculation.pdf.

[126] Tabb (2012), p 53; MacKenzie, D. (2011) 'How to make money in microseconds', *London Review of Books*, 33(10), pp 16–18; Lanchester, J. (2014) 'Scalpers Inc. review of *Flash Boys: Cracking the money code*', *London Review of Books*, 36(11), pp 7–9.

[127] Norfield, T. (2012) 'Derivatives and capitalist markets: the speculative heart of capital', *Historical Materialism*, 20(1), pp 103–32.

[128] Niederhoffer, V. (1989) 'The speculator as hero', *Wall Street Journal*, 2 October, http://www.dailyspeculations.com/vic/spec_as_hero.html.

[129] Cooper (2008). See also Henwood, D. (1998) *Wall Street*, London: Verso.

[130] Haldane, A. (2012) 'The doom loop', *London Review of Books*, 34(4), February.

[131] Blackburn, R. (2008) 'The subprime crisis', *New Left Review*, 50, pp 63–106.

[132] Shaxson, N. (2012) *Treasure islands*, London: Vintage, p 69.

[133] Cited in Ingham, G. (2012) *Capitalism*, 2nd edn, Cambridge: Polity, p 154.

[134] *The Economist*, 29 April 2006, p 78, cited in Ingham (2012), p 157

[135] Engelen, E., Ertürk, I., Froud, J., Johal, S., Leaver, A., Moran, M., Nilsson, A. and Williams, K. (2011) *After the great complacence: Financial crisis and the politics of reform*, Oxford: Oxford University Press, ch 3.

[136] 'America's billion-dollar-a-year men', *Too Much*, 4 April 2011, http://toomuchonline.org/weeklies2011/apr042011.html.

[137] Engelen et al (2011), ch 3.

[138] Inman, P. (2012) 'Black Wednesday 20 years on: how the day unfolded', *Guardian*, 13 September, http://www.theguardian.com/business/2012/sep/13/black-wednesday-20-years-pound-erm.

[139] Hutton, W. (2008) 'As we suffer, City speculators are moving in for the kill', *Observer*, 29 June, http://www.theguardian.com/commentisfree/2008/jun/29/investmentfunds.creditcrunch.

[140] On this see Randy Martin's (2007) *The financialisation of everyday life*, Houndmills, Basingstoke: Palgrave.

Chapter Eight: Don't the rich create jobs?

[141] Nick Hanauer, talk on inequality: http://www.youtube.com/watch?v=bBx2Y5HhplI. See also Dave Johnson, http://www.ourfuture.org/blog-entry/2011051913/do-we-depend-rich-create-jobs.

[142] The British website MoneyTerms notes that the term asset stripping 'is disliked because it is often associated with restructuring and job-losses, and it is seen as a less worthy way of making money than building a business. However, asset stripping does release value, improving the accuracy with which the constituent businesses are valued. This means that asset stripping does make financial markets more efficient': http://moneyterms.co.uk/asset-stripping/. No matter – apparently – that a firm that is broken up into bits and sold off is unlikely to produce anything. This argument assumes that making everything marketable and trading everything at its market price is the guarantor of efficiency and all good things. Whether they are making any goods and services is not seen as significant, as long as returns are maximised. This fits with the rentier's view of the world.

[143] http://www.csmonitor.com/Innovation/Latest-News-Wires/2012/0404/New-Yahoo-CEO-Scott-Thompson-cuts-2-000-jobs.

[144] Pettifor, A. (2006) *The coming first-world debt crisis*, Houndmills, Basingstoke: Palgrave.

[145] See Fairclough, N. (1991) 'What might we mean by "enterprise discourse"?', in Keat, R. and Abercrombie, N. (eds) *Enterprise culture*, London: Routledge, pp 38–57. See also Russell Keat's introduction to this edited collection.

[146] It might be argued that where the capitalist has to arrange the financing of production, as distinct from merely owning it, some work is involved in doing this.

[147] 'Rent seeking, often via activities such as litigation and takeovers, and tax evasion and avoidance efforts seem now to constitute the prime threat to productive entrepreneurship': Baumol, W.J. (1990) 'Entrepreneurship: productive, unproductive, and destructive', *The Journal of Political Economy*, 98(5), Part 1, pp 893–921, at p 915.

[148] Krugman, P. (2012) *End this depression now!*, New York: W.W. Norton, pp 78–9.

[149] Alperovitz, G. and Daly, L. (2008) *Unjust deserts*, London: The New Press, pp 68–9.

[150] Mazzucato, M. (2012) The Astellas innovation debate, Royal Society, London, 20 November; see also her 2013 TED talk, 'Government – investor, risk-taker, innovator', http://www.ted.com/talks/mariana_mazzucato_government_investor_risk_taker_innovator.html.

[151] http://www.nybooks.com/articles/archives/2012/jan/12/who-was-steve-jobs/?pagination=false. We also need to look at their business models, including, in the case of Apple, the domination of supply chains to take advantage of cheap, super-exploited workers in China.

[152] It's normal in information industries for employees to have to sign away intellectual property rights to their employer.

[153] Redwood, J. (2012) 18 August, http://politicsactive.blogspot.co.uk/2011/08/difference-is-means-and-why.html.

[154] New Economics Foundation (2009) *A bit rich*, London: NEF, p 22.

[155] John Redwood, Conservative MP, *Guardian*, 18. August 2011.

[156] United Nations Conference on Trade and Development Annual Report, 2012; Rowlingson, K. and McKay, S. (2011) *Wealth and the wealthy*, Bristol: Policy Press, p 32ff; Wilkinson, R. and Pickett, K. (2009) *The spirit level: Why more equal societies almost always do better*, London: Allen Lane.

[157] See below, Chapter Nineteen.

[158] Cited in Engelen, E., Ertürk, I., Froud, J., Johal, S., Leaver, A., Moran, M., Nilsson, A. and Williams, K. (2011) *After the great complacence: Financial crisis and the politics of reform*, Oxford: Oxford University Press. The quotation continues: 'And the dispersion of risk more broadly across the financial system, has, thus far, increased the resilience of the system and the economy to shocks. When proposing or implementing regulation, we must seek to

preserve the benefits of financial innovation even as we address the risks that may accompany that innovation.' No comment.

[159] There's a certain tendency in anthropology to romanticise pre-capitalist societies as not having any notion of economising or thinking of economic matters as separable from other social and spiritual activities. But even though this may be true, they must do things in a way that allows them to survive and that requires choices or conventions that enable this.

[160] No doubt, some would argue that the rich can justifiably outbid others because it is assumed that their wealth must result from performing some special function that many others need. But mere ownership produces nothing.

[161] If land were to be nationalised, no doubt landlords would claim compensation for their loss of rent. But, as Henry George argued, this would be a compensation for loss of future unearned income. Even just nationalising land without 'compensation' would actually let them off lightly, because they would still be able to keep the unearned income that they had appropriated up to that point. It would be like allowing someone who had continually burgled others to keep their past ill-gotten gains, provided they stopped now. The same goes for other appropriators of unearned income. From a political point of view, what action should be taken, however, is also a question of what is politically possible, given the prevailing balance of political economic power, which is of course very much in favour of rentier interests.

[162] Often they will invoke the claim that you can't derive value-judgements from facts and that it is irrational and unscientific to do so, and imagine that philosophical authorities are on their side in this matter; increasingly they're not: Sayer, A. (2011) *Why things matter to people*, Cambridge: Cambridge University Press.

[163] See Chapter Three, note 5.

[164] See Mirowski, P. (2013) *Never let a serious crisis go to waste*, London: Verso.

[165] This is why we need a relational theory of value, one that incorporates both the objectivity of goods and services and their subjective valuation.

Part Two

Introduction

[1] Hobson, J.A. (2012) [1929] *Wealth and life: A study in values*, Abingdon: Routledge, p 217.

[2] Bamford, L. and Horton, T. (2009) *Understanding attitudes to tackling economic inequality*, York: Joseph Rowntree Foundation. Miller, D. (1999) *Principles of social justice*, Cambridge, MA: Harvard University Press.

Chapter Nine: To what do we owe our wealth?

[3] Alperovitz, G. and Daly, L. (2008) *Unjust deserts*, New York: The New Press, p 151. Much of this section is indebted to Alperovitz and Daly's book.

[4] Cited by Alperovitz and Daly (2008).

[5] Alperovitz and Daly (2008), p 1.

[6] Williams, R. (2011) *The country and the city*, London: Spokesman, p 105.

[7] I'm alluding here to the work of Pierre Bourdieu, the French sociologist, who brilliantly analysed how inequalities are reproduced in education: Bourdieu, P. and Passeron, J.-C. (1990) *Reproduction in education, society and culture*, London: Sage.

[8] Tawney, R.H. (2004) [1920] *The acquisitive society*, Mineola, NY: Harcourt Brace and Howe. Describing the pre-capitalist understanding of property in England, he added: 'The idea that the institution of private property involves the right of the owner to use it, or refrain from using it, in such a way as he may please, and that its principal significance is to supply him with an income, irrespective of any duties which he may discharge, would not have been understood by most public men of that age, and, if understood, would have been repudiated with indignation by the more reputable of them. ... Property was an aid to work, not an alternative to it' (p 57).

[9] Tawney (2004) [1920], p 57. He went on to say: 'precisely in proportion as it is important to preserve the property which a man has in the results of his own labour, it is important to abolish that which he has in the results of someone else' (p 68).

[10] Sayer, A. (1995) *Radical political economy: A critique*, Oxford: Blackwell.

[11] Hayek, F.A. (1988) *The fatal conceit: The errors of socialism*, London: Routledge.

[12] But where the activity involves inherently unified systems, like railways or health provision, it makes no sense to fragment ownership into either capitalist firms or competing cooperatives.

[13] Piketty, T. (2014) *Capital in the 21st century*, Cambridge, MA: Belknap Press, especially ch 11.

[14] Rowlingson, K. and Connor, S. (2011) 'The "deserving" rich? Inequality, morality and social policy', *Journal of Social Policy* 40, pp 437-52. For an excellent discussion of the arguments for and against inheritance taxes (which concludes by defending such taxes) see Murphy, M. and Nagel, T. (2002) *The myth of ownership: Taxes and justice*, Oxford: Oxford University Press.

[15] Piketty, T. (2014), p 440.

[16] As usual in moral and political philosophy, we find that relying purely on a single principle of judgement ultimately produces undesirable or absurd results; practical judgement is a matter of weighing several criteria like entitlement, desert, need, equality and implications for the quality of life and the health of the planet. See Appiah, K.A. (2008) *Experiments in ethics*, Cambridge, MA: Harvard University Press; Williams, B. (1985) *Ethics and the limits of philosophy*, Oxford: Oxford University Press. See also: Geuss, R. (2008) *Philosophy and real politics*, Princeton, NJ: Princeton University Press; Putnam, H. (2004) *The collapse of the fact–value dichotomy*, Cambridge, MA: Harvard University Press; Dancy, J. (2004) *Ethics without principles*, Oxford: Oxford University Press.

[17] Toynbee, P. (2013) 'Jeremy Hunt's smoke and mirrors will not solve the care crisis', *Guardian*, 11 February.

[18] Inequality Briefings 14 and 15 (2014), http://inequalitybriefing.org/. See also Hills, J., Bastagli, F., Cowell, F., Glennerster, H., Karagiannaki, E, and McKnight, A. (2013) 'Wealth distribution, accumulation, and policy', Centre for the Analysis of Social Exclusion, CASEbrief 33.

Chapter Ten: So what determines pay?

[19] For a fuller discussion of these possibilities see Wright, E.O. (2000) *Class counts*, Cambridge: Cambridge University Press.

[20] Orton, M and Rowlingson, K. (2007) *Public attitudes to inequality*, York: Joseph Rowntree Foundation; Horton, L. and Bamfield, T. (2009) *Understanding attitudes to tackling economic inequality*, York: Joseph Rowntree Foundation; Miller, D. (1999) *Principles of social justice*, Cambridge, MA: Harvard University Press.

[21] See Robert Jackall's wonderful study of corporate managers in the US in his 1988 book, *Moral mazes*, Oxford: Oxford University Press.

[22] Gomberg, P. (2007) *How to make opportunity equal*, Oxford: Blackwell; Sayer, A. (2009) 'The injustice of unequal work', *Soundings*, 43, pp. 102–13.

[23] Horton and Bamfield (2009).

[24] Gomberg (2007).

[25] Gomberg (2007).

[26] Smith, A. (1976) [1776], *The wealth of nations*, ed. E. Cannan, Chicago, IL: University of Chicago Press, vol 2, bk V, ch i, pp 302–3.

[27] Murphy, J.B. (1993) *The moral economy of labor*, New Haven, CT: Yale University Press.

[28] Smith (1976) [1776], vol 1, bk I, ch ii, pp 19–20.

[29] Feinstein, L. (2003) 'Inequality in the early cognitive development of British children in the 1970 cohort', *Economica*, 70, pp 73–97. See also Bruenig, M. (2014) 'America's class system across the life cycle', *Demos*, 25 March, http://www.demos.org/blog/3/25/14/americas-class-system-across-life-cycle.

[30] Aldridge, S. (2004) 'Life chances and social mobility: an overview of the evidence', London: Prime Minister's Strategy Unit, Cabinet Office, http://www.cabinetoffice.gov.uk/media/cabinetoffice/strategy/assets/lifechances_socialmobility.pdf; Erikson, R. and Goldthorpe, J.H. (1992) *The constant flux: A study of class mobility in industrial societies*, Oxford: Clarendon Press; Inequality Briefing 39 (2014) 'What people in the UK earn depends on what their parents earned', http://inequalitybriefing.org/graphics/briefing_39_peoples_income_reflects_what_their_parents_earned.pdf.

[31] Lareau, A. (2003) *Unequal childhoods: Class, race and family life*, California: University of California Press; Walkerdine, V. and Lucey, H. (1989) *Democracy in the kitchen*, London: Virago; Bourdieu, P. and Passeron, J.-C. (1990) *Reproduction in education, society and culture*, London: Sage; Reay, D. and Ball,

S.J. (1997) "'Spoilt for choice': the working classes and educational markets', *Oxford Review of Education*, 23(1), pp 89–101.

[32] John Rawls, author of the most influential work of political philosophy of the 20th century, *A theory of justice* ((1971) Oxford: Oxford University Press), rejects 'desert' (roughly, ideas of what we deserve) as a criterion for the distribution of resources.

[33] For a critique of popular notions of intelligence, IQ and genetically determined intelligence, see Dorling, D. (2010) *Injustice: Why social inequality persists*, Bristol: Policy Press.

[34] Sayer, A. and Walker, R.A. (1992) *The new social economy*, Oxford: Blackwell.

[35] Tilly, C. (1999) *Durable inequality*, Berkeley, CA: University of California Press.

[36] In the Labour journal *Progress*, 21 March 2005, http://www.progressonline.org.uk/2005/03/21/weve-got-to-carry-this-on/.

[37] Even when people buy a product or service the making of which they can witness, such as counselling or a piano lesson, such that they can guess how much they are contributing to the worker's income and consider whether they deserve it, they may still be mainly concerned with saving their own money.

[38] Ruskin, J. (1997) [1862] *Unto this last: And other writings*, London: Penguin, p 227.

[39] A similar effect is found where the service is sold for money, as in private nurseries for children. Also, most such workers are women, and gender discrimination depresses pay too.

[40] Hayek, F.A. (1976) "'Social" or distributive justice', in his *Law, legislation and liberty, vol 2*, p 74. Similarly: 'the value which a person's capacities or services have for us and for which he is recompensed has little relation to anything we call moral merit or deserts': Hayek, F.A. (1960) *The constitution of liberty*, Chicago: The University of Chicago Press, p 94.

[41] Philip Mirowski calls this division between what neoliberals say in private and what they say in public neoliberalism's 'double-truth'. Mirowski, P. (2013) *Never let a serious crisis go to waste*, London: Verso. The quotation from Hayek encapsulates it.

[42] Some enlightened employers may try not to favour applicants according to their accent and demeanour and social background, but the applicants have already been made unequal by being brought up in a society of wide economic and social inequalities, so they are usually competing unequally for unequal positions.

[43] Wright (2000).

Chapter Eleven: The myth of the level playing field

[44] Mills, C.W. (2000) [1956] *The power elite*, new edn, Oxford: Oxford University Press, p 14.

[45] Wilkinson, R. and Pickett, K. (2009) *The spirit level: Why more equal societies almost always do better*, London: Allen Lane.

[46] Aldridge, S. (2004) 'Life chances and social mobility: an overview of the evidence', London: Prime Minister's Strategy Unit, Cabinet Office, http://www.cabinetoffice.gov.uk/media/cabinetoffice/strategy/assets/lifechances_socialmobility.pdf.

[47] Rawls, J. (1971) *A theory of justice*, Oxford: Oxford University Press, p 104.

[48] See, for example, Sher, G. (1987) *Desert*, Princeton, NJ: Princeton University Press. For what it's worth, I would recommend a pluralist view of desert, that is, one that acknowledges *all* these measures as morally relevant in assessing what *recognition* people should get (that is, those who do well on these criteria through their own efforts should definitely be acknowledged and praised). Further, we can say little useful about the subject unless we consider contributive justice. I suggest that the different measures of desert should be used not so much for influencing what people get in economic rewards, but in assessing whether to call upon them to contribute more (or less) work.

Part Three

Chapter Twelve: The roots of the crisis

[1] To explain fully how the crisis developed over the last 40 years would require a major work of global historical economic geography, analysing the shifting interdependencies between economic processes in different parts of the world.

[2] Pettifor, A. (2006) *The coming first-world debt crisis*, Houndmills, Basingstoke: Palgrave, p 21.

[3] Haldane, A. (2012) interview on BBC 4, 3 December, http://www.bbc.co.uk/news/business-20585549. Estimates of the cost of the crisis are extremely difficult given that they involve counterfactual judgements about what would have happened in its absence, but Haldane estimates the loss to the UK economy at possibly as high as £7.4 trillion.

[4] See Chapter Eight.

[5] See Chapter Five.

[6] Jordan Brennan shows in the case of Canada how rising union membership in the early post-war period was strongly correlated with an increased proportion of national income going to labour in wages and salaries and how, from the 1980s, both fell as profits rose, and with that the incomes of the top 1%: Brennan, J. (2012) 'A shrinking universe: how concentrated power is shaping income inequality in Canada', Canadian Centre for Policy Alternatives. See also Oxfam (2014) 'Working for the few: political capture and economic inequality', 178 Oxfam Briefing Paper, 20 January.

[7] There are other possible reasons for this decline in profitability – for example, the labour- and capital-saving character of the emerging information

technology and the tendency for the benefits of technological innovations to be restricted by intellectual property rights and the pursuit of economic rent. See Shutt, H. (2010) *Beyond the profits system: Possibilities for a post-capitalist era*, London: Zed Books.

[8] This was matched by shifts in unearned income as income from interest rose from 1.4% of total US income in 1950 to 6.5% in 1979 and to a peak of 10.9% in 1986, before falling to 7.2% in 2005. Dew-Becker, I. and Gordon, R.J. (2005) 'Where did the productivity growth go?', National Bureau of Economic Research, Working Paper 11842, http://www.nber.org/papers/w11842.

[9] Oxfam (2014).

[10] Buchanan, J., Dymski, G., Froud, J., Johal, S., Leaver, A. and Williams, K. (2013) 'Unsustainable employment portfolios', *Work, Employment and Society*, 27, pp 396–413.

[11] Piketty, T. (2014) *Capital in the 21st century*, Cambridge, MA: Belknap Press.

[12] Resolution Foundation (2012) *Gaining from growth: The final report of the Commission on Living Standards*, http://www.resolutionfoundation.org/media/media/downloads/Gaining_from_growth_-_The_final_report_of_the_Commission_on_Living_Standards.pdf. The authors of this report also argue that increased non-wage benefits, particularly employer pension contributions, help to explain the divergence too.

[13] Peters, J. (2010) 'The rise of finance and the decline of organised labour in the advanced capitalist countries', *New Political Economy*, 16(1), pp 73–99, at p 93. See also Perrons, D. (2012) '"Global" financial crisis, earnings inequalities and gender: towards a more sustainable model of development', *Comparative Sociology*, 11, pp 202–26.

[14] Kristal, T. (2010) 'Good times bad times: postwar labor's share of income in 16 capitalist democracies', *American Sociological Review*, 75(5), pp 729–63. According to Harry Shutt, at the same time returns on 'investments' have been 'higher than in any period of comparable length since the Industrial Revolution', with an estimated 75% of this resulting from appreciation of assets in the US and Britain, compared with well under 50% on average from 1900 to 1979: Shutt, H. (2009) *The trouble with capitalism*, London: Zed Books, p 124.

[15] UNCTAD (2012) *Trade and development* report, p 52.

[16] ILO (2008) *World of work* report.

[17] The same trends of falling labour shares are reported in IMF (2007) *Spillovers and cycles in the global economy*, p 168, though workers in sectors employing a large proportion of graduates increased their shares.

[18] IMF (2007), p 168; OECD (2011) *Divided we stand: Why inequality keeps rising*, Paris: OECD. I am grateful to Diane Perrons for alerting me to these reports. See also Oxfam (2014).

[19] Keynes, cited in Ingham, G. (2008) *Capitalism*, Cambridge: Polity, p 85.

[20] This is only part of a much more complex story. For a fuller introduction, see Pettifor (2006).

[21] Ingham (2012).

[22] *The Economist* (2006) 'Sounding the Retreat', 13 July.

[23] Pauly, D. (2004) 'General Motors and Ford won't survive as bankers', *Bloomberg*, 15 October , http://www.bloomberg.com/apps/news?pid=newsarchive&sid=amuO_75ObjIM.

[24] Harvey, D. (2007) *A brief history of neoliberalism*, Oxford: Oxford University Press; Crotty, J. (2005) 'The neoliberal paradox: the impact of destructive product market competition and "modern" financial markets on nonfinancial corporation performance in the neoliberal era', in Epstein, G. (ed) *Financialization and the world economy*, Northampton, MA: Edward Elgar, pp 77–110; Glyn, A. (2007) *Capitalism unleashed: Finance, globalization and welfare*, Oxford: Oxford University Press; Shutt (2010).

[25] Pettifor (2006). US financial sector profits rose from 10–15% of total US profits in the 1950s and 1960s to over 40% by the late 1990s.

[26] Henwood, D. (1998) *Wall Street*, London: Verso, p 73. James Crotty commented: 'Financial market payments [by non-finance sector firms] rose from relatively low levels in the 1950s to average about 30 percent of cash flow from the mid-1960s through the late 1970s. But from 1984 to 2000, with the exception of three years in the recession of the early 1990s, NFCs paid out well over half their cash flow to financial agents. From 1984 to 1990 and again from 1997 to 2001 this ratio never fell below 50 percent, peaking at 76 percent in 1989 and again at 74 percent in 1998' (Crotty, 2009, p 99 in Epstein et al).

[27] For a detailed analysis of this process, see Langley, P. (2009) *The everyday life of finance: Saving and borrowing in Anglo-America*, Oxford: Oxford University Press, and Martin, R. (2002) *Financialization of everyday life*, Philadelphia, PA: Temple University Press.

[28] OECD (2011), ch 9. Germany and Spain were the main major exceptions over the last two decades.

[29] Chang, H.-J. (2011) *23 things they don't tell you about capitalism*, London: Allen Lane, p 145.

[30] Dumenil, G. and Levy, D. (2001) 'Costs and benefits of neoliberal policies: a class analysis', *Review of International Political Economy*, 8(4), pp 578–607.

[31] Dumenil, G. and Levy, D. (2004) 'Neoliberal income trends: wealth, class and ownership in the USA', *New Left Review*, 30, pp 105–33.

[32] Alternet (2012) '"The Dumbest Idea in the World": Corporate America's False – and Dangerous – Ideology of Shareholder Value', 29 August, http://www.alternet.org/economy/dumbest-idea-world-corporate-americas-false-and-dangerous-ideology-shareholder-value.

[33] *Financial Times* (2009) 12 March, http://www.ft.com/cms/s/0/294ff1f2-0f27-11de-ba10-0000779fd2ac.html#axzz29IJX9vvb.

[34] William Lazonick, cited in Chang (2010), p 20.

[35] Tabb, W.J. (2012) *The restructuring of capitalism in our time*, New York: Columbia University Press, p 49.

[36] Mazzucato, M. (2013) 'From bubble to bubble', *Guardian*, 16 January.

[37] According to Stuart Lansley, Debenhams and the AA both stopped paying corporation tax after a private equity takeover: Lansley, S. (nd) 'Do the super-rich matter?', TUC Touchstone Pamphlet No 4.

[38] Crotty (2008) and Erturk, I. et al (eds) (2008) *Financialization at work: Key texts and commentary*, London: Routledge.

[39] In leading firms, stock options formed over two-thirds of managers' remuneration. One commentator described the methods used to maximise management's gains as 'legal embezzlement' (John Plender, cited in Tabb, 2012, p 44).

[40] Engelen, E., Ertürk, I., Froud, J., Johal, S., Leaver, A., Moran, M., Nilsson, A. and Williams, K. (2011) *After the great complacence: Financial crisis and the politics of reform*, Oxford: Oxford University Press, p 49.

[41] Piketty, T. (2014), p 458.

[42] Froud, J., Johal, S., Haslam, C. and Williams, K. (2001) 'Accumulation under conditions of inequality', *Review of International Political Economy*, 8(1), pp 66–95.

[43] Shutt (2009), pp 128–9.

[44] See Chapter Eighteen.

[45] Lysandrou, P. (2011) 'Global inequality as one of the root causes of the financial crisis: a suggested explanation', *Economy and Society*, 40(3), pp 323–44.

[46] At the time of writing, European Union citizens' bank deposits were protected up to €100,000 (£85,000) in any one banking group.

[47] Turner, A. (2009) *The Turner Review: A regulatory response to the global banking crisis*, London: Financial Services Authority, p 18.

[48] For a definition of debt deflation, see Chapter Four. On how Wall Street engineered asset inflation at the end of the 20th century and enhanced the unearned income of the top 1% in the US who were bondholders, see Canterbury, E.R. (2000) *Wall Street capitalism: The theory of the bondholding class*, Singapore: World Scientific Publishing Company.

[49] Merryman, J. (2012) *Occupying money*, 17 May, http://source.yeeyan.org/view/430335_f43/Occupying%20Money.%20-%20welcome%20to%20exterminating%20angel%20press. See also Amato, M. and Fantacci, L. (2012) *The end of finance*, Cambridge: Polity, p 15.

[50] Leyshon, A. and Thrift, N. (2007) 'The capitalization of almost everything: the future of finance and capitalism', *Theory Culture Society*, 24, p 97. Doug Henwood comments: 'debts, mere promises to pay, are nonetheless transformed into commodities in the eyes of the creditors. This capitalization of promised incomes enables nearly everything, from an industrial plant to an unspoiled wilderness to a human life, to be modelled as a quasi-credit, whose value today is the value of its future earnings stream – profits or

wilderness services or wages, adjusted for value over time using prevailing interest rates and maybe an estimate of risk' (Henwood, 1998, p 22).

[51] Engelen et al (2011), p 61. See also Turner (2009), ch 1 and Barba, A. and de Vivo, G. (2012) 'An "unproductive labour" view of finance', *Cambridge Journal of Economics*, 36, pp 1479–96.

[52] Yes, he did write that. Marx, K. (1998) [1894] *Capital*, vol III, London: Lawrence and Wishart, p 547.

[53] In the inquests that followed the crash in 2007, several CEOs admitted they didn't understand the derivative products their own companies were selling. See Crotty, J. (2010) 'The bonus-driven "rainmaker" financial firm: how these firms enrich top employees, destroy shareholder value and create systemic financial instability', pp 74ff, http://people.umass.edu/crotty/RMFC%20paper%20-%20July%202010.pdf.

[54] Münchau, W. (2010) 'Time to outlaw naked credit default swaps', *Financial Times*, 28 February.

[55] Hildyard, N. (2010) 'From US sub prime to London prime: shadow bankers in London', The Corner House, http://www.thecornerhouse.org.uk/resource/us-subprime-london-prime. See also Münchau (2010).

[56] Anrig, G. (2010,) '"Strategic deficit" redux', *The American Prospect*, 26 January, http://prospect.org/article/strategic-deficit-redux-0. See also Dumenil and Levy (2001).

[57] Meek, J. (2012) 'Human revenue stream', *London Review of Books*, 5 April. Thanks to John Allen for drawing this reference to my attention.

[58] On how UK privatised train services are still heavily subsidised by the state, with much of the subsidy going to shareholders, see Bowman, A. et al (2013) 'The conceit of enterprise: train operators and trade narrative', http://www.cresc.ac.uk/sites/default/files/The%20Conceit%20of%20Enterprise.pdf.

[59] Charles Rowley's Blog, http://charlesrowley.wordpress.com/2012/05/10/bond-market-vigilantes-rule-across-the-eurozone/.

[60] Hilferding, R. (2010) *Finance capital*, London: Routledge, ch 7, http://www.marxists.org/archive/hilferding/1910/finkap/ch07.htm.

[61] In the US, the top 0.5%, who dominate bondholding, got half of all the interest payments by the Federal government going to households. See Canterbury (2000).

[62] Stevenson, T. (2012) 'Bond market vigilantes turn on Italy', *Telegraph*, 12 November.

[63] *Time* (1989) 'Top 10 tax dodgers'. She was imprisoned for tax evasion. http://content.time.com/time/specials/packages/article/0,28804,1891335_1891333_1891317,00.html.

[64] European Central Bank (2014) 'Long-term interest rate statistics for EU Member States', http://www.ecb.europa.eu/stats/money/long/html/index.en.html.

[65] *Wall Street Journal* (2011) 30 September, http://online.wsj.com/article/SB 10001424053111904332804576538363789127084.html.

[66] Cited in Canterbury (2000).

[67] Stevenson (2011).

[68] Krugman, P. (2009) 'Invisible bond vigilantes', *New York Times*, 19 November 2009; see also Wolf, M. (2010), 'Why the Balls critique is correct', *Financial Times*, 2 September, http://www.ft.com/cms/s/0/119c59ac-b6c3-11df-b3dd-00144feabdc0.html.

[69] Cited in Leyshon, A. and French, S. (2010) '"These f@#king guys" (1): the terrible waste of a good crisis', *Environment and Planning A*, 42, pp 2549–59. Actually, most of the holders of British government bonds were British.

[70] Shifferes, S. (2009) 'Can banking regulation go global?', BBC News, 18 March.

[71] These banks were heavily involved in fuelling the Irish property boom. *The Journal* (2012) 'AIB repays €1 billion to unsecured bondholders today', 1 October, http://www.thejournal.ie/aib-bondholder-payment-617526-Oct2012/.

[72] http://www.golemxiv.co.uk/2010/10/who-are-the-bond-holders-we-are-bailing-out/ He is also a friend of Jose Manuel Barroso, EU President, whom he invited for a week's trip on his luxury yacht, a fact revealed in a corruption scandal involving Barroso in 2005, http://spirolatsis. crazybillionaire.org/spirolatsis.php.

[73] *International Viewpoint* (2011) 'Why agreements with the troika are odious', 31 August, http://www.internationalviewpoint.org/spip.php?article2267.

[74] It may be possible for private organisations as bondholders to sue national governments for defaulting, by appealing to the World Bank's International Center for the Settlement of Investment Disputes. If debtors are not allowed to default, then this quite clearly means that the risk is all on their side: *Real News* (2011) 'The tyranny of the bondholders', 29 July, http://therealnews.com/t2/index.php?option=com_content&task=view&id=31&Itemid=74&jumival=7062.

[75] Tsipras, A. (2013) 'Austerity is wreaking havoc, but the left can unite to build a better Europe', *Guardian*, 'Comment is free', 27 November, http://www.theguardian.com/commentisfree/2013/nov/27/austerity-left-unite-europe-alexis-tsipras.

[76] Blackburn, R. (2011) *Age shock*, 2nd edn, London Verso, p xxix. Goldman Sachs had not only bet on a Greek default but previously helped the Greek government to disguise its debts with derivatives so that it could take on more debt! Words like 'stitch-up' and 'heist' come to mind.

[77] Savage, M. and Williams, K. (2008) *Remembering elites*, Oxford: Blackwell, p 13.

[78] Froud, J., Johal, S., Haslam, C. and Williams, K. (2001) 'Accumulation under conditions of inequality', *Review of International Political Economy*, 8(1), pp 66–95, at p 83.

[79] Canterbury (2000), pp 196–7.

[80] As Geoffrey Ingham notes, taking companies private can be interpreted as a return to a purer form of capitalism, in which ownership and power are more concentrated (Ingham, 2012, p 161).

[81] http://andersred.blogspot.co.uk/. In some cases the buyers in leveraged buyouts are the managers of the target firm themselves; as such, they are in a good position to lower share prices by manipulating the company accounts by delaying booking of profits and bringing forward expenditures so they can buy them up more cheaply. See also Dore, R. (2008) 'Financialization of the global economy', *Industrial and Corporate Change*, 17(6), pp 1097–112.

[82] Clark, I., Appelbaum, E. and Batt, R. (2011) 'Financial capitalism, breach of trust and collateral damage', www.birmingham.ac.uk/Documents/college.../ian-clark-inaugural.pdf.

[83] IUF (2012) 'Kraft and Cadbury: victors and spoils', 31 January, http://www.iufdocuments.org/buyoutwatch/2010/02/kraft_and_cadbury_victors_and.html#more.

[84] Wachman, R. (2008) 'Utilities at risk from debt timebomb', *Observer*, 20 April, http://www.theguardian.com/business/2008/apr/20/utilities.creditcrunch.

[85] Not all buyouts were asset-stripping ventures – some may have enabled long-term benefits, but as William Tabb puts it, 'It's difficult to distinguish between a reasonable euthanasia and a murder-for-profit of a viable entity' (Tabb, 2012, p 121). See also Ferguson, C. (2012) *Inside job*, Oxford: Oneworld, pp 233 ff.

[86] Wolf, M. (2009) 'Why Britain has to curb finance', *Financial Times*, 29 May, http://www.ft.com/cms/s/0/24bfcb30-4636-11de-803f-00144feabdc0.html#axzz26SMfanvo.

Chapter Thirteen: Key winners

[87] Folkman, P. et al (2006) 'Working for themselves? Capital market intermediaries and contemporary capitalism', CRESC Working Paper No 25.

[88] Savage, M. and Williams, K. (2008) 'Elites: remembered in capitalism and forgotten in social science', *The Sociological Review*, 56(s1), pp 1–24.

[89] Cited in New Economics Foundation (2009) *A bit rich*, p 26. Van der Veer was facing criticism for receiving a €1.35 million bonus from an incentive scheme and a 58% pay increase to €10.3 million in 2008, even though the company failed to meet performance targets for 2006–08: *Financial Times*, 8 June 2009, http://www.ft.com/cms/s/0/d8ed7afa-5458-11de-a58d-00144feabdc0.html#axzz29IJX9vvb.

[90] Cited in Partnoy, F. (2004) *Infectious greed: How deceit and risk corrupted the markets*, London: Profile Books, p 83.

[91] Peppard, A. (2008) 'Oil in the family', *Vanity Fair*, http://www.vanityfair.com/politics/features/2008/06/hunt200806.

[92] Stanford University Centre on Poverty and Inequality, http://www.stanford. edu/group/scspi/cgi-bin/facts.php.

[93] Haldane, A. (2012) 'The doom loop', *London Review of Books*, 34(4), 23 February, pp 21–2.

[94] Smith, E.B. and Kunt, P. (2013) 'CEO pay 1,795-to-1 multiple of wages skirts U.S. law', *Bloomberg News*, 30 April, http://go.bloomberg.com/ multimedia/ceo-pay-ratio/.

[95] Tabb, W.J. (2012) *The restructuring of capitalism in our time*, New York: Columbia University Press, p 45.

[96] Froud, J., Johal, S. and Williams, K. (2005) 'Pay for corporate performance or pay as social division', *Competition and Change*, 9(1), pp 49–74. Tabb argues that in the US stock options have shifted ownership towards CEOs relative to outside shareholders.

[97] Tabb (2012), p 44.

[98] Tabb (2012), p 47.

[99] Tabb (2012), p 50.

[100] This was confirmed in a survey reported by Deborah Hargreaves of the High Pay Centre, http://www.highpaycentre.org/blog/it-is-obscene-for-bosses-to-continue-to-take-big-bonuses, 24 September 2012.

[101] *Guardian* (2012) 'Executive pay up 27% despite backlash', 6 November, http://www.theguardian.com/business/2012/nov/06/executive-pay-up-27-percent. In practice, the difference between long-term incentive plans and bonuses for short-term performance is smaller than the name would suggest.

[102] Krugman, P. (2012) *End this depression now!*, New York: W.W. Norton, Ertürk, I. et al (2006) 'Agency, the romance of management pay and an alternative explanation', CRESC Working Paper No 23.

[103] Bowman, A., Ertürk, I., Froud, J., Johal, S., Moran, M., Law, J., Leaver, A. and Williams, K. (2012) 'Scapegoats aren't enough: a Leveson for the banks?' CRESC Discussion Paper, p 8.

[104] *New York Times* (2006) '"Bonus heaven" at Goldman Sachs after record year', 13 December, http://www.nytimes.com/2006/12/13/business/worldbusiness/13iht-goldman.3884286.html?_r=1&.

[105] *New Statesman* (2011) 'Bank bonuses make a mockery of the Tories' rhetoric', 20 July, http://www.newstatesman.com/blogs/the-staggers/2011/07/unacceptable-bonuses-block

[106] BBC (2011) 7 January, http://www.bbc.co.uk/news/business-12131092

[107] Clark, A. (2011) 'Goldman Sachs in the firing line over predicted $15.4 bn wage bill', *The Observer*, 16 January.

[108] Cited in Crotty, J. (2010) 'The bonus-driven "rainmaker" financial firm: how these firms enrich top employees, destroy shareholder value and create systemic financial instability', pp 74 ff, http://people.umass.edu/crotty/RMFC%20paper%20-%20July%202010.pdf. This section owes much to this article.

109 *Financial Times* (2012) 'Banks ready to claw back more bonuses', 27 August, http://www.ft.com/cms/s/0/01ab1656-eadc-11e1-afbb-00144feab49a.html#axzz28nNe7PiO.

110 Crotty (2010) pp 74 ff.

111 *Financial Times* (2008) 'Curbing the excess of bankers' pay', 7 March.

112 J.-C. Trichet, cited in Crotty (2010), p 109.

113 Haldane, A. (2010) 'The £100 billion question', Speech, Bank of England, March.

114 Wolf, M. (2010) 'The challenge of halting the financial Domesday machine', *Financial Times*, 20 April, http://www.ft.com/cms/s/4351118c-4cdc-11df-9977-00144feab49a.html#axzz37d7uu0nR.

115 *New York Times* (2012) 'Top hedge fund managers earn over $240 Million', 24 April, http://www.nytimes.com/2007/04/24/business/24hedge.html.

116 'Don't lower taxes for billionaires. Double them', http://ourfuture.org/blog-entry/2012104109/dont-lower-taxes-billionaires-double-them, 9 October 2012.

117 Farrell, G. (2009) 'Blankfein defends pay levels for "more productive" Goldman staff', *Financial Times*, 11 November, http://www.ft.com/cms/s/0/c99bf08e-ce62-11de-a1ea-00144feabdc0.html#axzz34du1m4BI

118 Speech by the Chancellor of the Exchequer at the Lord Mayor's Banquet, Mansion House, 16 June 2004, http://www.wired-gov.net/wg/wg-news-1.nsf/54e6de9e0c383719802572b9005141ed/97132678f0af3244802572ab004b99f7?OpenDocument.

119 Gieve, J. (2007) 'The City's growth: The crest of a wave or swimming with the stream?', Speech at the Bank of England to the London Society of Chartered Accountants, http://www.bankofengland.co.uk/publications/Pages/news/2007/038.aspx.

120 Christophers, B. (2011) 'Making finance productive', *Economy and Society*, 40(1), pp 112–40.

121 Haldane, A.G. and Madouros, V. (2011) 'What is the contribution of the financial sector', VOX, http://www.voxeu.org/article/what-contribution-financial-sector. See also Christensen, J. and Shaxson, N. (2013) *The finance curse*, Tax Justice Network, http://www.taxjustice.net/cms/front_content.php?idcat=150.

122 '[M]uch financial innovation has been of minimal social value, representing instead economic rent extraction which has swollen some parts of the financial sector beyond their economically efficient size': Turner, A. (2009) Turner Review press conference speech.

123 CRESC (2012) 'An alternative report on UK banking reform', http://www.studyblue.com/notes/note/n/cresc-report-on-banking-reform1pdf/file/6164790.

124 In the UK, when the regional distribution of public spending is measured, it's normal to ignore the huge defence sector, which is heavily concentrated in the south-east of England. Public spending on transport also heavily favours

London and suburbs. See also Massey, D. (2007) *World city*, Cambridge: Polity.

[125] Wolf, M. (2009) 'Why Britain has to curb finance', *Financial Times*, 29 May.

[126] Marx, K. (1998) [1894] *Capital*, vol III, London: Lawrence and Wishart, p 596. Note, however, the cautionary note on page 63 of this volume.

[127] Hudson, M. (2012) *The bubble and beyond*, Dresden: ISLET.

[128] Blackburn, R. (2011) *Age shock*, London:Verso

[129] Monbiot, G. (2011) 'The corporate welfare state', blog, 2 November, http://www.monbiot.com/2011/11/21/the-corporate-welfare-state/.

[130] Just how big is the bailout is unclear, as, despite the fact that the public has had to foot the bill, little information is available on amounts and conditions – a telling fact in itself. RBS had an insurance scheme worth £60 billion – more than the UK's entire education budget! – to insure £200 billion of toxic loans and mortgages, for which it pays a fee of £500 million per year to the government. Lloyds TSB received £20 billion and has paid back £2.5 billion. Other banks that weren't directly bailed out benefitted from this stabilisation (New Economics Foundation, 2010).

[131] Alessandri, P. and Haldane, A. (2009) 'Banking on the state', London: Bank of England.

[132] Haldane, A. (2010) 'The $100 billion question', Bank of England, http://www.bankofengland.co.uk/archive/Documents/historicpubs/news/2010/036.pdf.

[133] IMF data, cited in Chang, H.-J. (2011) *23 things they don't tell you about capitalism*, London: Allen Lane, p 235.

[134] Blackburn, R. (2008) 'The sub-prime crisis', *New Left Review* 50.

[135] Philip Coggan comments:'bad-debts have been passed up the chain – from private-sector borrowers to banks, from banks to governments, and from weak governments to strong ones' (Coggan, P. (2011) *Paper promises*, London: Allen Lane, p 209).

[136] See http://www.bloomberg.com/apps/news?pid=newsarchive&sid=aAdP3tUMTdVE, 5 September 2010.

[137] Leyshon, A. and French, S. (2010) '"These f@#king guys" (1): the terrible waste of a good crisis', *Environment and Planning A*, 42, pp 2549–59.

[138] Kunkel, B. (2012) 'Forgive us our debts', *London Review of Books*, 34(9), pp 23-9.

[139] Cited in New Economics Foundation (2010).

Chapter Fourteen: Summing up

[140] Reich, R. (2011) *Aftershock*, New York: Vintage Books, p 141.

[141] http://www.youtube.com/watch?v=_mzcbXi1Tkk.

[142] Epstein, G. and Jayadev, A. (2005) 'The rise of rentier incomes in OECD countries', in Epstein, G. (ed) *Financialization and the world economy*, Cheltenham: Edward Elgar, pp 46-75.

[143] Engelen, E., Ertürk, I., Froud, J., Johal, S., Leaver, A., Moran, M., Nilsson, A. and Williams, K. (2011) *After the great complacence: Financial crisis and the politics of reform*, Oxford: Oxford University Press, p 206.

[144] New Economics Foundation (2010) *Where did our money go?*, London: NEF.

[145] Collinson, P. (2006) 'On reflection', *Guardian*, 26 August, http://www.theguardian.com/money/2006/apr/15/consumernews.moneysupplement2.

[146] CRESC (2009) *An alternative report on UK banking reform*, p 65, http://www.cresc.ac.uk/sites/default/files/Alternative%20report%20on%20banking%20V2.pdf.

[147] See Eureka Report, 'G10 debt distribution', http://www.eurekareport.com.au/graphs/2012/2/22/g10-debt-distribution.

[148] Cited in New Economics Foundation (2010).

Part Four

Introduction

[1] Brandeis was an American lawyer and Associate Justice on the Supreme Court of the US from 1916 to 1939.

[2] Smith, A. (1976) [1776] *The wealth of nations*, ed. E. Cannan, Chicago, IL: University of Chicago Press, bk I, ch v, p 35. Thomas Hobbes (1588–1679) was an early theorist of politics, society and power.

[3] Actually, in the US, that's becoming less true, as more marginalised people are being excluded from voting.

Chapter Fifteen: How the rule of the rich works

[4] For elaboration see Engelen, E., Ertürk, I., Froud, J., Johal, S., Leaver, A., Moran, M., Nilsson, A. and Williams, K. (2011) *After the great complacence: Financial crisis and the politics of reform*, Oxford: Oxford University Press. The authors describe the success of finance in achieving dominance of economics and politics as an 'elite debacle', a debacle being a *confused rout*.

[5] Williams, H. (2006) *Britain's power elite*, London: Constable.

[6] Henwood, D. (1998), *Wall Street*, London: Verso, p 23. As Colin Ley puts it, 'global financial markets are supposed to register the collective judgement of the owners of capital about how profitable it is to operate in a given country where all factors, including the risk of adverse government policies, are taken into account' (Ley, C. (2001) *Market driven politics*, London: Verso, p 21).

[7] Johnson is the Mayor of London and, like Cameron, a former member of the exclusive Oxford Bullingdon Club (in other words, gang), whose members used to get drunk and run round Oxford and smash up restaurants – with impunity. See also *Huffington Post UK* (2013) 'Is being a banker genetic? Boris Johnson looks to intelligence to explain equality gap', 28 November,

http://www.huffingtonpost.co.uk/2013/11/28/iq-intelligence-boris-johnson-_n_4355372.html.

[8] Bourdieu, P. (1993) *Sociology in question*, London: Sage, p 14.

[9] Chakrabortty, A. (2013) 'Looking for a party funding scandal: try David Cameron's Conservatives', *Guardian*, 8 July, http://www.guardian.co.uk/commentisfree/2013/jul/08/party-funding-scandal-david-cameron-conservatives.

[10] Froud, J. et al. (2012) 'Groundhog Day: elite power, democratic disconnects and the failure of financial reform in the UK', CRESC Working Paper No 108, University of Manchester, p 16, http://www.cresc.ac.uk/sites/default/files/Groundhog%20Day%20Elite%20power,%20democratic%20disconnects%20and%20the%20failure%20of%20financial%20reform%20in%20the%20UK%20CRESC%20WP108%20(Version%202).pdf.

[11] The Bureau of Investigative Journalism (2011) 'Tory Party funding from City doubles under Cameron', 8 February, http://www.thebureauinvestigates.com/2011/02/08/city-financing-of-the-conservative-party-doublesunder-cameron/.

[12] The Bureau of Investigative Journalism (2011) 'Hedge funds, financiers and private equity make up 27% of Tory funding', 30 September, http://www.thebureauinvestigates.com/2011/09/30/hedgefunds-financiers-and-private-equity-tycoons-make-up-27-of-tory-funding/.

[13] Hutton, W. (2010) *Them and us*, London: Little, Brown, p 179.

[14] Powerbase (2001) 'New Labour: donors', http://www.powerbase.info/index.php/New_Labour:_Donors.

[15] Peston, R. (2008) 'Pointing fingers at the plutocrats', *Telegraph*, 26 January, http://www.telegraph.co.uk/finance/economics/2783334/Pointing-fingers-at-the-plutocrats.html.

[16] Wintour, P. (2013) 'Labour backer says £1.65m donation was given in shares to avoid tax', *Guardian*, 6 June, http://www.guardian.co.uk/politics/2013/jun/06/labour-party-backer-donation-tax. Giving shares was also a smart way of making sure New Labour supported his business, as the value of the shares would have fallen if it didn't.

[17] Chakrabortty (2013).

[18] However, according to Robert Reich, the identities of many of the donors are hidden: hundreds of millions of dollars are poured into political advertisements without a trace of where the money is coming from. Only 32% of groups paying for election ads disclose the names of their donors. Reich, R. (2010) 'The perfect storm that threatens American democracy', 18 October, http://inlightofrecentevents.wordpress.com/rule-of-super-rich-privileged-plutocracy/. See also Brenner, M. (2013) 'Plutocracy in America', *Counterpunch*, 1 April, http://www.counterpunch.org/2013/04/01/plutocracy-in-america/.

[19] Pizzigati, S. (2013) 'Why can't democracy trump inequality?', *Too Much*, 19 August, http://www.toomuchonline.org/tmweekly.html.

[20] McGregor, R. (2014) 'US Supreme Court strikes down donation limits', *Financial Times*, 2 April, http://www.ft.com/cms/s/0/70f806b4-ba78-11e3-aeb0-00144feabdc0.html#axzz34du1m4BI.

[21] Monbiot, G. (2010) 'When corporations bankroll politics, we all pay the price', *Guardian*, 29 October, http://www.theguardian.com/commentisfree/2012/oct/29/capitalism-bankrolls-politics-pay-price. For information on Goldman Sachs' role in US politics, see http://my.firedoglake.com/fflambeau/2010/04/27/a-list-of-goldman-sachs-people-in-the-obama-government-names-attached-to-the-giant-squids-tentacles/.

[22] Monbiot, G. (2012) 'Stop this culture of paying politicians for denying climate change', *Guardian*, 2 August, http://www.theguardian.com/environment/georgemonbiot/2012/aug/02/climate-change-political-funding-us. Inhofe sits on and previously chaired the Senate Committee on Environment and Public Works.

[23] Berners-Lee, M. and Clark, D. (2013) *The burning question*, London: Profile Books, p 128. For contributions to US political parties by industry, see data from OpenSecrets.org: http://www.opensecrets.org/industries/index.php and http://www.opensecrets.org/industries/background.php?cycle=2012&ind=E01.

[24] Ferguson, C. (2012) *Inside job*, London: Oneworld.

[25] World Economic Forum web pages: http://www.weforum.org/our-members.

[26] Green Governance (2013) 'To Save The World', 22 January, http://www.bibliotecapleyades.net/sociopolitica/sociopol_globalelite123.htm.

[27] Law governing lobbying in the US requires more transparency.

[28] Ferguson (2012), p 298.

[29] For further information on politicians' connections to private health interests, see http://socialinvestigations.blogspot.com/2012/02/nhs-privatisation-compilation-of.html, and more recently, http://socialinvestigations.blogspot.co.uk/2014/03/compilation-of-parliamentary-financial.html. Sadly, though it's consistent with the neoliberal corruption of universities, Milburn has recently been appointed as Chancellor of my own university. Hewitt was caught out by the *Dispatches* TV programme advising a fictional US company on how best to lobby the UK government, obligingly offering five key routes. See: http://www.powerbase.info/index.php/Patricia_Hewitt.

[30] Alleyne, R. (2012) 'NHS cuts may not be sustainable, says spending watchdog', *Telegraph*, 13 December, http://www.telegraph.co.uk/health/healthnews/9741705/NHS-cuts-may-not-be-sustainable-says-spending-watchdog.html. In the news reports and inquests of successive failings of NHS hospitals since 2012, these cuts are never mentioned. The inevitable suspicion is that the NHS is being set up to fail.

[31] Macalister, T. (2013) 'Ministers' oil industry ties prop up high-carbon policy, report alleges', *Guardian*, 10 March, http://www.guardian.co.uk/business/2013/mar/10/oil-industry-links-and-high-carbon-energy-

policy?INTCMP=SRCH;World Development Movement (2013) 'Carbon capital handbook', http://www.wdm.org.uk/carbon-capital/web-of-power.

32 Mulgan, G. (2013) *The locust and the bee*, Princeton, NJ: Princeton University Press, and Mendick, R. and Watts, R. (2012) *Telegraph*, 30 June, http://www.telegraph.co.uk/news/politics/tony-blair/9367302/Im-not-one-of-the-super-rich-says-Tony-Blair-despite-being-worth-20m-a-year-and-owningsix-homes.html. See also Hall, R. (2012) *Independent*, 18 April, http://www.independent.co.uk/news/world/middle-east/kuwaiti-finance-minister-faces-questions-over-deal-to-pay-millions-to-tony-blairs-company-for-advising-royal-family-7654711.html; Bennett, A. (2014) 'Tony Blair enjoys "best year yet" with over £13m in bank', *Huffington Post*, 6 January, http://www.huffingtonpost.co.uk/2014/01/06/tony-blair-fortune_n_4547935.html.

33 Cohen, M. (2012) 'Tony Blair's moral decline and fall is now complete', *Observer*, 27 May, http://www.theguardian.com/commentisfree/2012/may/27/nick-cohen-tony-blair-kazakhstan.

34 Quoted in Krugman, P. (2012) *End this depression now!*, New York: W.W. Norton, p 88.

35 Mathiason, N., Newman, M. and McClenaghan, M. (2012) 'Revealed: the £93m City lobby machine', The Bureau of Investigative Journalism, 9 July, http://www.thebureauinvestigates.com/2012/07/09/revealed-the-93m-city-lobby-machine/.

36 *Telegraph* (2013) 'Mervyn King: banks lobbying at highest level against regulator's demands', 25 June, http://www.telegraph.co.uk/finance/newsbysector/banksandfinance/10141142/Mervyn-King-Banks-lobbying-at-highest-level-against-regulators-demands.html.

37 McClenaghan, M. (2010) 'How big four get inside track by loaning staff to government', The Bureau of Investigative Journalism, 10 July, http://www.thebureauinvestigates.com/2012/07/10/how-big-four-get-inside-track-by-loaning-staff-to-government/. For a revealing analysis of the growth of the power of the City and its domination of politics, see Ertürk, I. et al (2011) 'City state against national settlement', CRESC Working Paper No 101, http://www.cresc.ac.uk/sites/default/files/City%20State%20and%20National%20Settlement%20CRESC%20WP101.pdf.

38 Mathiason, N., Newman and McClenaghan, M. (2012) 'Revealed: the £93m City lobby machine', The Bureau of Investigative Journalism, 9 July, http://www.networkedblogs.com/zS43z.

39 Treanor, J. (2012) 'Bleak day for British banking as Libor arrests follow record fine for HSBC', *Guardian*, 11 December, http://www.theguardian.com/business/2012/dec/11/banking-libor-fine-hsbc.

40 Ball, J. and Taylor, H. (2013) '"Buddy" scheme to give more multinationals access to ministers', *Guardian*, 18 January, http://www.theguardian.com/politics/2013/jan/18/buddy-scheme-multinationals-access-ministers.

41 Carrington, D. and Sparrow, A. (2013) 'Gas industry employee seconded to draft UK's energy policy', *Guardian*, 10 November, http://www.

theguardian.com/environment/2013/nov/10/gas-industry-employee-energy-policy.

[42] Monbiot, G. (2013), 12 November, http://www.monbiot.com/2013/11/11/why-politics-fails/.

[43] *Washington Monthly*, cited in Shaxson, N. and Christensen, J. (2013) *The finance curse*, Taiwan: Commonwealth Publishing, p 55.

[44] http://www.policyexchange.org.uk/corporate-engagement

[45] Investigative journalists at Spinwatch discovered that another one of the Policy Exchange's funders is a company called Tribal, which wants to get into providing health service commissioning for general practitioners – a potentially vast business involving charging fees for directing public money to 'any willing provider' of health services, public or private. (GPs are being given control of the majority of finance for health services, so that they can use whatever providers they wish, though in practice many lack the time to do so and will subcontract this allocation work to private companies: http://www.powerbase.info/index.php/Health_Portal.) Spinwatch itself does list its funders on its website, and how much they give: http://www.spinwatch.org/.

[46] http://www.sourcewatch.org/index.php?title=State_Policy_Network and http://stinktanks.org/what-stinks/.

[47] Cave, T. and Rowell, A. (2014) *A quiet word: Lobbying, crony capitalism and broken politics in Britain*, Oxford: The Bodley Head.

[48] Bartels, L. (2005) 'Economic inequality and political representation', Working Paper, August, http://www.princeton.edu/~bartels/economic.pdf. See also Gilens, M. (2014) *Affluence and influence*, Princeton, NJ: Princeton University Press.

Chapter Sixteen: Hiding it

[49] Hume, D. (1777) *Political discourses*, Co 19, Mil 266, http://www.davidhume.org/texts/pd.html. Thanks to John Christensen for this quote.

[50] This section draws substantially from Nicholas Shaxson's superb (2012) *Treasure islands: Tax havens and the men who stole the world*, London: Vintage. See also Urry, J. (2014) *Offshoring*, Cambridge: Polity.

[51] Research by Actionaid: 'FTSE 100 tax haven tracker', http://www.actionaid.org.uk/tax-justice/ftse-100-tax-haven-tracker.

[52] Murphy, R. and Christensen, J. (2014) 'Tax us if you can', 2nd edn, London: Tax Justice Network, available at: http://www.taxjustice.net/cms/front_content.php?idcatart=134&lang=1.

[53] Palan, R., Murphy R. and Chavagneux, C. (2010) *Tax havens: How globalization really works*, Ithaca, NY: Cornell University Press, pp 5–6.

[54] Channel 4 News, 14 June 2013.

[55] See Palan et al (2010), pp 38–40.

[56] Said, S. (2011) 'The 10 biggest tax havens in the world', *The Richest*, 15 September, http://www.therichest.com/expensive-lifestyle/location/the-10-biggest-tax-havens-in-the-world/.

[57] http://www.financialsecrecyindex.com/index.html.

[58] The Bureau of Investigative Journalism (2012) 'City of London Corporation reveals its secret £1.3bn bank account', 20 December, http://www.thebureauinvestigates.com/2012/12/20/city-of-london-corporation-reveals-its-secret-1-3bn-bank-account/.

[59] The Bureau of Investigative Journalism (2012) 'Streets paved with gold', 9 July, http://www.thebureauinvestigates.com/2012/07/09/streets-paved-with-gold-the-local-authority-that-works-for-the-banks/.

[60] Shaxson (2012), p 265; Nelson, F. (1996) 'Labour rift over city overhaul', *Independent*, 7 April, http://www.independent.co.uk/news/labour-rift-over-city-overhaul-1303565.html. In 2002 an Act was passed to allow the Corporation to enlarge the business vote! See Froud, J. et al (2011) 'Groundhog Day: elite power, democratic disconnects and the failure of financial reform in the UK', CRESC Working Paper No 108, University of Manchester, http://www.cresc.ac.uk/sites/default/files/Groundhog%20Day%20Elite%20power,%20democratic%20disconnects%20and%20the%20failure%20of%20financial%20reform%20in%20the%20UK%20CRESC%20WP108%20(Version%202).pdf.

[61] http://democracy.cityoflondon.gov.uk/mgUserInfo.aspx?UID=136.

[62] Neville, S. and Treanor, J. (2012) 'Starbucks to pay £20m in tax over next two years after customer revolt', *Guardian*, 6 December, http://www.theguardian.com/business/2012/dec/06/starbucks-to-pay-10m-corporation-tax.

[63] http://www.twnside.org.sg/title2/resurgence/2012/268/cover02.htm. I've calculated the effective tax rate at July 2013 exchange rates: $11.6 billion = €8.9 billion. There are also other ways of moving money to escape tax: see Palan et al (2010) and Shaxson (2012).

[64] http://blogoscoped.com/files/hamburg/large/7.jpg.

[65] Murphy and Christensen (2014).

[66] Mason, C. (2014) 'Treasury anger over Margaret Hodge "grandstanding"', BBC News, 23 January, http://www.bbc.co.uk/news/uk-politics-25858447.

[67] Sikka, P. (2009) 'Shifting profits across borders', *Guardian*, 12 February, http://www.guardian.co.uk/commentisfree/2009/feb/11/taxavoidance-tax.

[68] Brown, G. (2005) Speech to the CBI annual conference. Available at: http://www.guardian.co.uk/business/2005/nov/28/economicpolicy.budget2006.

[69] Guardian Tax Reporting Team (2009) 'The top gamekeeper', *Guardian*, 6 February, http://www.theguardian.com/business/2009/feb/06/tax-gap-gamekeeper-inland-revenue.

[70] Provost, C. (2013) '£180m aid to developing countries routed through tax havens last year', *Guardian*, 15 August, http://www.oxfam.org.uk/blogs/2013/05/tax-haven-cash-enough-to-end-extreme-poverty.

[71] Kar, D. and Freitas, S. (2012) 'Illicit financial flows from developing countries: 2001–2010', Washington, DC: Global Financial Integrity Unit, http://iff. gfintegrity.org/documents/dec2012Update/Illicit_Financial_Flows_from_ Developing_Countries_2001-2010-WEB.pdf.

[72] http://www.oxfam.org.uk/blogs/2013/05/tax-haven-cash-enough-to-end-extreme-poverty.

[73] Forbes (2012) 'Forget the drug dealers and Iran, HSBC is having a great year', 12 December, http://www.forbes.com/sites/nathanvardi/2012/12/12/ forget-the-drug-dealers-and-iran-hsbc-is-having-a-great-year/. See also http://blog.ourfuture.org/20130628/believe-it-or-not13-mind-blowing-facts-about-tax-evading-corporations.

[74] Howker, E. and Malik, S. (2012) 'Cameron family fortune made in tax havens', *Guardian*, 20 April, http://www.guardian.co.uk/politics/2012/ apr/20/cameron-family-tax-havens.

[75] http://www.taxresearch.org.uk/Blog/2013/09/10/david-cameron-takes-leave-of-his-senses-as-he-declares-the-uk-has-no-tax-havens-left/#sthash. PMFksAlX.dpuf.

[76] Watts, R. and Ungoed-Thomas, J. (2009) 'Minister in charge of offshore clampdown ran tax haven firm', *Sunday Times*, 22 March, http://www. thesundaytimes.co.uk/sto/business/article157241.ece. Myners was already in trouble for approving a £703,000-per-year pension for Fred Goodwin, head of the failed bank RBS. Worryingly, Myners was more recently appointed as an independent director to reform the failing Cooperative Group.

[77] Newman, M. (2012) 'Conservative peer hired as tax haven lobbyist', The Bureau of Investigative Journalism, 17 April, http://www. thebureauinvestigates.com/2012/04/17/conservative-peer-hired-as-tax-haven-lobbyist/.

[78] Sayal, R. and Williams, M. (2012) 'Tory treasurer wants UK to become more like a tax haven', *Guardian*, 21 September, http://www.guardian. co.uk/business/2012/sep/20/tory-treasurer-make-uk-tax-haven.

[79] Mason, R. (2012) 'Britain could prevent the use of tax havens by ending "archaic" business rules', *Telegraph*, 21 September, http://www.telegraph. co.uk/news/politics/conservative/9557273/Britain-could-prevent-the-use-of-tax-havens-by-ending-archaic-business-rules.html.

[80] Drucker, J. (2013) 'Europe eases corporate tax dodge as worker burdens rise', *Bloomberg News*, 13 May, http://www.bloomberg.com/news/2013-05-13/europe-eases-corporate-tax-dodge-as-worker-burdens-rise.html.

[81] Murphy, R. (2013) 'For a man who says he thinks tax evasion is repugnant George Osborne is doing his utmost to promote it', *Tax Research UK*, 23 March, http://www.taxresearch.org.uk/Blog/2012/03/23/for-a-man-who-says-he-thinks-tax-evasion-is-repugnant-george-osborne-is-doing-his-utmost-to-promote-and-assist-it/.

[82] Palan et al (2010), p 7.

[83] Centre for Economics and Business Research (2011) 'The 50p tax – good intentions, bad outcomes: the impact of high rate marginal tax on

government revenues in a world with no borders', http://conservativehome.
blogs.com/files/cebr-report---final.pdf.

Chapter Seventeen: Legal corruption

[84] From http://www.nakedcapitalism.com/2012/10/john-kenneth-galbraith-on-the-moral-justifications-for-wealth-and-inequality.
html#qvYXvQ1HKPM5ihYI.99.

[85] Hobbes, T. (2005) [1666] *A dialogue between a philosopher and student of the common laws of England*, Oxford: Oxford University Press.

[86] Jessop, B. (2013) 'The complexities of competition and competitiveness: challenges for competition law and economic governance in variegated capitalism', in M.W. Dowdle, J. Gillespie, and I. Maher (eds) *Asian capitalism and the regulation of competition: Towards a regulatory geography of global competition law,* New York: Cambridge University Press, pp 96–120.

[87] Kaufmann, D. (2012) 'Rethinking the fight against corruption', *Huffington Post*, 28 November, http://www.huffingtonpost.com/danielkaufmann/rethinking-the-fight-corruption_b_2204591.html.

[88] Hudson, M. (2012) 'Financial conquest or clean slate?', http://michael-hudson.com/2012/09/financial-conquest-or-clean-state/.

[89] Engelen, E., Ertürk, I., Froud, J., Johal, S., Leaver, A., Moran, M., Nilsson, A. and Williams, K. (2011) *After the great complacence: Financial crisis and the politics of reform*, Oxford: Oxford University Press.

[90] As Gillian Tett and other close observers of the financial sector have observed, the efficient markets thesis – routinely used to legitimise the financialisation of everything – has become a kind of religion: 'There is a real sense of intellectual confusion. Over the past year I have been talking to former true believers and they're like a priest who has lost faith in the Bible, but still has to go to church, and the congregation is sitting there but he doesn't know what the Bible is any more …' Adair Turner adds: 'Yes, the fact is that intellectual systems – the whole efficient market theory, Washington consensus, free market deregulation system – can become like a religion': Turner, A. (2009) 'How to tame global finance' *Prospect*, 27 August, http://www.prospectmagazine.co.uk/magazine/how-to-tame-global-finance/.

[91] Mirowski, P. (2013), *Never let a serious crisis go to waste*, London: Verso. It has been heterodox economists, largely excluded from major economic journals, who have blown the whistle on economists acting on behalf of companies.

[92] It's worth asking economists who profess this whether they believe it because they think it's true or because it's in their self-interest to believe it. If the former, then acting on the basis of what is true is an exception, and if the latter, then why should we take their ideas seriously as an account of human motivation?

[93] Hume, N. (2005) 'PM's attack angers City watchdog', *Guardian*, 6 June, http://www.guardian.co.uk/politics/2005/jun/06/uk.business.

94   Blair, T. (2005) Speech on Risk and the State, University College, London, 26 May, http://www.astrid-online.it/Qualit--de/Studi--ric/Archivio-21/ Blair_Risk_State_Speech_26May05.pdf. See the 23 March 2013 blog of Rowan Bosworth-Davies, a former detective and legal consultant dealing with financial crime, on his submission to the Parliamentary Commission on Banking Standards, at: http://rowans-blog.blogspot.ch/2013/03/why-british-banking-industry-has-become.html.

95   Pickard, J. (2011) 'Miliband's business crusade draws fire', *Financial Times*, 28 September, http://www.ft.com/cms/s/0/e81a446a-e932-11e0-af7b-00144feab49a.html#axzz2ZyHQEJlx.

96   Massey, D. (2007) *World city*, Cambridge: Polity

97   Hudson (2012).

98   Lanchester, J. (2013) 'Are we having fun yet?', *London Review of Books*, 4 July, 35(13), pp 3–8.

99   Meacher, M. (2012) 'When are banksters going to be punished?', blog, 23 September, http://www.michaelmeacher.info/weblog/tag/hsbc-money-laundered-for-iran-mexico-drug-cartels/.

100 Smith, G. (2012) 'Why I am leaving Goldman Sachs', *New York Times*, 14 March, http://www.nytimes.com/2012/03/14/opinion/why-i-am-leaving-goldman-sachs.html?pagewanted=2&_r=2&hp.

101 See Shaxson, N. and Christensen, J. (2014) *Finance curse*, Taiwan: Commonwealth Publishing, for examples and elaboration.

102 Wallace, C. (2012) 'Keep taking the testosterone', *Financial Times*, 9 February, http://www.ft.com/cms/s/0/68015bb2-51b8-11e1-a99d-00144feabdc0.html#axzz34du1m4BI.

103 Marx, K. and Engels, F. (1848) *The Communist Manifesto*.

104 They are also shockingly ignorant about ordinary people's lives and basic social facts: see Toynbee, P. and Walker, D. (2008), *Unjust deserts*, London: Granta.

105 Smith, A. (1759) *The theory of the moral sentiments*, Indianapolis: Liberty Press, pt VI, sec ii, ch 3.1, p 235 (6th and final edition published in 1790, a year *after* the 5th and final edition of *The wealth of nations*).

106 Hudson (2012).

107 http://www.rollingstone.com/politics/news/the-great-american-bubble-machine-20100405. See also http://my.firedoglake.com/fflambeau/2010/04/27/a-list-of-goldman-sachs-people-in-the-obama-government-names-attached-to-the-giant-squids-tentacles/ and http://www.salon.com/2009/04/04/summers/.

108 Engelen et al (2011), p 171. See also Johnson, S. (2009) 'The quiet coup', *The Atlantic*, May, http://www.theatlantic.com/magazine/archive/2009/05/the-quiet-coup/307364/2/.

109 Foley, S. (2011) 'What price the new democracy? Goldman Sachs conquers Europe', *Independent*, 18 November, http://www.independent.co.uk/news/business/analysis-and-features/what-price-the-new-democracy-goldman-sachs-conquers-europe-6264091.html.

[110] Marshall, A.G. (2013) 'Global power project Part V: banking on influence with Goldman Sachs', 15 July, http://truth-out.org/news/item/17563-global-power-project-part-v-banking-on-influence-with-goldman-sachs.

[111] http://www.publiceye.ch/en/news/public-eye-awards-2013-naming-and-shaming-awards-go-goldman-sachs-and-shell/.

[112] For further information, see Engelen et al (2011), chs 6 and 7.

[113] Ferguson, C. (2012) *Inside job*, London: Oneworld, pp 248–53.

[114] *Bloomberg* (2009) 'Harvard swaps are so toxic even Summers won't explain, (update3)', 18 December, http://www.bloomberg.com/apps/news?pid=n ewsarchive&sid=aaZGpGgHsVGw.

[115] Murphy, R. and Christensen, J. (2014) 'Tax us if you can', 2nd edn, London: Tax Justice Network, available at: http://www.taxjustice.net/cms/front_content.php?idcatart=134&lang=1.

[116] White, A. (2012) 'PwC fined record £1.4m over JP Morgan audit', *Telegraph*, 5 January, http://www.telegraph.co.uk/finance/newsbysector/supportservices/8995981/PwC-fined-record-1.4m-over-JP-Morgan-audit.html.

[117] Thanks to John Christensen for this information.

[118] https://www.gov.uk/government/organisations/hm-revenue-customs/groups/hmrc-board.

[119] http://www.ushistory.org/us/24d.asp.

[120] Bowman, A., Ertürk, I., Froud, J., Johal, S., Moran, M., Law, J., Leaver, A. and Williams, K. (2012) 'Scapegoats aren't enough: a Leveson for the banks?', CRESC Discussion Paper, p 8.

[121] Canada, US, Mexico, Peru, Chile, New Zealand, Australia, Brunei, Singapore, Malaysia, Vietnam and Japan.

[122] Wikileaks (2013) 'Secret Trans-Pacific Partnership agreement (TPP)', https://wikileaks.org/tpp/pressrelease.html.

[123] Wikileaks (2013).

[124] Monbiot, G. (2013) 'The lies behind this transatlantic trade deal', *Guardian*, 2 December, http://www.theguardian.com/commentisfree/2013/dec/02/transatlantic-free-trade-deal-regulation-by-lawyers-eu-us.

[125] Corporate Europe Observatory (2013) 'A transatlantic corporate bill of rights', 3 June, http://corporateeurope.org/trade/2013/06/transatlantic-corporate-bill-rights.

[126] McDonagh, T. (2013) 'Unfair, unsustainable and under the radar', San Francisco: Democracy Center, http://democracyctr.org/new-report-unfair-unsustainable-and-under-the-radar/.

Chapter Eighteen: What about philanthropy?

[127] Blair, T. (2012) Speech to conference on philanthropy, China Philanthropy Forum, Beijing, 28 November.

[128] Wikipedia Hélder Cámara, http://en.wikipedia.org/wiki/Hélder_Câmara

[129] According to research by Barclays Bank, 97% of the world's 'high net worth individuals' give annually to charity. But only one third of these give away over 1% of their net worth: *Too Much* (2013) 'A Whistleblower for Philanthropy', 5 August, http://toomuchonline.org/weeklies2013/aug052013.html. See also Brennan, P. and Saxton, J. (2007) 'Who gives to charity?', nfpSynergy report, and Rowlingson, K. and McKay, S. (2011) *Wealth and the wealthy*, Bristol: Policy Press, pp 136 ff.

[130] Buffett, P. (2013) 'The charitable-industrial complex', *New York Times*, 27 July, http://www.nytimes.com/2013/07/27/opinion/the-charitable-industrial-complex.html?_r=1&.

[131] Blair, T. (2012) Speech to the Global Philanthropy Forum in Washington, DC, 16 April, http://www.tonyblairoffice.org/news/entry/tony-blair-global-philanthropy/.

[132] In a speech to the Labour Party Conference, 28 September 2004, http://news.bbc.co.uk/1/hi/uk_politics/3697434.stm. '

[133] An exception might be made where they give to foundations that distribute money according to scientific, expert advice, but even here we have still to ask whether the donors' wealth is legitimate. My thanks to Michael Edwards for advice on philanthropy and, with the usual disclaimers, to Balihar Sanghera for comments on this point and others in the chapter.

[134] Buffett, P. (2013). Tony Blair's speech to the Global Philanthropy Forum (see note 131) provides illustrations of this philanthropic colonialism. See especially his comments on his Africa Governance Initiative.

[135] Edwards, M. (2010) *Small change: Why business won't save the world*, San Francisco, CA: Berrett-Koelher.

[136] http://www.toomuchonline.org/tmweekly.html

[137] Edwards (2010), p 13.

[138] Edwards (2010), pp 40–3.

[139] Edwards, M. (2013) 'From love to money: can philanthropy ever foster social transformation?', Paper for international symposium: New Philanthropy, Social Justice, and Social Protection Policy, University of Bradford, 25–26 March.

[140] Piller, C. and Smith, D. (2007) 'Unintended victims of Gates Foundation generosity', *Los Angeles Times*, December 16, http://fairfoundation.org/news_letter/2008/01march/criticism_of_gates_foundation.pdf.

[141] Edwards, M. (2011) 'The role and limitations of philanthropy', Institute of Development Studies, University of Sussex, UK, http://opendocs.ids.ac.uk/opendocs/bitstream/handle/123456789/3717/The%20Role%20and%20Limitations%20of%20Philanthropy_summary.pdf?sequence=2.

[142] See Graeber, D. (2012) *Debt: The first 5000 years*, New York: Melville House Publishing.

Chapter Nineteen: Class

[143] The reports can be downloaded at http://pissedoffwoman.wordpress.com/2012/04/12/the-plutonomy-reports-download/.

[144] Citigroup (2006) Plutonomy Report Part 2, 5 March.

[145] In the *Chattanooga Times Free Press*, http://2.bp.blogspot.com/-Xq6TMq8_X70/Tn6mxnjj8vI/AAAAAAAANtY/84rDSYW2EBw/s1600/Class_War_t618.jpg.

[146] The Plan, including the controversial appendix, is available at: http://www.margaretthatcher.org/archive/displaydocument.asp?docid=110795. Nicholas Ridley was the father of Matt Ridley, the scourge of the state whom, as Chair of the failed and bailed-out Northern Rock, we met in Chapter Thirteen.

[147] Milne, S. (2014) 'Who's to blame for the crisis, bankers or benefits claimants?', *Guardian*, 16 January, http://www.theguardian.com/commentisfree/2014/jan/16/crisis-bankers-benefit-claimants-class.

[148] There's now a big literature on this: for example, Sayer, A. (2005) *The moral significance of class*, Cambridge: Cambridge University Press; Jones, O. (2011) *Chavs*, London: Verso; Skeggs, B. (1997) *Formations of class and gender*, London: Sage; Tyler, I. (2012) *Revolting subjects: Social abjection and resistance in neoliberal Britain*, London: Zed.

[149] See for example: Sveinsson, K.P. (ed) (2009) 'Who cares about the white working class?', Runnymede Trust; Skeggs, B. (2004) *Class, self, culture*, London: Routledge.

[150] Baumberg, B., Bell K. and Gaffney, D. with Deacon, R., Hood, C. and Sage, D. (2012) *Benefit Stigma Report*, Turn2Us, http://www.turn2us.org.uk/PDF/Benefits%20stigma%20Draft%20report%20v9.pdf.

[151] The ambiguities of the word 'poor' combined with the wider culture of blaming the poor also make it unsurprising that the poor resist including themselves in the category. See Shildrick, T, and McDonald, R. (2013) 'Poverty talk: how people experiencing poverty deny their poverty and why they blame the poor', *The Sociological Review*, 61, pp 285–303, and Unwin, J. (2013), *Why fight poverty*, London: London Publishing Group.

[152] Tax Research UK (2013) 'Benefit errors cost £1 million a day. Tax avoidance and evasion cost £260 million a day', 13 September, http://www.taxresearch.org.uk/Blog/2013/09/13/benefit-errors-cost-1-million-a-day-tax-avoidance-and-evasion-cost-260-million-a-day/.

[153] For readers outside Britain, 'public school' actually means *private* school, not state school, although, extraordinarily, these schools for the children of the rich are publicly supported indirectly by being allowed charitable status!

[154] Lamont, M. (1990) *Money, morals and manners: The culture of the French and American upper-middle class*, Chicago, IL: Chicago University Press

[155] Jones, O. (2013) 'The truth about class', Royal Television Society Lecture, 18 November, http://www.bbc.co.uk/programmes/p01lqx74.

156 See Skeggs, B. and Wood, H. (2011) *Reality television and class*, London: Palgrave; Mirowski, P. (2013) *Never let a good crisis go to waste*, London: Verso.

Part Five

Introduction

1 World Bank, estimates for 2010, http://www.worldbank.org/en/news/press-release/2013/10/10/report-finds-400-million-children-living-extreme-poverty.

Chapter Twenty: Spending it

2 Sunday Times Rich List, 2013.

3 http://www.bornrich.com/.

4 *Mail Online* (2007) 'World's most expensive cocktail launched at £35,000 a glass', 8 December, http://www.dailymail.co.uk/news/article-500581/Worlds-expensive-cocktail-launched-35-000-glass.html.

5 Peppard, A. (2008) 'Oil in the family', *Vanity Fair*, http://www.vanityfair.com/politics/features/2008/06/hunt200806.

6 Much of the house-buying by the rich in London is purely speculative, especially after the UK government obligingly fuelled a new housing bubble in 2013.

7 http://medberths.com/mbm-apr2013/?utm_source=DP+All&utm_medium=email&utm_campaign=MedBerths+April+2013.

8 Williams, R. (2011) *The country and the city*, London: Spokesman Books.

9 Gorz, A. (1983) *Critique of economic rationality*, London: Verso. Note that such a division of labour, involving specialisms in different functions, like car maintenance, plumbing or medicine, is different from the unequal division of labour discussed earlier, in which *within* such activities there is a division of workers between skilled/interesting/pleasant tasks and unskilled/boring/unpleasant tasks.

10 Cox, R. (2006) *The servant problem: Domestic employment in a global economy*, London: I.B.Tauris; Ehrenreich, B. and Hochschild, A.R. (eds) (2002) *Global woman: Nannies, maids and sex workers in the new economy*, London: Granta; Tronto, J. (2002) 'The nanny question in feminism', *Hypatia*, 17, pp 34–51; Gregson, N. and Crewe, L. (1994) *Servicing the middle classes: Class, gender and waged domestic labour in contemporary Britain*, London: Routledge.

11 Veblen, T. (1994) [1899] *The theory of the leisure class,* Dover Thrift Editions.

12 Frank, T. (2012) *Pity the billionaire*, New York: Harvill Secker, Random House, p 30.

13 Jackson, T. (2010) 'Re-imagining investment for the whole human', video lecture, http://www.ted.com/talks/tim_jackson_s_economic_reality_check.html/.

14 Schor, J. (2010) *Plenitude*, New York: The Penguin Press, p 26.

[15] Schor (2010), p 29.

[16] http://england.lovefoodhatewaste.com/node/2163.

[17] Tawney, R.H. (2004) [1920] *The acquisitive society*, Mineola, NY: Harcourt Brace and Howe, p 41.

[18] Smith, A. (1759) *The theory of moral sentiments*, Indianapolis: Liberty Fund, I.iii.2.III, p.61

[19] Layard, R. (2005) *Happiness: Lessons from a new science*, London: Allen Lane.

[20] Schor, J (2010), p 177, updating Layard's figures.

[21] Skidelsky, R. and Skidelsky, E. (2012) *How much is enough?*, London: Penguin, p 103.

[22] Wilkinson, R. and Pickett, K. (2009) *The spirit level: Why more equal societies almost always do better*, London: Allen Lane.

[23] Wilkinson and Pickett (2009). See also Lane, R.E. (1991) *The market experience*, Cambridge; Cambridge University Press.

[24] Layard, R. (n.d.) 'Action for happiness', www.actionforhappiness.org/why-happiness.

[25] Layard (2005).

[26] Source: UNICEF (2007) 'An overview of child well-being in rich countries', http://www.unicef-irc.org/publications/pdf/rc7_eng.pdf; UNICEF (2013) 'Report Card 11: Child well-being in rich countries', http://www.unicef-irc.org/publications/pdf/rc11_eng.pdf.

[27] Schor (2010), p 96.

[28] Global Footprint Network, http://www.footprintnetwork.org/en/index.php/GFN/.

[29] BBC News (2012) 'Electronic waste: EU adopts new WEEE law', 19 January, http://www.bbc.co.uk/news/world-europe-16633940.

[30] Spash, C.L. (2013) 'New foundations of ecological economics', presentation at Conference on Kritische Soziologie meets Critical Realism: A Dialogue between Social Research, Social Theory and Philosophy of Science, Jena, Germany, 2 February.

[31] Peter Mandelson, a highly influential figure in the New Labour government, is known for seeking the company of the rich and for his infamous remark that New Labour was 'intensely relaxed about people getting filthy rich – as long as they pay their taxes'.

[32] Monbiot, G. (2009) 'Stop blaming the poor. It's the wally yachters who are burning the planet', *Guardian*, 28 September, http://www.theguardian.com/commentisfree/cif-green/2009/sep/28/population-growth-super-rich.

Chapter Twenty-One: The twist in the tail

[33] Kahn, S.R. (2014) 'The ease of mobility', in Birtchnell, T. and Caletrio, J. (eds) *Elite mobilities*, London: Routledge, pp 136–48, at p 136.

[34] This characterisation of neoliberalism as zombie-like is developed by Jamie Peck in his 2010 article, 'Zombie neoliberalism and the ambidextrous state', *Theoretical Criminology*, 14(1), 104–10.

[35] UN Intergovernmental Panel on Climate Change (2013), http://www.climatechange2013.org/images/uploads/WGIAR5-SPM_Approved27Sep2013.pdf.

[36] Methane degrades within a few years into CO_2 and ground-level ozone.

[37] Carrington, D. (2103) 'Global carbon dioxide in atmosphere passes milestone level', *Guardian*, 10 May, http://www.theguardian.com/environment/2013/may/10/carbon-dioxide-highest-level-greenhouse-gas.

[38] Global Humanitarian Forum (2009) *The anatomy of a silent crisis*, http://www.ghf-ge.org/human-impact-report.pdf.

[39] See Urry, J. (2011) *Climate change and society*, Cambridge: Polity, p 148, for this and other scenarios.

[40] Carbon Dioxide Information Analysis Centre, Oak Ridge National Laboratory, USA. http://cdiac.ornl.gov/trends/emis/overview_2010.html.

[41] Pacala, S. (2009) 'Equitable climate solutions', lecture, at: http://www.youtube.com/watch?v=2X2u7-R3Wrc. See also http://edition.cnn.com/2008/BUSINESS/02/17/eco.class/.

[42] Urry (2011), p 53, citing research by Stephen Burman and Richard Heinberg. Nevertheless, Mark Jacobson at Stanford University has calculated ways in which each US state could replace its fossil fuel energy supply with renewable energy by 2030, without recourse to nuclear of bio-power. http://news.stanford.edu/news/2013/march/new-york-energy-031213.html.

[43] Steinberger, J.K. and Roberts J.T. (2010) 'From constraint to sufficiency: the decoupling of energy and carbon from human needs, 1975–2005', *Ecological Economics,* 70, pp 425–33, and Lamb, W.F. et al (2014) 'Transitions in pathways of human development and carbon emissions', *Environmental Research Letters*, 9, pp 1–10. To be sure, the countries that combine low emissions with high life expectancy and HDI have warm climates and are less affluent than the core (mostly cooler) rich countries, but this is precisely why cleaner energy and less wasteful, more moderate consumption are needed in the latter.

[44] Gough, I. et al (2012) 'The distribution of total greenhouse gas emissions by households in the UK, and some implications for social policy', Centre for Analysis of Social Exclusion, London School of Economics; Jones, C.M. and Kammen, D.M. (2011) 'Quantifying carbon footprint reduction opportunities for U.S. households and communities', *Environmental Science and Technology*, 45(9), pp 4088–95. In their book, *A climate of injustice: global inequality, North-South politics, and climate policy* (Cambridge MA: MIT Press, 2006), J.Timmons Roberts and Bradley C. Parks point to a 1996 study that showed that people in the US who earned more than $75,000 emitted nearly four times as much CO_2 as those who earned less than $10,000. Greenhouse gases emitted at high levels in the atmosphere do more damage than those emitted at low levels,

yet measures of emissions from aircraft often fail to take this into account. See also UNDP Human Development Report, 2011.

[45] Global Commons Institute, 'Contraction and convergence (C&C). Climate justice without vengeance', http://www.gci.org.uk/.

[46] Global Commons Institute, http://www.gci.org.uk/

[47] Jackson, T. (2007) *Prosperity without growth*, London: Earthscan, pp 68 ff.

[48] If energy prices were raised to reduce consumption, then that would hit the poor far harder than those with more money. The problem here is the inequality, not high prices for energy. We need to redistribute so as to reduce inequalities for many reasons, but one benefit is that such burdens would be more equally shared.

[49] Urry (2011), p 78.

[50] Interview with Natalie Bennett (2013) *Soundings*, 53, pp 33–43.

[51] While it would increase the 'horizontal division of labour' – between different kinds of activity – it would probably reduce the vertical (and unequal) division of labour within activities or sectors, because operations would be smaller scale and less able to support this kind of specialisation.

[52] Berners-Lee, M. (2010) *How bad are bananas? The carbon footprint of everything*, London: Profile Books, p 86.

[53] Berners-Lee (2010), p 95.

[54] This is known as the 'Jevons parodox', after William Stanley Jevons, the economist who first identified it.

[55] For example, see http://carboncalculator.direct.gov.uk/index.html, http://www.nature.org/greenliving/carboncalculator/index.htm, http://www.carbonfootprint.com/calculator1.html, http://www.carbonstory.org/?ref=google_footprint&gclid=CMy0x5velroCFZMdtAod8iAAzw. There are also eco-footprint calculators, so you can estimate your wider impact on the earth: http://footprint.wwf.org.uk/home/calculator_complete, http://www.earthday.org/footprint-calculator?gclid=CPK0tu XdlroCFXMbtAodrGYAtg,

[56] Marriot, J. (2008) 'BP and the fuelling of Heathrow', *Soundings*, 39, pp 56–66 and http://www.thisismoney.co.uk/money/pensions/article-1695211/Pension-funds-sunk-by-BP-oil-spill-chaos.html.

[57] Interestingly, this is now less prominently advertised on BP's website than in the past: http://www.bp.com/en/global/corporate/sustainability/bp-energy-lab.html.

[58] Marriot (2008).

[59] Jones, J. (2013) 'How can we live with it?', *London Review of Books*, 35(10) 23 May, pp 3–7.

[60] Berners-Lee, M. and Clark, D. (2013) *The burning question*, London: Profile Books, p 43.

[61] See, for example, Goldenberg, S. (2013) 'Secret funding helped build vast network of climate denial thinktanks', *Guardian*, 14 February, http://www.theguardian.com/environment/2013/feb/14/funding-climate-change-denial-thinktanks-network.

[62] Mirowski, P. (2013) *Never let a serious crisis go to waste*, London:Verso.

[63] In effect, this is Will Hutton's solution in his 2010 book, *Them and us*, London: Little, Brown, ch 9.

[64] Cited in Mirowski et al (2009), and with a telling response by David Roberts,'Why Branson and SuperFreakonomics are wrong, in pictures', 17 October, http://grist.org/article/2009-10-16-why-richard-branson-and-superfreakonomics-are-wrong-in-pictures/. The reference to Copenhagen is to the Climate Change talks in the city in 2009.

[65] Pettifor, A. (2014) *Just money*, Taiwan: Commonwealth Publishing.

[66] Kempf, H. (2008) *How the rich are destroying the earth*, Totnes, Devon: Green Books, p 74.

Conclusions

Chapter Twenty-Two: So what now?

[1] Keynes echoed this, writing that the love of money 'as a possession' and not just 'as a means to the enjoyment and realities of life' was 'one of those semi-criminal, semi-pathological propensities which one hands over with a shudder to the specialists in mental disease': Keynes, cited in Skidelsky, R. and Skidelsky, E. (2012) *How much is enough?* London: Penguin, p 91.

[2] Sen, A. (1999) *Development as freedom*, Oxford: Oxford University Press; Nussbaum, M. (2012) *Creating capabilities*, Cambridge, MA: Harvard University Press.

[3] Some kinds of suffering aren't avoidable, for example, bereavement.

[4] Tawney, R.H. (1952) [1931] *Equality*, 4th edn, London: George Allen and Unwin, p 291.

[5] Martha C. Nussbaum's *Political emotions* (Cambridge, MA: Belknap, Harvard University Press, 2014) is a good antidote to the narrow economic view of politics, emphasising the importance of well-being, including compassion, enjoyment and love.

[6] Friedman, M. (1978) 'An interview with Milton Friedman', *Human Events* 38(46), p 14. See also Hudson, M. (2005) *Global fracture: The new international economic order*, 2nd edn, London: Pluto Press.

[7] New Economics Foundation (2010) *Where did our money go?*, London: NEF.

[8] For example, see 'Investing in Community Shares', Co-operatives UK, Development Trusts Association, http://www.communityshares.org.uk/sites/default/files/resources/investing_in_community_shares.pdf; and Murray, R. (2011) 'The co-operative movement: where now?', talk given

to Co-operatives UK, http://www.uk.coop/congress/co-operative-movement-where-now-robin-murray.

[9] Davis, J. and Tallis, R. (eds) (2013) *NHS SOS*, London: Oneworld.

[10] Chang, H.-J. (2013) 'Irresponsible and beyond blame: the new fat cats', *Guardian*, 10 July; Green New Deal Group (2013) 'A national plan for the UK: from austerity to the age of the Green New Deal', http://www.greennewdealgroup.org/wp-content/uploads/2013/09/Green-New-Deal-5th-Anniversary.pdf. See also the interview with Adair Turner, Chair of the UK's Financial Services Authority, in *Prospect*, 27 August 2009, at: http://www.prospectmagazine.co.uk/magazine/how-to-tame-global-finance/; Murphy, R. (2010) 'Why is country-by-country financial reporting by multinational companies so important?', Tax Justice Network, UK, http://www.taxresearch.org.uk/Documents/CountrybyCountryReporting.pdf.

[11] I refer those who think this will inevitably cause hyper-inflation, as in Argentina or Weimar Germany, to Mellor, M. (2010) *The future of money*, London: Pluto, and (forthcoming) *Debt or democracy?*, and to Turner, A. (2014) 'Creating money – for what purpose?', lecture, London School of Economics, 24 March, http://www.lse.ac.uk/newsAndMedia/videoAndAudio/channels/publicLecturesAndEvents/player.aspx?id=2356. See also Wolf, M. (2014) 'Strip private banks of their power to create money', *Financial Times*, 25 April, http://www.ft.com/cms/s/0/7f000b18-ca44-11e3-bb92-00144feabdc0.html#axzz34zGZwF7d.

[12] Dolphin, T. (2010) 'Financial sector taxes', Institute of Public Policy Research, http://www.ippr.org/images/media/files/publication/2011/05/Financial%20sector%20taxes_1779.pdf, p 4.

[13] Cited in Chang, H.-J. (2010) *23 things they don't tell you about capitalism*, London: Allen Lane, p 241.

[14] Dolphin (2010), p 18.

[15] For further analyses and proposals on tax, see the Tax Justice Network. http://www.taxjustice.net/.

[16] Hume, D. (1777) *Political discourses*, http://www.davidhume.org/texts/pd.html.

[17] Piketty, T. (2014) *Capital in the 21st century*, Cambridge, MA: Belknap Press, chs 15 and 16. For the record, while this is a remarkable and indispensable book for its analysis of wealth and income data in the history of capitalism, I disagree with some of its basic concepts (for example, the equation of wealth with capital, the treatment of ownership as in itself deserving of yielding an income) and I would argue that climate change needs much more attention, especially given his highly questionable assumption that growth should continue in rich countries.

[18] Inequality Briefing 26 (2014) 'Almost one third of wealth in the UK is inherited, not earned', 11 April, http://inequalitybriefing.org/brief/briefing-26-almost-one-third-of-wealth-in-the-uk-is-inherited-not-earned.

[19] Tax Research UK (2013) 'Benefit errors cost £1 million a day. Tax avoidance and evasion cost £260 million a day', 13 September, http://

www.taxresearch.org.uk/Blog/2013/09/13/benefit-errors-cost-1-million-a-day-tax-avoidance-and-evasion-cost-260-million-a-day/.

[20] Indiviglio, D. (2011) 'In Norway everyone's income is public – and so is tax paid', *The Atlantic*, 23 July, http://www.theatlantic.com/business/archive/2011/07/in-norway-everyones-income-is-public-and-so-is-tax-paid/242386/; Tax Justice Network (2011) 'Finland publishes all tax receipts in public', 2 November, http://taxjustice.blogspot.co.uk/2011/11/finland-publishes-all-personal-tax.html.

[21] There are also smaller subsidies that benefit the rich, which could be cut, including subsidies to landowners of grouse moors (£56 per hectare); these actually damage the environment by damaging peat, by CO_2 emissions from burning heather and by limiting biodiversity. See Monbiot, G. (2014) 'This cash for grouse scandal shows how Britain became a plutocrats' paradise', *Guardian*, 29 April, http://www.theguardian.com/commentisfree/2014/apr/28/britain-plutocrats-landed-gentry-shotgun-owners.

[22] Smith, A. (1976) [1776] *The wealth of nations*, ed. E. Cannan, Chicago, IL: University of Chicago Press, vol 1, bk I, ch IX, p 110. This fits Apple perfectly, for example.

[23] In Britain, the Living Wage Foundation defined a living wage – geared to the cost of living – as £7.65 per hour (London £8.80) in January 2014, while the government's minimum wage was set at £6.31: http://www.livingwage.org.uk/what-living-wage.

[24] Richard Duncan argues that an increase in low hourly wages from $3 to $4 would boost demand by a third but would increase export prices much less – 2–3%, he estimates (in Blackburn, R. (2011) *Age shock*, London: Verso). See also van Staveren, I., Elson, D., Grown, C. and Cagatay, N. (eds) (2007) *The feminist economics of trade*, London: Routledge.

[25] This was suggested to me by Erik Olin Wright.

[26] Royal Society (2012) *People and the planet report*, London: Royal Society, http://royalsociety.org/uploadedFiles/Royal_Society_Content/policy/projects/people-planet/2012-04-25-PeoplePlanet.pdf.

[27] Morgan, K.J. (2014) 'The new urban foodscape', in Bohn, K. and Viljoen, A. (eds) *Second nature urban agriculture: Designing productive cities*, London: Routledge. For more details see http://www.esrc.ac.uk/news-and-events/videos/celebrating-impact-prize-winners-2013.aspx?media-component=tcm:8-26076&type=video.

[28] Pizzigati, S. (2012) *The rich don't always win*, New York: Seven Stories Press.

[29] Marquand, D. (2014) *Mammon's kingdom: An essay on Britain, now*, London: Allen Lane.

[30] *Huffington Post* (2012) 'Rupert Murdoch pushed Tony Blair over Iraq war, claims Alastair Campbell', 16 June, http://www.huffingtonpost.co.uk/2012/06/16/rupert-murdoch-pushed-tony-blair-over-iraq-war-claims-alastair-campbell_n_1602091.html.

[31] Aitchison, G. (2012) 'How capitalism is turning the internet against democracy and how to turn it back', *OpenDemocracy*, http://www.opendemocracy.net/guy-aitchison/how-capitalism-is-turning-internet-against-democracy-and-how-to-turn-it-back.

Afterword

[1] World Economic Forum (2015) *World Economic Forum Annual Meeting 2015: The New Global Context*, http://www3.weforum.org/docs/WEF_AM15_Report.pdf; and WEF, 'Inequality and climate change: 2015's challenges', https://agenda.weforum.org/2015/01/inequality-and-climate-change-twin-challenges-of-2015/.

[2] IMF (2015) 'All will benefit from steps to cut excessive inequality—Lagarde', *IMF Survey Magazine*, 17 June, available at: http://www.imf.org/external/pubs/ft/survey/so/2015/NEW061715A.htm and http://www.imf.org/external/pubs/ft/sdn/2015/sdn1513.pdf.

[3] OECD (2015) *In it together: Why less inequality benefits us all*, OECD Publishing, Paris, http://www.keepeek.com/Digital-Asset-Management/oecd/employment/in-it-together-why-less-inequality-benefits-all_9789264235120-en#page1.

[4] You can download it here: http://liberationtheology.org/pope-franciss-encyclical-on-ecology-june-2015/. I recommend it.

[5] Wikipedia entry: https://en.wikipedia.org/wiki/Tax_evasion_and_corruption_in_Greece; C. Koulovatianos and J. Tsoukalas (2015) 'Why debt sustains curruption in Greece and vice versa', Vox, 20 July, http://www.voxeu.org/article/why-debt-sustains-corruption-greece-and-vice-versa; Smith, H. (2014) 'Corruption still alive and well in post-bailout Greece', *Guardian,* http://www.theguardian.com/world/2014/dec/03/greece-corruption-alive-and-well; Robinson, A. (2013) 'Political corruption and media retribution in Spain and Greece', *The Nation*, 21 February, http://www.thenation.com/article/political-corruption-and-media-retribution-spain-and-greece/; Armitstead, L. (2012) 'Debt crisis: Greek government signs €330m settlement with Siemens', *The Telegraph*, http://www.telegraph.co.uk/finance/financialcrisis/9502146/Debt-crisis-Greek-government-signs-330m-settlement-with-Siemens.html.

[6] Touissant, E. (2011) 'The debt in the north: some alternative paths', *Latin America in Movement online*, 1 January, http://www.alainet.org/en/active/44773.

[7] Jubilee Debt Campaign (2015) 'ECB to make between €10 billion and €22 billion profit out of loans to Greece', 10 July, http://jubileedebt.org.uk/blog/ecb-to-make-between-e10-billion-and-e22-billion-out-of-loans-to-greece; Jubilee Debt Campaign (2015) 'IMF has made €2.5 billion profit out of Greece loans', 8 April, http://jubileedebt.org.uk/news/imf-made-e2-5-billion-profit-greece-loans.

[8] Müller, J.W. (2015) 'Rule breaking', *London Review of Books* 37(16), 3–7, http://www.lrb.co.uk/v37/n16/jan-werner-muller/rule-breaking.

'According to the Stockholm International Peace Research Institute, Greece continued to buy large quantities of weaponry from the two countries between 2010 to 2014, some of the worst years of its economic depression. During this time, Athens bought $US551 million worth of military equipment from Germany and $US136 million of equipment from France': see Bender, J. (2015) 'Here's why Greece's military budget is projected to grow in 2015 – despite the country's economic mayhem', *Business Insider*, 30 June, http://www.businessinsider.com.au/why-greeces-military-budget-is-so-high-2015-6.

[9] *Financial Times* (2015) 'Greek bakers rise to reform challenge', 15 July, http://www.ft.com/cms/s/0/832f1e24-2af9-11e5-8613-e7aedbb7bdb7.html#axzz3lErxkLDb.

[10] http://ourfuture.org/20150713/reaction-to-greece-austerity-deal-thisisacoup.

[11] http://www.lse.ac.uk/researchAndExpertise/researchImpact/PDFs/germany-hypocrisy-eurozone-debt-crisis.pdf.

[12] Provost, C. (2013) 'Susan George on the secret capitalist cabal behind European austerity', *Guardian*, http://www.theguardian.com/global-development/2013/dec/30/susan-george-secret-capitalist-cabal-behind-european-austerity.

[13] Murphy, R. (2015) 'The tragedy of Greek debt', Tax Research UK, http://www.taxresearch.org.uk/Blog/2015/06/20/the-tragedy-of-greek-debt/.

[14] Grist (2011) 'Obama administration announces massive coal mining expansion', *Guardian*, 24 March, http://www.theguardian.com/environment/2011/mar/24/obama-coal-mining-expansion.

[15] McKibben, B. (2013) 'Obama and climate change: The real story', *Rolling Stone*, 17 December, http://www.rollingstone.com/politics/news/obama-and-climate-change-the-real-story-20131217#ixzz3lFgtwuG8.

[16] https://www.whitehouse.gov/climate-change.

[17] Vaughan, A. and Macalister, T. (2015) 'The nine green policies killed off by Tory government', *Guardian*, 24 July, http://www.theguardian.com/environment/2015/jul/24/the-9-green-policies-killed-off-by-tory-government; Ecotricity (2015) 'Husky-hugging Conservatives show their true colours', https://www.ecotricity.co.uk/news/news-archive/2015/husky-hugging-conservatives-show-their-true-colours.

[18] See Klein, N. (2014) *This changes everything: Capitalism vs the climate*, London: Allen and Lane.

[19] Capgemini and RBC Wealth Management, *World Wealth Report 2015*, https://www.worldwealthreport.com/.

[20] Monbiot, G. (2015) 'The City's stranglehold makes Britain look like an oh-so-civilized mafia state', *Guardian*, http://www.theguardian.com/commentisfree/2015/sep/08/britain-civilised-mafia-state

[21] *Private Eye* (2015) 'How to speak Corbyn: A headline-writer's guide to twisting a politician's words', 16 September, http://i.imgur.com/UZlDEuP.jpg.

[22] Media Reform Coalition (2014) 'The elephant in the room: a survey of media ownership and plurality in the United Kingdom', http://www.mediareform.org.uk/wp-content/uploads/2014/04/ElephantintheroomFinalfinal.pdf.

Index